Underdogs

The Making of the Modern Marine Corps

Aaron B. O'Connell

Harvard University Press • Cambridge, Massachusetts • London, England

Library of Congress Cataloging-in-Publication Data

O'Connell, Aaron B., 1973–
Underdogs : the making of the modern Marine Corps / Aaron B. O'Connell.
pages   cm
Includes bibliographical references and index.
ISBN 978-0-674-05827-9 (cloth : alk. paper)
ISBN 978-0-674-41681-9 (pbk.)
1. United States. Marine Corps—History—20th century.
2. United States. Marine Corps—Military life—History—20th century.
3. Sociology, Military—United States—History—20th century.   I. Title.

VE23.O25   2012
359.9'609730904—dc23   2012006344

FOR MY FAMILY'S CASUALTIES OF WAR:

Colonel Anthony J. Touart, U.S. Army
January 1, 1892–March 1, 1945

Lieutenant Colonel George R. Barnes, U.S. Army
January 24, 1908–October 18, 1942

Joan Touart-Barnes O'Connell
June 18, 1936–June 23, 2006

Contents

Illustrations

My students at the U.S. Naval Academy in Annapolis, Maryland, usually laugh when I tell them I joined the Marine Corps because of *Top Gun*. It seems silly at first—not least because Tony Scott's 1986 film starring Tom Cruise is about Navy pilots, not Marines—but most are nodding in agreement by the time I finish my explanation. When *Top Gun* came out, I was thirteen, short and slight, and probably a little more awkward than most thirteen-year-olds, if such a thing is possible. The film's opening credits, run against a background of real Navy pilots launching real planes from a real aircraft carrier, were enough to hook me for life. Like many young boys, I was enamored of big machines, but I remember being equally impressed with the characters and the plot. Maverick's (Tom Cruise) brotherlike friendship with his navigator, Goose (Anthony Edwards); the search for the truth behind Maverick's father's disappearance in Vietnam; Goose's death in a flying accident, and finally an eventual triumph over the Soviets in a spectacular aerial dogfight all convinced me that the military was a place of adventure, danger, and, of course, women like Meg Ryan and Kelly McGillis. My own father, a conscientious objector during the Vietnam War, suffered patiently through the ordeal, remarking only at the end that while he didn't care for the film, he could see why I did. My mother didn't go to the movies with us and never would have consented to seeing a film about the military in the first place.

Once I got interested in the military, the shift to the Marines was a quick one. Films played some part—the boot camp scenes from

Stanley Kubrick's *Full Metal Jacket* (1987) in particular—but recruiting commercials were probably the bigger influence. I tried to join
right out of high school, but as I was under eighteen, I needed my
parents' consent, and they refused to give it. The recruiter offered to
talk to my parents, but I knew there was no hope of changing their
minds. I went to college instead, and after I turned eighteen I spent a
summer at Officer Candidates School in Quantico, Virginia, which
made me eligible for an officer's commission upon graduation.

After five years on active duty, I left the Corps as a captain and
started a Ph.D. program just two weeks before the September 11 attacks. Shortly thereafter, I joined the reserves and spent the summers
serving as a staff officer in various commands inside the United
States. As a result, until recently, I have had only indirect contact
with the wars that have shaped the past decade. Even now, serving in
the International Security Assistance Force (ISAF) headquarters in
Kabul, Afghanistan, I feel far too safe to claim any privileged status
as a combat veteran, and I expect I will still feel uncomfortable when
I return for not having done my full share.

John Keegan, whose book *The Face of Battle* revolutionized military history in the 1970s, famously wrote that he had "not been in a
battle, not near one, nor heard one from afar, nor seen the aftermath."
I have never felt that way. Even in my youth, war's aftermath was pain-
fully obvious to me. When my mother was six, her father was killed
in the Pacific; when she was eight, her maternal grandfather died
during the assault into Germany. These two losses ruined both my
mother and my grandmother; neither woman ever fully recovered
from the war that broke their family apart. I grew up in a house with
ghosts, where the stories of two men and the war that took them inspired me but haunted my mother. I am convinced that these legacies
of loss are more common and enduring than most Americans like to
acknowledge. Particularly today, after eleven years of continuous military operations in Afghanistan and eight in Iraq, and with living
veterans from three other previous wars, the aftermath of battle is
everywhere. Most of us, however, are not willing to confront it fully.

Every book is the product of a specific time and place; this one is no exception. Except for this preface and the final edits, I wrote every chapter between 2002 and early 2010—a time when I felt an enormous obligation to serve in combat yet did not volunteer for mobilization. That has undoubtedly colored some of the interpretations that follow, though in what specific ways, I cannot say. These were also years when the prestige of military service gained the added fuel of real sacrifice, which has led various politicians, pundits, and organizations to try to appropriate that prestige and sacrifice for their own purposes. As a result, the military's cultural apparatus—its symbols, images, ideologies, and texts—have grown markedly more present and powerful in American society over the past decade. That too has operated in the background of my writing, for good or for ill.

I have dedicated this book to my mother, her father, and her grandfather—three individuals who are all, to my mind, casualties of war in one way or another. But I would also like to dedicate it to the living, and in particular to my wife, Brigitte, who has supported me both in the writing and in the military career that has taken me away from her for the past eight months. And finally, this book is for the many Marines and their families who have shared their stories with me during my seventeen years in the Corps, and whose sacrifice has been so much more significant than my own. *Semper Fidelis.*

Kabul, Afghanistan
May 2011

Underdogs

Introduction:
Culture Warriors

You Marines don't trust anybody, do you?

—President Harry S. Truman to the Commandant of the
Marine Corps, 1947

Before World War II, the United States Marine Corps was tiny, unpopular, and institutionally disadvantaged. Numbering just 50,000 men, it accounted for only 3 percent of the active-duty military in June 1941. As a separate naval service inside the Department of the Navy, the Marines had little control over their budget or equipment purchases, and always came second in the secretary of the Navy's attention. Their highest-ranking officer—the Commandant of the Marine Corps—was a two-star major general and had no seat on the newly created Joint Chiefs of Staff. Nor were they as popular or well respected as they are today. In a wide-ranging national opinion survey conducted just before Pearl Harbor, both young men of enlistment age and their parents named the Marines as the least attractive military service, attributing to them a reputation for rowdiness and hard living.[1]

By the start of the Vietnam War, the Marines' position in American society and the Department of Defense was quite different. The Commandant was, by this point, a four-star general with a seat on the Joint Chiefs of Staff. A strong, bipartisan coalition of lawmakers in Congress had authored a series of legislative protections for the Corps, which prevented the President from making major cuts to its manpower or funding. A broad network of journalists who had served in the Corps defended its interests in print. The things the Navy bought for the Marines' use—aviation and amphibious ships, in particular—had increased significantly since the start of the Cold War, as had the Marines' own budget. As a result, by 1965, the Corps was roughly four times as large as it had been in 1941, and it was considerably more powerful inside the Department of Defense.

The Marine Corps' mission also had changed since World War II. Then, it had one principal purpose: to seize temporary bases for the Navy by attacking enemy-held islands from the sea. By 1965, the Marines had transformed themselves into a multipurpose quick-reaction force that floated throughout the world's oceans on Navy ships. When ordered into action, they arrived in days, or even hours. These were not the naval landing parties that had existed in ages past; these Marines came equipped with their own helicopters, jets, tanks, artillery, engineers, and mechanics, plus enough supplies to sustain themselves for fourteen days of fighting. They were global shock troops who provided the President with on-call military power for any contingency ranging from a natural disaster to sustained, non-nuclear combat. The technical name for these units was "Marine Air-Ground Task Forces," or more generally, the "amphibious force-in-readiness." Marines today refer to it as "America's 9-1-1 force."

This is a cultural history of the United States Marine Corps—a study of the stories, assumptions, and habits of mind of this smallest of the four armed services.[2] It relates how, over a period of twenty-five years, the Marines created a set of narratives for and about themselves that attained wide legitimacy within their organization and without. The Corps' stories strengthened its solidarity, binding Marines together in a community as strong as any in the world. Stories helped them expand their alliances with politicians, journalists, and other civilians who rallied to their defense in times of need. Stories energized and focused the Corps' members, albeit sometimes against civilians and other inappropriate targets. The Marines' ideology even shaped their preparations for Cold War defense, making their organization one of the sharpest and swiftest tools of American power. Ultimately, the Corps' culture has been its greatest asset, supporting both its internal cohesion and its institutional expansion.[3]

Most historians attribute the Marines' institutional growth to their heroics in combat, particularly in World War II and Korea. That is only part of the story. From 1941 to 1965, the Marines did not just fight wars and rest on the laurels they earned in them; they played an active and interventionist role in American society and politics. They recruited newspapermen into their ranks and nurtured relationships with civilian journalists, editors, and publishers. They sent veterans into politics and built a grassroots network of supporters across the country. Friends in Hollywood kept the Corps' name in the limelight; political operatives in Washington orchestrated congressional support. Through careful marketing, public relations spectacles, and bare-knuckle politics, the Marines insinuated themselves into American media, government, and everyday life.

The Marines did not grow their power by foisting themselves on an unwilling public, however. They formed alliances with civilians that yielded benefits for both sides. Newspaper editors used Marine stories to sell papers; filmmakers did the same to bring viewers to theaters. Political candidates advertised their Marine Corps connections to get elected; once in office, they made common cause with the Corps for a variety of reasons. These coalitions were critical to the Corps' growing cultural power, but the Marines did not control the relationships. Civilians had a say, and sometimes they were the most prolific distributors of Marine Corps stories and images.

Other studies have tried to explain the Marines' cultural power by comparing them to samurai, Spartans, or other warrior castes.[4] This one does not. Cultural similarities may exist across services (indeed, even across centuries and continents), but every military organization exists in a specific time and place, and while comparisons have their benefits, they also often require distortions to make the subjects fit the argument.[5] I am content instead to argue the following three general points. First, in the twenty-five years studied here, the Marines thought and acted differently than the other American armed services, a point accepted as obvious by those who know Marines but left largely unexplored by historians. Marine culture may not have been entirely unique or exceptional, but it was so to them, and in the end, that made all the difference. At the root of the Marines' ideas about themselves were narratives of exceptionalism— an ideology that made them feel separate from and superior to everyone else, both soldiers and civilians. This exceptionalism, with its attendant sentiments of insularity and mistrust of outsiders, was the first principle of Marine Corps culture.

Second, the Marines' sense of their own exceptionalism, which existed before World War II, grew stronger in the years studied here and became an increasingly valuable asset for their institution. Motivated by a combination of loyalty, pride, and fear, the Corps built a robust infrastructure of political and public relations support that protected its interests during wartime and peacetime. While all the armed services attempted similar moves, the Marine Corps was arguably the most successful at it. The outreach infrastructure the Marines built in the 1940s remains in place to this day and is one of the sources of their contemporary popularity and power.

Finally, the Marines' culture not only helped their organization but also has had long-lasting effects on American society, national defense, and eventually the United States' role in the world. The modern Marine Corps—an elite force of military first responders with a global reach—came of age in the first decade of the Cold War.[6] Since then, it has grown more popular in American society and more powerful inside the national security establishment. Over the past eleven years, in times of war and peace, Americans have routinely ranked the Marine Corps as the most prestigious military service by a healthy margin.[7] In the past four presidential administrations, Marines and former Marines have held some of the highest positions in American national security leadership, including secretary of state, national security advisor, chairman and vice chairman of the Joint Chiefs of Staff, secretary of the Navy, and a host of other senior military positions.[8] The Marines now comprise roughly 14 percent of the active-duty armed forces and 26 percent of all ground forces.[9] Over the past twenty years, the number of military operations involving Marine amphibious forces has more than doubled.[10] And while they still rely on a close partnership with the Navy, the Marines have moved well beyond service aboard ships. Indeed, if there is any country on earth where amphibious forces should be irrelevant, it is Afghanistan. And yet the Marines are heavily engaged there today, and the commander of all U.S. and NATO forces in the country is a United States Marine. The Corps' cultural operations in World War II and the early Cold War established the preconditions for this global system of amphibious military power.

THE NARRATIVES OF MARINE EXCEPTIONALISM

Among those who know Marines, the most commonly acknowledged characteristics are their reputation for physical toughness, extremely short haircuts, unabashed arrogance, and shameless self-promotion. Some members of the other armed services occasionally dispute the first of these four points but never the last two. Since at least World War I, there have been running jokes in military circles about the Marines' preoccupation with their public image, summarized best by a quip attributed to an army officer: "In the army a squad consists of thirteen men. In the Marine Corps it consists of twelve men and a press agent."[11] Marines make few apologies for this active self-promotion; most view it as necessary for their service's survival. But even devotees of the Corps have occasionally shaken their heads at the efforts the service makes to sell itself to the public. As one aspiring Marine poet put it in 1944:

> The Marines, the Marines, those blasted Gyrenes,
> Those sea-going bellhops, those brass-button queens.
> Oh! They pat their own backs, write stories in reams.
> All in praise of themselves—the U.S. Marines.[12]

It is true that the Marines orchestrated an extraordinary amount of favorable publicity for themselves during World War II and in the years that followed. But the number of stories the Marines told about themselves is not what gave their culture its power. Rather, it was the nature of the stories that mattered, the assumptions behind them, and the emotional and social bonds that they generated in both Marines and civilians. Running through nearly every artifact of Marine Corps culture in this era were regular, almost compulsive affirmations of the Marines' inherent superiority over everyone else, coupled with a wariness of outsiders that bordered on paranoia. They imagined themselves as a small and loyal tribe of warriors who were outnumbered, disrespected, and persecuted, even by their sister service, the Navy. They built high ideological walls around their community and had little patience for rules imposed on them from outside.[13] Perennially obsessed with losing status or being polluted by outside influences, they displayed many of the traits of what anthropologists call a fundamentalist or enclave culture.[14] And while it goes too far to call them a monastic order, the Marines of this era drew regularly on the language of religion, practices of extreme discipline, and intricately scripted rituals to mark themselves as different, separate, and superior to every other organization around them.

Because the Marines enforced such rigid boundaries between themselves and everyone else, those inside their cultural universe shared a remarkable degree of solidarity, cohesion, and commitment. That emotional commitment had several names. Marines called it variously "esprit de corps," "Marine Corps spirit," or "Marine Corps feeling"; civilian admirers usually explained it with references to the Marine Corps motto, *Semper Fidelis*, meaning "Always Faithful."[15] No matter what it was called, its effect was the same: to bind Marines to each other in extremely effective ways, both on the battlefront and on the home front.

The Marines' stories about themselves did more than create loyalties between living members of the Corps, however. They also invested Marines in the past, creating attachments to a mythology and a deep historical community that included all who had ever worn the Marine Corps uniform, both living and dead. This belief in an enduring family of Marine ancestors, legible in nearly every Marine Corps ritual, tradition, and narrative, only grew stronger when friends passed violently from one world to the next in combat. Being "always faithful" to the Marine Corps required more than swearing an oath to the U.S. Constitution; it demanded fealty to a historical narrative and family that claimed to predate the nation itself.

Surprisingly, this attachment to the past did not prove an obstacle to innovation. The Marine Corps of this era was institutionally agile and adaptable, and here too, culture was an asset. Distrust of outsiders helped the Marines reject the other services' conventional wisdom and chart new paths; their ideas about themselves and warfare shaped the direction they took. While their organization's small size explains something of their dynamism, other cultural factors mattered as well. More than the other services, Marines were comfortable with chaos and uncertainty. They disdained the rational and quantitative modes of thought that increasingly dominated the military in the twentieth century. Theirs was the least bureaucratic culture, the most emotional, and it was shot through with the experiences and aftereffects of trauma. They were the service least enamored with machines and computers and most committed to intimate, spiritual, and transcendent themes. They, more than the Army and particularly the Navy and Air Force, understood the world and warfare through the language and logic of art rather than those of science. This attention to emotion, mythology, spirit, and community made them particularly good at understanding cultural forces and deriving benefits from that understanding.[16]

The Corps' cultural traits also generated friction. As President Truman's remark to the Commandant of the Marine Corps indicates, the Marines didn't trust anybody and saw enemies everywhere—particularly in the White House and in the Army.[17] This led them to lobby Congress and the public vigorously, an effort Truman would later criticize as "a propaganda machine that is almost equal to Stalin's."[18] President Truman was not wrong—even the Commandant of the Marine Corps later agreed with the President's characterization—

but propaganda alone does not account for the Marines' successes on the cultural front.[19] The Corps did excel at selling itself to Americans, but sufficient numbers of Americans also wanted what the Corps was selling. Others used the Corps' stories to sell something of their own. The public did not accept the Corps' stories uncritically; it negotiated, interacted with, and in some cases rejected them. On balance, however, it celebrated far more than it criticized for a variety of reasons that these pages explore.

One reason deserves mention at the outset. When supporters of the Marine Corps—both veterans and civilians—spoke of its charms, they used words such as "tradition," "history," "family," and "community."[20] Underlying these words was a certain type of longing that the Marine Corps knew well how to fill. There has always been a long-standing tension in American society between tradition and progress, between attachment to the past and breaking with it.[21] Like most modern Western nations, the United States has always been more focused on the future than the past, more interested in creating new things than in preserving the old. This has produced a remarkable record of innovation and technological progress but also deep historical amnesia and, for some, a sense of rootlessness. Particularly in times of great change and danger, people yearn for stability, continuity, and strong social networks. World War II and the early Cold War were just such a time.

Many Americans today remember the 1950s as a time of placidity, safety, suburbanization, and economic growth. This memory obscures the unsettling elements of that era. World War II uprooted millions of Americans from their homes; the years that followed brought pervasive anxieties about Communists and a world-ending nuclear war. In this environment, all the armed services tried to give the public reassuring messages that emphasized their strength, devotion, and ability to protect. However, each service used different messaging strategies to do so and positioned its messages at different points on the continuum between commemorating the past and celebrating the future. The youngest and most popular service, the Air

Force, was the most invested in science and technology and, not surprisingly, gave the greatest emphasis to future-focused narratives of progress. The Army and the Navy, coupling deep attachments to tradition with heavy emphases on nuclear and computing technologies, tried to celebrate both the past and the future, with varying degrees of success. All of the three largest services gave extensive coverage to their machines. Their recruiting literature is littered with pictures of jets, ships, missiles, tanks, and, by the early 1960s, computers. Their stories are peppered with reminders of past exploits but also feature equal, and often greater, reference to the newness of the present and the promise of tomorrow.[22]

The Marine Corps took a different approach. Using language suffused with nostalgia, the Marines told a type of story more often heard in church than in a science fiction film. They privileged the collective over the individual, venerated sacrifice and suffering, and spoke often of their service's unique sense of community. They presented their junior Marines—the privates in particular—as their principal war-fighting asset instead of the machines that those privates operated. While not overtly opposed to technology, they were skeptical of it, preferring more human-centered and romantic narratives of warfare. Almost all of their public relations products privileged the warm bonds of the Marine Corps "family" over the sleek, cold feel of jets, missiles, and computers. At a time when Americans had to grapple with so much uncertainty and change, this public relations strategy offered something that the other services' emphasis on technology and the future could not.

If the Corps' stories were the vehicles for spreading its culture into American society, the trauma of two wars was the fuel. More than any other subculture in the United States, the Marines of this era saw the most violent aspects of American foreign policy. In World War II, Korea, and Vietnam, they had the highest casualty ratios of the four armed services and, in most cases, the highest percentages of combat participation.[23] The psychological effects of exposure to such extreme violence, though rarely acknowledged or verbalized, operated continuously in the background of Marines' daily lives, with both positive and negative results. Trauma unified the Corps, energized its networks, and brought passion and focus to arguments about the Marines' role in national defense. Real fights for survival in World War II and Korea gave way to metaphorical ones in Washington, D.C., and in the media. Marines brought the same intensity to both, with beneficial results for their institution. However, what helped the Corps was not always good for its members. Anger and alcohol abuse were also legacies of Marines' combat experiences, as were emotional collapses and violent outbursts that could sometimes turn deadly. And while the public understood that such difficulties could emerge in combat, their continuation on the Cold War home front was a well-guarded secret.

This underlying trauma and the Marines' skillful manipulation of their own image come together in the title of this book. "Underdogs" is an adaptation of the Marine Corps nom de guerre "Devil Dogs," which the Corps claims to have taken from a 1918 German newspaper lamenting defeat at the hands of American *Teufel Hunden* or "hounds from hell." (No German newspaper bearing the term ever came to light to corroborate the tale, but the Corps appropriated the nickname nonetheless and put it on a recruiting poster.)[24] Most Marines—then and today—accept without question the Devil Dogs story, much as they do the equally tall tales of the Marine Corps' ostensible creation on November 10, 1775, and its combat heroics in its first hundred years of existence.[25] Perhaps because they accept the Corps' mythology so readily, they miss what lies underneath. This study seeks to probe under the Devil Dog mythology, to separate its truths from its fictions, and to understand the things that gave the culture such force in Marines' lives.

Calling Marines "underdogs" also emphasizes the minority status, sense of persecution, and paranoia that have always been a dominant cognitive frame in Marine Corps culture. Perhaps the most recurrent theme in the Marine Corps of the early Cold War was a notion of being under siege from without, both by enemies in combat and by other forces in the executive branch of the U.S. government. A feeling of being persecuted, already well established in their service history, instilled in Marines a feeling of hypervigilance, to which the experiences of combat added an undisputable experiential basis. That hypervigilance and the group cohesion that flowed from it were the engines of the Marines' cultural power and institutional success.

A "Devil Dogs" recruiting poster from the World War I era: an early example of Marine Corps mythmaking. (United States Marine Corps)

THE MARINE CORPS AND INTERSERVICE RIVALRY
BEFORE WORLD WAR II

In many ways, the Marine Corps was the least likely candidate for institutional expansion in the second half of the twentieth century. Ever since the first Marine officer was commissioned on November 28, 1775 (five months after the Army commissioned its first officer and one month before the Navy did the same), the Corps has always been the smallest and most insular of the armed services. Serving primarily as guards aboard ships, the Marines saw their numbers fluctuate throughout the nineteenth century from as few as 300 to as many as 3,000 men. Fluent in naval lingo but possessing army ranks, they were truly "soldiers of the sea," a hybrid status that made them vulnerable to the predations of presidents seeking to economize or of Navy admirals and Army generals looking to increase their services' power. Legislation passed in 1798 made the Corps a separate service inside the Department of the Navy, but this did little to stop the other services' abolition attempts. As early as 1820, the Commandant of the Marine Corps grumbled in a letter to the secretary of the Navy that his "isolated Corps, with the army on one side and the navy on the other (neither friendly), has been struggling for its existence since its very establishment. We have deserved hostility from neither, more especially the navy."[26]

The Marine Corps Act of 1834 reaffirmed the Corps' status as a separate service but did not improve interservice relations aboard ship.[27] Part of the problem was the Marines' very purpose: to enforce order aboard naval vessels, to mete out punishments for infractions, and, when required, to put down mutinies. These duties created regular and enduring friction between Marines and sailors, which was exacerbated by the fact that Marines lived aboard ship but did none of the hard work of sailing, cleaning, or maintaining the vessels. As the Navy professionalized in the late nineteenth century and lost the need for armed guards, it tried repeatedly to remove the Marines from its ships or disband the Corps altogether. Four such attempts occurred between 1894 and 1909 alone.[28] Junior naval officers took to voicing their displeasure in print. One writing in 1896 argued that the word "Marine" was nothing more than a "synonym for idleness, worthlessness, and vacuity of intellect."[29]

Relations with the War Department and the President were often no better. In addition to their guard mission aboard ship, Marines were occasionally detached to serve as infantry ashore with the Army. To Army officers and economizers in government, having two separate infantry forces seemed duplicative; their solution was to either merge the Marine Corps into the Army or abolish the Corps. Between 1829 and 1932, there were four such attempts, the last coming at the urging of then chief of staff of the Army Douglas A. MacArthur.[30] Like the Navy's efforts, these attempts failed, but not before convincing Marines that their only trustworthy allies lay outside the executive branch: Congress, the public, and their own veterans.

Interservice rivalry with the Army escalated in the twentieth century. The Marines' performance in World War I established their reputation as an elite infantry force, but it was a reputation built more on luck than on superiority over the Army troops they fought alongside.[31] During their largest battle of the war, a censoring error resulted in droves of good publicity for the Marines but excluded the Army, furthering the acrimony between the two services.[32] In the 1920s and 1930s, Marines gained additional acclaim by serving as occupation forces in Haiti, Nicaragua, and the Dominican Republic, where they practiced an earlier, more brutal version of what is now called counterinsurgency. By the start of World War II, Marine officers and noncommissioned officers had far more combat experience than their counterparts in the U.S. Army, a fact they likely pointed out to anyone who would listen.[33] Yet few Americans were impressed. As late as November 1941, fully 86 percent of boys of enlistment age and 90 percent of parents preferred one of the other military services over the Marines.[34]

During these same years, the Marines pioneered the tactics for seizing defended islands that would make them famous in World

War II. Convinced that war with Japan was likely, several prescient Marine officers in the 1920s and 1930s pushed their service away from counterinsurgency missions and guarding ships and toward amphibious operations. Unable to generate much interest from the Navy or the Army, the Corps did most of the work alone, researching equipment needs, conducting exercises, and formalizing tactics. Here too, poor interservice relations slowed the process. While the Marines authored the first tentative doctrine for assaulting islands from the sea in 1934, it took the Navy four years to approve it. The Army copied the Marines' document almost to the letter and published it as the Army's own in 1941, which further irked the Corps' senior planners.[35]

This long history of interservice rivalry had a pronounced effect on how the Corps operated in American society during World War II and the early Cold War, but not in the way one might think. Instead of isolating themselves from outsiders, the Marines worked to extend bridges across the wide ideological moat that separated their world from the rest of American society. Those bridges led to networks of allies and proxies in Congress, Hollywood, the news media, and other key constituencies. Like an expanding inkblot or oil stain (metaphors well known to historians of counterinsurgency), the Corps' culture moved into civilian society with ease, where it found a warm welcome from a broad base of admirers and supporters.[36] This expansion was a form of militarization—no other term suffices—but military forces were not its only drivers.[37] Civilians played a role too, either by cooperating with the Corps or by appropriating its prestige for their own purposes. The result was a gradual but steady growth of the Marines' cultural capital, which would eventually bring their reputation to its current height.

The Marine Corps may seem an unlikely candidate for arguments about militarization; as the smallest armed service, it possessed only a fraction of the manpower and resources of the Army, Navy, or Air Force. It was these larger and more technology-dependent services that changed the character of the American economy and society the most in this era, particularly as aviation, computers, and telecommunications became such a large part of the military's procurement. World War II provided the initial catalyst, but the Cold War normalized a state of permanent preparation for war. American government, economics, and foreign relations all became increasingly influenced by national security concerns. Peacetime defense spending rose from 17 percent of the federal budget in 1940 to 33 percent in 1950 and to 52 percent in 1960.[38] Missile silos and military bases proliferated across the country and around the globe.

But militarization means more than large standing armies, a global basing system, and the creation of military products instead of civilian ones.[39] Militarization is also a *cultural* phenomenon: a fascination with war stories and military technology, an increased reliance on martial metaphors and cognitive frames, and a growth of the military's prestige in political and social life.[40] These were the years when Americans abandoned the skepticism about the armed forces that had emerged after World War I. Military service, infrastructure, and ideas all became ordinary parts of their everyday lives. The notion of national security expanded to include issues of race, gender, sexuality, and family life.[41] It was in these cultural arenas that the Marines had certain advantages, which they used to increase their power in American society and inside the Department of Defense.

CULTURAL OPERATIONS IN CULTURAL FIELDS

Any study of culture must give some attention to definitions and methodology. What exactly is culture, and how do historians document its effects? Previous scholarship on the Corps has made occasional reference to the Marines' cultural power, but no study has attempted to explain it with anything other than formulas or platitudes.[42] Sociological studies may shed some light on military institutions and values, but they cannot explain why individuals commit themselves to those values in such intense and sustained ways.[43] This study attempts a more in-depth investigation of civil-military relations, one that takes account of the unquantifiable influences that were so central to the

Marines' rising prestige. The Corps' culture was not grounded in science or systematic thinking. Attempts to understand and explain it must not be either.

It is an animating assumption of this book that culture is a form of power. Like gravity, culture operates everywhere in ways both obvious and invisible. The mental and emotional architecture we carry within us—our identity narratives, values, ideologies, and underlying assumptions—do not just help us interpret the world; they *frame* it, coloring our choices, shaping our priorities, and privileging some interpretations while excluding alternatives. This does not happen by accident. People and media (newspapers, radio, advertisements, fashion, books, film, and television) promulgate narratives and assumptions throughout the cultural landscape, and thinking individuals accept, reject, ignore, and even absorb these unwittingly.

The cultural landscape is no benign marketplace of ideas where consumers shop for values and identities; it is a set of interconnected battlefields where individuals and groups fight constantly for attention, endorsement, or passive acquiescence.[44] Whether marketing experts call it "branding" or political consultants call it "shaping the message," the intent is the same: to make one agenda or interpretation desirable, authoritative, or, better yet, widely accepted "common sense." Culture is thus one of the subtlest and softest tools of power, for it persuades rather than coerces, managing consent rather than demanding it.[45] It gives individuals and organizations the power to exert influence by shaping the very assumptions people carry on a day-to-day basis.

Much like physical battlefields, cultural fields can be mapped. While no culture has real fences around it, there are discernible conceptual boundaries between groups and ways to evaluate the cultural operations occurring within and between them. The evidence is often suggestive rather than definitive, and the linkages between cause and effect are occasionally unclear. In wars of ideas, as in conventional battles, the winners and losers are fairly easily determined; the reasons for victory are not.[46]

In the pages that follow, I discuss four types of cultural "operations"—four ways that culture functions both in general and in the Marine Corps of midcentury America. First, within all of us, culture operates as the stories we tell ourselves and others about ourselves.[47] It is the beliefs and practices we commit to intentionally in order to identify ourselves and to advertise our identity to those around us.[48] And while I use the words "stories" and "narratives" interchangeably, culture exists not only in the realm of the verbal. Fashion, military uniforms, and silent gestures are culture too. The things one buys, wears, or does—even a style of walking or shaking hands—are ways to communicate the set of commitments made to specific identities and beliefs. In this first sense, culture operates primarily by marking out differences. It is the whole host of ways that individuals and groups differentiate themselves from other individuals and groups.[49]

Culture also ties members of groups together. As Benedict Anderson argued years ago, there is an intimate link between culture and social organization, for it is through stories that individuals feel and mark their connections to the larger imagined communities of nation, church, ethnic group, or military brotherhood.[50] Being in community with others means co-owning stories with them; with that shared ownership come both ties of affection and bonds of mutual responsibility. There are unwritten contracts underlying the stories we share with others, informal and often-changing agreements that frame what it means to be Irish or Italian, a New Yorker or a Texan, Catholic or Jewish, a soldier, sailor, or civilian. This second operation of culture is particularly powerful when it concerns the military, for those who serve in the nation's defense are, for many Americans, emblems of the entire nation. This leads some—both within the military and without—to try to control what stories are told about them and to dictate who may do the telling.

But culture is more than the beliefs we intentionally endorse and advertise to others. It is also the beliefs we don't even know we hold, the assumptions and ideologies that operate in the background of consciousness as common sense.[51] As Isabel V. Hull explains in one of the few fine cultural histories of a military service, culture is the whole range of "habitual practices, default programs, hidden assumptions, and unreflected cognitive frames" that shape our understanding of ourselves and affect the choices we make.[52] It is the patterns and practices we revert to unconsciously, much the way a computer reboots its operating system when it crashes or restarts. This third type of cultural operation is, at times, covert—hidden from outside view and sometimes beyond the awareness of the individual on whom it is operating. These covert operations of culture are perhaps the hardest for historians to document. Oftentimes the very forces shaping choices and actions are assumptions that are never spoken, penned, or recorded in the archives.

Finally, culture has a disciplinary function: it operates by policing the boundaries within and between groups. It provides signs and rules for what is "inside" or "outside," normal or abnormal. This type of cultural operation is readily apparent in the Marines, for they have always been explicit, unsubtle, and even aggressive about marking the boundaries of their group and policing behavior within it.

Of course, Marine Corps culture was not monolithic in the early Cold War. Officer culture was not the same as enlisted culture; there were cultural differences between pilots and infantrymen; women Marines had different stories and identities than men did. But compared to the other services—and, indeed, other subcultures in American society—there was an extraordinary amount of consensus inside the Marine Corps of this era. When one digs below the topsoil in different places in the Marines' cultural field, one finds remarkably consistent ground underneath.

Perhaps more than any other group in America, the Marines have always been cultural warriors, open and unapologetic about advertising their identity, preserving and sustaining it, and policing the boundaries that separate them from the uninitiated. They seem almost addicted to their own paraphernalia: wherever a Marine appears, Marine Corps hats, sweatshirts, and jackets are never far behind. Marine Corps flags fly outside their homes; the eagle, globe, and anchor emblem adorns cars, boats, backpacks, and biceps. Few military organizations think of their culture as a form of power; the Marines do so explicitly, protect it zealously, and deploy it offensively. It is almost a type of weapon or armor—an armored personhood carrier that protects them in both war and peace.[53] While other services may sport similar trappings of identity and community, many Marines do so obsessively. Aaron Sorkin's 1992 film *A Few Good Men* summed it up well: to a certain degree, Marines are fanatical about being Marines.

Metaphors of culture as a weapon or armor carry us only so far, however. Weapons can be aimed and controlled; culture, much less so. A celebratory story can backfire; an image meant to criticize can instead be appropriated by the very target at which it is aimed. Cultural products do not always operate according to their producers' intentions, any more than military forces do according to the campaign plans of the generals. In short, the environment is relevant, whether it is the literal terrain of the battlefield or the figurative terrain of a cultural field. Therefore, to understand the power of Marine Corps culture, we cannot limit the investigation to the cultural products themselves; we must also examine how the products were received by different audiences. Doing so shows that more often than not, the Marines read the cultural terrain well, adapted their stories to it, and thus were able to project their power into the surrounding cultural fields.

Much as farmers do for their crops, the Marines of this era worked constantly to prepare the cultural landscape so that their stories might take root and flourish. They did so most assiduously inside their own cultural field, the internal world of the Marine Corps. But they also cast seeds into other, non-Marine fields, where some narratives thrived and others did not. Some stories required constant cultivation; others emerged despite the Corps' best efforts to weed them out.

As a result of these operations, the Marines expanded their power, authority, and influence inside the military and the country.

The method of that expansion was to build alliances and establish cultural settlements in fields outside their own. The activating engine of their expansion was not just success in battle or a superior public relations machine; it was the deep mistrust, trauma, and fear of outsiders that were pervasive inside the Corps community. The following chapters explore the origins of the Marines' cultural power, as well as its maneuvers, contradictions, and effects on midcentury America.

The first chapter analyzes the Corps' best stories about itself and the rules and conditions operating inside the Marines' own cultural universe. It chronicles the Corps' growth in World War II and the formative experiences of recruit training and combat in the Pacific. It also explains the narratives of Marine exceptionalism—a set of shared stories about the Corps' superiority that constituted the meta-narrative of Marine identity. Tracing their influence on Marines young and old, officer and enlisted, active and long retired, I argue that Marine culture functioned much like a religion, one grounded in practices of violence, experiences of trauma, and narratives of persecution. Those identity narratives and the experiences that empowered them go far to explain why Marines made such strong commitments to their service culture and remained attached to it for the rest of their lives.

Chapter 2 charts the extension of Marine Corps culture into civilian society from the start of World War II until the Korean War. The success of that cultural operation depended on both institutional and cultural factors—on how the Marines organized their publicity apparatus and the environment in which it operated. By maintaining close contact with editors of both major daily newspapers and small local papers, they spread their stories far and wide, in ways the larger services did not duplicate. Similar efforts occurred in the field of radio and film. By the end of the war, the Corps had an effective coalition of civilian publishers, editors, and writers who served as a resource for the Corps for decades thereafter. The types of stories they told also mattered. Unlike the other services, the Marine

Corps focused its storytelling on its youngest members, the privates, and emphasized the deeply personal themes of family and community. In so doing, they mastered the rhetoric of "tender violence"—a discursive strategy that used domestic themes to soften warfare and reframe it in a more family-friendly light.[54] This emphasis on domestic themes continued long after the war's end. The Toys for Tots charity program (begun in 1947) and Republic Pictures' blockbuster film *Sands of Iwo Jima* (1949) are two later examples of how Marine publicists managed the Corps' image by speaking the language of American family life.

The following chapter traces the Corps' expansion into Congress and explains how the Marines transformed their wartime cultural capital into political power. Immediately after the war, the Corps helped elect a disproportionate number of Marine veterans to Congress, often bending (and in some cases breaking) rules to do it. Illegalities continued in the Corps' political lobbying during the reorganizations that unified the War and Navy Departments into a single Department of Defense. A small group of Marines known as the "Chowder Society" took creative liberties with the law and naval regulations in order to protect the Corps from the President's economizing efforts. Here and elsewhere, the Marines' impassioned belief in their own persecution was essential to their success.

Chapters 4 and 5 examine the aftermath of war. I first explore the cultural terrain of post–Korean War America, a landscape that was filled with civil-military friction. That friction helped make Korea the "forgotten war," but it did not impede the movement of Marine Corps stories into the surrounding cultural geography. Of all the services' stories, the Marines' Korean War narratives enjoyed the best mobility in the post-Korea cultural terrain. The success of those narratives bolstered the Corps' reputation, giving it increased legitimacy and prestige with journalists, historians, and national security experts.

Korea also exacted a heavy toll on Marines' minds, bodies, and families, much as World War II had done less than a decade before.

Because Marines committed themselves so completely to their service's culture, failing to measure up to the Corps' own unrealistic ideals could precipitate identity collapse. The cultural gulf between the Marines' world and civilian society made it difficult to leave the former and reenter the latter, and the civil-military friction of the 1950s only widened that gulf. The inability to generate usable stories about their service led some to relive the war for years thereafter as victims of post-traumatic stress.

Chapter 5 explores one of the unacknowledged "default programs" of Marine Corps culture: the propensity to use aggression and violence when faced with uncertainty or stress. Using four incidents of abuse in the Corps of the 1950s, I demonstrate how the habits of mind Marines learned inside the Corps also made unwelcome advances into other areas of their lives. On the Freedom Train Tour of 1948 and in the Devil Pups Citizenship Project (a Marine Corps camp for teenagers modeled on recruit training), Marines lashed out at children and taught them that violence was a critical component of manhood. In the recruit training environment of the 1950s, unauthorized violence was rampant and at times deadly. The final story of the chapter is one of domestic violence and murder, which returns to the theme of the lasting effects of war on families.

The final chapter explains how the Corps' culture affected its strategic assumptions, its role in national defense, and America's role in the world. As early as 1948, the Marine Corps disputed the other services' assumptions about the types of military operations the Cold War would entail and began building forces for a wider range of military operations. Their predictions proved prescient in numerous short-of-war contingencies in the Middle East, Caribbean, and Asia, and the Corps' ideas about armed conflict are the reason these capabilities developed. Because the Marines worried incessantly about their institutional survival, they became convinced that they could not follow the strategic path outlined by the other services. Only by doing something different would they avoid charges of duplication and irrelevance. This led them away from nuclear weapons and toward the lower end of the conflict spectrum, to missions such as peace-keeping, counterinsurgency, and non-nuclear crisis response. Their service's antiscientific mind-set and predilection for romantic, human-centered narratives pushed them away from the growing bureaucracies, computers, and data-driven techniques that were proliferating throughout the Cold War military. These cultural dynamics shaped the type of forces they built, forces that have been increasingly in demand since the Cold War ended.

The book ends at the start of the Vietnam War, at which point the Marines were more firmly entrenched in American society and the Department of Defense than at any previous time in their history. And while Vietnam damaged the reputation of all the services, the Marines bounced back quickly in the 1980s. The infrastructure they had built in World War II and the early Cold War—the networks of media support, the political allies, the Marine Air-Ground Task Forces, and a set of stories with lasting legitimacy and power—was integral to that comeback. That infrastructure has made the modern Marine Corps what it is today.

1 A Harsh and Spiritual Unity

There's a magical feeling about being a United States Marine. I can't describe it to you or to anyone. But other Marines, they understand.

—Major Rick Spooner, U.S. Marine Corps (retired)

Rick Spooner is eighty-six years old and still gets a regulation "high and tight" haircut every week. In public he wears what Marines call "appropriate civilian attire": a collared shirt neatly tucked into trousers, belt buckle in perfect alignment with his trousers' centerline. Neither age nor the three wars he participated in show any effect on his body: it is trim, athletic, and ramrod straight. His mustache, white and pencil thin, is also regulation, neither touching the lips nor extending beyond the corners of the mouth. He calls civilians "sir" or "ma'am" unless he knows them well. But fellow members of the Corps are almost never addressed by rank. "When they walk in the door, it's always 'Hello, Marine,'" he explains. "Because that's more important than being a general or a private or a lieutenant. They're Marines. That's what's important." His smile is engaging and genuine, his speech quick and articulate. When he talks about friends lost in World War II, even the youngest ones, his voice does not modulate much; he has long since made his peace with the dead. But when he speaks of the Corps itself—of its history, traditions, and unique spirit—his face reanimates and his voice gets quiet and impassioned. "The Marine Corps is not a job," he insists, "it's a vocation."[1]

Rick owns and operates the Globe and Laurel Restaurant, which sits just outside the main gate of Marine Corps Base Quantico in northern Virginia. The Globe and Laurel is part restaurant, part museum, and part Marine Corps shrine. Almost every inch of wall space is covered with exhibits: captured weapons from two centuries of wars, medals, flags, and Rick's own Japanese souvenirs from the Pacific. Every night, Marines come from the base and the surrounding areas to eat and to admire the living tribute to their organization. Rick visits with everyone: listening to the Marines, chatting with their friends, and, when asked, telling something of his nearly thirty years in the Corps and his service during World War II, Korea, and Vietnam.

Like most of the Marines who fought in World War II, Rick was not drafted. He volunteered. When the war broke out, he never had any doubt which service he would join. He fell in love with the Corps the first time he ever saw a Marine. Working as a shoeshine boy on the docks of San Francisco, he would often see servicemen coming off the battleships in San Francisco Bay. The Marines always stood out: "Always in blues, marching down the street, looking tall and squared away, and never letting me shine their shoes, always referring me to the sailors. . . . The Marines were too proud to let a kid shine their shoes. And I thought, 'Wow, they're special, they're different, they're wonderful!'"

At fourteen, Rick dropped out of school and tried to enlist in the Corps by doctoring a birth certificate. He was caught and discharged after three days. By seventeen, he was in the Corps legally; by eighteen, he was an infantry rifleman fighting in the South Pacific. Before he was twenty-one, he had been wounded four times and seen many of his fellow Marines killed on the islands of Saipan, Tinian, and Okinawa. He was discharged when the war ended but missed the Corps too much to stay out. Three months later, he reenlisted at the same rank he had held for most of World War II: private first class.

Rick's career in the Corps was unusual—he stayed twenty-nine years and rose to the rank of major—but his experience in World War II was not. Nor is his continued attachment to the Corps as a retiree atypical. There's no such thing as an ex-Marine, veterans are fond of saying, only *former* Marines. People leave the Marine Corps, but it does not leave them. While Rick's restaurant and the two autobiographical novels he wrote are uncommonly public displays of devotion, few veterans would disagree with his assertion that "there's a magical feeling about being a United States Marine."[2]

Rick Spooner at the bar of his restaurant, the Globe and Laurel, in Quantico, Virginia, 2011. (Photo by author)

THE "MAGIC" OF MARINE CORPS CULTURE

World War II did not create the Marine Corps feeling. As long as there have been Marines, they have insisted that they are superior to the other services and have located that superiority in transcendent nouns such as "esprit," "spirit," "mystique," and "feeling." But even though these stories and feelings existed before Pearl Harbor, the combat in the Pacific had a pronounced effect on them. There was a deep compatibility between the stories Marines brought to the war and the experiences they found once in it. Perceptions of mistreatment strengthened their claims of uniqueness and elitism, even though they and the Army performed, at times, almost identical missions.[3] Their culture grew stronger because the fighting confirmed their best ideas about themselves and their worst fears about the other services, particularly the Army.

The most important stories Marines carried into war with them were a set of claims asserting unconditionally that Marines were, and always have been, unique and superior to all other military services. On the surface, these narratives of Marine exceptionalism were simple and almost tautological: Marines are special, better than any other armed service, its members claimed, and it is the feelings, traditions, and spirit of the Marines that make them so. Underneath this circular logic, however, lay an unspoken contract between the Marine and the Corps, one that traded comfort for prestige and lionized suffering and self-sacrifice as quintessential acts of devotion. This contract of suffering only grew stronger as the costs of war mounted in the Pacific. The result was a lasting bond, formed by shared stories and a broad network of kinship that encompassed both the living and the dead. And while some Marines probably considered the Corps nothing more than a job, for the majority it was much more: a vocation, an identity, and even a new family.

At its most basic level, Marine Corps culture functioned through a process of symbolic exchange.[4] Being a Marine meant elitism, an intimate community, and access to a set of stories granted only to a few. But those benefits were not free. The costs of belonging to the Corps were more than the typical restrictions on freedom and autonomy found in any military culture. More so than in the other services, membership in the Marine Corps required an ideological commitment, the abandonment of previous civilian identities, and the adoption of a new set of stories and priorities. One officer put it well a decade after World War II: "The Marine Corps must seek to possess the souls of its personnel as earnestly as it strives to condition their bodies."[5] As Rick Spooner and so many other veterans attest, once adopted, the Corps' stories and priorities often lasted a lifetime.

Violence was an essential component of the Marines' cultural contract. What made Marines different, new recruits quickly learned, was an impressive capacity to endure discomfort. That capacity was tested and proved in boot camp, where the suffering was usually limited to verbal abuse, exhausting exercises, and perhaps the occasional beating. But once in combat, the process of exchanging suffering for prestige came at a higher cost. As the price of Marine prestige grew, so too did its members' valuation of that title. The Corps' steadily increasing casualties in World War II—which were twelve times greater in the last year of fighting than they were in the first—further convinced Marines that their service was superior to the others around them.[6]

At first glance, this claim that increasing suffering created greater attachment and dedication to the Corps may seem counterintuitive. The costs of the war, in terms of lives and limbs lost, friendships and minds shattered, would seemingly prompt disaffiliation with the Marines' community, not deeper attachment to it. As casualties grew steadily worse, cohesion should have decreased as the gulf between costs and benefits widened. Instead, the reverse occurred: the dedication to and insularity of the Corps only grew stronger throughout the war even as the final and most violent battles exacted so high a price. When blame needed assigning, it fell almost always on other services, not on the organization that demanded so much of its members. The narratives of Marine exceptionalism continued to function, even when the service's principal marker of difference was greater suffering and dying.

This reframing of suffering and sacrifice as devotion to one's community is not unique to the Marine Corps. Similar cultural maneuvers exist in societies the world over and are particularly overt in religious communities. The basic cultural operation of such practices is to reconfigure a cost into a symbolic benefit, to recode pain or loss as a mark of devotion, distinction, or prestige. In the Marine Corps, these quasi-religious elements had both positive and negative attributes. They led some to sacrifice themselves unhesitatingly, but gave others a way to understand and to explain the violence and death surrounding them in the Pacific. Above all else, the Marines' greater suffering and sacrifice gave them proof positive that their own best stories about themselves and their Corps were true.

THE NEW CORPS AND THE "DEMOCRATIC ARMY"

The Marine Corps in 1939 was small and selective, with only 1,400 officers and 18,000 enlisted men.[7] Recruiters took just one of every five applicants, and many officers and non-commissioned officers (NCOs) were already battle-hardened from fighting insurgencies in Haiti, the Dominican Republic, and Nicaragua.[8] Most officers and senior enlisted men knew each other, either personally or by reputation. Marines also had a strong shared sense of place, as there were just a handful of bases, ships, and overseas stations available for assignment. Theirs was still an imagined community—no one knew *everyone* in the Marine Corps as they would in an actual family—but it was a tight-knit organization nonetheless, where networks of friendship and camaraderie were easy to establish.[9]

This culture remained cohesive during the war despite the fact that the Corps expanded to twenty times its prewar size. Even at its largest—just under 500,000 men in 1945—Marines remained connected to each other by just one or two degrees of separation.[10] Two enlisted men of the same grade would have gone through one of the two recruit training depots at Parris Island, South Carolina, or San Diego, California. Officers all went through training at Quantico, Virginia, and served under the same handful of regimental and division commanders. At its largest, the Corps had just 72 general officers; the Army had more than 1,500.[11]

Even in the "New Corps" (as the prewar Marines called it), there was a palpable sense of elitism and community that was impossible to duplicate in the larger services. This was not an accident—whereas the other services gave more attention to ships, planes, and the machines of war, Marine recruiters specifically marketed the Corps' traditions, history, and reputation as an all-volunteer force.[12] The emphasis on elitism worked: in the first six months of the war, the Marine Corps doubled in size and had a faster rate of growth than either the Army or the Navy.[13] Weekly enlistments, which had peaked at a pre–Pearl Harbor one-week high of 552, jumped to 6,000 per week.[14]

The all-volunteer Corps did not endure long in World War II, however. In late 1942, President Roosevelt required the War and Navy Departments to procure personnel through the Selective Service System, thus halting the Marines' direct recruiting of draft-age men. Fortunately, President Roosevelt's executive order pertained only to those between eighteen and thirty-five, which allowed the Marines to still enlist seventeen-year-olds. Between 1943 and 1945, the Corps recruited and enlisted 60,000 seventeen-year-old volunteers, as well as some younger than seventeen who, like Rick Spooner, forged papers.[15] The Corps also staged "Marine liaisons" at the Selective Service induction centers, where they persuaded draftees to request assignment to the Marine Corps.[16] As a result, of the 669,000 who served in the Marine Corps in World War II, roughly one-third came in through the Selective Service System, but only 70,000 exercised no choice in choosing the Marines.[17] The rest volunteered in one way or another—either joining the Corps voluntarily before 1943 or choosing the Marines over the other branches once drafted. This system of partial choice allowed the Corps to maintain the fiction of an all-volunteer Marine Corps and to preserve its elitist image. The

Army, which contained more than 70 percent draftees, could not make a similar case.[18]

The volunteers of 1942 and the partial volunteer system that existed thereafter made the World War II Marine Corps a self-selected group. Unlike the prewar Marine Corps, in which the South was overrepresented, World War II Marines came disproportionately from the Northeast and Mid-Atlantic states. The South was underrepresented.[19] The most overrepresented states—Pennsylvania, Massachusetts, Michigan, and Illinois—all had large urban populations, which tended to send more recruits to the Marines than did the more rural areas. (West Virginia was a notable exception.)[20] African Americans were segregated and severely underrepresented, accounting for only 3 percent of all who served in the Corps during the war.[21] Women served in equally small numbers, totaling just under 20,000 by war's end.[22] Hispanics and American Indians were integrated into combat units with whites, though they too encountered regular racial discrimination. The Marine Corps in World War II was still essentially a club for white men, and there was serious resistance in all ranks to making it otherwise.

The most significant demographic characteristic of the World War II Marine Corps was its youth. In the testosterone-infused environs of the recruiting and induction stations, it was the younger men who were most vulnerable to the pressure to join the toughest outfit, whether the influence was coming from the Marine recruiting liaisons or from their own comrades. Many Marine recruits were fresh out of high school, and like most young men, they yearned for tests of manhood. In the Army, where more than 80 percent of the soldiers were over twenty-one, identities were more fully formed.[23] These men had greater experience with responsibility and adulthood; they needed no drill instructor to tell them they were men. But the younger Marine recruits did. For these boys, still in search of themselves and desperate for role models in the new social universe of wartime America, the Corps offered a compelling narrative of self, community, and, most important, manhood. By the end of the war, the Marines would fill 40 percent of their ranks with men age twenty-one or younger.[24]

Though some friction existed between the prewar Marines and the New Corps, the rifts were minor in comparison to the Army. Recruits entering the Marine Corps understood they were leaving civilian culture behind; indeed, if memoirists' descriptions are to be trusted, many chose the Marine Corps because of its distinctiveness from civilian society. Most recruits respected their NCOs, many of whom had had combat experience in Central America or the Caribbean or had been stationed in Asia during the interwar years. Even relations between officers and enlisted men—always fractious in military organizations—were less problematic in the Marines because so many of the prewar officers had been commissioned from the enlisted ranks. These "Mustangs," as prior-service officers were called, made up 62 percent of the second lieutenants in 1942 and 49 percent of the lieutenant colonels.[25] They and the enlisted leaders passed on the sense of community and elitism that were integral to the narratives of Marine exceptionalism.

The Army also had a prewar service culture steeped in martial tradition, but it did not weather the wartime expansion as successfully as the Marines' culture did. The influx of so many draftees forced civilian mores into the Army, creating deep rifts between the prewar regular soldiers and the new draftees. Educational differences between draftees and the prewar regulars exacerbated the tensions, particularly since so few regulars had combat experience to bolster their authority with the new recruits.[26] The size of the Army proved another obstacle. With so many men and units, the Army's identity narratives were formed around individual regiments or divisions; no single, unifying story for the entire Army ever gained authority.[27]

Army soldiers in World War II had a firm sense of patriotism and agreed on one goal: to win the war. Beyond that, there was little to bind them together. Some entered by choice, others because they were drafted. Some fought in the Pacific, others in Europe, the Mediterranean, or the Middle East. Almost a quarter stayed in the United

States. Service-wide cohesion was hindered further by the fact that infantry divisions were separated by type: regular, reserve, and National Guard, with no small amount of interunit rivalry between them. Across the service, there was a relatively low density of common experience. The wide variation of Army experiences in the war, the deployment to many theaters, and the sheer number of units made it impossible to create a uniform culture across the whole service. With such weak bonds of commonality, few draftees found a strong sense of martial identity in the Army. They were citizens first, soldiers by necessity.[28]

The Army's only attempt at a service-wide identity narrative was that of the "democratic army," which further diluted martial tradition by asserting that the military was a natural extension of civilian life.[29] As explained by the nation's political and military leaders, America's strongest advantage in the war was an armed force of citizen-soldiers, whose greater individualism and creativity would outthink and outfight their totalitarian enemies. Conscription was not a deviation from American tradition but a mere "change in circumstances, demanding a redirection of the skills and efforts of every American, but allowing even those men drafted into the armed forces to continue revised versions of their civilian lives."[30]

This reframing of military service as an extension of civilian life created persistent friction within the Army. Recruits came in expecting the right to voice dissent and believing that civilian values of meritocracy and individualism could coexist with military hierarchy and discipline. The culture clash that resulted not only undermined the "democratic army" narrative but also diluted the Army's prewar martial tradition and thwarted the development of a single cohesive service culture.[31]

The Marine Corps made no effort to adapt its culture to civilian society. Rather than downplaying the costs of moving from civilian to military life, it emphasized them. Instead of noting similarities, the Corps insisted on its own radical difference from every other group—the Japanese and German enemies, the other American services, and even the civilian society whence it came. In boot camp, recruits experienced a total break with civilian society and entered an environment of absolute discipline, transcendent narratives, and, most of all, ritualized violence. Together, these practices not only built effective military men but also gave recruits a new identity and symbolic universe that they would carry with them onto the battlefields of the Pacific theater.

RECRUIT TRAINING AND THE MARINE CORPS RELIGION

Recruit training (also called boot camp) was the central locus of cultural indoctrination for enlisted Marines. The lessons imparted there by drill instructors (DIs) were intense and at times brutal. And while combat training was an essential component of the experience, the primary purpose of recruit training was to effect "the transition from a civilian to a Marine"—to instill in recruits a new culture, complete with its own language, myths, heroes, and rituals.[32]

This experience was drastically different—in content and purpose—from the Army's initial training program, which occurred at 242 different training centers around the country.[33] Because the Army's basic goal was to build and then integrate all the component parts of an entire division, the training philosophy was Taylorist: it emphasized rational and efficient classification rather than cultural transformation. After a month-long orientation in basic military subjects, classification officers sorted and segregated the new soldiers by military specialty. For the remainder of their training, soldiers trained in specific technical skills: engineers worked demolitions, clerks learned administrative procedures, signalmen strung wire, and infantry units conducted tactical exercises. The primary methods of instruction were lectures, films, and practical demonstrations. None of this was easy, and, at thirteen weeks, Army basic training was longer than the six to eight weeks of Marine boot camp. However, two-thirds of Army basic was devoted to technical subjects and small-unit training; the single month of common training was hardly enough to effect the type of cultural transformation experienced by those entering the Marine Corps.[34]

The Marine recruit's first contact with the Corps was designed not for orientation, as in the Army, but for shock and disorientation. Upon arrival at Parris Island or San Diego, Marine recruits received what former recruit depot commander General Victor H. Krulak later called an "ego-ectomy":

> Initiation starts with a reduction of all to a common denominator. Stripped naked in a group for a physical examination, they are bathed together, their heads clipped, civilian clothing and jewelry removed, all dressed exactly the same. From this moment, none is different from any other. None is better than any other.... [T]hey start from an initial zero and they are rebuilt from there.[35]

Unlike the other services, which bestowed the label "soldier" or "sailor" upon induction, the new recruits could not yet call themselves Marines. Officially, they were "recruits" or "boots"; more colloquially, they were "shitbirds." Neither civilian nor Marine, they were like novitiates in a religious order, consigned to a liminal status until they completed recruit training.[36]

To emphasize the abrupt shift away from civilian life, drill instructors resorted readily to "rigorous physical punishment" to imprint the culture of the Corps on the new initiates.[37] The first step was to learn the Marines' language, some of which dated from the age of sail. "It was unwise," remembers one World War II recruit, "to call a deck a 'floor,' a bulkhead a 'wall,' an overhead a 'ceiling,' a hatch a 'door,' or a ladder 'stairs.' . . . On Parris Island these and all other customs of the boot's new way of life were flouted at great risk."[38] DIs corrected mistakes with physical exercises performed in flea-ridden sandpits, and sometimes with slaps, kicks, or worse. Particularly in the early years of the war, when the DIs were often corporals or privates first class just a year or two senior to the new recruits, the discipline could lead to beatings and concussions.[39] The harshest punitive measures were most often used to correct cultural gaffes—mistakes in terminology, failures in military courtesy, or symbolic mistreatment of one's rifle.

Of all the subjects in the training schedule, weapons instruction received the most attention—more than twice as many hours as any other subject. Field training ranked second in total hours; physical training ranked fourth. The physical components of boot camp were intense: in 1943 they included thirty minutes of "body contact exercises" and thirty minutes of "massed bare-handed boxing" every day.[40] There were twice-weekly training sessions in hand-to-hand and unarmed combat, as well as bayonet drills, judo, and wrestling. Though much of this training was pragmatic in nature, the violence of the process served another function as well. The punitive exercises, hand-to-hand fighting, and disciplinary violence not only prepared the recruit for combat but also linked the measure of his worth to his capacity to suffer. Recruits learned, in ways they would not forget, that what made Marines exceptional was their ability to endure more pain than members of their sister services. "We soon gloried in the hardships heaped upon us and in our ability to endure them," remembered one World War II Marine who would later be elected to Congress. "We also developed a fierce loyalty to each other and pride in being members of a Corps that asked for tough and dangerous duty."[41]

Though physical conditioning was an obvious priority for combat, it accounted for less than one-tenth of the total scheduled hours.[42] Nearly twice as much time was spent on garrison subjects, and much of it was devoted to close-order drill: the highly ritualized art of maneuvering a military unit around a parade ground in perfect unison. Up to three hours a day were spent marching, during which DIs would single out the poor performers and assign them extra exercises.[43] (By contrast, initial training in the Army involved only forty-five minutes of close-order drill daily, and only for the first month.)[44] Regular rifle and uniform inspections, which were also highly ritualized affairs, gave the DIs further opportunities to find innumerable (and often fictional) flaws in their recruits. Though seemingly irrelevant for modern combat, drill, inspections, and other "spit-and-polish" traditions of military service were essential for effecting the transition from civilian to Marine. They taught recruits to submit to authority, to venerate tradition, and to sacrifice comfort, safety, and even life, all in the name of Marine Corps discipline.

The Marines' emphasis on violence, drill, and inspections was not the only method of imprinting the culture of the Corps on new recruits. The Marines' unique admixture of history and mythology was another critical component. In addition to receiving lectures on Marine Corps customs and courtesies, recruits also received ad hoc history lessons from their DIs. This oral history gave recruits new stories about themselves and their community to replace the civilian identity they had left behind. As Rick Spooner explained it:

> The thing that makes Marines different is our esprit de corps. And the esprit de corps comes from several things, but one of the contributing factors is a knowledge of our heritage.... Whenever we were marching somewhere or taking a break from close-order drill . . . they [the DIs] would just give us a two- or three-minute vignette about some individual in Marine Corps history or some great battle. And we listened . . . we'd hear it again a week later, two weeks later, three weeks later, from another DI or a different instructor. By the time we graduated from boot camp, we knew a lot about Marine Corps history.... [T]he heritage and history—you just absorbed [it], you soaked it up. By the time you left boot camp, you were really a Marine. Not just because you could wear the emblem, but in your heart, you were a Marine.

As the hours Marines spent on ceremony, tradition, and history demonstrate, much of recruit training during World War II was designed not to impart specific combat skills but to ritualize the recruit's induction into a new culture. This is not to say that drill and inspections had no practical military purpose. They did. But the pragmatic goals of such training—to instill discipline, promote teamwork, and encourage proper care of equipment—were only part of their purpose. Their greater effect was symbolic. The endless drill, specialized jargon, and monastic strictures concerning the proper way to wear the uniform gave the narratives of Marine exceptionalism visible markers: upon graduation, Marines looked, talked, and even walked differently than everyone else. As Rick first noted as a youngster, it was not just the uniform but their manner of striding proudly down the docks of San Francisco that made Marines "special," "different," and "wonderful."

The violence of recruit training also filled a deeper need in young men seeking to transition from boyhood to manhood. The haranguing DIs seemed at times excessive to some, but for many of the younger recruits the violence was not only tolerated but expressly desired.[45] "Boot camp was wonderful!" remembers Rick. "I thought it would be very demanding and that was fine with me. I wanted to be a Marine."[46] Boot camp "is a process of surrender," wrote Private Robert Leckie, who joined immediately after Pearl Harbor. "We were having it rough, which is exactly what we expected and what we signed up for. That is the thing: having it rough. The man who has had it roughest is the man to be most admired. Conversely, he who has had it the easiest is the least praiseworthy."[47]

While the desire to prove oneself was probably strongest among the teenage recruits, it was not only the young who willingly tolerated the excesses of the DIs. Dan Levin, who entered the Marines at age twenty-nine, remembered boot camp as a "gift." By giving "fond obedience to the playfully brutal routines of boot camp," he wrote, the recruit entered "a harsh and spiritual unity. Stripped of higher education, of past, and of future ambitions for myself, I was becoming one of the anonymous many. I was happy. . . . I was part of a totality and felt a great collective will working on me and shaping me."[48] Sergeant William Manchester, whose *Goodbye, Darkness* is one of the finest memoirs of the Pacific War, also entered Parris Island in his twenties. As he describes it: "Astonishingly, I adored Parris Island. . . . How could I enjoy this? Parts of it, of course, I loathed. But the basic concept fascinated me. I wanted to surrender my individuality, curbing my neck beneath the yoke of petty tyranny. . . . Everything I saw seemed exquisitely defined—every leaf, every pebble looked as sharp as a drawing in a book. I knew I was merely becoming a tiny cog in the vast machine which would confront fascism, but that was precisely why I had volunteered."[49]

The spiritual tone of Levin's, Manchester's, and Spooner's descriptions—the pleasures of surrender and the deep feeling of community that resulted—is commonplace in memoirists' descriptions of Marine Corps boot camp. Descriptions of initial training in the Army are quite different. Instead of emphasizing feeling, emotion, and spirit, Army veterans more commonly used the language of pragmatism and rational organization. Soldiers remembered their training in terms of its efficiency or inefficiency, its practicality, and the value of the skills. Even in the more elite units, such as the armored and airborne divisions, where one would expect a higher degree of tradition and community, training focused almost exclusively on transmitting combat skills.[50] Compared to Marines, soldiers had far less interest in martial tradition; they derided the lessons in drill and ceremony as irrelevant and distracting from the business of learning to fight.[51]

In the Marine Corps, the emphasis on spirituality pervaded the ranks, from the lowest private to the highest general. "War," the Commandant of the Marine Corps said in 1943, "is about one fifth body, four fifths mind and spirit. That's the proportion I want in the Marines."[52] "The first requirement" of being a Marine, noted a 1942 leadership pamphlet for lieutenants, is to "know our Corps. We must be proud of its traditions. It must be our religion, our main spring, our very soul. We must be willing to sacrifice, suffer and die—just as Marines have done since the capture of Fort New Providence in the Bahamas in 1776, to the defense of Wake Island."[53] For Sergeant Dan Levin, that willingness to sacrifice, which he called a "pride in a prodigal throwing away of the self," was "at the bottom of the psychology of those who became Marines."[54]

In fact, references to spirit, sacrifice, and the pleasures of surrendering to a higher authority are found throughout the culture of the Marine Corps, from World War II through the Cold War. Writers in the *Marine Corps Gazette* spoke of a "Jesuitical zealousness in the profession of arms" in the 1950s; generals in the 1960s called Marine esprit de corps "a way of life, a religion . . . the fountain at which annually we renew our strength."[55] Gerald Averill, a World War II private who rose through the ranks to lieutenant colonel, gave the idea its fullest expression in a memoir published at the end of his career: "To the Marine, the *Corps* is his religion, his reason for being. He cannot be committed up to a point. For him, involvement is total. He savors the traditions of his Corps and doubts not the veracity of them. He believes implicitly that he must live up to those epics of physical and moral courage established by those who preceded him. . . . His is an unsworn oath, an unspoken promise, a conviction that he must never betray the trust of his comrades and that his individual safety, his very life must be secondary to the attainment of the unit's assigned objective."[56]

This notion of the Marine Corps as a "religion" would probably not sit well with anthropologists of religion, but it does help explain why Marine Corps culture was so strong in World War II, and why it grew more cohesive thereafter. The physical suffering of boot camp and the constant emphasis on history and tradition gave recruits the same thing that most religions provide their members through less extreme rituals: a connection to a larger family that reaches across time and space. This was one of the principal benefits of membership in the Marine Corps: a broad and deep sense of kinship that encompassed all Marines, past and present, living and dead. While devotion to actual (living) buddies was always paramount in motivating Marines in battle, this larger imagined community provided an additional feeling of connection, above and beyond the commitments to one's squad, platoon, company, or battalion.[57] What historian Jay

Winter calls "fictive kinship"—a set of ties with the same affective strength of family but applied to a larger group—thus bound Marines together in ways not experienced by members of the larger and more diversified services.[58] It was not only to the members of their unit that Marines remained *Semper Fidelis,* "always faithful." It was to an idealized and timeless community of ancestors—the entire "family" of the Corps.

The proof of Marines' belief in a timeless community of the living and the dead lies in the many cultural products of the period that featured Marine Corps ancestors and ghosts visiting the living. Sometimes this was done lightheartedly, as in the 1944 story "A Marine Never Dies," which features the ghost of Major Samuel Nicholas (the first Commandant of the Marine Corps, who died in 1790) visiting a twentieth-century training base to check up on his Corps.[59] However, more serious variations on the theme existed as well. A corporal writing for the *Marine Corps Gazette* in 1960 promised young Marines that if they served the Corps faithfully, they would "hear the voices of all the other good Marines who have gone before whisper the greatest commendation of them all—'well done, Marine.'"[60] A sterner warning appeared repeatedly throughout the Cold War in newspapers, in films, and on signs above office doors reading "Let no man's ghost say your training let him down."[61] Rick Spooner's first novel captured a similar sentiment when one Marine explains to another that "no one is really dead until they are forgotten."[62] And Jack Lucas, who went through boot camp at age fourteen and would win the Medal of Honor on Iwo Jima, later wrote that his spirit "was forever changed. . . . To complete basic was to accomplish immortality."[63]

These spiritual components of Marine Corps culture—the surrender of individuality "to a great collective will," the deeply felt sense of the Corps as a calling or vocation, and the notion of a Marine Corps "family" that transcended time and place—do not make the Marine Corps a religion. They merely show that it functioned like one.[64] Together, these ideas and feelings did exactly what the etymological root of the word "religion" means: they bound people together in a system of shared obligations and beliefs.[65] As the above passages show, the ideas binding Marines together were explicitly transcendental, encompassing both the mundane world and another, nonmaterial realm of spirit, ancestors, and an idealized past. This system of meaning making was entirely unique in the cultures of the American military in World War II. While members of the Army, Navy, and Army Air Forces did speak approvingly of tradition, morale, and the bonds of fraternity, their training literature, memoirs, and service journals make no mention of "spiritual unity" or ghosts, and they do not refer to their service as a "religion," as the literature of the Marine Corps did. Nor did the other services have quite the same deep veneration of suffering, which offered prestige in exchange for a demonstrated capacity to endure hardship. Together, these ideas produced the sense of reverence that still flows through retired Marines such as Rick Spooner—a "magical feeling" of being a United States Marine.

Recruit training may have armed new Marines with a strong sense of family, tradition, and devotion, but it was the fighting in the Pacific that convinced them that their stories about themselves were true. The interservice rivalry of the Pacific theater and the trauma of the amphibious assaults provided the evidence for the narratives of Marine exceptionalism, fulfilling and reinforcing the logic of boot camp, where "the man who has had it roughest is the man to be most admired."[66] The wartime abuses (both real and perceived) suffered at the hands of both the Japanese enemy and the other American services only strengthened the Marines' ethos during the war and afterward. If recruit training introduced new Marines to the Corps' cultural contract, the fighting in the Pacific ensured that the contract was fulfilled.

"A LOP-SIDED WAR": FIGHTING IN THE PACIFIC

In the six months after the Pearl Harbor attack, the Japanese seized a maritime empire extending as far south as the Solomon Islands and almost as far east as the American-held island of Midway. On the myriad islands in between, they built a network of bases from which they could repair and rearm their ships, launch their planes, and supply their forces throughout the Pacific. As long as they possessed these islands, they also controlled the seas. The job for the United States was to attack and seize select islands from the Japanese, establish American bases on them, project military power west toward Japan, and win the war by either blockading, bombing, or invading the home islands.

The Marines' job in the Pacific was to do exactly what they had trained for, on and off, for almost two decades: to assault the Japanese-held islands and overwhelm the defenders in close combat. Because of the dangers inherent in such operations, the Marines had the most homogeneous and violent experience of the war: they all went to the same places, performed the same types of mission, and saw the same kind of combat in higher percentages than did the larger and more widely dispersed Army, Navy, or Army Air Forces. More than 90 percent of the Marine Corps served overseas during World War II; the average for all U.S. forces was just 73 percent.[67] With negligible exceptions, the Marines all went to the Pacific, where they had the highest casualty ratio of any American service.[68] Across the entire U.S. military, 6 percent of those who served during World War II were either killed or wounded in combat. In the Marine Corps, the casualty ratio was 13 percent.[69]

Despite their high casualties, the Marines were unquestionably skilled in the brutal form of close combat that the Pacific theater required. In all of their island operations, the Marines not only seized the beach and prevailed over the defenders but also, in most cases, destroyed almost the entire Japanese force. In most operations, Marines killed twice as many Japanese soldiers as they lost themselves, and in some cases almost ten times as many.[70] Rifles, machine guns, hand grenades, and bayonets were the principal weapons. Hand-to-hand fighting was common; surrenders were not. In the final year of the war, when the Japanese fought from caves, tunnels, and bunkers,

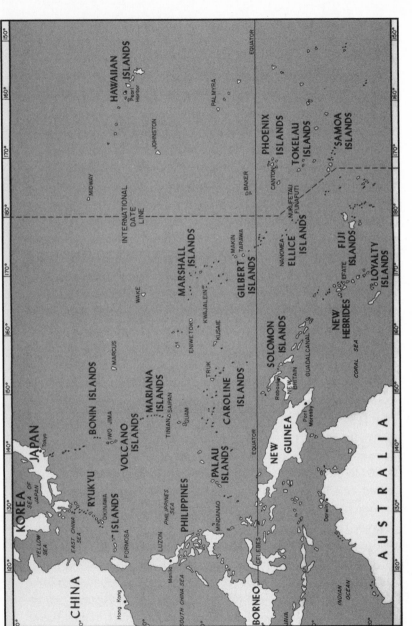

The Pacific theater of World War II. (United States Marine Corps)

flamethrowers became one of the Marines' most effective weapons. In such environments, the physical and emotional hardening of recruit training was essential precombat conditioning. It allowed Marines to stay focused, intense, and effective under the most horrific circumstances. This string of brutal victories had an effect on the Corps' culture: it yielded a consensus within the Corps about the war and the Marines' role in it. A dominant narrative, one asserting that the Corps fought better and suffered more than the other services, became widely accepted in most Marine units.[71] Bolstering this common sense were regularly rehearsed litanies of the unfair treatment received by the Marines at the hands of the Army and the Navy. Together, these narratives strengthened the Marines' internal cohesion by deflecting blame away from the Corps and onto the other services.

The Marines' first piece of evidence of their hardship was their location. Compared to Europe, the islands of the South and Central Pacific were wastelands. Temperatures rose to over 100 degrees with high humidity. The jungles hosted parasites, stinging plants, and poisonous snakes. Coral reefs and kunai grass cut and infected the skin; volcanic ridges and cliffs exhausted the infantry. The water caused intestinal cramps and diarrhea. Malaria, dengue fever, and scrub typhus gave the Southwest Pacific theater the second highest disease rate of the war.[72] For those serving in the Pacific, the most common infectious or parasitic condition was malaria. In the European and Mediterranean theaters, it was gonorrhea.[73]

Campaigns in Europe lasted much longer than in the Pacific but also were closer to the relative comforts of civilization. After Paris was liberated, it became an oft-visited liberty destination for the troops. In the Pacific, men languished in barren island camps, with little to distract them besides poker and, if they could find it or make it, alcohol. To these men, fighting in Europe at least meant *being* in Europe, with the important ancillary benefit of being able to meet, or even just look at, European women. The severe loneliness, harsh conditions, and intense combat of the Southwest Pacific help explain why the men stationed there had the highest rate of hospital admissions for psychiatric conditions during the war.[74]

Soldiers have an easier time in combat when the rules that govern it make sense and are followed. Although fighting on the Eastern front and Germany's race war against the Jews degenerated into utter brutality, the Americans' contact with the Germans did not. Ninety-nine percent of American prisoners of war survived their captivity, and more than half of the men fighting in Europe believed that the Germans "are men just like us. It's too bad we have to be fighting them."[75] No such standards existed in the war against Japan. The racial and cultural differences between the two enemies removed all constraints on conduct in battle.[76] The Japanese beat more than 90 percent of their American prisoners of war; 35 percent died in captivity.[77] Americans rarely took prisoners, and souvenir gathering turned quickly to corpse mutilation and trophy hunting. This was not only the result of the brutalization that combat brings—even before the first land campaign of the war, shipboard Marines were talking about pickling "Jap ears" and making necklaces of their gold teeth.[78] Human souvenir hunting got so bad that in 1943 the First Marine Division issued a directive that "no part of the enemy's body may be used as a souvenir. Unit commanders will take stern disciplinary action against any person acting contrary to this directive."[79] It didn't work. By 1944, human souvenir hunting had become prevalent enough for the Archdiocese of St. Louis to warn American Catholics in Missouri not to accept Japanese body parts mailed from the front.[80]

Marines did not just compare their experience to the greener pastures they assumed lay in the European theater, however. They compared themselves with the other branches serving alongside them in the Pacific. The first operation of the now-famous "island-hopping campaign" occurred on Guadalcanal, in the Solomon Islands, in August 1942. Problems began on the first night after the landing, when the United States and Australia lost four heavy cruisers in a surprise attack by the Japanese. Rightly concerned with protecting the fleet, the Navy weighed anchor and departed before the First

Marine Division could finish offloading its supplies. As a result, the Marines began the campaign with roughly half their equipment and only four days' worth of ammunition. They lacked food, radio equipment, and basic defensive materials such as barbed wire. The division immediately went on short rations, which meant the troops received only two small meals a day, much of which were captured Japanese rations that quickly rotted. The enemy attacked regularly from the sky and sea, launching daily raids on the airfield while their ships shelled the beach. Artillery and mortars hidden in the areas surrounding the Marines' positions became active every night. The Marines held only a small enclave around the airfield, in a dense jungle that provided excellent cover for Japanese snipers. Malaria, dysentery, malnutrition, and parasitic infections made life miserable. The Japanese repeatedly landed reinforcements and surrounded the Marines. With no naval support, the Marines felt abandoned. Major victories over the Japanese in late August and September improved morale, but the Marines retained a sense that they were fighting the war entirely alone.[81] In addition to 4,400 physical casualties, 526 Marines broke under the mental and emotional strain of the operation and were diagnosed with "combat fatigue."[82]

After holding off repeated Japanese land assaults, the Marines received reinforcements from the Army in the third month of the operation. The Army formally relieved the Marines in early December, but Marine-Army relations suffered another blow when General MacArthur billeted the war-weary division near Brisbane, Australia, in a marshland infested with malaria-carrying mosquitoes. Cases of malaria and related fevers quickly reached "epidemic proportions," surpassing the already high rates that had occurred on Guadalcanal.[83] Repeated efforts to convince MacArthur to move the Marines failed until the Navy agreed to provide all the transportation. These two incidents set the tone for the remainder of the war. MacArthur's slights, the supply failures, and the months of hard fighting with little outside help gave the First Marine Division plenty of evidence that they were undervalued by their sister services. The five other Marine divisions found similar evidence of mistreatment in the later amphibious assaults of the war.

The landing at Guadalcanal had surprised the Japanese defenders; they did not oppose the landing at the water's edge. Other landings on New Georgia, Bougainville, and New Britain also encountered challenging weather and geography but relatively light resistance.[84] The majority of Marine operations thereafter, however, were conducted against defended beachheads. The landing at Tarawa, in November 1943, shocked the American public: more than 3,000 Marines were killed or wounded in just seventy-six hours of fighting. Each of the ensuing operations on Saipan, Guam, and Peleliu in 1944 caused two, sometimes three times as many casualties. The last six months of the war were the worst: roughly half of the Marines' 87,000 combat casualties in World War II occurred in the final two assaults on Iwo Jima and Okinawa.[85]

The division of labor between the services was one reason for the Marines' higher casualties: in combined operations with the Army, the Marines landed in the first waves and consequently suffered the heaviest losses. Once the assault phase concluded, the Marines would turn the island over to the Army and Navy to mop up the remaining resistance and convert the island into an Allied base or staging point. This earned the other services no small amount of disrespect from the Marines: from their perspective, they were the shock troops, and everyone else was the cleanup crew.

Relations with the Navy were more amicable than with the Army, but difficult nonetheless. The Navy chaplains, surgeons, and corpsmen (medics) who served ashore with the Marines were all beloved, but disagreements between Marine and Navy planners caused regular conflict. Naval doctrine for amphibious landings dictated that the Navy would retain control of the landing forces until a beachhead had been established. This gave Marines little control over major elements of the landing: the targeting and duration of pre-landing naval gunfire, the pre-landing air bombardments, and even the location of the landing were controlled by the Navy. Navy and Marine planners fought constantly over how much ordnance should be dropped on the islands before the landings. On Peleliu and Iwo Jima, two of the costliest landings of the war, the Marines felt the Navy shortchanged them. At Iwo Jima, they asked for ten days of pre-landing bombardment. They received only three.[86]

The greatest source of interservice friction was with the Army, which conducted amphibious assaults just as the Marines did, but with different tactics. Schooled in a long tradition of ground warfare, the Army believed in conserving manpower at the expense of time or terrain seized. When they encountered stiff resistance, they would prudently regroup or attempt a different avenue of attack. Their methods were effective but slow. The Marines, by contrast, trained for quick, decisive engagements. Bypassing an enemy position or waiting for reinforcements depleted momentum and left more forces packed into the exposed areas of the beach and landing zone. Delays also placed the Navy at further risk, because ships were particularly vulnerable to submarine and aerial attack while supporting landing operations. From the Marines' perspective, success was best achieved by a continuous assault: landing quickly and pushing through the defenses, even when it meant confronting the enemy's strongest positions.[87] Speed of conquest was critical; the carnage it produced was the unfortunate but necessary price for victory. The Army found the Marines' direct approach reckless and unimaginative; the Marines thought the Army lacked tenacity. The differences were never resolved. In all of their combined operations, the Marines had higher casualty ratios but took more ground; the Army worked more slowly but conserved lives in ways Marine tactics did not.

For the junior soldier or Marine, an amphibious landing began with the movement to shore in an amphibious tractor or landing craft. More so than in the European landings, the size of the islands, beach conditions, and tidal and reef patterns greatly restricted where the Marines could land. This allowed defenders to predict where the landing would occur and to concentrate their fire on the arriving forces. In the landing craft and ashore, the assault force faced direct fire from Japanese rifles, machine guns, and large caliber antiship and antiarmor guns. Mortar and artillery rounds fell on them from above. With so many troops packed into so small a space, casualties were severe. A single artillery round could kill five or ten men.

In the November 1943 assault on Tarawa Atoll in the Gilbert Islands, the Second Marine Division suffered more than 1,000 dead and 2,200 wounded in just three days.[88] One commander counted 105 dead Marines in a space of twenty yards.[89] Despite the heavy losses, the Marines secured the island in seventy-six hours, killing the entire Japanese garrison of almost 5,000 men. The Army's objective in the Tarawa operation, nearby Makin Island, contained only 800 defenders. The Army took the island carefully, suffering only 218 total casualties, with only 66 killed.[90] However, it took the soldiers four days to do it—a fact that was noted with contempt by the Marines. The Navy concurred with the Marines, particularly after a Japanese torpedo sank the escort carrier *Liscome Bay* on the fourth day of the operation. The carrier's losses, 53 officers and 591 men, might have been avoided, some later argued, had the Army adhered to the Marines' practice of continuously pressing the attack.[91]

After Tarawa came Kwajalein, Roi-Namur, and Eniwetok in the Marshall Islands during the winter of 1944. On Kwajalein and Eniwetok, the Army again moved more slowly than the Marines would have liked.[92] Marines secured the island of Roi in under a day, Namur in two days. The Army took four days to seize Kwajalein, even though it had the lightest defenses.[93] Interservice tensions finally boiled over in June 1944 on Saipan, in the Mariana Islands. The operation, the largest thus far in the Pacific, involved 71,000 Marines and soldiers under the command of Marine lieutenant general Holland M. "Howlin' Mad" Smith. In one month of fighting, the Corps suffered more than 11,000 killed or wounded, and another 304 were diagnosed with combat fatigue.[94] "We had so many dead Marines, we were having a hard time not stepping on dead bodies," remembers Rick Spooner. "They blanketed the beach."

In three days of hard fighting, the Marines secured the beach-head, after which the Army's 27th Infantry Division came ashore. Maneuvering in the interior of the island was challenging. The jungle was thick and the terrain ideal for defenders. General Smith was impatient with his commanders, demanding, as he had on Tarawa, that they continuously press the attack—a tactic whose utility was questionable in the rugged island interior. Unhappy with the progress of the Army division, Holland Smith relieved Army major general Ralph Smith of command for his lack of aggressiveness and "defective performance."[95] The "Smith versus Smith" controversy soured Army-Marine relations for the remainder of the war. The Army convened an investigation that found the relief legal but unwarranted. Howlin' Mad Smith, never one to mince words, stood his ground. The 27th Division's performance, he claimed, was due not only to a difference in tactics but also to cowardice, pure and simple: "They're yellow. They're just not aggressive. They've held up the battle and caused my Marines casualties."[96] Holland Smith was never allowed to command Army troops again, a fact that only strengthened the Marines' belief that they were being mistreated by the other services.

The controversies over who seized more ground, how quickly, and at what cost did not exist just among officers and strategists but trickled down to the most junior ranks. Marines "get the shitty end of the deal," remembered Sergeant Dan Levin. "You bury your dead and send the wounded to the hospitals and those of you that are still alive go someplace else and get knocked off yourselves while the army comes in and gets the glory. . . . But that's the Marines. There's the kind of outfit it is. You asked for it, didn't you, so don't look for no pity."[97] Even in the rest camps, usually built on the islands the Marines had seized, friction abounded: "All the army does around here is construction, building PX's, officers clubs and recreational facilities," wrote home one lieutenant. "They are also the military police of the island and [they] sure do push the Marines around."[98] A platoon sergeant who fought in the battle for Guam returned to find the island populated with Army support troops, which only furthered his sense that the Marines were being mistreated. He wrote in his diary:

> Late afternoon we were trucked back to our area with our hearts full of bitterness. All along the roads were barracks, mess halls, even movie screens. . . . [O]ur nights were spent in the darkness of our fox holes waiting for sudden death, our days in the steaming jungle on patrol . . . making it possible for those dog-faces [Army] and Seabees [Navy construction engineers] less than two miles from us to live a life of luxury. This is a lop-sided war.[99]

As another historian has noted, the constant friction between the services hampered operations in the Pacific theater: it affected logistics and command arrangements, and it led to massive duplications of effort.[100] But while it may have hurt the overall war effort, interservice rivalry strengthened the Corps' culture. The presence of a rival service performing similar missions but with fewer casualties did not degrade the Marines' esprit de corps; it increased it. The timetable of the island operations—Marines in first, Army to follow, and then Army and Navy rear-echelon forces last—proved to the Marines that they were "having it rough" and consequently were deserving of the most admiration. The speed at which they took their objectives, regardless of the losses, only reinforced this view.

The constant interservice rivalry of the Pacific theater explains something of the strength of the Corps' culture, but the Marines' loyalty to their organization did not depend on comparisons to the Army. It stayed strong whether they operated alone or with other services. Even on Iwo Jima, an all-Marine operation, the junior members of the Corps continued to obey the mandates of their service culture, even as the demands of the continuous assault drove some to madness.

The age of the Marines in the Pacific is one of the reasons this was so. "The Marine Corps knew what it was doing, concentrating on eighteen-, nineteen-, and twenty-year-olds," recalled Sergeant Dan Levin. "How ready they were to do what was asked, and sometimes more. How careless of their existence. . . . It takes the very young to fling themselves forward, to die in battle, because they do not really know yet what life is about."[101] The young privates and privates first class, sometimes ten years younger than their Army counterparts, had a level of idealism absent in most older men. Just as it led recruits to tolerate the harassment and abuse of boot camp, idealism helped combat Marines sacrifice themselves with greater ease than older men could muster. "We were still dreamers," remembers Rick Spooner. Soldiers in the Army were "more mature, more realistic. . . . [They] were old enough to be wise and not want to be killed, and the Marines were teenage kids."

Youth was not the only reason, however; the Corps' unspoken contract of suffering and sacrifice mattered too. Reconfiguring loss of life as proof of devotion gave Marines a way to understand and explain the violence they confronted; venerating sacrifice allowed them to derive symbolic benefit from suffering and loss. As Private Leckie later explained in a memoir, "It is to sacrifice that men go to war. They do not go to kill, they go to be killed, to risk their flesh, to insert their precious persons in the path of destruction."[102] This "exultation, the self-abnegation, the absolute freedom of self-sacrifice" gave Marines ideological tools for coping with the increasing losses that the last months of the war brought.[103] The result was a culture that not only endured but grew stronger as the suffering grew more severe in the final year of the war.

By mid-1944, the Japanese had given up trying to defeat the invaders at the water's edge; instead, they dug extensive cave networks from which they planned to take as many American lives as possible before being killed themselves. The Marines' propensity to continuously press the attack proved costly in these later operations. Tarawa took three days to secure; Iwo Jima, by contrast, took thirty-five days and Okinawa eighty-two. Everywhere in these final operations, explained one correspondent, the Marines "died with the greatest possible violence. Nowhere in the Pacific War have I seen such badly mangled bodies. Many were cut squarely in half. Legs and arms lay fifty feet away from any body. Only the legs were easy to identify— Japanese if wrapped in khaki puttees, American if covered by canvas leggings. In one spot on the sand, far from the nearest clusters of dead men, I saw a string of guts fifteen feet long."[104]

The severe terrain of the islands gave a natural advantage to the defender and exhausted the attacker. Platoon Sergeant Thomas O'Neill saw his forty-man platoon reduced to twelve in the first five days of the battle for Guam, and was still ordered back into the attack. He wrote in his diary:

> I couldn't believe my ears when informed that we would continue the attack. For the past few days we've heard scuttlebutt that the elements of the Army's 77th Division had landed and we had hoped to be relieved and with only a few men left, over half the company gone and other companies worse than we were. I just couldn't see how we could go on. When I informed the platoon of the plan of attack, Duravelo and Watts both broke down and cried.[105]

The recapture of Guam lasted another twenty days, and a total of 532 Marines were diagnosed with combat fatigue before the island was secured.[106]

After Guam came Peleliu, in the Palau Islands, which planners estimated would be secured in a week. It took more than a month. Temperatures on the island rose to as high as 115 degrees; the coral ground made it impossible to bury the dead. Largely because of the duration of the operation, Peleliu broke the minds of more men than any Marine operation thus far in the war: 748 were evacuated for combat fatigue.[107] Total Marine casualties numbered close to 7,000 by the battle's end.[108]

As traumatic as it was, the losses on Peleliu paled in comparison to those on Iwo Jima and Okinawa, where the Marines suffered more than 42,000 casualties in just four months. Like Peleliu, both operations lasted over a month. At Iwo Jima, 23,203 Marines were killed or physically wounded on an island that measured just eight square miles.[109] The small size of Iwo and the lack of protective terrain ensured that even the rear-echelon Marines lived under constant shellfire. "There were no lines, nowhere to be safe. It was so small that you couldn't maneuver," wrote Second Lieutenant Robert Schless in March 1945, whose job as an embarkation officer should have kept him away from the worst of the violence.[110] Americans lived with the dead; it was impossible to bury them all. The closeness to so much death—most caused by mortars, artillery, and other high-caliber weapons that tore the body apart—wore down the psychological defenses of the troops. As Lieutenant Schless wrote in a letter just weeks after the battle:

> Some men became senile; really they seemed to age forty years before your eyes. Some turned into idiots and forgot where they were and began walking around upright and laughing and yelling and not knowing his old buddies. Some just sat down and stared until you thought their eyes would pop out. Most just sank down on the ground on their hands and knees and cried like babies, shaking all the while, and they'd look up at you with eyes full of tears and so full of uncontrollable anguish that you couldn't stand looking at them. Remember, these were big grown men, the pick of the nation; our toughest fighters. And so very many cracked up.[111]

Because of these extreme conditions, 2,448 Marines left Iwo Jima as combat fatigue casualties. Another 1,268 joined them from Okinawa, in states ranging from "dull detachment seemingly unaware of their surroundings, to quiet sobbing, or all the way to wild screaming and shouting." Together these two battles accounted for over half the Marines' combat fatigue casualties for the entire war.[112] And yet the narratives of Marine identity continued to function. Even those who were evacuated from Iwo Jima and Okinawa for combat fatigue felt guilty about leaving and asked to be sent back to their units in numbers that surprised the psychiatrists treating them.[113]

Even as these experiences broke men's minds, they also strengthened the emotional bonds between Marines. Because the Marines' culture relied so heavily on a notion of community that incorporated the dead as well as the living, it gave Marines a way to make sense of death and to carry on in otherwise unimaginable circumstances. As First Lieutenant David Tucker Brown Jr. explained in a letter to his mother: "I have seen a spirit of brotherhood, more evident in the most tattered companies, that goes with one foot here amid the friends that we see, and the other with those we see no longer, and one foot is as steady as the other. This is that 'we.' "[114] The notion that the combat Marine's bond with the dead was as strong and steady as his bond with the living is found elsewhere too. Lieutenant Schless wrote home that "you gradually got used to [the dead], and as you did you got the feeling that you were the living dead; that you belonged with them."[115] As Sergeant Dan Levin explained after the battle of Iwo Jima:

> A part of me had gone into that poem of the dead Marines and would always pipe along with them for youth destroyed. But in return for this bondage had come many rewards: the pride—ironic for me who once claimed to believe in an egalitarian world—of having been part of an elite of those more ready than the rest to "lay ourselves down at freedom's altar."[116]

The statistics for the nation's highest award for heroism give one indication of how ready Marines were to lay themselves down at that altar. Even though the Marine Corps comprised just 4 percent of the total American forces to serve in the war, eighty-two Marines earned the Medal of Honor—roughly 20 percent of the total medals awarded. Almost two-thirds of the Marines' medals were awarded posthumously. The culture's emphasis on suffering and self-sacrifice is one of the reasons for these high numbers.[117]

The effects of the Corps' culture can also be seen in the actions of the least articulate: the dazed and traumatized privates fighting both the Japanese and their own descent into madness in the final weeks of the Iwo Jima campaign. As Lieutenant Schless described his men:

> On the last attack they'd just stood up and walked bolt upright, waiting to get shot. After walking ten or twelve yards they'd fall flat on their faces, get up and walk again, straight into criss-crossing machine gun fire. They no longer cared whether they lived or died, those few that were left. Almost half of those left—and there were hardly any when I came up there—were just about to crack anyway. They were all standing up and walking around and getting shot.[118]

What is significant about the Marines' behavior is not that they were in shock or temporarily mad—some doubtless were by this point—but that so many continued to advance directly into the enemy's strength. For fifteen months, a debate had raged in military circles concerning the best tactics for seizing the islands, with the Army voicing regular condemnations of the Marines' habit of advancing directly into the teeth of enemy resistance. And yet, even by the end of the war, none of the Marines seemed to support the Army's safer tactics. In fact, junior officers scorned them: "My impression serving with the soldiers is very unfavorable," wrote Second Lieutenant Richard Kennard in a letter to his father during the battle of Okinawa. "Most of the men are old, lacking initiative and fortitude. They don't care whether it takes two days or two months to take the ground to their front and are always wanting to be relieved."[119]

Why wouldn't Lieutenant Kennard and his men—those who experienced the horrible effects of the continuous assault—adopt (or at least favor in private correspondence) the Army's safer approach? One answer is that they could not. If Marines disobeyed orders or refused to advance, they risked being disciplined: beaten, court-martialed, or, in extreme cases, shot. But Lieutenant Kennard's letter shows that another form of discipline was also in operation on the islands of the Pacific—a cultural discipline that framed the continuous assault as a course of action that was preferred to safer but less Marine-like tactics. In short, the Marines continued forward because their ideas about proper Marine behavior gave them no alternative. Death was not unimaginable; it could be incorporated into the Marine's stories about his own identity. Failing one's comrades or appearing to prefer the Army, however, could not. As one Marine noted in his last letter to his wife before being killed in the assault on Tarawa: "The Marines have a way of making you afraid—not of dying but of not doing your job."[120]

As soon as the war ended, the ideological bonds holding men together in the Army began coming apart. Draftees long inculcated with the rhetoric of the "democratic army" took to protesting the pace of demobilization. Marches, letter-writing campaigns, and even riots swept through Army bases in the Pacific.[121] In April 1946, a War Department review of Army public relations complained that "the people have turned on the army since the war" and blamed the Army for not inculcating sufficient morale among its soldiers.[122] Veterans, particularly from the Army, voiced deep displeasure with service life. "Seven million GIs, particularly those with discharges safely in their pockets, are telling us the Army stinks. . . . They are glad to escape from it and that they never again want any part of it," wrote one officer in the pages of the Army's *Infantry Journal*.[123] "Bitterness, unparalleled in scope in any victorious army of recent times, is today the earmark of the discharged GI," wrote a Navy veteran. "The same phenomenon is noticeably among the men who wore the navy blue—though not to so great or so vocal an extent; the Marines, blessed with exceptional esprit, suffer from it far less than either of their sister services."[124]

Rick Spooner is just one of the many Marines who remains "blessed with exceptional esprit." When he returned to the United States in December 1945, he quickly got a job in San Francisco, purchasing office equipment for an insurance company. It was a well-paying executive position, filled normally by college graduates, but the hiring officer was a former Marine and gave Rick the job. Rick had every reason to be happy. He liked his coworkers and joined their bowling league. The women in the office were pretty. His salary was far above what most enlisted veterans were making. When not filling out purchase orders, he would flirt with the secretaries, "drink coffee, and wonder what the hell I was supposed to be doing for all this money I was making. . . . [It was] a hell of a racket. It could've been a great thirty-year career."

Three months later, on a routine trip to the bank, Rick saw a military parade marching through downtown San Francisco. All the services were represented; the Army, remembers Rick, didn't march very well. By the time the band passed by, playing "The Marines' Hymn," he was sobbing. "Those lucky bastards [are] in the Marine Corps, and I'm standing here in a civilian suit!" he said to himself. He walked directly to the recruiting station, started the paperwork to reenlist, and then quit his job. His boss seemed to understand. "You lucky son of a bitch. Back to the Corps, huh?" was all he said.

What propelled Rick back into the Marine Corps? Why would he abandon a lucrative career to rejoin an organization that had heaped on him such hardship and suffering? "There are some things in life that are so much more important than money and status," he explained. "But other Marines, they understand. Even the ones that are getting out of the Corps know that they're leaving the Corps, but the Corps will always be a part of them. . . . It's just something that grows within your spirit."

Previous scholarship on the Corps' culture has focused on how the stories Marines brought to the battlefield affected their conduct in the Pacific.[125] The reverse was also true: the experience of the war changed the Marines' culture, making it stronger, even as the service expanded to meet wartime manpower requirements. The Corps' smaller size, youth, and system of partial volunteerism ensured that the Marines remained distinct from the Army, even as they performed similar missions on the islands of the Pacific. Recruit training imprinted the prewar service culture on the new Marines, instilling in them an ethos that valorized tradition and suffering both in boot camp and on the battlefields of the Pacific.

More than anything else, however, it was the island combat of the war with Japan that empowered the Marines' culture. The tremendous casualties of the Pacific reinforced the Corps' spirituality; interservice rivalry strengthened its insularity. The narratives of Marine exceptionalism gave men a way to interpret trauma as devotion, thus converting the costs of war into symbolic benefits. Their culture's broad network of fictive kinship bound them together in a community of remembrance, one that kept them connected to those who did not survive the war. That sense of a Marine Corps "family" continued long after the war's end and was integral to the Marines' success in the postwar era.

2

The Privates' War and the Home Front in the 1940s

There is something about the Marines—I don't know what it is—
that draws them together and makes them one.

—Frances Newman, age eighteen, June 22, 1945

The eighteen candles on Frances Newman's birthday
cake had to be lit twice. The first time, she blew them out too quickly
and the photographers crowding around her missed the shot. Perhaps
she was unaware of the time needed to frame a good photograph, or
maybe she was nervous about all the attention and the guests. The
handsome Marine in dress blues standing next to her—her "substitute brother," the newspapers would call him—probably increased
her anxiety, for she had met him just hours before. She may even have
rushed through the ceremony on purpose. All the parties, gifts, radio
interviews, and celebrity trips to New York would not bring her real
brother back; Bob had been killed four months earlier on the island
of Iwo Jima. Nevertheless, she smiled through the entire party the
Marines had organized for her. "There was a lump in my throat for a
long time," Frances wrote later, "but I just swallowed it, closed my
eyes, and in dreams Bob and I danced just as we used to do."[1]

The next day, Frances, a farmer's daughter from outside Lump-
kin, Georgia, made the front page of both the *Atlanta Journal* and
the *Atlanta Constitution*. The Associated Press picked up the story
and it appeared around the country, from Los Angeles, California, to
Lowell, Massachusetts. The papers and radio shows told a story of a
courageous young girl's letter to a Marine general, his response, and
a promise fulfilled. They explained the $100 dress and the flowers
the Marines sent Frances from the Pacific, as well as the handsome

Marine escort sent down from Atlanta, who, for one night, "will be Bob, come back to fill his promise" to dance with her on her eighteenth birthday.[2] Fan mail flooded the general's division in the Pacific, as well as the Marine Corps Division of Public Relations in Washington, which had orchestrated the spectacle. Some of the nation's biggest newspapers ran editorials. "Few incidents of this war have so struck home with Americans. It is not the mere pathos of it— there have been many other equally touching," wrote the *Christian Science Monitor*. Rather, what made Frances' birthday party so special was that "it talks so clearly and genuinely the language of American family life."[3]

Frances would agree. Though she had always admired her brother's branch of service, the party and her brother's death brought her closer to the Marine Corps, making it a second family. She began to call the Marines her "brothers" and herself "their kid sister." In a thank-you note to her brother's commanding general, written just a week after the party, she remarked:

> In the past week and a half, I've become more and more acquainted with the United States Marines and the great work they are doing. There is something about the Marines—I don't know what it is—that draws them together and makes them one. I don't what that is about the Corps, but there is something and I've gotten it too. I'm proud that I have been associated with them, and I have elected myself an honorary member. I'll be good and I'll be content to stay a private. I won't ask for any rank but I'll do the best job I can in the Army and proudly say that I am a Marine.[4]

Why would Frances—who was not in the Army but a civilian war worker on an Army Air Forces base—elect herself an honorary Marine? Was her loyalty to the Corps just the result of the Marines' expert public relations, or was there something more? Marines such as Rick Spooner grew increasingly attached to the Corps through traditions, rituals, and the violence of recruit training and combat. What made some civilians similarly committed?

Much has been written on the successes and excesses of Marine Corps public relations during World War II.[5] Most works focus on another event that occurred the very day that Bob Newman died: the raising of the American flag over Mount Suribachi, which was immortalized in black and white by Associated Press photographer Joe Rosenthal.[6] Rosenthal's photo has given the Corps its best-known story about itself, one rehearsed in several films and books, the Marine Corps War Memorial, a postage stamp, and numerous recruiting commercials.[7] But even though the Iwo Jima photograph has become the Marines' most reproduced image, both its creation and its initial distribution were done by civilians. Employees of the Associated Press shot the photo and sent it to papers around the country; the Department of the Treasury chose it as the centerpiece of the seventh war loan drive and then demanded the participation of the three surviving flag raisers (at least two of whom were reluctant to give it).[8] Considered in isolation, this image tells us little about the tactics of Marine public relations or, more important, about why they were so successful.

A wider treatment of the Corps' public relations in the 1940s shows that the Marines succeeded for reasons both structural (how they organized their storytelling apparatus) and cultural (the nature of the stories they told). At the start of the war, they had just a handful of public relations officers and no journalists; by the end, they had hundreds of professional newsmen in uniform writing stories about the Corps. The Marines also built alliances with a host of civilian organizations: radio stations, film studios, and even art galleries. After the war, they entered into new alliances with department stores, fraternal organizations, unions, and the Walt Disney Company. By the end of the decade, they had expanded their outreach further to libraries, schools, and parent-teacher associations. The actions of these civilians were as important as those of the Marine public relations officers, as the enduring success of Republic Pictures' hit film *Sands of Iwo Jima* would later attest.

The Marines also had a unique storytelling style. Unlike the Navy and Army Air Forces, which focused on the exploits of ships and planes, or the Army, which mostly covered officers and tactics, the Marines focused their storytelling on their youngest enlisted members, both in and out of combat. They gave the public the "privates' war": the stories told by privates and about the deeply private themes of home and family. By 1945, as public fatigue with the war reached a peak, Marines did more than talk about family—they traveled to homes like Frances Newman's to take up the familial duties the dead had left unfulfilled. This reliance on narratives of private obligation (duties owed to family) rather than public obligation (duty to the country) remained an integral part of the Marines' public relations throughout the Cold War.[9] The result was a cultural maneuver similar to the ones used on recruits in boot camp. While ritualized violence did not enable public relations as it did recruit training, the underlying themes of family, intimate community, and obligations to the fallen remained the same.

There were numerous variations on these themes. Because of their coalitions with civilian editors and publishers, the Marines received regular feedback on the public's changing mood and were thus able to tailor their products to specific audiences. Coverage of their earliest battles performed a balancing act: emphasizing the Corps' ferocity in combat while attributing that ferocity to their service's quasi-religious faith in its traditions, culture, and mystical notions of community. As the war grew more costly, the Marines' messages grew increasingly intimate and were tailored to women, mothers in particular. After the war, they used the Toys for Tots program and Hollywood to adapt their image yet again. In so doing, the Marines managed concerns about returning veterans and spread the Corps' influence into nearly every sphere of American social life.

Popular memory recalls the World War II home front as one of great solidarity and common purpose, and in many ways it was. Less remembered, however, is how badly the conflict disrupted American families and their sense of community. Even before American casualties skyrocketed in the final year of the war, the process of building and supplying the armed forces severely strained the social fabric of the country. In just five years, 27 million people left their homes—12 million for the military, and another 15 million for war work or other reasons. The war industries made cities badly overcrowded and depopulated rural areas. Nearly every urban school suffered teacher shortages; many major cities saw race riots. All the standard measures of a society's health showed strain and decline: by 1944, child labor had tripled and divorce rates had almost doubled. Juvenile delinquency rates soared, as did rates of violent crimes such as assault. Nationally, crime rose by 10 percent in 1943 alone.[10]

In the final year of the war, a massive increase in casualties further destabilized the home front. After the invasion of France, casualties ran into the tens of thousands every week.[11] "One cannot walk down the street without meeting some heart broken mother who is sobbing her heart out," wrote one anguished parent to the secretary of the Navy in the spring of 1945. "Can't something be done to stop all this? Don't we have no voice at all in our sons' lives?"[12]

The Marines' emphasis on community and tradition had particular appeal in this era of instability and violence. Their stories gave the public something—a vicarious sense of solidarity and perhaps even kinship—that the larger military services could not duplicate. By the end of World War II, there would be widespread agreement on the home front that Marines were not only effective combat troops but also a deeply loyal community—more a family in some ways than an impersonal and bureaucratic military service. The result was lasting coalitions of loyal civilians such as Frances Newman who believed it their duty to remain *Semper Fidelis*—always faithful to the Marine Corps.

"A FIERCELY UNITED GROUP":
THE MARINES OF WAKE ISLAND

The Marines should not have outpaced the public relations efforts of the Army or the Navy. They had the smallest public relations budget and staff of all the services and did not even activate a division of public relations at Headquarters Marine Corps until July 1941. At the time of the attack on Pearl Harbor, it was staffed with only three officers.[13] (Navy public relations, by comparison, had a staff of about a dozen officers; the Army had more than a hundred.)[14] The sheer numbers of soldiers and sailors in uniform also gave the other services more contact with the public: by 1944, an average city block in Chicago had roughly seven men or women in uniform, but only one in twenty would be a Marine.[15] Except in the major cities and base towns, seeing a Marine in uniform was rare, and many small communities had just one or no Marines serving in the war.

These disadvantages were evident in the public's opinion of the Marines just before the war. A nationwide poll conducted in November 1941 showed the Marines to be the least well-known and least popular branch of service. Among boys of enlistment age, the Marines ranked dead last, after the Navy, Army Air Forces, and Army, respectively. Only 14 percent of all boys surveyed preferred the Marines over the other services; the Navy—the favorite service—got 26 percent. Parents liked the Army best, preferring it over the Marines by a ratio of almost three to one. Both college men (future officers) and boys from farms rated the Marines lower than did the general survey population. Even those boys giving serious consideration to a military career ranked the Marines last, with only 5 percent naming the Corps as their preferred service.[16]

The most common unfavorable impressions of the Marines were that they were a "tough, rowdy, rough" lot and that service with them was a "hard type of life." Parents liked the Marines even less than their children did: only 10 percent of parents preferred the Marines over the other services, and less than 3 percent reported "serious consideration of the Marines" as a career for their child. Both parents and boys named the Corps' reputation for being "poor associates [and] rough" as a "leading disadvantage of [the] Marines."[17] It was not an entirely unfair characterization, since in 1940 and 1941, one in five Marine recruits had a minor police record.[18]

When the war began, the Marines reinvented themselves, and they used civilian journalists to do it. The Marines kept their traditional selling points of toughness, manliness, and fighting spirit, but wrapped them in new, more family-friendly packaging. Much as the DIs did with their recruits, the World War II publicists argued that Marines' characteristic toughness stemmed from loyalty and commitment to the community of the Corps. This strategy of reframing ferocity as faith in the Marine "family" would be used throughout the war to distinguish the Corps from its sister services.

The public's first impression of the Marines in World War II came in the battle of Wake Island. Attacked the same day as Pearl Harbor, the 400 Marines on Wake enjoyed an early success, repelling the initial Japanese landing force by sinking two destroyers and damaging a number of other ships.[19] They would hold out for two weeks before surrendering on December 23, 1941. Unfortunately, at this early stage, the Marines had no journalists in their ranks and precious few resources for distributing the story to the public. Everything fell to the handful of Marines at the Division of Public Relations, and to one junior officer in particular, Lieutenant John W. Thomason III. Thomason, son of a prominent Marine colonel who had authored several volumes of the Corps' sea stories in the interwar period, conducted all of the press outreach for Wake, and naturally, he focused on what he knew: the history, customs, and mythology passed down to him by his father.[20]

Fed both facts and yarns by Lieutenant Thomason, civilian reporters described the Marines as an anthropologist would a foreign tribe. Marines, they insisted, were simply different from other men, and it was their service's culture that made the difference. They wrote about Marine lingo, a language even more confusing than the Navy's.

They explained the iconography—the eagle, globe, and anchor emblem that was stenciled on the uniform and tattooed on the biceps. They claimed—inaccurately—that the Marine Corps was the nation's oldest armed service.[21] In all the coverage, a simple equation was present: more than a hundred years of tradition had created an entrenched sense of community among Marines, which in turn gave them their characteristic tenacity. "The Marine Corps is an impressive denial of wave-of-the-hand contentions that 'tradition' is not needed in a fighting service," wrote Army veteran Samuel T. Williamson for the *New York Times*.

> It is tradition which has sharpened the fighting spirit of the Marines and given them an almost fanatical pride in their history and customs. The army has its fighting traditions, but they are rooted in famous old regiments and in arms of the service. A soldier thinks of his regiment before he does of the army. A sailor thinks first of his ship. But rarely does a Marine boast first of his ship or his regiment; the Marine Corps is first with him.... [They are] a fiercely united group.[22]

This emphasis on solidarity likely struck a chord with the public because it eased concerns over the supposed military advantage of totalitarian societies. In much of the early coverage of the war, reporters commented on the lockstep uniformity of the Germans and Japanese and wondered if a democracy could generate a similar degree of commitment. America's "biggest lack in fighting World War II [is] a great dynamic faith," cried *Time* magazine just months after the attack on Pearl Harbor.[23] "Does our spiritual dynamic move our people to the degree that the spiritual dynamic of the enemy has moved the Germans and the Japanese?" asked Emmet Lavery in *Commonweal*. The Japanese had more than patriotism, Lavery continued; they had "love of country plus a high pressure form of political mysticism."[24]

The Marines had a great dynamic faith in themselves and "high pressure" notions of community too, which the public learned about through Lieutenant Thomason and a cooperative civilian press. Nearly every story about the Marines at Wake celebrated that faith with regular reference to the Corps' motto.[25] When the public learned on Christmas Day of the Marines' possible surrender, one newspaper editor opined:

> Whether they have lost the island, as the Japanese claim, or are still holding on, their place in our annals is secure. They have lived up to the Marine motto to be "ever faithful" whatever has happened to the island. That motto is the lodestar of all civilized men. Few live up to it, but those few know the beauty of life or the glory of death. This is the grand gift that the men on Wake have given to the Nation this Christmas. It will instill into us all a fresh inspiration, a realization of a destiny in us as individuals as a Nation which has somehow been overlooked in our everyday living.[26]

The other services tried to emphasize their tradition and cohesion too, but at this early stage of the fighting, the Marines cornered the market. Marines "are never allowed to forget that they are Marines—and that is a distinction which sets them apart from other men," wrote Navy veteran Hanson W. Baldwin in mid-1942.[27] The Marine Corps "does not know what to believe in . . . except the Marine Corps," wrote *Time* correspondent Robert Sherrod in 1943. "The Marines fight solely on esprit de corps. It simply is inconceivable to a Marine that he would let another Marine down."[28]

By repackaging pugnacity as the Marine's faith in his community, Lieutenant Thomason and the civilian journalists rescued the Marines from their poor prewar image, taking them from the nation's least desirable associates to a model of wartime solidarity. After Wake, the public not only knew who the Marines were but understood what made them different from the other services: loyalty to their Corps, its traditions, and its members. As the war grew more costly, Marines would emphasize the same communal themes and would build an impressive grassroots network to distribute their messages to the public.

DENIG'S DEMONS: MARINE CORPS COMBAT
CORRESPONDENTS

Although the Marines benefited immensely from the newspaper coverage of Wake Island, they did not intend to leave their public relations to civilians any longer than necessary. Immediately after Wake fell, the Corps' director of public relations, Brigadier General Robert L. Denig, sent his only sergeant around Washington to encourage professional newspapermen to join the Marines. He had tremendous success. "I prepared for this mission by putting on my blues, my decorations, probably took a few short ones [drinks], and then went to the city editors for permission to talk to their personnel—and got it in each case," First Sergeant Walter J. Shipman later remembered.[29] Sam Stavisky and Al Lewis of the *Washington Post* joined in the first year, as did eleven other Washington-based reporters.[30] Rhodes scholar Herbert Merillat, screenwriter and Hollywood producer Milton Sperling, and future Pulitzer Prize winner Jim Lucas also signed up. First Sergeant Shipman recruited so much of the Washington press corps that the owner of the *Washington Times-Herald* complained to President Roosevelt, who relayed his concerns to the Commandant of the Marine Corps. First Sergeant Shipman received orders to canvass elsewhere for recruits, and proceeded to rob other cities of their most ambitious reporters.

Shipman's recruiting visits were the first steps in creating "Denig's Demons"—the collection of journalists, artists, radio broadcasters, filmmakers, photographers, and authors who would work under General Denig in the Division of Public Relations at Headquarters Marine Corps. Known collectively as combat correspondents, or CCs, Denig's Marines revolutionized military public relations, earning the Corps the best publicity of the war as well as the enmity of the other services. The secret to their success was their networking: because the journalists brought their professional contacts with them when they entered the Corps, General Denig got advice and support from the nation's leading editors, publishers, and public relations experts. The result was a coalition of professional writers and publicists who stayed committed to the Marine Corps, even after they left the service.

By putting journalists in uniform, the Marines also lessened the distrust and animosity traditionally present between those who fight wars and those who write about them. The Marines' correspondents were both professional newsmen and enlisted Marines, usually sergeants. They went through boot camp and were trained to fight, which earned them their fellow Marines' trust. "The CC had access to and sympathy for the enlisted men, who, in turn, had empathy for the CCs," remembered one correspondent. "The CCs were much closer in many ways to the enlisted Marines, because they lived, suffered, and went on liberty with them."[31]

Before the CC program, all the services' public relations officers did what Lieutenant Thomason had done during Wake: serve as liaisons to civilian journalists. They may have authored some press releases and communiqués, but most of their work in wartime involved censoring civilian reporters' articles and serving as the commander's representative to the press. As a result, journalists' contact was almost exclusively with officers, and distrust abounded on both sides. Many units had no public relations officer, which made liaison with reporters an additional duty assigned to already overworked officers who were unfamiliar with the press. "An officer on a combatant ship suddenly being designated as Public Relations Officer usually reacts about as follows: 'Here comes a g—— d—— newspaper man. Now what am I supposed to do?'" admitted a Navy public relations bulletin as late as 1943. "Your newsman may be an evil, but he is a most essential evil."[32] Conditions in the Army were equally frustrating. Army public relations officers were "working under many and heavy handicaps," claimed the acting director of the Army's Office of Public Relations at a conference in 1941.[33] Distrust of the press within the Army, poor chain of command, and lack of coordination were just a few of the obstacles mentioned.[34]

Bureaucratic inefficiency posed other problems for military publicists at the outset of the war. Both newspapers and the military had convoluted procedures for sending reporters overseas, and many who wanted overseas press credentials did not receive them. As of August 1943, the entire War Department (which was then almost thirty times the size of the Marine Corps) had accredited only 367 civilian correspondents. The Navy Department had accredited less than half that number.[35] Once with the troops, the civilian journalists encountered further obstacles: "They do not welcome us as private photog[rapher]s and would feel a lot better if we were either not here or [were] in the army," reported one to his editor during the Army's campaign in North Africa.[36] The Marines' system avoided most of these problems. By 1943, they had more than 130 CCs in uniform, and most of them were already overseas writing stories.[37] In the first two weeks of August 1943, the CCs placed 339 stories in local and national newspapers, and by April 1944 they were publishing an average of 38 stories per day.[38]

Marine public relations operations ran smoothly because the Marines made their publicity a priority, but also because the entire operation was centralized, streamlined, and under the direction of one man: General Denig. Once cleared and censored in the field, the CCs' stories went straight to General Denig's office at Headquarters Marine Corps, where they were edited and placed with a local paper. His clerks sent additional copies to the families of the Marines featured in each story and also forwarded editors' and readers' feedback to the writers in the field. Monthly newsletters went out to every CC in the Corps, with requests for specific stories and topics. The CCs had all the advantages of a professional newsroom with almost none of the military's characteristic red tape.

In the Army and the Navy, by contrast, bureaucracy abounded. There was no centralization in either service: each naval district and Army corps had its own separate procedures and rules for dealing with the press. While major stories of national interest often made it into the news, hometown coverage—accounts of promotions or awards, or just a short story on a corporal's life in the service—was almost always neglected. Hometown coverage of enlisted men was "perfectly legitimate news," admitted the Army's acting director of public relations, but "it's the function of the public relations officer in the unit to which that corporal belongs to send that to the home town paper. He has got to know the general set up of the news. He has got to, and many of them don't, unfortunately. They are groping in the dark."[39]

Whom the journalists spoke to also mattered. In the larger services, reporters got most of their information from officers, and consequently their coverage emphasized the themes those men knew well. Articles covering Army operations were filled with language of tactics—delaying actions, secondary main efforts, and pincer movements.[40] They gave the public a view from the map, one that emphasized the profession of arms and the complexities of maneuvering large units on the battlefield. Coverage of the Navy and Army Air Forces was deeply technocentric: it made heroes of the ships and planes, and of the officers who controlled the great machines of war.[41] The Marines left tactics and technology aside and focused almost exclusively on the wartime experience of the average private—"Joe Blow," they called him—both in and out of combat. As the CCs' official style book explained with characteristic Marine emphasis:

> *Individuals,* not *things,* provide the *human interest* material that the people at home are hungry to have and that editors want to give them. . . . Let the communiqués and the civilian correspondents outline the action—yours is the privilege of telling about the flesh-and-blood men who make it click. Between the lines of every paragraph

of their [civilians'] report are from a dozen to a hundred stories about boys from Kansas and Georgia and Maine that cry for the telling. Any one of these stories will carry a more powerful impact upon families, relatives, neighbors, friends and townspeople back home than that paragraph could possibly suggest.[42]

Though some Joe Blow stories gave extremely graphic depictions of combat, many others focused on the humdrum routine of military life and the boyish pranks of the young Marines in the rear areas. The latter stories softened the former, and editors began requesting more human interest pieces as the war progressed. Because Joe Blow stories were about local boys and always mentioned hometowns, parents' names, and even street addresses, they did not need to run in the national section, where competition for space was high. Editors could place them under local news. Joe Blow stories were also less time sensitive than battle coverage, which allowed editors to run them whenever they needed to fill a few columns. By the end of the war, managing editors and public relations firms agreed that the Marines' stories were superior to "any copy from the other services," most of which was too general or impersonal to be run in local papers.[43] "This is the kind of copy and pictures we can use," wrote the publisher of the *Advocate-Hamiltonian* in Hamilton, Missouri. "Leave it to the Marines to lead, and others try to follow."[44]

Even with these early successes, General Denig took the relationship with publishers and editors to a new level in 1943 when he invited them "to give assignments to our combat correspondents for specific or general stories and features about individuals, groups, or incidents that you want covered for your paper."[45] This was particularly attractive to the smallest papers, which lacked the funds to send their own writers overseas, and their editors responded with alacrity. "The offer seems almost too good to be true," wrote the editor of the *Daily Independent* in Murphysboro, Illinois. "I don't want to be hoggish, but stories like these are just what we have been wanting."[46] By 1945, the CC clipsheet of stories would go out to 4,900 small daily and weekly newspapers every week.[47]

Denig's Demons did not focus only on newspapers. They supplemented print coverage with radio broadcasts, comic strips, photo exhibits, and newsreel coverage. Radio shows such as *The Halls of Montezuma* re-created famous moments in Marine Corps history with an all-enlisted cast who vowed to "let a private tell you about it."[48] Magazines published the CCs' longer feature stories. A traveling exhibit of Marine combat art opened at the Museum of Modern Art in New York and toured hundreds of small towns. Headquarters also mailed families copies of these longer stories and the photos of their children that appeared in print. When interviews with Marines aired on the radio, the Division of Public Relations called parents to alert them to tune in.

The Marines' Joe Blow stories had another advantage over the other services: they appealed particularly to women. In 1944, advertising researchers compared male and female readership of two stories: a front-page combat story and a story about two hometown Marines meeting in the Pacific that appeared on page thirteen. They found that men were the primary consumers of the page-one coverage: 50 percent of men but only 28 percent of women read the entire story. But with the Marines' hometown story, the statistics were rather different. Seventy-two percent of women and 66 percent of men read the Joe Blow story in its entirety.[49]

Women were three times more likely to read the Marines' hometown coverage than the combat accounts because the Joe Blow stories covered material other than tactics, technology, and strategy, which were skewed toward male readers. The advantage of the Marines' hometown stories was that they dealt as much with local news as they did with the war, and thus straddled both the domestic and political realms. As a result, the Marines' coverage reached across gender lines in ways that the other services' war stories did not.

As the war progressed, the CCs began deliberately tailoring their coverage to families, and mothers in particular. As soon as the Marine Corps opened its ranks to women in 1943, General Denig started a women Marine section at the Division of Public Relations and recruited Louise Stewart, an editor of the *Ladies' Home Journal,* to run it. Over the next two years, Lieutenant Stewart trained twenty-six women Marines to do public relations work for the Corps in both Washington and the recruiting districts.[50] In General Denig's office at Headquarters, women—both military and civilian—did the bulk of the administrative work, including the personal contact calls to parents when a radio broadcast of Marines aired. The *Combat Correspondents Memorandum,* which passed editors' and parents' feedback to the writers in the field, ran a regular column devoted to the coverage of women Marines and specifically instructed CCs to dramatize "the job being done by the women."[51] The Division of Public Relations further instructed men overseas to write specifically for families and women: "Keep in mind the fathers, mothers, sisters, and sweethearts, who want very much to know every scrap of information about their loved ones. . . . [W]hen you go out to get a story, look about you again and think of these things and these people."[52]

The CCs' most intimate and effective method of connecting families to the Marine Corps was via radio. Early in the war, archivists at the Library of Congress approached all the services seeking cooperation in recording war songs. Only the Marines agreed to participate. After training his men on the large Presto recording machines, General Denig told them to forget the songs and to record Joe Blow interviews and battle sequences instead. The most popular broadcasts were the holiday messages, recorded by Marines in the field for Valentine's Day, Mother's Day, Father's Day, and Christmas. In 1944, thirty states received the Marines' Christmas broadcasts; one station aired more than six hours of the Marines' messages to their families. Headquarters presented phonograph records of the interviews to the parents as mementos.[53] The following year, Headquarters sent seventy-three personalized Mother's Day recordings to radio stations in twenty-five states across the country.[54] Papers published photos of the recording sessions, which featured young privates and privates first class; women Marines at Headquarters kept parents informed of the air times. "The Mother's Day greetings did big business," boasted one CC. "They were even better received than the Valentine shows."[55] "I can't begin to tell you how wonderful it was to hear his voice again after two long years," wrote Mrs. Mary Murray of Dalton, Massachusetts, after hearing her son on the radio. "It seemed as if he was right in the room with us. The whole town listened to the broadcast [and] also several of his friends in Berkshire County."[56]

None of the other services made such personalized contact with the enlisted men's families and hometown communities. In the Navy, hometown coverage usually meant sending stories about a ship to newspapers in the city after which it was named.[57] A Navy public relations guide published during the war offered a list of sixteen potential sources for news. Officers were listed in half of the sources; enlisted sailors were not named at all.[58] The Army tried to re-create the Marines' success with its own combat correspondent program in 1944, but this never reached the proportions of what the Marine CCs accomplished. In fact, the Army's greatest publicity came not from military correspondents but from a civilian: Ernie Pyle. Like the CCs, Pyle gave the public "the little guy's war," but Pyle was just one man writing two or three columns a week.[59] By 1944, Marine CCs were writing more than 3,000 stories a month and publishing between 30 and 40 pieces every day. When the Marines invaded Saipan in June 1944, the CCs put out 185 stories in a single day.[60]

KEEPING FAITH WITH THE FALLEN

Despite the CCs' regular and intimate appeals to families, by 1945 the public was tired of war. During the worst months of fighting, Americans were dying at a rate of more than 400 per day.[61] During the month-long battle of Iwo Jima, grief and shock were widespread.

Joe Rosenthal's triumphant photo of the Iwo Jima flag raising lifted the public's spirits temporarily, but the battle would continue for another four weeks and would take the lives of three of the six flag raisers. A mother's letter to the secretary of the Navy, reprinted in *Time*, gave voice to the grief of many: "Dear Sir: Please for God's sake stop sending our finest youth to be murdered on places like Iwo Jima. It is too much for boys to stand, too much for mothers to take. It is driving some mothers crazy. Why can't objectives be accomplished some other way? It is most inhumane and awful—stop, stop."[62] Other parents saw the Marines as victims of an inattentive government. "Our Marines have been given all those suicide invasions," wrote Mrs. George Lambina from Steubenville, Ohio. "Why should the smallest branch of the services be selected for all the tough spots? . . . These boys are paying for the mistakes in Washington and the parents know this."[63]

This was the public mood in March 1945 when Frances Newman learned of her brother's death on Iwo Jima. Frances first wrote Bob's friends, hoping for more information, but none came. A Marine in her town advised her to write to her brother's commanding general, Major General Clifton Bledsoe Cates, who would later become the Commandant of the Marine Corps. "He is one of the grandest guys there is," the Marine told her. "He will answer your letter."[64]

General Cates received Frances' letter and about a hundred others like it. "My most difficult job at the present time," he wrote to his wife shortly after the battle, "is replying to letters written by mothers who lost sons at Iwo. Every mail brings more and more." When he got to Frances' letter, however, the general did more than read it. He wept.[65] Then he showed the letter to his division staff—including, no doubt, his public relations officer—and wrote two letters: one to Frances and one to the mayor of Macon, Georgia, asking for a favor.

It was not just Frances' grief that touched the fifty-two-year-old general, penetrating the thick layer of emotional armor he had built up to protect himself from the losses of the previous weeks. There was something more, something General Cates might expect of a Marine but not of a heartbroken seventeen-year-old girl: devotion to the Corps. "My heart is still there with the Fourth Marine Division and will always be," she wrote. "I love the Marines, even though they took all that I hold dear. . . . I was so close to Bob and could almost feel when he went into battle."[66] The only request in her letter (and so many letters carried requests—for answers, mementos, and explanations) was to know if Bob's friends had survived the battle. She closed with the story of her last moment with her brother, a moment that carried a promise she knew now would never be fulfilled.

> He left a few days before my sixteenth birthday. He told me that on my seventeenth birthday he would be back. He didn't make it, but he told me when my eighteenth birthday came around he would be home on furlough (he never did get one) and he would buy me a beautiful orchid, a lovely evening dress and take me dancing just as if I were his best girl. But June thirteenth (my eighteenth birthday) is not far away and I know now that he will never come back. But I'm going to buy the prettiest evening dress I can find, and I'm going dancing just as I planned. But just for a few hours, the boy I am dancing with will be Bob, come back to fill his promise. I know he'd want me to go on because we both planned on it so. The boy I go with is going to have to be awfully nice because the boy I was to have gone with was the sweetest in the world to me.
>
> Good bye sir, and Good Luck,
>
> Sincerely,
> Frances Newman[67]

Frances never expected the general to reply. As she later explained to the general's mother, "I expected at the most to get a form letter written by one of the general's aides. I didn't dream that a general who gets thousands of letters every month would take time out to write to me himself." But General Cates did respond. "In over twenty-eight years in the Marine Corps, I have received thousands of letters but I can truthfully say yours was the most beautifully written and the finest of them all. . . . It has touched us all deeply, very deeply," he wrote.[68]

When General Cates showed Frances' letter to her brother's friends, they took up a collection and bought her an evening dress. The mayor of Macon agreed to deliver orchids to Frances on the general's behalf. One of his combat correspondents typed up the story and alerted the Division of Public Relations of General Cates' plan. Once in the hands of General Denig's Marines, the story quickly turned into a spectacle. They contacted Warner Robins Army Air Forces Base, where Frances worked as an administrative clerk, and planned a birthday party. They arranged for Frances to appear on the *We the People* radio program in New York the week before her birthday and on a local radio program, *Runway to Victory*, the week after. The night of the party, the Marines sent a photogenic combat veteran down from Atlanta to serve as a replacement for Bob. Reporters played up the familial theme. "Marine Acts as Proxy for Dead Brother," one headline read. "Substitute Brother . . . Keeps a Pledge Made to Frances Newman by Her Brother," read another. The Associated Press and United Press news services picked up the story and ran it from coast to coast. A comic strip rendered the tale in color and schmaltz.[69]

Both Frances and the general were swamped with fan mail. General Cates received requests for similar parties, flowers, and mementos. Frances received a marriage proposal, which she did not accept. "You and your men could have found no better way to show your appreciation for the sacrifice of Sgt Newman, nor a more eloquent manner to honor true American womanhood," wrote one Marine wife from Virginia.[70] "The Marine Corps," opined one United Press staff writer, "has a heart as well as a punch."[71] Other letters to the general came from shut-ins and widows, some of whom he characterized as "strangers and crackpots. One [letter came] from a lady in Los Angeles wanting an orchid and wrist watch—a very lonely lady, so she said."[72]

The reason for the deluge of letters and public sentiment surrounding this event lies in the unbalanced nature of the relationship between Americans and their military after three and a half hard years of war. After Pearl Harbor, the energies of the vast majority of Americans went into supporting the military, but the families of those who served received very little in return. While they eventually

Frances Newman and her "substitute brother" at her eighteenth birthday party, June 1945. The Marines arranged the party for her after her brother was killed on Iwo Jima on February 23, 1945, the same day as the famous flag raising. (From *The Atlanta Journal*, June 14, 1945, © 1945 *The Atlanta Journal-Constitution*. All rights reserved.)

saw steady progress toward the end of the war, parents had almost no contact with the organizations that controlled their children's lives. Military bureaucracies were impersonal, full of hurried officers who had little time for civilians. As Mrs. Lambina's letter attests, some civilians' faith in the government had begun to wane. The news of a child's death, coming by simple telegram, lacked a personal touch. Families did not even receive their children's remains: naval casualties were buried at sea, and soldiers and Marines were interred in temporary cemeteries on the islands where they fell. Parents seeking further information could only write letters, which overworked and emotionally exhausted officers such as General Cates may or may not have answered. The exigencies of war made the social contract between the soldier's family and the state horribly lopsided. Parents gave their children to the country; in return, they got bureaucracy, empty rhetoric, and silence.

For many on the home front, the Marines' decision to send Frances a dress, a party, and a "substitute brother" was a rare instance in which the military balanced that social contract. By honoring Bob Newman's promise to his sister, the Corps had stayed "always faithful" both to their Marine and to the sister he loved. Her birthday party affirmed a claim that the wasteful carnage of Iwo Jima had almost disproved: that the Marine Corps cared as much for the fallen as did America's mothers, fathers, and siblings. As one fourteen-year-old girl who had lost a brother in the Army wrote, the Marines understood that "the boys who are giving their lives everyday aren't 'just mere soldiers,' but dear friends and fellow comrades. You may not know them all personally, for that would be improbable, but they're still dear to you, just as they are to us."[73] This basic message of community—which the Marines had been telling in various forms since Wake Island—resonated with many whose families were ripped apart by the war.

The Marines did not throw Frances Newman a party just to help her, however. They did it to help themselves. General Cates and General Denig knew full well the value of good publicity. (Indeed, General

Denig kept a sign on his office wall that read, "If the public becomes apathetic about the Marine Corps, the Marine Corps will cease to exist.")[74] In the aftermath of Iwo Jima's 23,000 Marine casualties, General Denig, probably more than General Cates, saw a publicity opportunity in the sorrows of a heartbroken girl. The party they arranged thus pushed back against the claim that Marines did not value the lives of their men, and recast the Corps as an organization that honored and preserved families rather than one that broke them apart.

Frances' own words show how the birthday party served as a form of damage control for the bad press of Iwo Jima. In her first letter to General Cates, she admitted doubting that any political goal was worth the loss of her brother: "I cannot say I am glad we had him to give for our country, for I'm not. Sometimes I wonder if it is worth the sacrifice the boys are making."[75] But after she learned of her upcoming party she regretted her doubts: "The hundreds of other things that have been done for us in our time of grief makes me feel very much ashamed of the fact that, when my first shock of knowing Bob was dead came, I wondered just for an instant, if it was worth it. But I would be a coward to say that, and Bob would not want me to be a coward."[76] She still had a thousand broken things in her heart, she confessed to the general, but they were "broken things that have been rebuilt by the faith and love of a bunch of war-weary Marines in the jungles of the Pacific. I'm their kid sister now."[77]

Even in a necessary war, patriotic rhetoric serves as a poor explanation for the loss of a son or brother. Some people require thicker, more intimate narratives of community, ones that incorporate their lost loved one into something other than a political goal. This is what Frances Newman's party did, giving her access to the very networks of fictive kinship to which her brother belonged. "I felt that I, in getting this party and the trip to New York, represented the entire Marine Corps and things they would like to do for each 'kid sister.' I hope I've made my big brothers proud of me, for I did try to. I'm proud of every one of them."[78] In short, Frances' birthday party did for her what the Corps' culture did for Marines fighting in the Pacific: it extended her notion of family and community beyond the living, giving her a strategy for mourning and a way to cope with loss. "I have found a strange peace, it seems," she wrote in her last letter to the general, just four months after her brother's death. "I can almost hear him say 'It's all right . . . don't worry.'"[79] She imagined Bob living on in the afterlife of the Corps, guarding the streets of heaven in his uniform, just as "The Marines' Hymn" promised.[80]

While a general's letter and a birthday party may have helped a grieving young girl, other civilians were more skeptical. One week after the party, the letters were still flowing into General Cates' headquarters, but not always with praise. "The Frances Newman story has started to backfire," the general wrote to his wife. A Marine widow wrote the general and, in his words, "bawled me out saying it was cheap publicity. I must admit, it got a little too much but that wasn't my fault."[81] Even Frances' mother, Sarah Newman, seemed unconvinced by the Marines' spectacle. Sarah accompanied her daughter to the party but said almost nothing, cried once, and stood "watching quietly from a darkened corner." "This is a big night!" a reporter crowed at her when they arrived. "Well," Sarah said slowly, "it's a sad one."[82]

Although some civilians resisted the Marines' propaganda, far more responded positively to it, and not only because such narratives helped to mediate bereavement. Jean De Marranza—the "Marines' Mother," she called herself—was perhaps the Marine Corps' biggest fan: between 1942 and 1968, she wrote more than 30,000 letters to Marines. She, like Frances, felt the Marine Corps belonged as much to her as to her son. Starting in 1942, she began writing letters to her seventeen-year-old son and other members of his unit in the Pacific. After he was evacuated home with malaria, she continued writing the Marines in his unit, and sent 13,000 letters to "her boys" in the Pacific during World War II alone.[83] Every year she wrote the Commandant on the Marine Corps birthday, sometimes including a poem. It is "our Corps," she wrote in 1946. "*My* Corps too. A civilian true, but inside of me I'm *all* Marine. I know them. I should. I've been close to them for nearly five years."[84] "I had a feeling that the whole Marine Corps was behind me, instead of my being behind them," she wrote in 1947. "I feel that the whole Marine Corps was mine."[85]

Frances Newman and Jean De Marranza had very different experiences in World War II. Frances lived in a small farming town in Georgia, Jean in the crowded industrial city of Detroit. Frances' family was torn apart by the war; Jean's emerged largely unscathed. And yet both women felt a deep kinship with the Corps, which both described as more of a family than a military service. This was not an accident; it was the deliberate product of General Denig's public relations campaign since the earliest days of the war. It worked because it imbued the war with narratives of private obligation—duties owed to family—which supplemented and empowered the public obligations present in the discourses of citizenship and patriotism.[86] Marine publicists went further than talking about family: with acts such as Frances Newman's birthday party, they extended their culture's networks of kinship to the families of the fallen, ensuring that promises made by brothers to sisters were kept, even in death. This gave survivors such as Frances strategies for living with loss and made them loyal supporters of the Corps for years to come.

THE LANGUAGE OF AMERICAN FAMILY LIFE

The public relations infrastructure built during World War II did not disappear after the war. It remained in place and proved essential for adapting the Marines' image to peacetime. The "language of American family life" that the Marines had become so fluent in during the war became an oft-used resource afterward for mitigating public anxiety about returning veterans and standing militaries. What historian Laura Wexler calls "tender violence"—a strategy of softening and legitimizing war by reframing it through a feminine and domestic lens—helped the Corps obscure its more aggressive traits and present itself instead as a community organization of fathers and siblings.[87] The Toys for Tots program, begun in 1947, and the 1949 Republic Pictures film *Sands of Iwo Jima* serve as two examples of how the Marines continued to use domestic themes in order to manage public perception of their image.

Patriotism and respect for the armed forces remained widespread in American society after the war, but so too did fatigue with military matters. Those who had fought and survived wanted to forget what they had seen; those who had lost loved ones often aimed their grief and anger at anything military. Even those untouched by the casualties of war were ready for the military to play a less prominent role in American society. For most Americans, the dominant worries of the immediate postwar period concerned finding jobs and housing. In these areas, returning veterans were more the problem than the solution. Psychiatrists warned that returning veterans would carry emotional scars as well as physical ones. Many family members feared their veterans would not be able to shed their military identity and take up a civilian one again.[88]

Such fears were not unfounded. By one historian's estimate, "troubled reunions" after the war outnumbered happy ones by a ratio of four to one.[89] Nor did the problems disappear with time. Between 1944 and 1948, the number of psychiatric beds at Veterans Administration hospitals grew by 33 percent, and more than half of the veterans receiving disability payments in the postwar period were classified as requiring "emotional adjustment."[90] In the same period, suicides increased nationally by 20 percent and homicides by 30 percent.[91]

The Marines likely provoked the most anxiety during demobilization. Americans understood that the Marines had been overseas the longest and had seen the worst combat. The racial dynamics of the Pacific War only added to these fears, as four years of propaganda had convinced the public that the only way to fight the Japanese was to abandon Western notions of morality. While Marine public relations had worked hard to build a domestic-friendly image of its members, the realities of island combat continued to saturate newsreels and papers until the final days of the war. If recruits needed weeks of intensive indoctrination to become a Marine, what could unmake one?

This question grew only more pressing during demobilization as newspapers reported on Marine veterans committing extremely violent crimes. In Los Angeles County, where Toys for Tots began, police arrested Marines in the first years after the war for kidnapping, spousal abuse, robbery, assault, and murder.[92] Several of the arrests were spectacular—two for mutilation murders, one for beating a man to death with a hammer, and another for setting a booby-trapped grenade in an effort to kill a girlfriend.[93] Suicides and suicide attempts also made the news.[94] Alcohol was usually involved, and papers made regular mention of the lingering psychological effects of combat on the Marines in question.

These problems did not go unnoticed by the Corps' publicists. However, they could not simply return to their wartime practice of inundating the papers with the combat correspondents' feel-good stories. That strategy had worked because almost the entire Marine Corps was outside the country; by late 1946, Marines and former Marines were dispersed throughout the nation on bases, in reserve units, and as demobilized veterans. The Corps thus needed new strategies for mediating between the privates and the public, ones that could still emphasize its softer side using the resources available in the United States. California Marines associated with the film industry developed one of the most successful efforts.

Toys for Tots began in 1947 as an ad hoc effort by Marine reservists to collect and distribute Christmas presents to war orphans and needy children in Los Angeles. The program's founder was Major Bill Hendricks, who, when not in uniform, was the director of public relations for the Warner Bros. film studio. Using his contacts in the film industry, Major Hendricks organized sufficient publicity in the program's first year to collect 5,000 toys. The following year, the Marine Corps Reserve formally adopted the program and Headquarters Marine Corps began tracking its success. Walt Disney designed the official logo, and John Wayne—who never served in any branch of the military—was one of its first celebrity spokesmen. The program grew exponentially: in 1956, Marines collected and distributed more than 5 million toys in more than 250 communities, and received more than 1,200 hours of radio air time. General Denig's office—now renamed the Division of Public Information—estimated the campaign's publicity in that year to be worth $25 million.[95]

Toys for Tots was not just a publicity stunt; it was a genuine effort to care for the children the war had orphaned. But the program had another effect too. The many photographs of Marines with children helped reinforce the Marines' postwar image as parents, siblings, and mentors—all of which served to deemphasize their combat experiences and problems with reintegration. "To many, the image of the Marine Corps and its members is one of hardened, rough and tough military men," warned a Toys for Tots community relations guide designed for Marines. "Yet, the 'Toys for Tots' program presents to the community a truer picture of the Marines—that of men in every city who have the same compassion, the same aims as other citizens with one exception—that they are Marines."[96] Radio broadcasts distributed the same message to civilians. "What's this? Marines with Teddy Bears? Veterans of Iwo Jima and the Chosin Reservoir, sorting gaily-wrapped gift packages? This is not an incongruous picture," insisted a radio script from 1952.[97] "Because Marines gravitate toward kids, wherever they go, they want to give all the kids a break."[98] One unit in Indiana went beyond collecting toys by organizing Operation Santa Claus Land—a field trip to a local holiday park for sixty orphans who were chauffeured and escorted by Marines in their dress blues.

Commanding officers of reserve units followed a similar strategy as General Denig's outreach program to editors and publishers during the war: they formed coalitions with civilians. Toys for Tots press kits instructed Marines to contact town officials, presidents of large companies, movie theater managers, department stores, newspapers, and radio and television studios. Marines partnered with the Salvation Army, the Boy Scouts of America, and local business and fraternal organizations. If possible, advised the press kits, Marines should combine efforts with "service clubs, churches, schools, unions, etc. This is your chance to reach the general public, yet on a more personal basis. Have your unit members talk about 'Toys for Tots' to their teachers, their bosses, their union heads, etc. . . . Do not overlook any publicity media."[99]

A Toys for Tots publicity photograph from the early 1960s. (United States Marine Corps)

Besides softening their image by pointing up family themes, Toys for Tots also helped manage public concern over the military's expanded role in civilian society. By the late 1940s, reserve units had sprung up all throughout the country, bringing the equipment and uniforms of military life to towns that had never before had them. The casualties of the last war and the real fears of a new one made the public uninterested in glamorizing combat or the military. Congressional debates over reorganizing the armed services made militarism a central theme in 1947 and again in 1949. By the mid-1950s, reserve Marines were warning that there had even been instances of "bitterness towards the Marine Corps and its Reserve in individual communities."[100] Toys for Tots helped to dilute that bitterness by civilianizing the Marine Corps Reserve—portraying it as a civic organization as much as a military service. As one of the Corps' radio promotions put it, Marines participated in Toys for Tots because "our homes are here, we work or go to school here. We feel . . . [our unit] is a community organization."[101] Marine publicists noticed the difference. "There are numerous examples on record," boasted a public relations memorandum, "in which 'Toys for Tots' has overcome the hostility of a community and gained its complete cooperation."[102]

The Marines also worked to influence the public through film, and here too the alliance with civilians in Hollywood was critical. However, that alliance did not bear fruit immediately after the war. Perhaps because the major studios had made so many patriotic combat pictures during the war, most were uninterested in doing so once the fighting stopped. Most studios refused to even consider combat film scripts until 1947.[103] But as the military's interservice competition became more intense in Washington and defense budgets grew lean, each service pressed Hollywood for help in mobilizing public support. In 1948, the Corps' director of public information contacted Paramount Pictures to discuss the prospects for a feature-length picture about the Marine Corps. His proposed subject was Frances Newman's correspondence with General Clifton Cates (now Commandant of the Marine Corps), which he thought would appeal specifically to "mothers, sisters, and brothers."[104] Frances, now married to an Air Force sergeant and still waiting for her brother's remains to be shipped home from Iwo Jima, agreed to participate. When nothing came of the project, the Marine Corps signed on to support another film: Republic Pictures' box-office smash *Sands of Iwo Jima*.

Sands of Iwo Jima was among the first batch of war films to be made in the postwar period, shot the same year as the Navy's *Task Force*, the Army's *Battleground*, and the Air Force's *Twelve o'Clock High*. Though all the films received support and cooperation from the military, *Sands of Iwo Jima* received the most.[105] The Marines helped select the combat footage to be used in the film, ran a boot camp for the actors, and loaned the production company equipment and personnel. More than a thousand Marines appeared in the film. Several famous Marines made cameo appearances, including future Commandant David M. Shoup, Lieutenant Colonel Henry P. "Jim" Crowe, and the three surviving Marines from Rosenthal's photograph, who reenacted their flag raising in the final scene of the film. Edmund Grainger, the film's producer, valued the Marines' assistance at $2.5 million and admitted that without them, the picture could not have been made.[106]

At first glance, the film seems to emphasize all the Marine Corps wanted to downplay in the postwar era. The plot follows Sergeant John Stryker (John Wayne), an abusive, alcoholic squad leader, as he trains his men for battle on Tarawa and Iwo Jima. John Wayne's iconic depiction of Stryker is the embodiment of Marine toughness: he solves problems with his fists and quells his anger with the bottle. This has led him into trouble in more ways than one: he has been busted in rank for fighting and is estranged from his wife and child. Most of Stryker's anger is focused on the young, uncooperative Private First Class Pete Conway (John Agar), who has joined the Corps because it is a family tradition. (Like many Marine films, the plot is a family melodrama: Stryker served in the Corps under Conway's now deceased father, whom the son still resents for being too tough and remote.) Friction ensues between the two until the grizzled squad leader finally softens toward his surrogate son and Conway embraces his Marine identity. Each saves the other's life, but Stryker is shot dead by a sniper just before the flag goes up over Mount Suribachi. Inspired by the flag raising, and now reconciled with both Stryker and his father, Conway takes up the leadership of the squad and exhorts the men to "get back in the war."

None of this seems to follow in the footsteps of Toys for Tots or Frances Newman's birthday party, where the Marines used familial themes to soften the Corps' wartime image. And yet, if one probes beneath the surface, a different story emerges. Producer Edmund Grainger claimed he wanted "no Hollywood version of the Marine Corps" and insisted that the Marine liaisons assigned to the film had had no editorial input other than correcting terminology and technical issues.[107] The Marine advisor's production notes tell another story.[108] In fact, the Marines raised objections to two scenes where Sergeant Stryker resorts to violence—one against a Marine private and the other against a woman. After extensive debate, the Marines allowed the first scene, which showed Sergeant Stryker smashing a private in the jaw with a rifle during bayonet practice. A Marine in the Division of Public Information completely rewrote the second scene, inserting domestic themes to present the Corps in a more family-friendly light.

As had drill instructors in recruit training, World War II squad leaders did use violence to maintain discipline, but it was rare that a sergeant would hit a Marine with anything other than his fists. The film's technical advisor, Captain Leonard Fribourg, objected to the bayonet practice scene both on grounds of accuracy and because he felt it hurt the Marine Corps' image. The director wanted the scene left intact, arguing that it was in character for Stryker and made good drama. Eventually the two sides struck a compromise. The scene would remain, but a humorous vignette followed where

Sergeant Stryker taught the clumsy private how to use a bayonet by dancing with him.

In the second objectionable scene, Stryker encounters Mary, likely a prostitute, in a bar, and she suggests they return to her apartment. Once there, the drunk and angry Stryker hits Mary. In a memo to the producers, one of the script screeners wrote: "In this case having a man smash a woman in the face ruins your character build up of the man. A good push with her landing in a chair would be better with other action and expressions."[109] The Marines then offered to do a rewrite. "The scene with Stryker and the woman in the apartment has been rewritten in its entirety," Marine liaison Major Andrew Geer reported to the director of public information. "In the revision the woman is made a sympathetic character and the ugly undertones in her life removed."[110] "There's no question that Marines had hit women before," a Marine script screener later remembered, "but we wouldn't approve anything like that."[111]

Once rewritten, Stryker's scene with Mary becomes the turning point in the film, as Stryker begins changing from an angry abuser into a surrogate father toward his men.[112] The initial encounter is still the same: Mary solicits him in the bar and the two return to her apartment. Once there, Mary leaves to buy more liquor, and in her absence, Stryker discovers an infant in the adjoining room. When she returns and finds her secret revealed, she suggests that they continue their evening regardless. Stryker demurs and helps her prepare a bottle for the child. "I know about babies," he admits grudgingly as a lullaby plays in the background. He gives Mary all his money to care for her son and departs, cheerful and sober. "I'm about five years smarter than I was a half hour ago," he tells a comrade waiting for him outside. The two Marines return to the bar, where for the first time in the film, Stryker takes a kind and fatherly tone toward Conway, who rebukes and insults him. "I don't understand why you don't belt that guy," Stryker's comrade grumbles. "I've mellowed in my old age," he replies. In the original script, the scene ended with a bar fight between

Marines. In the final version, it ends with Stryker calmly musing on how proud Conway's father must have been of his son.[113]

Most scholarship on *Sands of Iwo Jima* reads it as a farewell to the World War II fighting man and a harbinger of the new Cold War military. Stryker, heroic but brutal, must die with the war; Conway, the citizen-soldier, is the military man of the future.[114] But rather than breaking away from the Marines' World War II storytelling strategies, the film is really a continuation of them. The revisions to Stryker's scene with Mary do exactly what Frances Newman's party and Toys for Tots did: reframe the violence of military life with a domestic lens. Stryker's character is no fading symbol of the past; he is emblematic of the Marine Corps in 1949, an organization that used narratives of home and family to quell public nervousness about the lingering effects of the war.

Even more revealing of the Marines' concern with preserving a family-friendly image are the "exploitation manuals" authored by the Division of Public Information to publicize Grainger's film. As they had done with Toys for Tots, Marines spread the word about *Sands of Iwo Jima* by targeting social spaces dominated by women and children: schools, libraries, department stores, and parent-teacher associations. Marine reservists received orders to hand out roses to Marine wives in the theaters, hold "cutest Marine baby" contests, and host underprivileged kids for a base tour and film screening—"all with photo coverage, of course." Other stunts included holding a party for the Marine veteran with the biggest family, a letter-writing contest for youngsters (the theme was "My Pop's the best Marine in the world because . . ."), and a "War Bride phone stunt" in which a Marine wife originally from New Zealand would be photographed calling her family long distance from the States.[115]

Schools received special emphasis. "It has become increasingly difficult for Marine Corps Recruiting Officers to gain entry into high schools," one officer complained just months before the film's release.[116] *Sands of Iwo Jima* provided a way in: "The flag-raising scene fan photo [which was distributed to teachers] and the entire patriotic subject matter of 'Sands of Iwo Jima' should give you an entrée into the schools not usually available to other commercial films," the exploitation manual advised. "We urge you to take advantage of this fact to vigorously publicize your show to students, teachers and parent-teacher associations." Marines were told to organize coloring contests for younger students and a patriotic essay contest for the older ones, and to give free passes for the best film review written by students. "This sort of contest always has wide appeal for the kids. . . . Maybe you could also give passes to the teacher in whose class the winner is enrolled."[117]

While the publicity campaign in schools focused on domestic themes, the Marine-initiated efforts in the theaters were more

A Marine Corps theater display for *Sands of Iwo Jima*, December 1949. Note the flamethrower, rifles, and high-explosive mortar round on display in the background. (United States Marine Corps)

militaristic. "The U.S. Marine Corps will lend you every legitimate cooperation," the exploitation manual promised theater managers, "whether it be the provision of Marines for a parade, the loan of guns or equipment . . . or tanks, amtracks, and other equipment for parade and display in front of your theater." Some units re-created Pacific islands inside theater lobbies, with "Jap trophies . . . machine guns, mortars, hand grenades, walkie-talkie equipment [and] flamethrowers," all of which were guarded by Marine sentries. Even the film reels became part of the military spectacle, as the manual recommended having a group of Marines take possession of them when they arrived in town and then escort them to the theater with "a procession of jeeps . . . [and] with a lot of ceremony."[118]

The film would receive four Academy Award nominations, earn John Wayne a *Photoplay* award for most popular male star, and go on to become the eighth-highest-grossing film of 1950.[119] And while *Sands of Iwo Jima* was more of a civilian cultural product than a military one, the Corps' extensive cooperation with Republic Pictures and theater owners reveals nonetheless how the Marines managed their image in the uneasy peace of the early Cold War. What began as a desire to give Americans personalized contact with young Marines overseas had become by 1950 a pervasive campaign that reached into libraries, schools, churches, department stores, and movie theaters. With Toys for Tots, Frances Newman's birthday party, and the publicity campaign for *Sands of Iwo Jima,* Marines not only gave the public the "Privates' War" but also spread their influence deep into the public sphere.

The Marines' public relations successes in the 1940s were due to two principal factors. An effective coalition with civilian news organizations brought experienced newsmen into their ranks and allowed the Corps to adapt to different audiences on the World War II home front. A messaging strategy that privileged intimate narratives of community and the experience of the junior Marines differentiated the Corps from the other services. As a result, the Marines' cultural capital increased dramatically during World War II and remained high during the difficult years of demobilization. Speaking the "language of American family life" helped them establish a public relations infrastructure that would endure through the 1950s.

Not all the services were so lucky. The Army struggled with disgruntled veterans and the poor press of the 1946 demobilization riots; the Navy soon found itself embroiled in the affair that has come to be known as the "Revolt of the Admirals." Several years after the war, the Army was still trying to repair its reputation and looked to the Marines for pointers. "A shortage of red-blooded young Americans never plagues the Marine recruiting officer. There is no question of support by the public and the Congress," wrote Lieutenant Colonel Donovan Yeuell in the pages of the Army's *Infantry Journal.* "The success of the Marine Corps in gaining and holding the public fancy is a tradition with history to support it. The army can learn much from the [Marine] Leathernecks."[120]

3

The Politicians and the Guerrillas

We had a loyal bunch of Marines out there on the Hill, and they moved freely across party, committee boundaries, and everything; they were everywhere.

—Colonel Robert Debs Heinl, "Minister of Propaganda," Chowder Society

In 1952, Paul H. Douglas of Illinois was arguably the most liberal member of the United States Senate. Joseph R. McCarthy of Wisconsin was one of the most conservative. Although the two men detested each other, they had one thing in common: both were former Marines and staunch supporters of the Corps. So when Senator Douglas was gathering support for a bill that would strengthen the Corps' position in the Department of Defense, he was surprised when Senator McCarthy did not agree to be a cosponsor. Douglas already had forty-six senators sponsoring the bill and needed forty-nine to guarantee passage, but McCarthy and a small cohort of the most conservative senators were holding out. Using a retired Marine as a back channel, Douglas learned that McCarthy would cosponsor and would encourage others to do so for nothing more than a handshake in front of the press gallery. It "was a high price to pay," remembered Douglas, "but my love for the Corps was such that I would do even that." Douglas strode down the aisle of the Senate and in full view of the gaping reporters in the press gallery sat down next to his political enemy and shook his hand. "Within ten minutes four other signatures were obtained, and I filed the bill with fifty-one cosponsors, two more than a majority," Douglas later wrote. The Douglas-Mansfield Act, also called the Marine Corps Bill, passed both houses with overwhelming support. "I never knew why Joe wanted this public recognition from me in view of his known feelings about me. But apparently he did, and that ultimately saved the Corps."[1]

For the Marines and their supporters, Senator Douglas' words were no hyperbole. From their perspective, the postwar defense reorganizations known as "unification"—which combined the War and Navy departments into a single Department of Defense—were a "struggle for survival," requiring almost the same degree of commitment and tenacity as combat in the Pacific.[2] They felt surrounded by enemies and untrustworthy allies, both in the military and in the White House. The Army was openly hostile; the Navy was more preoccupied with protecting naval aviation than with supporting the Marines. Without a seat on the Joint Chiefs of Staff, the Marines had no direct line to President Truman, who himself was eager to reduce the Corps' size, its funding, and the scope of the missions it would perform. Consequently, the Marine officers who managed the Corps' political relations after the war viewed themselves as alone, outnumbered, and facing a President bent on their destruction.

But even as most Marines remember the postwar years as ones of political attacks and near abolition, they typically underemphasize how deeply their service insinuated itself into the political arena. Throughout the Truman and Eisenhower administrations, the Corps created and nurtured a broad, bipartisan coalition in Congress that worked tirelessly to protect the Marine Corps from the President and the other services. The efforts of that coalition were an unqualified success. In the National Security Act of 1947, Congress wrote the Marines' roles and missions into law, which prohibited the President from transferring their duties and funding to another service. In 1949, Congress added further provisions to control how the President funded the Marines. The 1952 Douglas-Mansfield Act was Congress' most aggressive intervention into the President's powers as commander in chief, giving the Marines a seat on the Joint Chiefs of Staff, reaffirming their status as a separate armed service, and legislating a minimum size and structure for the Corps—a protection no other service enjoyed. President Eisenhower tried repeatedly to reclaim the roles and missions authority lost in the 1947 fight but never succeeded. In the 1958 Defense Reorganization Act, Congress again expanded its authority over the Department of Defense by allowing the service chiefs to bypass the President and bring their roles and missions concerns directly to the legislature. Eisenhower derided the provision as "legalized insubordination" but could do little save accept it.[3]

Because of these protections, the Corps not only survived the Truman and Eisenhower presidencies but thrived, growing its numbers, assets, and political power. In 1945, the Corps contained less than 4 percent of the total manpower of the active-duty armed forces. By 1950, it had risen to 5 percent; by 1960, 7 percent. If Congress had had its way, the Corps would have been even bigger: on three occasions in the Eisenhower administration, Congress tried to increase the size or funding of the Corps over the objections of the President.[4] By 1960, the Marine Corps' active duty end strength had doubled in just ten years.[5]

The Corps' budget tripled during the same period, growing from $302 million to $955 million.[6] Marine aviation assets increased by more than 40 percent between 1950 and 1960, growing from 815 platforms to 1,156.[7] The number of amphibious ships—which are built by the Navy primarily for the Marines' use—also increased at the same rate.[8] And while the Marines were the primary beneficiaries of these planes and amphibious ships, they paid for none of them. All the funds for amphibious shipping, Marine aviation, and the related aviation equipment and maintenance came entirely from the Navy's budget.

These facts disprove the claim that the Marines barely survived the early Cold War. They also counter two other arguments about the military and American government in that era. First, most Cold War historians believe that public opinion and Congress were largely permissive actors in this period—that both allowed the President to organize the military and conduct foreign and defense policy with minimal interference.[9] This was not the case with the Marine Corps. Congress and the public challenged Presidents Truman and Eisenhower repeatedly on the size, structure, and role of the Marine Corps in national defense; more often than not, the commander in chief had to yield to those challenges. Second, in the realm of civil-military relations, most historians agree that the general trend of these years was toward increased civilian control and decreased power for the individual military services.[10] Again, the Marines were the exception. In the first decade of the Cold War, the Corps grew larger, stronger, and more institutionally entrenched than either President desired. The Marines' coalition with Congress was a primary reason for these developments.

The Marines' victories in the interservice battles over defense unification occurred on two fronts: one inside Congress and the other in the broader collection of veterans, journalists, and defense experts who influenced debates on national security. On the political front, the Marines' strategy was one of deception, delay, and irregular warfare. On the cultural front, they launched a direct attack against the President and the Army. Both strategies succeeded.

Inside Congress, the tiny postwar Marine Corps built coalitions with civilians and fought using proxies. Headquarters helped Marines get elected and took steps to bolster their reputations once there. When legislation affecting the Corps came under consideration, the Marines used their most intelligent and well-connected officers to reach out to Congress in ways both legal and illegal. In a manner characteristic of Marines, they treated the legislative arena as a theater of war, seeing the other services, particularly the Army, as the enemy. Survival was the only rule. Departmental directives, orders from the President, regulations, and laws either contributed to that objective or were ignored. "We were in a fight for our lives," explained one of the Corps' most active propagandists, "and a man fighting for his life doesn't very much question the intellectual or moral alignments of someone who steps in and fights on his side."[11]

Outside Congress, Marine publicists read the cultural landscape well and adapted their arguments constantly to a variety of different audiences. Here their methods were more aggressive. Their most useful rhetorical weapon was fear; their strategy was to reframe external threats as internal ones. Rather than arguing their case on the merits of national security, they took an essentially domestic position, arguing that the President's efforts to unify the services into a single Department of Defense would alter the proper relationship between the private citizen and the government. They reconfigured the most boring and bureaucratic aspects of defense policy into simple and emotional arguments about the lurking dangers of militarism and dictatorship. As they had done with their wartime public relations, they represented themselves and their interests in deeply personal and affective terms, which brought journalists, politicians, and ordinary citizens into the fight on their behalf.

There was a great disparity between these two strategies—between what the Marines did inside Congress and how they represented their actions and motives to the rest of the country. They argued against militarism and excessive military influence in politics, even as they became the most politically activist branch of the armed services. They claimed to defend civilian control of the military but resisted every attempt to reduce their own role in national defense, whether coming from the other services, the secretary of defense, or the commander in chief. Despite these contradictions, the Marines' political and cultural strategies were complementary. Together, they helped the Corps augment its power in the Defense Department and obtain a degree of political influence disproportionate to its size and budget.

THE POLITICAL FRONT: THE MARINE COALITION IN CONGRESS

The Marine Corps built relationships with three main groups in Congress. The most important of these were the Marine veterans who went on to elected office and the non-Marine congressmen who, for various reasons, became stalwart supporters of the Corps. A third, less obvious group were undercover Marines: reservists who had civilian jobs on congressional staffs and who worked across parties, committees, and houses of Congress to advance the interests of the Corps with their employers. Together these three groups formed the Marines' congressional coalition.

If numbers of veterans in Congress are any indication of a military service's power in the legislature, the Marines should have had the least influence of all the services. During the interwar years, there were, on average, five former Marines serving in Congress in any given session.[12] In the Truman and Eisenhower administrations, that number rose to over twenty. The Air Force had twice as many veterans in the legislature; the Navy had five times as many. The Army had the most veterans: almost 150 former soldiers served in Congress in 1947, a number that would grow to almost 200 by 1960.[13] What they lacked in numbers, however, the congressional Marines gained in cohesion. Though it sometimes involved political bargaining, as Senator Douglas learned from Senator McCarthy, in the main the congressional Marines stuck together on issues of importance to the Corps.

Marine congressmen were of every possible stripe and political persuasion. Of the twenty-seven Marine veterans who served during this period, fourteen were Democrats and thirteen were Republicans. Most were in the House; only six served in the Senate. They came from across the country, with the South having the most (nine, of whom eight were Democrats) and the Northeast the least (only four). The most powerful members were all from the Midwest and West: Senators Mike Mansfield (D-Mont.), Paul Douglas (D-Ill.), Joe McCarthy (R-Wisc.), Francis Higbee Case (R-S.D.), and Charles Wayland Brooks (R-Ill.).[14] Besides being regionally diverse, they had wide ideological differences. There were conservative anti-Communists such as Senator George Smathers (D-Fla.) and Joe McCarthy, and voices of tolerance such as the Quaker Paul Douglas. There were liberal internationalists such as Representative James Patterson (R-Conn.) and Mike Mansfield, and isolationists such as Francis Case and Charles Brooks. There were two former university professors and a similar number of war heroes, including President Roosevelt's son James.[15] There were also four dual-service veterans, who had served first in the Army and then later joined the Marine Corps or the Marine Corps reserve.[16]

Democrats Paul Douglas and Mike Mansfield were perhaps the strongest and most consistent supporters of the Marine Corps. Both were liberal internationalists—the ideological and temperamental opposites of Senator Joe McCarthy. Neither man had the typical background for politics. Both grew up in poor and broken homes. Douglas earned money by clearing forested land in rural Maine; Mansfield ran away at age fourteen and joined the Navy. He was discharged for enlisting fraudulently, served a tour in the Army, and then became a private in the Marines. Of the two, Douglas was the more liberal and Mansfield the more bipartisan. Douglas was eloquent and voluble; Mansfield was quiet to the point of taciturnity. Mansfield served in the tiny Marine Corps of the 1920s and left to become a copper miner in Butte, Montana, before entering college and politics. Douglas joined in World War II as a fifty-year-old private and won a Bronze Star and Purple Heart on Peleliu and Okinawa. Both men wore their love of the Corps openly. Douglas displayed the Marine Corps colors behind his desk, and Mansfield was almost never seen in a suit without a Marine Corps lapel pin or tie clip.[17]

Joining the Marine veterans in the Corps' congressional coalition were a number of members who had never served in the Marine Corps or even in the military at all. Members in this second group in the Marines' coalition all found something appealing in the Marine Corps that went beyond party politics and service affiliation. Senators Leverett Saltonstall (R-Mass.) and Henry Styles Bridges (R-N.H.) were Army veterans, yet both took strong anti-Army positions in favor of the Marine Corps during the unification fights. Midwestern isolationists Clare Hoffman (R-Mich.) and George H. Bender

(R-Ohio) had no military experience at all but did as much or more to protect the Corps than most of Congress' Marine veterans did. Leslie Arends (R-Mich.), a Navy veteran, was another anomaly. As the House minority whip and a golfing partner of President Eisenhower, Arends knew much about the importance of party loyalty, yet he broke with the Republican President on the controversial Defense Reorganization Act of 1958 and supported the Marine Corps position because he felt a principle higher than party loyalty was at stake.

Democrats who had never served in the Corps were also strong supporters. Georgians Carl Vinson and Richard B. Russell, who served as chairmen of the House and Senate Armed Services Committees, respectively, were consistent supporters of the Marine Corps, as were Representatives Carter Manasco (D-Ala.) and Daniel J. Flood (D-Penn.). Despite his total lack of military service, Flood was such a flamboyant supporter of the Corps that his colleagues in the House were said to occasionally sing the opening lines to "The Marines' Hymn" when he rose to speak.[18]

Marine reservists serving on the professional staffs of congressmen and committees made up a less well-known but critical element of the Marine coalition. These men maintained the back channels between Headquarters Marine Corps and Congress and helped write much of the legislation that protected the Marine Corps. The list of their members is extensive. Reserve lieutenant colonels held full-time civilian positions on the Senate Armed Services, Judiciary, and Government Operations Committees.[19] In the House, the top lawyer for the House Armed Services Committee was another reserve lieutenant colonel; still another reserve Marine served as a staff member on the House Appropriations Committee.[20] Senator Leverett Saltonstall—one of whose sons was a Marine killed in World War II—had two reserve Marines on his staff as assistants; Senators Styles Bridges and Hubert Humphrey had one each, both lieutenant colonels.[21] The clerk of the House, the Honorable Ralph R. Roberts, and the House reading clerk, Joe Bartlett, were former Marines as well. All of these Marines actively supported the Corps' interests and made no apologies for it. Lieutenant Colonel Russell Blandford, the top lawyer for the House Armed Services Committee, made this clear when he was offered the job after completing Yale Law School. "Don't ask me to give up my prejudice for the Marine Corps because I can't do it. . . . It's part of me."[22] Even though the Marine staffers served congressmen of both parties and chambers, they kept in close contact. By 1953, they had even formed a "Congressional Marines Breakfast Group" that met monthly and operated according to a set of published bylaws. (Both the Commandant and his legislative assistant were charter members, despite having no formal affiliation with the legislative branch.)[23] Together, the staffers did everything from serving as liaisons between Congress and Headquarters to conducting outreach to veterans organizations. One staffer, Lieutenant Colonel Blandford, even helped orchestrate a charade to convince congressmen visiting the Quantico base that the Marines were underfunded. "First of all, get all the horses out of there [the stable] and take 'em out to the remote pasture," he advised the Marines at Headquarters.

> Don't let any member see any one of those horses going up and down the road there . . . because you're going to lose 'em if they see 'em. Secondly, close the Post Exchange for inventory the day they arrive, because as soon as they get off that bus somebody's going to say "oh, I'd like to run into the Post Exchange for a moment." That always endangers the Post Exchange because Quantico happens to have one of the best exchanges in the country. . . . Finally—and you're gonna think I'm crazy—I said, you're going to have a reception afterwards. . . . Have crackers and cheese, and the cheapest brands of whiskey you can find. . . . I don't want you to put on one of these lavish displays of food and whiskey and shrimp and crab meat and lobster and all that sort of thing. . . . And on the bus going home that night I heard several of the members saying "My god! These guys sure do need a pay increase. Did you ever see such cheap whiskey in your life?" And literally, it did make an impact on them. . . . They never saw a horse.[24]

Lieutenant Colonel Blandford's horse-hiding operation was not unusual for the Marine Corps—or, indeed, for any military service— in the lean-budget years of the Truman and Eisenhower administrations. All the services employed tactics of a questionable nature in an effort to secure the best funding and future for their institutions.[25] The Marines were simply the most effective at it, and their service culture helps explain why. Discipline and respect for authority were paramount values inside the Corps, but following the orders of outsiders was not. The Marines' intense distrust of the President and other services solidified their cohesion and led them to take creative liberties with regulations and the law. The Corps' small size and heightened awareness of threats helped it adapt, react, and outmaneuver the larger services and their own commander in chief.

BUILDING THE COALITION: "SILENT GEORGE" AND "TAIL-GUNNER JOE"

In the 1946 congressional elections, the public sent fifty-five veterans of World War II to Washington as freshman congressmen. Nine were Marines—three times more than their proportion of World War II veterans in American society.[26] The reasons for the Marines' victories are numerous, and local politics were usually the primary drivers of each candidate's success. But one thing that helped was the fact that Headquarters Marine Corps allowed active-duty officers to campaign in uniform, a practice that violated the spirit, if not the letter, of the naval regulation prohibiting officers from participating openly in political activities. In cases such as that of the youngest member of the House in 1947, twenty-seven-year-old Representative George Sarbacher Jr. of Philadelphia, it is clear that his status as a Marine led to his election.

Sarbacher did not seek out the Republican Party's nomination for his district. The party bosses came to him. When ward boss Austin Meehan learned in early 1946 that the Democrats' pick for the fifth district would be a veteran who had not served overseas, he knew immediately what to do and how to win: "We decided that if they wanted to make it a veterans' fight . . . we'd give them a real veteran."[27] Meehan approached George's father (who was also a Republican ward boss in Philadelphia) and asked if his son would run. The elder Sarbacher agreed that his son had strong military credentials—he had served two years overseas as a bomb disposal officer in the Pacific—but reminded the boss that George had no political experience. Furthermore, a House run was impossible because his son was still on active duty. But the political bosses were persistent and contacted Headquarters Marine Corps seeking an exception to the naval regulations. The Marine Corps quickly found a compromise: campaigning, a lawyer in Headquarters decided, meant making speeches, so George could run for office, appear in campaign literature in uniform, and even wear his uniform at rallies, as long as he stayed off the stump.[28]

Sarbacher's campaign for Congress was political theater of the highest order, and the star was not George but the Marine Corps. Each rally opened with the band playing "The Marines' Hymn," and out would march George in uniform, his chest gleaming with ribbons. Though Headquarters had barred him only from making formal speeches, "Silent George," as the papers called him, would rarely speak at all; he would simply take a bow and stand on the stage while professional Republican campaigners spoke about him. "I was afraid that if I opened my mouth, I might accidentally say something about the issues, and the opposition would be all over me like a four-alarm fire for violating regulations," he explained to reporters. The message, even if it did not come from his lips, was effective: he was fighting for Philadelphia as a Marine, not as a Republican or even as a politician. The advantages of this campaign strategy became abundantly clear one evening at the Kensington Labor Lyceum, as a loud pro-union crowd booed down each Republican candidate who tried to speak. "Suddenly, a tinkling of glockenspiels and the music of banjos and violins were heard. In marched the Ferko String band . . .

playing the Marine[s'] Hymn," reported the *Saturday Evening Post*. "Behind the band, in uniform, came George Sarbacher, Jr. The boos died down. A Republican in the Kensington district of Philadelphia is as fair game as a New York Giant at Ebbets Field, but a Marine in uniform was something else."[29]

The youngest member of the Senate in 1947 was also a Marine, though one far less honorable than George Sarbacher Jr. Wisconsin's youngest judge, Joseph R. McCarthy, had political aspirations even before the war started, and he considered joining the Army to boost his credentials. A mentor advised differently. "If you want to be a politician," his mentor told him, "be a hero—join the Marines."[30] McCarthy claimed to have enlisted as a private, as Paul Douglas did, but in fact, he applied for and received a direct commission as a first lieutenant and served as an intelligence officer for an aviation squadron in the Pacific. He never attended boot camp.[31] His duties kept him at a desk, but because he knew that combat service would be necessary for his political career, he wheedled his way into the tail gunner's seat of a combat plane and was allowed to fly on a few combat missions that were expected to be relatively safe and uneventful. McCarthy did see some action, but most of his time as a tail gunner was spent blindly shooting at trees, which earned him a joke award from his squadron for "destroying more coconut trees than anyone else in the South Pacific."[32] He later lied about the number of flights he made, doctored logbooks in order to qualify for military awards he did not earn, and forged his commanding officer's signature on a citation he wrote for himself.[33] McCarthy also claimed to have injured a leg while crash-landing a plane, but his only war injury occurred when he fell off a ladder during a shellback ceremony—a Navy hazing ritual that celebrates the crossing of the equator aboard ship.[34]

McCarthy made friends in the Corps by plying them with liquor, which he smuggled aboard ship and onto the islands where the squadron was based. (The smuggling operation later collapsed because of a dispute over profits with a partner. The result was a fistfight in which the two men beat each other bloody.)[35] None of these details came out in his 1944 campaign for Senate, however, because McCarthy convinced the combat correspondents attached to his unit to write a plethora of positive stories about him, which he and the public relations officer mailed to Wisconsin newspapers.[36] At McCarthy's urging, the CCs also took photos of him sitting in the tail gunner's seat, wearing a flying helmet and staring at the sky—pictures that McCarthy would use later to create the label that would win him his seat in Congress: "Tail-Gunner Joe." As soon as he returned to the United States, he used his uniform to campaign for office and would

Marine Lieutenant Joseph R. McCarthy poses for a photograph in the Pacific, 1943. Although he was not a pilot or a tail gunner, he would later use this image to run for Congress as "Tail-Gunner Joe." (Wisconsin Historical Society, WHi-8005)

later preside over trials in uniform, all with no admonitions from Headquarters Marine Corps. One of his most frequently distributed campaign posters read "The Spirit of Our Fighting Men: Elect Captain Joseph R. McCarthy of the U.S. Marines."[37]

The Marine Corps not only allowed McCarthy to use the Corps for political gain but also helped him do it. In June 1944, as the Corps was still accepting draftees to fill their combat units for the Pacific, it took the unusual step of transferring McCarthy back to the United States, where he campaigned tirelessly for the Senate. Headquarters offered McCarthy the same deal that it would give George Sarbacher Jr. two years later, allowing him to campaign in uniform as long as he made no overt political statements. In December 1944, after his first Senate run failed, the Corps allowed McCarthy to resign from the Marine Corps, even though the need for men had only grown since the previous summer. (McCarthy told supporters the reason for his exit was the leg wound he suffered in the Pacific and would occasionally feign a limp to prove it.)[38] McCarthy's 1946 campaign depended almost entirely on his fabricated war record, and this time, with the Corps' reputation still at a high from the victories on Iwo Jima and Okinawa, McCarthy prevailed. He defeated Robert La Follette Jr.—largely by accusing the forty-six-year-old of evading military service—and became the junior senator from Wisconsin.

Once McCarthy was in the Senate, Headquarters again bent rules by recommending him for an Air Medal with four stars and a Distinguished Flying Cross (which ranks above both the Purple Heart and the Bronze Star). To qualify for these awards, McCarthy needed to show documentation of at least twenty-five combat flights or an act of genuine heroism in air combat. Of course, he could not. When he first returned from the Pacific, he claimed to have made fourteen flights. By 1952, when he applied for the Distinguished Flying Cross, the number had jumped to thirty-two, and he provided his own doctored logbooks, which he claimed were signed by his commanding officer, Major Glenn Todd, as evidence. (Major Todd's log showed only eleven flights by McCarthy, the same number certified by Headquarters Marine Corps.) Even once it had been alerted to the problems with McCarthy's flight logs, Headquarters supported McCarthy's petition for the awards, and Major Todd "received what he considered a 'very strange' order from Marine Corps headquarters forbidding him to comment on McCarthy's missions or citations."[39]

Headquarters also continued to promote McCarthy while in the Senate, though as an inactive reservist, he did nothing to warrant advancement. He entered the Senate as a captain; by the time of his death, he was a lieutenant colonel. Nor was McCarthy the only one to receive unearned promotions. Senator George Smathers of Florida, who served only three and a half years in the Marine Corps, received so many promotions that he protested to Headquarters Marine Corps. "When I got retired I was still a captain. After I got elected to Congress, all of a sudden I get a notice that I had been promoted to major. . . . I went to the Senate, and I got a notice that I was now a lieutenant colonel," he later explained. When he got promoted to colonel, he decided to confront the Commandant. "I love the Marine Corps. I thought it was a great outfit. . . . But I am embarrassed by the fact that since I've gotten into Congress and haven't done a damn thing, I get promoted three times. I couldn't get promoted once when the war was going on and I was really doing something. Now this is ridiculous." The Commandant agreed to halt the promotions, but Senator Smathers had already risen to a rank that took most Marines two decades to obtain. "They were really pretty bad about that," Smathers admitted.[40]

The Corps' creative interpretations of regulations concerning political campaigning and medals are one indication that it was willing to overlook rules in order to increase its political power. But the Corps' real disregard for both regulations and federal law came during the legislative battles over the 1947 National Security Act and its subsequent amendments. The story of how the Marine Corps won its congressional protections during unification is a tale of intrigue, theft, and subterfuge.

"A BUNCH OF GUERRILLAS"

Marines did not just build support in Congress by getting their veterans elected. They pursued other, more surreptitious stratagems as well. They mobilized the former combat correspondents who worked in the Washington press corps; they sent out secret mailings to influential allies around the country; and they lobbied congressmen directly, both openly and in secret. The Marines of the "Chowder Society"—an unofficial organization of brilliant and well-connected Marine officers—maintained the congressional coalition almost single-handedly. They were, as one of their more voluble members put it, "just a bunch of guerrillas and almost fugitives."[41] They worked in the shadows, trusted no one, and concealed much of what they were doing, even from their own superiors. Although they had deep devotion to their country and the Marine Corps, they operated at the limits of the law and sometimes beyond them. They were insurgents inside the defense establishment, a small cadre of officers who used political pressure and asymmetric tactics to upset the status quo and delegitimize their larger, more institutionally entrenched opponents. Throughout the 1940s and 1950s, this small group of relatively junior officers obstructed and in some cases defeated the plans of the President and, in so doing, strengthened the Marine Corps' position inside the Department of Defense.[42]

Calling the Chowder Marines "guerrillas" is hyperbole, of course, but it is an appropriate label nonetheless. Guerrillas and insurgents—whom the two senior members of the Chowder Society had fought in Nicaragua and Haiti in the interwar period—do not obey traditional rules of war or use conventional tactics.[43] Being smaller and less well-resourced than their opponents, they work outside existing power structures and choose unconventional strategies. They are dynamic and decentralized, organizing themselves in informal networks rather than rigid hierarchies. Because they are less saddled by bureaucracies and regulations, they are highly adaptable and flexible. They pursue indirect means, turn weaknesses into strengths, and use proxies and the media to win public support. Secrecy and surprise are their greatest weapons, innovation and adaptability their most critical assets.[44]

Such were the very tactics of the Chowder Society during the legislative battles that would eventually produce the National Security Act of 1947. Their members operated incognito, occasionally wearing civilian clothes instead of uniforms. When caught and chastised for interfering in political matters, they suspended operations temporarily or lied to their superiors and continued them. Because they were young and of relatively junior rank (most were lieutenant colonels—the Army and Air Force usually used generals as their lobbyists), the Corps' senior leadership could maintain both distance from their activities and plausible deniability of wrongdoing. The result was a series of networked and decentralized operations, all of which occurred well below the level of the Commandant. "The Commandant never saw any of us personally," remembered then-Lieutenant Colonel Robert Debs Heinl, one the Chowder Society's most active and talkative members. "There were no briefings, no charts, none of the formal decision-making apparatus, the way things are mostly done now in the Defense Department. . . . We operated much more like the CIA."[45]

The Chowder Marines worked in two groups, one in Quantico, Virginia, under the leadership of Colonel Merrill B. Twining and the other in Washington under Brigadier Generals Gerald C. Thomas and Merritt A. "Red Mike" Edson. They took the name Chowder Society from a comic strip containing a character that resembled the shortest and most aggressive member of the group, Lieutenant Colonel Victor H. "Brute" Krulak. The group had other names as well. Edson called his team the "Termites," because they worked to bring down a huge bureaucracy in the executive branch by weakening key points in the structure.[46] Colonel Twining called them the "dirty tricks department."[47] Truman referred to them crossly as just "those lieutenant colonels."[48] Despite the many nicknames, however, the Chowder Society was not a club or a formal organization, although most of the officers had served in General Archer A. Vandegrift's First Marine Division on Guadalcanal. It was a loose affiliation of thinkers, lobbyists, and war heroes who shared the conviction that the Marine Corps was in danger of being reorganized out of existence.

Not only were the Chowder Marines some of the Corps' greatest officers, they ranked among its most privileged. Colonel Twining

Lieutenant Colonel Robert Debs Heinl Jr., the self-proclaimed "Minister of Propaganda" of the Chowder Society, 1945. (United States Marine Corps)

came from a wealthy Quaker banking family in Wisconsin and attended the U.S. Naval Academy, an alma mater shared by two other Chowder Society members, Lieutenant Colonels Samuel R. Shaw and Victor H. Krulak (the latter's son would become the Commandant of the Marine Corps in 1995). The Twining family had a long military tradition that was unusual for Quakers, but Merrill was not the most successful family member; his brother Nathan would become the chief of staff of the Air Force and, later, the chairman of the Joint Chiefs of Staff.[49] Lieutenant Colonel James D. "Don" Hittle also came from the Midwest. His was a well-connected political family in Michigan, and after retiring from the Marine Corps, Hittle would become an assistant secretary of the Navy in the Nixon administration and a senior vice president of Pan Am Airways. Lieutenant Colonel Robert Debs Heinl had the most interesting pedigree: he was the grandnephew of socialist presidential candidate Eugene V. Debs but had a bank president for a grandfather, and everyone in his family besides Eugene was what Heinl called "brass collar Republicans." Son of a Washington press correspondent, Heinl was educated at St. Albans Academy in Washington, D.C., and then at Yale (as was another Chowder member, Lieutenant Colonel James C. Murray). Heinl would use his father's contacts with the Washington press corps to become what he described as the Chowder Society's "Minister of Propaganda."[50] He also promoted the Corps' interests as a regular contributor to the *Marine Corps Gazette* and as the director of the Historical Section at Headquarters Marine Corps, which oversaw the official historical monographs the Corps produced.

Brigadier General Edson did not share the refined upbringing of most of the Chowder members. Raised poor in rural Vermont, he was a crack shot on the Marine Corps Rifle Team, and a Medal of Honor winner on Guadalcanal. A member of the Grange (his father had founded the local chapter in Chester, Vermont), Edson grew up as a farmer's son and had a lifelong antipathy to monopolies and the concentration of power in the hands of the few. After dropping out of the University of Vermont, Edson enlisted in the National Guard and then joined the Marines. He fought guerrillas in Nicaragua in 1928 and was a driving intellectual force behind the Corps' 1940 doctrinal publication *Small Wars Manual,* which was the most innovative and detailed set of tactics yet penned for fighting insurgencies.[51] A self-described "rock-ribbed Republican" and, later, the president of the

Chowder Society member Lieutenant Colonel Victor H. "The Brute" Krulak in the Pacific, 1945. The youth and relatively junior rank of Chowder Society members helped them to lobby Congress without attracting unwanted attention. (United States Marine Corps)

National Rifle Association, he was a staunch antimilitarist, a populist, and distrustful of what he called the "high hat" class of Washington Republicans.[52] Short in stature, with a quiet demeanor and piercing blue eyes, he was considered a front-runner for the Commandancy. Instead, however, he resigned his commission at the height of the unification controversy and committed suicide some eight years later.[53]

The other major character in the unification story is not a person at all but a set of classified papers, known as the Joint Chiefs of Staff

Congressional Medal of Honor winner Brigadier General Merritt A. "Red Mike" Edson, the most passionate leader of the Chowder Society. (United States Marine Corps)

(JCS) Series 1478. Authored by the chiefs of the Army, Navy, and Army Air Forces just after the war, these studies set out each service's point of view on a unified Department of Defense. In them, the Army and Army Air Forces made a strategic error in committing to print their vision for the future of the Marine Corps. The Army study in particular, authored by chief of staff of the Army Dwight D. Eisenhower, recommended disbanding all six Marine divisions and confining the Marines to their prewar role as naval landing parties, ships' guards, and guards for naval bases. The Navy argued forcefully against the reduction of the Marine Corps but focused more attention on the question of naval aviation. As the Commandant of the Marine Corps did not yet sit on the Joint Chiefs of Staff, the Marines could only offer advice to the Navy, and did not prepare a 1478 study of their own.

As Congress began considering how to unify the separate services, two coalitions quickly emerged, with the Army and Army Air Forces on one side and the Navy and Marine Corps on the other.[54] The Army coalition argued for full unification, which required dismantling the duplicative bureaucracies the war had created and establishing a single, hierarchical system of staff organization for all the armed services. Naturally, the Army viewed its own model of staff organization as the most efficient and recommended that it be extended over the other services. At the head of the military chain of command would be a chief of staff of the armed forces—a single military officer, serving under the secretary of defense, but with considerable control over the services underneath.[55]

The Navy and Marine Corps feared this staff system would concentrate too much power in the hands of the Army, and so they argued for a "merger" of the services instead, which would preserve more autonomy for each service, even while keeping them subordinate to a single civilian secretary of defense. Beyond this, however, the Navy coalition was divided, with the Marine and Navy leadership disagreeing on priorities. The Navy's primary concern was preserving its naval aviation, which they knew the soon-to-be independent

Air Force would try to appropriate for itself. This was not only concerning to the Navy's pilots; officers throughout the Navy understood that without carrier planes, the Navy would have no claim to the most important weapon and funding source of the postwar era, nuclear weapons. In the Navy's view, unless aviation could be protected, a unified Department of Defense meant underfunding and the slow destruction of the Navy.[56]

The bigger issue for the Marines was whether the specific roles and missions of each service would be spelled out in the law or decided later in an executive order signed by the President. If left to the executive branch, the President would have total control over which military service performed which functions; by a mere stroke of a pen, the President could eliminate the Marine Corps' missions or reassign them to another service. After reading the 1478 studies, the Marines became convinced that this was exactly what President Truman planned to do.[57]

The Marines' lobbying during unification was made harder by the fact that almost no one inside the armed forces agreed with them. The President, Secretary of War Robert Patterson, the entire Joint Chiefs of Staff, and almost every military officer who testified on the bill all argued for presidential control of roles and missions, claiming that the right to determine and transfer duties from one service to another belonged to the commander in chief. The press and the public were also strongly in favor of unification, with 60 percent of those polled endorsing the Army's plan for "unified command" of all the services.[58] Even the secretary of the Navy abandoned the Corps. Though he had been a strong ally early on, in January 1947 Secretary of the Navy James V. Forrestal met with Secretary Patterson and dropped his objections to an executive order on roles and missions in exchange for protections for naval aviation. The President announced the Forrestal-Patterson compromise the next day and sent a draft bill to Congress a month later. The Navy's capitulation to the War Department convinced the Marines that extreme measures were required to save the Corps from the President.[59] To prove to their allies in Congress that the Corps was in danger of elimination, the Chowder Marines needed copies of the JCS 1478 papers. Unfortunately, the President had classified the series as top secret and restricted access to a small number of generals and admirals working for the Joint Chiefs of Staff. The Commandant, General Vandegrift, knew of the papers' existence through General Edson, who served as a Marine Corps liaison to the chief of naval operations, but could not share the information with the Corps' supporters. The Commandant walked a fine line by even hinting at the papers' contents in his testimony to Congress, for in an open hearing, divulging the contents of classified documents even by summarizing them was a security violation.

Convinced that the 1478 series was the key to saving the Corps, General Edson took matters into his own hands. He stole the 1478 papers from the office of the chief of naval operations, made an illegal copy of them, and brought them to Headquarters Marine Corps. The Chowder Marines made additional copies and leaked their contents to key players in the unification fights—including journalists—which nearly caused the Commandant of the Marine Corps to be relieved of his duties. "It did look like a cloak-and-dagger kind of thing," admitted Chowder member Lieutenant Colonel Samuel R. Shaw. We "weren't supposed to copy JCS papers. But if we were going to work on it [unification] we had to have a copy."[60]

Most historical accounts of the Chowder Society treat their rule breaking with a wink and a smile, or even celebrate it as what one member called "the honorable art of institutional theft."[61] But besides stealing top-secret documents, the Chowder Marines broke a whole host of regulations during the unification fights, all in the name of protecting the Corps from the President and the Army. When the President announced the Forrestal-Patterson compromise in January 1947, Secretary Forrestal issued a department-wide message stating that "officers of the Navy and Marine Corps are expected to refrain from opposition [to the bill] in their public utterances."[62] An exception existed for formal testimony to Congress, though even that had to be cleared through the Department of the Navy. The Navy and Marines were further bound by Articles 94, 95, and 1252 of the U.S. Naval Regulations, which forbade informal contact with any member of Congress except with the explicit authorization of the Navy Department. The same regulations also prohibited the release of any information contained in government records "which for reasons of public policy, should not be disclosed to persons not of the Naval or other Military Establishments." Nor could a Marine "make any public speech or permit publication of any article written by him or for him which is prejudicial to the interests of the United States."[63] Once President Truman declared unification the policy of his administration and a necessity for the national security of the United States—which he did on numerous occasions from 1945 onward—any attempt by active-duty Marines to undermine the legislation constituted a violation of these regulations.

Despite these prohibitions, General Edson opposed the unification bill openly. He wrote a hefty briefing packet that named and summarized the 1478 papers as well as other documents he believed to be classified. The brief went out to thirteen members of Congress and at least three influential journalists.[64] He made allies of Republican senators Joe McCarthy, George Aiken, and Ralph Flanders of Vermont, and Edward Robertson of Wyoming, even after Robertson explained that his principal motive for opposing the legislation was simply that "it was a Truman sponsored bill."[65] Edson helped convince Senator McCarthy (who was not on the Armed Services Committee) to use his Senate prerogative to attend the hearings and to question witnesses forcefully on behalf of the Corps. When the bill came before the Senate Armed Services Committee, General Edson was the only active-duty officer to testify in opposition to it. Though several high-ranking naval officers were still unsatisfied with the Forrestal-Patterson compromise, none of them testified in opposition to the bill.[66]

Even though President Truman ordered the Commandant to "get those lieutenant colonels off the Hill and keep them off," the

Chowder Marines disregarded both the President's and their Commandant's orders.[67] Relations between General Edson and the Commandant grew strained. When General Edson leaked the results of a private meeting between General Eisenhower and the Commandant to a reporter, General Vandegrift threatened him with a court-martial. "It is not a very pleasant feeling," Edson wrote that night in his diary, to know that the Commandant "would abandon the ship immediately at the first sign of retaliation. It is a pretty lonesome feeling; and I am getting tired and weary of it—mentally, physically, and every other way."[68] He continued his outreach to the press nonetheless, and even described the contents of the classified 1478 papers to a reporter. The chief of naval operations, Chester W. Nimitz, under pressure from the White House, called the Commandant and requested an investigation.[69] General Vandegrift covered for Edson, but shortly afterward he resigned so that he could oppose the legislation without damaging the careers of the officers around him.

Even with Senators Robertson and McCarthy fighting it at every turn, the unification bill passed the Senate and headed to the House. There it was routed to the House Expenditures Committee, which was chaired by Representative Clare Hoffman of Michigan, a known isolationist who had little interest in the military or in foreign policy. This was a deliberate move by the President and the bill's supporters, who expected that Hoffman would turn the unification bill over to a subcommittee headed by representative James Wadsworth Jr. of New York. Quick hearings would ensure that the bill passed with few or no amendments, removing the need for a conference between the two chambers.

Instead, a dramatic reversal occurred. The father of Chowder member Lieutenant Colonel Don Hittle knew Clare Hoffman personally and got his son an audience with the congressman. Hittle showed Hoffman purloined copies of the 1478 papers that he had stashed in his basement in Quantico, and convinced the congressman that the President and senior leadership of the Army planned to disband the Marine Corps if the unification bill passed. Hoffman

adopted the Marines' cause with zeal and convinced other committee members to do the same. Though the President's unification bill
was a legislative priority for both the Republican and Democratic
leadership in Congress, several prominent committee members of
both parties joined ranks to fight for the Marines. On the first day of
the House hearings, Secretary of War Patterson found himself peppered with so many questions about the Marine Corps that he lost
his temper: "Marines, Marines! That's all I hear. They're not treated
any differently than any of the other branches."[70]

Technically, Secretary Patterson was correct, for at that point no
service had roles and missions spelled out in the bill; all the services'
functions were to be described in an executive order signed by the
President. Furthermore, the bill had already been amended in the
Senate to ensure "no alteration or diminution" of the Corps' relative
status.[71] But the fact that the President was withholding classified
papers from the Committee under a false pretense of national security
crystallized the committee's resistance to the bill. Hoffman demanded
the release of the 1478 papers, and once they were in his possession,
he seized the initiative. He got Secretary Forrestal to suspend the
naval regulations that Edson had already breached so brazenly, and a
flood of naval officers appeared to oppose the bill. Hoffman then
asked the Commandant to assign Lieutenant Colonel Hittle directly
to his committee as a special advisor to the chairman. General Vandegrift agreed, and Hoffman ensured that the bipartisan subcommittee drafting the new bill was overwhelmingly pro-Marine. Besides himself, Hoffman assigned two other pro-Marine Republicans:
Henry J. Latham of New York and isolationist George Bender of
Ohio. For Democrats, he chose the pro-Marine Alabaman Carter
Manasco and the minority whip, John W. McCormack of Massachusetts. Although McCormack was hesitant to support the Marines
fully at first, some hard pressure from Chowder member Major Lyford Hutchens and others brought him in line.[72] The subcommittee
voted five to one to specify the Marines' roles and missions in the
legislation. The law that resulted contained almost everything the

Marines had wanted, including the critical Section 206(c) (authored almost entirely by Chowder members), which defined the Marine Corps' roles and missions in national defense.[73]

Most explanations of the Marines' political victory in the 1947 fight emphasize the family connection between Chowder member Lieutenant Colonel Don Hittle and Representative Clare Hoffman, but this only provided the Marines their initial entrée to the congressman and his committee.[74] It was the Marines' political savvy that got Hoffman on their side. Hoffman was "a bitter-end conservative," remembered Robert Debs Heinl years later, so "when Don [Hittle] told him that there were a bunch of JCS papers . . . which disclosed the true intention of the other services toward the Marine Corps (which they were denying of course), this immediately inflamed Hoffman's feelings about government secrecy and hypocrisy by Executive Branch people up on the Hill."[75] The hearings became a power play between Hoffman and the administration, with the former fighting for Congress' rights as a coequal branch and the latter claiming weakly that national security required the 1478 series to stay classified. Hoffman won, and in the process became a powerful ally of the Corps and a constant stumbling block for both Democratic and Republican Presidents who tried to unify the military services further.

THE REVOLT OF THE ADMIRALS

The Marines' disruption of the President's unification agenda produced a National Security Act that was good for the Corps but bad for the nation. The new secretary of defense could not strip the Marines of their roles and missions, but neither could he exercise the most basic control over the nation's military services. Instead of a single unified department with a strong secretary, the 1947 law created the National Military Establishment—an organization that functioned as effectively as had the Articles of Confederation before the Constitution. The law preserved the Departments of the Navy and Army as executive departments and added a third: the Department of the Air Force. The secretaries of the military departments remained in the cabinet, served on the National Security Council, and could appeal directly to the President when they disagreed with decisions made by the Secretary of Defense. The entire system was loose, uncoordinated, and utterly unmanageable. The first secretary of defense, James V. Forrestal, found the system so unworkable that he drove himself to exhaustion, which led to a nervous breakdown and then suicide.

Forrestal's replacement, Louis Johnson, hated the Marines, and they hated him. Charged by the President with making dramatic reductions in defense spending, Secretary Johnson cut the budgets of all the services, but for the Marines he specified where the cuts should be made, ordering reductions to the manpower of the combat units. His goal was the same as General Eisenhower's in the 1478 series: to disband the Marine divisions, which he regarded as unnecessarily duplicative. Secretary Johnson also took aim at the Marines' pride and traditions. Because he believed the Marine Corps to be a subset of the Navy, he ordered the Commandant stripped of his limousine and tried to cancel the annual celebration of the Marine Corps Birthday. The Marines were furious but unsurprised. Secretary Johnson's insults were just further proof that the Corps was forever under siege by the President and other services.

In mid-1949, when Congress considered amendments to the National Security Act, the Chowder Marines returned to the guerrilla tactics they had used in the 1947 fight. They collected another store of stolen files; when they needed to hide them, Lieutenant Colonel Heinl buried them in the Marine Corps historical archives and, later, in the quartermaster's files.[76] At one point, several of the Chowder Society's most important files were stashed in the trunk of Colonel Shaw's car. The methods for distributing what Heinl called "collateral propaganda" were equally secretive. The Chowder Society enlisted help from former combat correspondents and from Hollywood allies like Major Andrew Geer, who had rewritten the script for *Sands of Iwo Jima* only a few months before. Heinl and Geer approached the quartermaster general of the Marine Corps and convinced him to direct secret funds toward a grassroots mailing effort to oppose the amendments. "We created a basic mailing list of friends of the Marine Corps nationwide, comprising several thousand people of serious influence, grass-roots people all through the United States," remembered Heinl. "We began sending them out in plain, white envelopes, un-headed mailings . . . [so that our supporters] knew where they were coming from, but any interceptor would know nothing."[77] They continued to wear civilian clothes when they went to Capitol Hill, to throw the other services off their trail. One member was tailed by Army or Air Force spies. Another was investigated by the Office of Naval Intelligence and subsequently labeled a "suspicious person."[78] Congressional staffer Russell Blandford found material slipped under the door of his home in the middle of the night "because nobody wanted to be seen coming over on the Hill with an envelope in their hand."[79] While the Commandant was always apprised of their general activities, in order to keep him out of trouble they withheld much of what they did. There was "an intentional obliquity in what we were doing," remembered Lieutenant Colonel Heinl, "so that up and down the line we could survive if real trouble came along."[80]

Real trouble did come along later that year, but luckily for the Corps, it was the Navy's. Like good insurgents, the Marines knew when to attack and when to lie low; the Navy, it seems, did not. Between April and October 1949, two interrelated scandals plagued the Navy—the B-36 controversy and the Revolt of the Admirals—tainting that service with a reputation for parochial politicking that belonged just as properly to the Marines. In the first scandal, Navy Department insiders authored an "anonymous document" alleging that the Air Force's procurement of the B-36 bomber was rife with corruption. When Congress investigated, the Air Force was vindicated and the Navy sources for the rumors revealed. The B-36 issue prompted another wide-ranging set of congressional hearings on unification and strategy, during which some of the Navy's most senior admirals publicly broke with Secretary of the Navy Francis P. Matthews and assailed the Air Force, the premises of strategic bombing, and the failures of unification.

As had General Edson during the 1947 fight, senior naval officers in 1949 disobeyed orders, leaked classified information, and aired their grievances against the other services to Congress and in the press. Like the Chowder Society, some in the Navy sought to undermine civilian control, in this case that of Secretary of Defense Johnson and their own Navy secretary. But unlike that of the Marines, the Navy's insurgency failed badly. As a result of the scandals, the President relieved the chief of naval operations, and morale throughout the Navy plummeted. The mainstream press lambasted the Navy for its supposed opposition to unification and civilian control. The Navy's senior leadership fell into disarray. In the middle of the hearings, the Navy's top policy committee was unable to agree on its goals for the hearings, or even if it should ask for them to stop or continue. Secretary of the Navy Matthews tried to muzzle those admirals who disagreed with him; they promptly leaked what he was doing to the press. When an enraged Matthews ordered his inspector general to investigate, they quickly discovered that the Organizational Research and Policy Division (OP-23)—the Navy's equivalent of the Chowder Society—was involved. OP-23 was raided and its members detained and interrogated. When the *Washington Post* learned of OP-23, it described it as "a secret publicity bureau almost solely dedicated to smearing the army and the air force and disrupting unification." Shortly afterward, the new chief of naval operations, Admiral Forrest P. Sherman, ordered OP-23 disbanded.[81]

At least one Chowder Marine worked in OP-23 and even helped hide some of the secret files the Navy's inspector general was pursuing. However, the Marines emerged from the Navy's scandals wholly unscathed.[82] In fact, the 1949 amendments to the National Security Act strengthened the Corps' position in the Department of Defense because they forbade the Secretary of Defense from using targeted funding cuts to reduce the Corps' combat units.[83] The final report on unification and strategy argued forcefully for less interservice bickering but also heartily endorsed the Marine Corps and recommended that the Commandant of the Marine Corps receive a seat on the Joint Chiefs of Staff. Three years later, he would get it.

The differences between the Navy's and the Marines' interservice warfare tactics are noteworthy. In the B-36 controversy and the Revolt of the Admirals, the large bureaucracy of the Navy eventually turned on itself, as disparate divisions and groups within the Navy began attacking each other and operating independently. Different officers pursued disparate agendas; members who perhaps meant well, such as the authors of the "anonymous document," caused great harm to their service's reputation. Cohesion collapsed. The Navy lost control of its public relations, and the very office designed to win interservice battles became a liability.

The Marine Corps had almost none of these problems. By using a decentralized network for their lobbying, the Chowder Society avoided the political attention that came when a senior officer publicly broke with his superiors. Being so much smaller than the other services also allowed the Marines to avoid unwanted scrutiny, work outside normal channels, and react quickly to change. Their political strategy was asymmetrical, turning ostensible weaknesses—the Marine Corps' small size, relative lack of senior officers, and ambiguous status in the Department of the Navy—into assets.[84] As a result, the Corps enjoyed stronger cohesion, a singleness of purpose, and less internal friction than the Navy.

The Chowder society never had a formal administrative designation like OP-23, but nor did Chowder disappear after 1949, as has been previously thought. In 1952, a Headquarters Marine Corps reorganization created the Policy Analysis Division and established the post of legislative assistant to the Commandant. Colonel Don Hittle was the first legislative assistant; two of the earliest directors of policy analysis were Chowder members Samuel R. Shaw and James C. Murray.[85] The Policy Analysis Division did not steal documents, as its predecessors had done, but it had the same general purpose.

The division monitored unification, roles and missions, the status of the Commandant in the Navy and Defense Department, and "the party lines of the army, navy and air force." It was further tasked with such former Chowder missions as developing "a plan to coordinate and effectively use the political potential of various Marine/ Service oriented friends and organizations" and evaluating "longrange policies related to the survival of the Marine Corps as a vital and useful military force."[86]

These more formal political organizations inside Headquarters Marine Corps proved helpful during the events leading up to passage of the Defense Reorganization Act of 1958, the final major unification effort of the 1950s. In his proposed bill, President Eisenhower sought to further streamline the chain of command, enhance the status of the Chairman of the Joint Chiefs, and, finally, "remove all doubts as to the full authority of the Secretary of Defense" over the individual services.[87] Privately, he explained to the National Security Council that a major goal of the legislation was "to eliminate those g. d. roles and missions," so that the executive branch could switch, alter, or abolish any service's missions as the President saw fit.[88] Lobbying by the Navy and the Marine Corps made his wish impossible to achieve.

The very day the 1958 reorganization bill was sent to the House Armed Services Committee, Chowder member Don Hittle, now a brigadier general and the Commandant's legislative aide, met with the committee's chairman, Carl Vinson. Present with them was the committee's counsel, reserve Marine lieutenant colonel Russell Blandford, who had earlier helped the Marines hide their horses on the base at Quantico. "What changes should we make?" Vinson asked the two Marines. Together, they "completely gutted the reorganization" and reversed much of what President Eisenhower had proposed.[89]

The problem then became how to mobilize bipartisan support for a bill that was in direct opposition to the President's agenda. "I need a Republican," Chairman Vinson told General Hittle. "Go over and talk to Les Arends." When Hittle approached the minority whip, he found him deeply skeptical: "I play golf regularly with the President. This is his bill . . . he'll be furious," Arends said. However, for reasons that will soon become clear, Arends agreed to cosponsor. Vinson introduced the bill in the House, and, as Hittle recalled, there was "a major shudder that went through the Pentagon and through some of the White House." The secretary of the Navy called the Commandant and demanded that he discipline Hittle for political interference, but the Commandant refused. Instead, he ordered Hittle to leave Washington until the bill passed. Hittle complied but continued to coordinate the Marines' efforts on the bill via telephone.[90]

A day after Vinson and Arends introduced the Marine-edited House bill, an identical version appeared in the Senate, sponsored by two other Marine allies: Senators Mike Mansfield and Styles Bridges, the senior Republican on the Senate Armed Services Committee. The result was a process of debate and compromise between the President's supporters and the Marines' allies that lasted for months. The Navy agreed to support most of the administration's proposals but confessed worry to the President about the reaction of the Marines, who, they warned, were "emotional."[91] After several weeks of wrangling between the President and Congress, the Defense Reorganization Act passed without the features most objectionable to the Marines. Instead of stripping Congress of its control over roles and missions, the final bill inserted a provision allowing either chamber the power to veto a transfer of functions, roles, or missions from one service to another. The final bill further increased the services' power by allowing the chiefs and service secretaries the right to appeal directly to Congress on a transfer of functions, a portion of the bill that the President detested but had to accept. Without the Marines' lobbying, President Eisenhower might have seized total control of the services' roles and missions, much as President Truman had tried to do a decade earlier.[92]

It was not just whom the Marines approached and their good relations with congressmen and staffers that led to success in 1958; how they talked about unification mattered too. The two senior Republicans who derailed the President's reorganization plan—Les

Arends of Michigan and Styles Bridges of Vermont—did so on behalf of deeply held beliefs, beliefs that the Marines understood and knew well how to manipulate. By being attentive to the cultural factors involved in unification, the Marines built a coalition that spanned both parties and stripped the President of some of his most loyal Republicans.

THE CULTURAL FRONT: FEAR AND LOATHING
AFTER WORLD WAR II

When the Chowder Marines approached politicians for favors, they were nuanced and discreet. When they advanced their agenda with journalists, defense experts, and veterans outside the halls of Congress, however, they were anything but. The Marines' efforts on the cultural front were blunt and aggressive: they smeared their enemies, questioned the patriotism of the other services, and frightened the public with hysterical claims of nonexistent threats. Attacks on the Marine Corps, they suggested, were attacks on the nation's traditions and would ultimately change America into a society like those of the very enemies it had just defeated. Sometimes they issued the charges themselves, but more often they used proxies: retired Marines and journalists. Examining how the Marines talked about unification—both inside and outside Washington—explains how they sustained their coalition of supporters and won further legislative protections.

Each service had a different rhetorical style for discussing unification that reflected its organization's core beliefs. The Army's rhetoric emphasized the central precepts of Army organizational culture: economy, efficiency, and the importance of centralized control and unity of command. The overriding goal of unification, argued General Eisenhower when the hearings first began, was to allow the country to buy "more security for less money" by streamlining the bureaucracy and eradicating waste and duplication.[93] A centerpiece of this argument was the Army's short-lived proposal for a single military chief of staff, a general or an admiral who would serve under the civilian secretary of defense and administer the armed forces through a national general staff. This, the Army leadership argued, would preserve civilian control of the military but would also centralize decision making, remove parochial competition between services, and give the entire department unity of command.

Officers in the Army Air Forces endorsed the Army's efficiency arguments but focused more on strategic arguments—mainly on the need for a separate Air Force to protect the country in the atomic age. They emphasized the contribution of airpower to winning World War II and claimed that the airplane had replaced the Navy ship as the first line of national defense. "As soon as airplanes are developed with sufficient range so that they can go any place that we want them to go," testified Lieutenant General James H. Doolittle to Congress just after the war, "there will be no further use for aircraft carriers."[94] Because they saw themselves as the principal military arm in any future conflict, they supported the War Department's proposal for a national general staff, certain that their place in the defense architecture was secure.

The Navy, which had the most decentralized bureaucracy, also had the least coherent message. It had numerous bureaus and semi-autonomous communities, and each argued for its own interests. Some admirals claimed that the atomic bomb augured a new role for the Navy; others insisted that nuclear weapons changed nothing. Aviators argued for naval aviation; others downplayed the role of airplanes. They made arguments for efficiency and reduced duplication, while arguing that competing research and development programs spurred innovation. They also made many of the same domestic arguments the Marines emphasized. They wanted more coordination between the services but feared that unification would lead to an Army-dominated Department of Defense.[95]

The Marines simplified the issue. Eschewing arguments of military strategy, where their position was weakest, they emphasized the domestic dangers of the proposed legislation. Unification, they argued, gave too much power to one military officer (first the Army's proposed single chief of staff, later the Chairman of the Joint Chiefs of Staff) and would lead invariably to dictatorship. Besides destroying the Marine Corps, this would constitute an unacceptable departure from American values and tradition. Unless checked, the "lust for power" of a militaristic President and War Department would destroy the nation's democratic institutions and traditions.[96]

The Marines' strategy worked, even though the merits of the argument were weak. Even after the War Department stopped lobbying for a single chief of staff and national general staff in 1947, it became the Marines' greatest weapon for smearing the Army. Ten years later, the Marines were still using both concepts to convince Representative Arends and Senator Bridges that more unification would lead to military dictatorship and destroy American democracy.

By linking their parochial concerns to broader strains of worry in both Congress and the country, the Marines gained access to a large coalition of organizations and individuals who would normally care little for the intricacies of defense policy. They made common cause with internationalists and isolationists, anti-Communists and antimilitarists, liberals and conservatives, connecting unification—often tenuously—to the most emotional issues of the day: universal military training, fear of militarism, and the still-present hatred of the nation's enemies in the recent war. All of these groups had disparate agendas but made similar arguments: the President, the executive branch, and the military were growing too strong and had become dangerous. Congress had a duty to resist.

These antistatist arguments played well both inside and outside Congress after World War II. The Depression and the war had yielded a massive expansion of the President's powers and an unprecedented intrusion of the state into private affairs. Calls for limiting the powers of the state came from all corners. Conservative southern Democrats feared that more interference from Washington would increase the pressure to alter the racial status quo in the South, business conservatives wanted price controls lifted and government management of the economy curtailed, and both liberals and libertarians deplored the draft and the calls for universal military training. Representatives from rural states—midwestern Republicans and southern Democrats, in particular—were particularly committed to reversing the decade-long expansion of the executive that occurred during Roosevelt's "Imperial Presidency."[97]

Although they were themselves a part of the executive branch of government, the Marines made the specter of growing executive power a centerpiece of their antiunification efforts. In the brief General Edson distributed around Congress, he argued that the President's desire to control all aspects of the military constituted "an unprecedented invasion of the fundamental rights of Congress" and thus "presents the greatest and most subtle threat to our form of democratic government and to the future welfare and safety of this nation that has been conceived since Washington took office."[98] In his famous "Bended Knee" speech to Congress in 1946, the Commandant took a similar line publicly, arguing that the Marine Corps' future is "a matter for determination by the Congress. . . . The Marine Corps believes it has earned this right—to have its future decided by the legislative body which created it—nothing more."[99] The argument was effective. When the Commandant finished, the entire committee and much of the audience rose to applaud. One Marine present heard Army Air Forces general Lauris Norstad grumble from the audience, "If they start singing the Marine Corps Hymn, I think I will throw up."[100]

To the warnings of expanding executive power, the Marines added a more general alarm concerning the dangers of militarism. If Congress passed the President's unification bill, argued General Edson, the result would be "an inordinate assumption of military and politico-military power" by the Army general staff. This "will constitute a serious threat to our principles of democracy; will inevitably result in a reversal of our traditional national policy of defense and security to one of offense and aggression; and will hasten the defeat and downfall of this nation."[101]

To journalists and the broader public, Chowder Marines offered any number of different arguments to mobilize a coalition. "We established relationships with a whole group of people: with liberal journalists, liberal periodicals, liberal intellectuals, who had their own reasons for not wanting to see a powerful authoritarian single Department of Defense," remembered Lieutenant Colonel Heinl. "We went on to the campuses; we talked to professors; we talked to historians; we dealt with the anti-conscriptionists, who had quite a powerful lobby here in Washington, and were surprised and pleased to find themselves singing the same tune as the people whom they had conceived of as being the most militaristic of the services."[102] To all these potential allies, General Edson argued that a strongly unified Department of Defense would "increase greatly the participation of the military in civilian affairs, extending its domination over the conduct of our foreign policy and assuming latent—if not actual—control of our national resources and economy." The result would be "a mass of half-trained conscripts on the European pattern" and would cause America to undergo "a complete reversal of our position throughout the past 158 years."[103]

Other Marine supporters made less dramatic arguments but with similar themes. Davis Merwin, a former Marine combat correspondent and newspaper editor, orchestrated a constant flow of editorials and newsletters that were mailed all over the country, some of which used bawdy rhymes to oppose unification:

> Now we all need more unification
> It solves all our problems, we hear;
> Let's unify both of the sexes,
> And all become happily queer.[104]

Though targeting different audiences, all of these arguments performed a similar function. They framed unification as a departure from American values and as an abandonment of the past and tradition. They presented change as frightening, radical, improper, or even unnatural. Such arguments were the Marine Corps' forte. As they had done inside their own culture and in their wartime public relations, during the struggle over unification the Marines described themselves as guardians of community, faithful to the past and to tradition. They framed themselves as a metaphor for the nation—as just one of the American traditions that would disappear if unification were allowed to proceed. "The one fear of most sensible democratic Americans," argued one retired Marine while speaking on unification, "is the likelihood that we may lose that good old-fashioned Americanism that has held us in such good stead in the past."[105]

This linkage—presenting threats to the Corps as threats to the nation and framing the Marines as an essential icon of American tradition—occurred at all levels of the Marines' public outreach. Internal public affairs memoranda strategized how to present the Marine Corps as "an expression of democratic American standards, values and modes of thought" and how to emphasize the Army and Navy's "distinct[ly] European and un-American cast."[106] The Commandant argued as much in front of Congress when he warned that "in sacrificing its Marine Corps, the country would lose more than a highly trained and thoroughly-proven body of fighting men. It would lose a symbol of real democracy—a truly American form of expression of military service."[107] One prominent retired Marine, speaking in Wilkes-Barre, Pennsylvania, in 1949, argued that

> to abolish the Marines would be to cut off a goodly portion of the tradition and heritage that is America. It would be like saying there will be no more Fourth of July; no Washington Monument; no Statue of Liberty; no more Brooklyn Dodgers; no more baseball; no Notre Dame football; no more Army and Navy annual classic; because they are all, and each of them, symbols of the American spirit. . . . Because the esprit de corps of the Marines, and the spirit of America have so much in common and are so intertwined, any attempt to abolish the United States Marine Corps, or set up a military dictatorship or a

military machine along Prussian or Hitlerian lines is not only a battle for Marines, but for all Americans.[108]

The public got the message. Articles and editorials such as "The Marine Corps Fights for Its Life" and "Save the Marines" ran in publications large and small.[109] The Onondaga County Veterans Council in upstate New York passed a resolution protesting the attacks on the Marine Corps and sent it to Secretary of Defense Johnson. Frances Imogene Kilgore, a thirteen-year-old girl from James A. Foshay Junior High School in Los Angeles, wrote a letter to the White House. "In my studies at school, I have been taught that the Marine Corps has always upheld the traditions for which they are famous," she wrote to President Truman in 1949. "Don't let the Marine Corps die—It is an American heritage."[110]

It is not difficult to understand why these arguments resonated with many Americans in the late 1940s and 1950s. Though victory in war had brought optimism about the future for some, the trauma and instability of the previous years had also made the public frightened of change and nostalgic for community. Politicians and journalists constantly harped on the dangers of the new Cold War, whether coming from Communists in Europe, homosexuals in the State Department, or nuclear bombs. The Marines knew well how to use these themes to their advantage. They broadened the conversation from the role of the Marine Corps to the role of the military in society, presenting the Corps' survival as essential to the survival of the nation's culture, democracy, and heritage.

REFIGHTING THE LAST WAR: UNIFICATION AS PRUSSIANISM

Framing the Marine Corps as "good old-fashioned Americanism" may have built some support in the public and Congress, but such a label should have applied to all of the military services. In fact, it did not. Remarkably, in just a few short months after the end of World War II, the Marines were able to rebrand the Army as un-American and dangerous. Focusing on the bureaucracy of the Army general staff rather than individual officers or men themselves, the Marines argued that the Army wanted to institute a Prussian military system, which would change America into something much like the militarized Nazi state it had just defeated.

This argument found a receptive audience in the postwar public, perhaps because so many who had served in the Army in World War II had chafed under the very brass and bureaucracy that the Marines were criticizing. The Marines took advantage of the anti-Army climate. The crux of their charge was the far-fetched claim that the Army general staff was a product of Prussian military theory and that a national general staff, or even a Department of Defense under Army leadership, would thus lead inexorably to a militarized Prussian state. The charges were patently false, and some of the loudest Marine critics of the Army knew it. Chowder member Don Hittle, a vocal critic of the Army and an expert on general staff development, admitted as much in his own history of military staffs when he argued that French military theory was the strongest influence on the U.S. Army general staff.[111] However, Hittle and other Chowder members knew an effective argument when they saw one, and so they reiterated constantly that adopting the Army's unification plan would lead the country toward Nazism and destroy American democracy.

Conservatives in Congress plucked the low-hanging fruit offered them by the Marines and threw it at the President and the Army. The "real intent of this bill," thundered Senator Robertson of Wyoming, who received much of his material from General Edson, "is to create a vast military empire, one in which ambitious men will wield greater power over the Military Establishment than has ever been heretofore granted to non-elected individuals . . . [giving them] untrammeled power over the entire social and economic structure of the nation."[112] Styles Bridges of Vermont and Thomas C. Hart of Connecticut claimed the bill was based on "militaristic and totalitarian doctrines in spirit and form" and would lead to "the prussianization of our military system."[113]

The 1949 amendments to the National Security Act provoked a similar response. Representative Gerald Ford of Michigan called them a choice between "a republican form of government," on one hand, and "an extreme concentration of authority and power of decision in a very small and carefully selected cadre of officers known as the general staff," on the other.[114] Colonel Hittle's strongest ally, Michigan representative Clare Hoffman, claimed the amendments were "the opening wedges for a Nazi-Prussian consolidation of military power."[115]

The Marines did more than charge the Army with German militarism, however. The Chowder Marines grabbed for any label that would equate the Army general staff with an American enemy, past or present. As Brigadier Hittle later framed the issue, "the chief of a general staff is an occidental equivalent of the Japanese Shogun. And when you establish a national general staff, you inevitably move toward some form of a shogun-ate."[116] General Edson went even further. In one sentence, he linked the Army's plans to nearly every totalitarian government ever to exist on the European continent. "This system embraces the general military principles that have guided Frederick the Great, Bismarck, Hitler, Mussolini, Franco and Stalin," he wrote. It is "bent on a program of calculated militarism in this country; not the partially-excusable accession of power incident to wartime necessity, but a progressive form of military dominance *in both peace and war.*"[117]

Not everyone was convinced. The editors of the *Saturday Evening Post* refused to publish one of General Edson's articles, claiming that the

> constant comparison of our American Army high command to the Politburo and the Prussian Authoritarians is hard to take.... Maybe they were over-reaching a bit in their plans for reorganization, but General Edson makes it sound as if General Marshall and his staff officers were more interested in grabbing power than in winning the war. We just don't believe that.[118]

An editorial in the *Wall Street Journal* acknowledged that growing militarism was of some concern, but it made the sensible point that the "far more menacing danger is not in the Pentagon, but in the Kremlin."[119]

The remarkable thing is that there weren't more who dismissed the Marines' arguments, given just how far-fetched and hypocritical those claims were. Though it claimed to defend civilian control, the Corps was more properly defending its own fiefdom and opposing any increase of power to any executive agency above its Commandant, whether civilian or military. In short, the Corps sought to preserve and grow, not restrict, its own military power. (This hypocrisy reached new heights after 1952, when the new Commandant of the Marine Corps instituted a general staff system for Headquarters Marine Corps, even while Marine lobbyists continued to accuse the Army of Prussianism for having a similar system of organization.)[120]

What the argument lacked in merit, however, it made up for with rhetorical power. The wounds of World War II were far from forgotten in the late 1940s, and any connection to German or Japanese militarism, no matter how feeble, caused alarm in the American public. As relations with the Soviet Union declined, the broader charge of totalitarianism became even stronger. One form of totalitarianism blended with another in the mind of the public; Nazism, Japanese militarism, and Stalinism all merged into a collectivist specter that the Marines exploited to oppose their political rivals.

THE CHARGES REVERSED: THE MARINE CORPS BILL OF 1952

The Marines would find themselves accused of totalitarian tactics as well during the unification debates, but the charge—leveled at them by the President himself—did not stick. In fact, General Clifton Cates, who had orchestrated the Frances Newman spectacle in 1945 and was now the Commandant of the Marine Corps, called the President's attack on the Marines "one of the luckiest things to ever happen to the Corps."[121]

In the summer of 1950, as North Korean forces crossed the 38th parallel and overwhelmed the ill-prepared South Koreans and Americans, the Marines sprang into action. They mobilized their reserves, deployed a reinforced regiment to Korea, and helped halt the advance along the Pusan perimeter. By all accounts, they performed marvelously.[122] In late August, congressman Gordon L. McDonough, a "fiercely partisan . . . confirmed member of the Republican party's right wing," wrote President Truman, asking that the Commandant be placed on the Joint Chiefs of Staff. Truman, perhaps still weary from the Marines' publicity barrage during the 1949 unification amendments, replied to his fellow Army veteran in a moment of unalloyed but ill-advised honesty. "For your information," he wrote, "the Marine Corps is the navy's police force and as long as I am President that is what it will remain. They have a propaganda machine that is almost equal to Stalin's."[123]

McDonough inserted the President's letter into the *Congressional Record,* and the response was immediate. Though the Marines and their partisans had accused the Army of everything short of membership in the Nazi Party during the 1947 and 1949 unification fights, none of that enraged the public as did Truman's reference to Stalin. "Hearing of the comparison of the Marines to the scum of the earth, Joe Stalin, I feel so sick—sick with disgust," wrote one mother with sons in both the Army and Marines. "Obviously, Harry is not the great politician I thought he was," wrote another parent. "No one but an idiot would make such a remark about the Marine Corps."[124] Marines in Korea mailed their Purple Hearts to the White House in a gesture of defiance. McDonough fanned the flames by selling the original letter to the highest bidder and donating the profits to a charity for Marines wounded in Korea.[125] The President retracted his remarks, wrote a letter of apology to the Commandant, and publicly apologized at the annual meeting of the Marine Corps League in Washington, D.C., a few days later. The story made the front page of the *Washington Post,* and a widely published photo appeared in other papers showing the Commandant smiling from ear to ear while the

President spoke at the podium. The raucous audience of veterans, most of whom had started the happy hour well before the President arrived, booed and groaned during the President's speech, and when he finished, they yelled, "Read it again!"[126]

Marine supporters in Congress saw this as a window of opportunity and mobilized the coalition. The day after Truman's apology, Representative Mike Mansfield introduced a bill in the House to fix the personnel strength of the Marine Corps at a minimum of four divisions and four air wings and to put the Commandant on the Joint Chiefs of Staff. Senator Paul Douglas introduced an identical bill in the Senate. Both men had introduced similar bills in 1949, but

President Harry S. Truman apologizes to the Marine Corps League, September 1950, after claiming that "the Marines have a propaganda machine that is almost equal to Stalin's." Seated at his right is the Commandant of the Marine Corps, General Clifton B. Cates. (United States Marine Corps)

neither effort had been successful. This time, however, the political climate had changed.

In the committee hearings that followed, the Marine coalition rehearsed once again the entire history of the threats to the Marine Corps. The JCS 1478 papers came back into the record, as did General Eisenhower's remarks about dismantling the Marine divisions. Though the President, all the service secretaries, and every member of the Joint Chiefs of Staff opposed the bill, their concerns fell on deaf ears. Senator Douglas' bargain with Senator McCarthy ensured that more than half of the Senate cosponsored the legislation, and the bill passed both houses by voice vote.[127] The final bill contained a few compromises: the Marines' minimum size was lowered to three divisions and three wings, and the Commandant was permitted a voice on the Joint Chiefs of Staff only on matters pertaining to the Marine Corps. Still, the law was the only time Congress dictated a minimum service size to either President Truman or Eisenhower, and thus it represented an unprecedented intervention into defense matters that had previously been left to the commander in chief.[128]

There is no question but that the Marine Corps did have a propaganda machine; even the Commandant admitted as much.[129] And yet the Marines could deploy the specters of totalitarianism and inappropriate military involvement in politics against their political enemies without being tarred with the same brush. Why? President Truman's timing was part of the reason: just days after his insult became public, the Marines landed at Inchon in an operation that revived memories of the amphibious landings of World War II. But perhaps there is another reason beyond inopportune timing. Because of their small size, their precarious role in the executive branch, and the history of threats against them, the Marines could represent themselves as victims, rather than perpetrators, of out-of-control state power. They felt under siege by their own government and knew well how to convey those sentiments effectively to the public. This earned them sympathy from civilians and journalists in ways not possible for the larger and more institutionally entrenched services. Their minority status, which at first appeared a liability for their institutional health, became a strength. It gave them rhetorical free rein: they could oppose militarism while working to grow their own influence in politics, and rail against insufficient civilian control even as they strove to weaken it.

The Marines' strategy for opposing further unification continued to serve them well throughout the remainder of the 1950s. In 1953, when President Eisenhower tried to further centralize authority in the Department of Defense with Reorganization Plan Number Six, he encountered entrenched resistance from Marine Corps allies in the press. Although the President claimed the "first objective" of the reorganization was "to strengthen civilian responsibility," defense correspondents friendly to the Marine Corps disagreed.[130] Eisenhower's 1958 Defense Reorganization Act encountered similar problems: House Armed Services Committee chairman Carl Vinson of Georgia assailed it as "militaristic" and leading to a "'Prussian-type' supreme high command"; Davis Merwin's Bloomington, Illinois, *Daily Pantagraph* fretted that the law would bring the country "one step closer to dictatorship."[131] The President grew exasperated with the constant charges of militarism and retorted testily that few who mentioned the Prussian general staff even knew what it was. When a reporter asked him directly if the plan would give one man his own "personalized military force," the President "blew his stack," which led to a spate of bad press on Eisenhower's temper.[132]

As other historians have shown, both the Truman and Eisenhower presidencies were characterized by increased unification of the armed forces, more civilian control, and a Cold War consensus with Congress on foreign policy.[133] When it came to the Marine Corps, however, there was far less consensus. Both Presidents wanted the Marine Corps reduced in size and its role in Cold War defense limited. The Marine Corps fought back, launching an insurgency that mobilized a powerful coalition of politicians, lobbyists, and public supporters to resist the President's intent. The Marine Corps' role in national defense grew, as did its share of military manpower, defense dollars, and resources. Both Presidents found it politically unprofitable to appear hostile or ungrateful to the Marines.

The Marines' irregular tactics are one of the reasons for their success; another was their cultural strategy of appropriating hot topics such as Prussianism, antistatism, and militarism. In 1945, the debates over unification began with how best to design a military to protect the nation from external attack. The Marine coalition in Congress changed the terms of that debate, making unification about how to fend off internal threats to both the Corps and American tradition. These arguments were so powerful that they could even be deployed against President Eisenhower—a true antimilitarist—who worked tirelessly to increase civilian control and weaken the power and partisanship of the individual armed services.

Political rhetoric works best when it stirs up emotion in the public, and here the Marines were particularly adroit. Throughout the unification controversy, the Marines' greatest asset was fear and exaggeration. While threats to the Marine Corps did exist, there was little danger of total abolition, as one of the Corps' congressional insiders, Russell Blandford, later admitted.[134] And yet, in politics and public relations, the simplest arguments are often the most effective, and the history of threats against the Corps, as well as President Truman's "police force" comment, gave the public enough evidence to believe the Corps' hyperbole. Both the 1478 papers and Truman's insult were, in this way, a gift to the Marine Corps, for they reinforced its public image as a small but loyal band of patriots surrounded by hostile forces that were bent on their destruction. This allowed the Marines to reframe unification using the still-powerful lens of World War II, to reanimate their wartime status as both heroes and victims, and to present themselves as just one of the American traditions under threat from an incautious and ill-meaning executive.

The Marines' fear-mongering also worked because the cultural terrain of the national security landscape was amenable to such arguments in the anxious years of the early Cold War. Threats of nuclear war, a real war in Korea, and the fear of Communist infiltration at home made large sections of the public feel under siege, just as the Marines felt in regard to the executive branch. The Corps exploited these fears with arguments about dictatorial executive power and a totalitarian Army bent on militarizing the nation. For a country still recovering from the wounds of a world war and ever conscious of the possibility of another, these charges resonated.

However, the Corps' sense of being under attack by the other services was not just a messaging strategy. The Marines of the Chowder Society fervently believed the threats were real. This too became an asset. Their fear for the future of their organization gave the Corps' lobbyists a sense of urgency, which kept them focused and nimble, able to outmaneuver the very executive branch to which they nominally belonged. The threat of attack—sometimes real but often exaggerated—strengthened their cohesion, both internally and with their allies in civilian circles. It pushed them to improvise, to break rules, and to fight for every measure of protection, whether fairly or unfairly gotten. Lieutenant Colonel Blandford's horse-hiding maneuvers, General Edson's theft of the 1478 papers, and the numerous machinations of the Chowder Society were all actions of people who felt the rules as written would not protect them. Because they were in a fight for the very existence of their organization, they had little compunction about sidestepping regulations and acting like a "bunch of guerrillas."[135]

4

> I don't know what I did. Did I do something to my own people or
> did I do something to the enemy? Why would it be blanked
> out? . . . Just what did I do?
>
> —Korean War veteran Sergeant Dick Bahr,
> U.S. Marine Corps (retired)

Dick Bahr looks like many retired Marines. He wears
a red Marine Corps hat and has a Marine Corps sticker on his car.
He goes to Marine Corps reunions and, until he retired, worked as a
carpenter outside of Milwaukee, Wisconsin. At eighty-two, he no
longer has the muscles he took to Korea, but he still has the haircut.
He also still has a sizable collection of Marine Corps paraphernalia:
hats, ties, jackets, and shirts, all emblazoned with the eagle, globe,
and anchor insignia of the Corps. One hat is unusual, though. The
inscription on it—"The Chosin Few"—marks him as a survivor of
one of the Corps' most famous battles of the Korean War: the escape
from the Chosin Reservoir in the winter of 1950.[1]

The Corps uses many names for Chosin. It was a "fighting withdrawal," an "epic retrograde," "an attack in another direction," and
even a "victory."[2] What it most certainly was *not* was a retreat, even
though it occurred during the 1950 Chinese offensive that pushed
United Nations forces out of North Korea in their most serious strategic defeat of the war. The battle began on November 27, when, as
temperatures dropped well below freezing, UN forces moved north
to the Yalu River and the Chinese border. In the frigid mountains
near the reservoir, between nine and twelve divisions of China's
People's Liberation Army surrounded the Americans and attacked.
In two weeks of fierce fighting, the First Marine Division fought

through six of the Chinese divisions, withdrew eighty miles south to the port of Hungnam, and evacuated by ship. In the process, it lost 700 men to enemy fire, 200 went missing, and another 3,500 were wounded. During the same period, the Chinese lost 80,000 men.[3] In the Corps' living mythology, the "Chosin Few" Marines symbolize everything good about the Marine Corps—tenacity, resolve, and fighting élan. But Dick Bahr's family knows a different legacy from that battle. They know that even now, sixty years later, they must never approach Dick from behind and surprise him, and that he still crouches instinctively when he hears a twig snap. They know that he stays away from fireworks and that he doesn't like to hug the minister at church. His children know that he often falls asleep in a chair in the living room rather than lie down on a bed. "He was afraid to go to sleep, because that's when the Chinese would attack," his daughter Dona remembered.[4] Even when he slept in the living room, he had nightmares and would panic if touched or awakened abruptly. "If he was sleeping in his chair, we could never come up from behind," Dona recalled. "If you came around from behind and touched him anyplace, or even ruffle[d] his hair, he would jump, and his arms would flare out, and he would be breathing hard." Instead, the children learned to approach from the right side of the room and stay out of arm's reach. Then, from a safe distance, they would turn the television's volume up, turn it down, and call their father's name to wake him.

When he first returned from Korea, Dick had nightmares almost every night. When they came, he would scream and thrash about. "I wake up from these things, and I'm maybe in the middle of them, and I never seem to finish them and they reoccur. I picture the faces of people and I never remember their names." Sometimes he would sob. Dona remembered one time when she was just eight years old and heard her father crying in his room in the middle of the night. "It was one of the pitiful kinds of cries, just helpless. As a kid you just didn't know whether to stay in bed or to find out what was going on. Then my mother would say, 'Go back to bed, go back to bed.'" Dick still has nightmares today, more than sixty years after coming home from Korea.

This is not a story most Americans, or indeed most Marines, know about the famous "Chosin Few." For even though Dick and his family will never forget Korea, in popular culture, it still holds the title of America's "forgotten war."[5] Although more than 33,000 Americans were killed and another 100,000 wounded in three years of fighting, for those without personal connections to the war, its history remains a blank.[6] In fact, as several scholars have noted, the difficulties in remembering Korea have become the war's most well-known legacy. For many Americans, the main thing remembered about the Korean War is that it has been forgotten.[7]

Claiming that Korea has slipped from American culture or memory is misleading, however, for no such thing as a single, national collective memory exists. States do not remember wars; individuals do.[8] Nor has the nation as a whole "repressed" Korea's legacy, as some scholars claim, for states do not experience psychological trauma the way Dick Bahr does.[9] Rather, Korea became the forgotten war because specific actors and groups wanted it forgotten and fought to make that label the dominant one. Understanding this battle over the war's legacy requires more than broad claims about the nation's so-called collective memory or psyche. It requires a thorough analysis of specific acts of remembrance—moments when individuals and groups wrote, spoke, or performed narratives about the war and its significance—and of the maneuvers they used to harness the war's legacies to their individual purposes.[10] That analysis shows that the military—in particular, the leadership of the three largest armed services—largely wanted to forget Korea. Only the Marines' leadership wanted to remember the war, and they used the stories of the "Chosin Few" Marines to do it.

THE FORGOTTEN WAR

Who wanted Korea forgotten and why? These two questions have been too long ignored by Korean War historians. Those who have attempted to answer them tend to blame the entire U.S. civilian population, who, the argument goes, were too disturbed or confused by the war and its contradictions to contextualize it into a broader narrative about their nation and themselves. Another theory argues that no one deliberately avoided the war but that for reasons of timing it was simply overlooked. Wedged between the triumph of World War II and the travesty of Vietnam, the public could find no room in its emotional and mental storehouses for a war as complex and unsatisfying as Korea. Only once the nation acknowledged the tragedy of Vietnam could it begin to consider Korea.[11]

There is truth to both of these arguments, but they do not suffice, either alone or together. For while it was difficult for many civilians to integrate Korea into their stories about themselves and their country, it was even more so for members of the military. Their role in Korea's forgetting has thus far been ignored. In fact, military members worked both to forget Korea and to blame its forgetting on civilians—a strategy that sought to deflect criticism aimed at them for the war's unsatisfying conduct. The very label "forgotten war"—which originated in military circles and was first promulgated by veterans and military journals—is one indication that their strategy worked.

All the services took different lessons from Korea, and most judged it an aberration, an "unreal war," or a mistake.[12] Only the Marines took a deliberately celebratory tone. For while Korea challenged the other services' assumptions about future war and strategy, it validated nearly every argument the Marines had made about themselves in the fractious debates over unification. Korea fit neatly into the Corps' stories about itself and thus strengthened its culture and power in American society. The war may have been a stalemate in the world of politics and Cold War strategy, but in the Marines' battle for public attention and approval, Korea was a victory.

Korea may have had salutary effects for the Corps as an institution, but not for Dick Bahr and many other men who did the actual fighting. For them, trauma was the most persistent legacy of the war, which they could neither forget nor incorporate into existing narratives about themselves. The result was constant, compulsive remembering, a reliving of events they needed to leave behind. Though it was not evident during the war, psychiatrists would later conclude that Korean War veterans experienced higher rates of suicidal thoughts, addiction, hostility, and post-traumatic stress than World War II veterans and, in some cases, Vietnam War veterans.[13] This aspect of the Korean War has too long been left untold. Even the Corps, which has generated an inordinate amount of historical writing on the Korean War, has left this history in the background. For sixty years, the Corps' historians have been telling the story of Dick Bahr's "Chosin Few" hat and ignoring or avoiding what lies underneath.

FRAMING THE WAR

Korea's forgetting is not entirely attributable to the military's deliberate attempts at erasure. Events live on in memory when they reinforce, or at least fit into, existing conceptual frames.[14] From the outset, the Korean War faced framing problems that hindered its assimilation into Americans' preexisting notions of armed conflict.[15] The result was persistent cultural friction between civilians and the armed forces, both during the war and afterward. That civil-military friction was also instrumental in forgetting Korea.

The framing problems began in the war's first days. President Truman did not ask for a congressional declaration of war before committing military forces in July 1950, and thus spent considerable time and effort insisting that Korea was not a war but a police action. (This reached its crudest point when the Department of Defense decided that tombstones in national cemeteries would bear only the label "Korea" instead of "Korean War" so that the practices of commemoration conformed to presidential politicking.)[16] The actors in the conflict were also ambiguous: it was not the United States but the United Nations that voted to intervene in Korea, generating confusion and even ridicule from Americans who knew they were doing the bulk of the fighting for that nascent organization. The Chinese intervention in November 1950, which caused a massive reversal and led to two years of stalemate, upset the categories of war further. Was this the same war, a different war, or just the wrong war? Truman's relief of General Douglas A. MacArthur for violating orders and making political statements generated further disunity. The war also ended unsatisfactorily, in a military armistice rather than a treaty, and with 58 percent of the American public believing that war would reignite in the near future.[17] For many Americans living through it, the Korean War lacked a legitimate beginning, had a cast of ambiguous actors, and ended in an ellipsis.

These problems of the war's categories and conduct had effects on the home front. Wars need political coalitions and strong domestic consensus to succeed; Korea had neither. In World War II, President Roosevelt built and maintained effective coalitions among the three branches of the government, between the two political parties, and between civilians and the military. During Korea, these three sets of relationships were strained almost from the start. The tensions between Congress and the executive appeared early in the war. Although there had been broad initial agreement between the President and both parties in Congress on the decision to intervene, a rift soon developed over the President's failure to ask for a declaration of war.[18] That rift widened to a chasm in 1951 and 1952 once the prospects for victory dimmed. The judiciary added its voice to the debate over presidential authority in wartime in 1952 when it declared Truman's seizure of the steel industry (ostensibly to prevent disruptions to war-related production) unconstitutional. These well-publicized power struggles made it clear that this was not a war like the previous one, if it was a war at all.

Cooperation between the political parties also disintegrated as the promise of victory waned. The twin blows of the Chinese intervention in November 1950 and President Truman's relief of General MacArthur in April 1951 poisoned relations between Democrats and Republicans for the remainder of the war. The President's popularity plummeted from 70 percent in October 1950 to a low of 22 percent by 1952.[19] Partisan journalism added to the discontent. Disdain for the President, the State Department, the United Nations, and the Democratic Party was a regular feature of the editorial pages of the *Chicago Tribune* and the *Wall Street Journal,* as were accusations of treason and calls for impeachment.[20] When MacArthur addressed a joint session of Congress shortly after his return, Republican leaders described him as "the reincarnation of Saint Paul" and "a great hunk of God in the flesh." Privately, Truman called the address "nothing but a bunch of damn bullshit."[21] One month after the signing of the armistice, polling showed that just 27 percent of Americans thought the Korean War had been worth fighting.[22]

After Truman relieved MacArthur, even ordinary conversation on the war's progress became difficult. For a nation of almost 20 million veterans, the dominant frame for interpreting the current war was the previous one, despite the obvious differences between Korea and World War II.[23] MacArthur's relief shattered that frame. The President rejected the World War II ideology of "unconditional surrender" (reframed by MacArthur as "no substitute for victory") and cashiered its most famous hero. But he did so using a narrative that had shown similar power in the unification debates: a defense of civilian control and opposition to power-hungry generals. The public thus had to choose between two utterly unsatisfying explanations of Korea: supporting MacArthur and rejecting civilian control, or defending the President and accepting appeasement. As these two narratives collided, the result was aporia, contradiction, and confusion. By a margin of roughly two to one, the public disapproved of the President's decision to relieve MacArthur, but support for MacArthur's proposed escalation of the war varied radically based on the wording of the poll.[24] By mid-1951, Americans' most popular answer for what to do in Korea was "no answer, don't know, couldn't say."[25]

This confusion and friction strained civil-military relations both during the war and afterward. The generals and admirals blamed the State Department and the President; the State Department and the President blamed MacArthur. Retired military officers published polemics in conservative magazines and wrote articles about the perils of political interference in military affairs.[26] Even after lengthy congressional hearings on MacArthur's relief, the debates continued. In 1954, some of the war's most senior commanders testified before Congress in support of MacArthur and minced no words on who was to blame for the failures in Korea. "I don't care what anybody says back home that I didn't have enough air [power] to do the job," testified former UN air commander Lieutenant General George E. Stratemeyer in front of the Senate Internal Security Subcommittee. "I had sufficient air to do just what General MacArthur wanted to do. But we weren't permitted to do it. . . . General MacArthur's hands were tied, I am sure, not by the Joint Chiefs of Staff, but by the then State Department.[27] At one point after his relief, General MacArthur leveled a veiled charge of treason against the President for entering into a secret deal with the Soviets; Truman replied coolly that the general was lying.[28]

Civil-military relations were strained at lower levels too. In 1954, an anonymous Army officer published an article decrying the influence of civilians in the Pentagon, claiming that "if patriotism is the last refuge of scoundrels, civilian control is a close competitor."[29] A junior Marine officer in Korea wrote a letter to President Truman and then sent it to the Fort Wayne (Indiana) *News-Sentinel,* warning Truman that

someday you will answer for this sellout of American manpower and materials. Unfortunately, on account of you and your administration, most of the boys over here won't be alive to register their righteous wrath against this sellout. . . . Two days ago I lost fifty percent of my men taking one hill—and for what? None of us know why we are here and none of us can understand why we stay.

Shortly after the letter was published, the Corps reprimanded the officer for criticizing the commander in chief, a move that almost certainly ended his military career.[30]

Divisions between the military and its civilian leaders were evident even in how each perceived the war's conclusion. For President Eisenhower and Secretary of State John Foster Dulles, the armistice was an unsatisfying but acceptable compromise; Secretary Dulles would later go so far as to call it "a triumph of collective security."[31] For the military, and the Army in particular, Korea was a defeat, one they felt keenly but were not allowed to admit. General Mark Clark, the American commander who had signed the armistice, voiced his service's frustration immediately upon his return from Korea in August 1953. In a Washington press conference, the soon-to-retire Clark commented that if the United Nations had done things differently it "could have won the war." At the use of this phrase, General Floyd L. Parks, the Army chief of public relations, jumped to his feet, visibly startled. "General Clark, seeing General Parks' apparent concern, said: 'What's the matter, am I getting too close here?'" reported the *New York Times*. "After a few seconds whispered conversation with General Parks, General Clark added that he was not intending to give the impression that the United Nations 'had lost a war.'"[32]

The friction between civilians and the military persisted long after the war's end. Even years after the armistice, talking about Korea inevitably meant discussing what had gone wrong, which veterans perceived as blame from the very population they had ostensibly fought to protect. *Not* talking about Korea was no solution, either, for avoiding the topic was a slight of a different kind, as a cartoon from 1952 depicts.[33]

The scenario depicted in this cartoon is not an accurate representation of how civilians treated veterans during or after the war. In fact, it is a full reversal of the prevailing civil-military dynamic. For the most part, civilians did talk about the war, and those who experienced close combat with the Chinese did not. But the cartoon is instructive nonetheless because it reveals the military's preferred

"Leatherhead in Korea," a cartoon from the *Marine Corps Gazette* that accused civilians of forgetting Korea, 1952. (Staff Sergeant Norval E. Packwood and the *Marine Corps Gazette*)

tactics in the battle over the war's memory. A quick tour of the cultural terrain of post-Korea America shows that journalists, academics, politicians, and filmmakers talked about the war endlessly and, on occasion, either implicitly or explicitly criticized the men who fought it. The military's response was to avoid the topic when it could, and when pressed, to fight back with accusations of forgetting.

FRICTION IN THE AFTERMATH: CIVILIANS REMEMBER KOREA

There was no shortage of cultural productions about Korea in the decade after the war. Newspapers frequently published articles imploring the public to remember the war and its veterans. Academics and social critics used Korea to attack the military and to lament a new softness among American youth. Politicians rehearsed and reinvented the war for political gain. Hollywood put out an average of four major feature films on Korea per year and in regular intervals thereafter.[34] Abundant criticism, much of which was felt by the military, continued to strain civil-military relations long after the armistice.

Journalists were some of the most prolific memory activists. "Recall Truce in Korean War," implored a *Chicago Tribune* headline on the one-year anniversary in 1954, using the imperative as would a teacher to a recalcitrant pupil.[35] "Remember Korea" demanded *Time* in 1955; "Are we in the process of forgetting Korea?" worried the *Washington Daily News* that same year.[36] On the ninth anniversary of the invasion, the *New York Times* ran a three-page feature on the war; on the tenth anniversary, the *Chicago Tribune* did a similar feature.[37]

While some journalists had praise for the military, remembering the war also meant assessing its effects and keeping open wounds that veterans hoped to heal. Most postwar coverage of the armistice was deeply critical, and negative assessments of the war persisted throughout the decade. The criticism began as soon as the war ended, as foreign policy and military correspondents argued over whether the armistice would keep the peace or embolden the Communists.

The Communist victory at Dien Bien Phu in French Indochina the following year reinvigorated the debate. Clamors over treasonous American prisoners of war continued for years. A recurring theme was the lack of finality or closure. The nation's obligations have "not yet been discharged," warned the *New York Times* in 1958. "Our pledges have not yet been redeemed. . . . We have not yet made a just and lasting—and free—peace."[38] In 1963, *Time* grumbled that the armistice had led to 800 hours of meetings, 10 million words, and little more.[39]

Some writers were even harsher. The war was "an ignominious political and military defeat," a symbol of "America's political immaturity, of her general military weakness, and of her refusal to live up to her greatest historical legacy," argued one historian in the *Washington Post* in 1958.[40] Defense and political correspondents invoked Korea in their lamentations over Indochina, the United States' contests with China over Formosa (Taiwan), and even the launch of Sputnik.[41] By the end of the 1950s, the war that Secretary of State Dulles had called a "triumph of collective security" was more often reframed as an emblem of failure and evidence of the nation's weakness and military inadequacy.

Accusations of prisoner of war (POW) collaboration and treason, which ran rampant through American society in the late 1950s, only added fuel to the fire.[42] Although only ten of the 7,190 POWs taken during the war were ever convicted of collaboration with their captors, a myth of POW disloyalty took hold in American society, with both civilian and military writers entering the debate.[43] A special advisory committee convened by the secretary of defense later debunked the myth, but the theme of military weakness and betrayal persisted well into the 1960s.[44]

Much like the debates over General MacArthur's relief, the public clamor over POWs damaged the military services' relationships with civilian society. Army psychiatrist Lieutenant Colonel William E. Mayer, who distributed hundreds of thousands of speeches and audiotapes on POW collaboration, laid most of the blame on civilian society.[45] The military should share some of the blame, Mayer argued, but mainly for allowing its culture to be improperly influenced by civilians, and by overbearing mothers, in particular.[46] Admiral Hyman Rickover blamed the education system, as did Army major Clarence Anderson, who argued that POW collaboration was "the result of some new failure in the childhood and adolescent training of our young men—a new softness."[47]

Civilian writers, in turn, blamed the military. Journalist Eugene Kinkead wrote first an article and then a book based on the scandalously inaccurate assertion that "almost one out of every three prisoners in Korea was guilty of some form of collaboration with the enemy."[48] "Lack of discipline" was the "critical deficiency," asserted Kinkead, quoting both named and unnamed military men as his sources. Though Kinkead agreed with Mayer that civilian society was also to blame, he emphasized the Army's failings, going so far as to call the POWs "cowards" and "opportunists."[49] Nor was he the only one. As late as 1959, *New York Times* military correspondent Hanson W. Baldwin wrote in the *Saturday Evening Post* that "our fighting men have gone soft" and that "inadequate leadership" and "physical pampering" were some of the reasons "Military Man has lost some of his zip." One pro-military reader fired back in a letter to the editor that "articles such as this make our good fighting men wonder if their fellow citizens are worth fighting for."[50]

The myth of widespread POW collaboration persisted throughout the 1950s not because they withstood rigorous evaluations of their accuracy but because they reinforced the political agendas of several powerful groups.[51] Calling American soldiers soft of body and weak of mind was useful to social conservatives and others who railed against the New Deal and other "Communistic" tendencies; liberals used the issue to highlight the perils of a culture of wealth and materialism. Emphasizing the hidden powers of Communist brainwashers bolstered the claims of hard-line anti-Communists, foreign policy hawks, and others who desired increased defense spending and a stronger stand against the Soviet Union. Boy Scout leaders, segregationists, and opponents of progressive education reform appropriated the story of POW collaboration for different purposes still.[52] Even Army leaders—with Mayer as just one of their spokesmen—used the specter of national softness to redirect criticism from themselves onto civilian society.[53] However, more important than why these stories persisted was their effect on veterans—both POWs and others—who had to endure the implicit or explicit questioning of their patriotism and fighting ability. As long as the public debated the POW issue and sought explanations for the military's betrayal, the men who fought in Korea would find it difficult to craft positive narratives about their wartime experiences.

Hollywood did not forget Korea either; it produced forty-two major motion pictures and fifteen documentaries on the war between 1954 and 1964.[54] *Pork Chop Hill* (1959) rewrote stalemate into victory in its depiction of one of the last major battles of the war; *Time Limit* (1957), *Prisoner of War* (1954), and *The Bamboo Prison* (1954) reframed POW collaborators as falsely accused patriots or American double agents. Even here, however, there was implicit criticism of the military. *Strange Intruder* (1956) depicted veterans as shell-shocked psychopaths; *The Rack* (1956) and *The Manchurian Candidate* (1962) portrayed POWs as traitors and weaklings.[55]

Nor did Congress forget Korea, and its politicization of the war generated still more civil-military friction. Congress held hearings on either the Korean War or the related POW issue every single year of the Eisenhower administration.[56] The Senate Internal Security Subcommittee tried in vain to show that Communist subversion in the State Department had led to the armistice; the Committees on Foreign Affairs, Appropriations, Government Operations, Armed Services, and Un-American Activities all probed the POW issue. Republicans used the war to blame Democrats for appeasement; Democrats countered that it was Eisenhower, not Truman, who had agreed to the hated armistice. "It was not this Republican administration which pulled out MacArthur when victory was within his grasp," thundered Representative Walter Judd of Minnesota in July

1954. "It was not a Republican administration that refused to let him win when he could win, and could thereby have prevented the war in Indochina. . . . We cannot be expected to remain silent when charged with responsibility for the bad results of decisions made by others."[57] The debates replayed annually when national security issues came before the Congress. By 1960, Democratic congressmen were still submitting articles to the *Congressional Record* claiming that Eisenhower's decision to end the war with an armistice "released Red Chinese troops to attack elsewhere as has been seen in Peiping's assaults on Quemoy, their role in wresting Indochina from France and their attacks on Tibet."[58] In the 1960 presidential election debate, Vice President Nixon scored one of his strongest rhetorical victories over Senator John F. Kennedy by calling his opponent's remarks on Asia "the same kind of wooly thinking that lead to disaster in Korea."[59]

Many thoughtful explanations of how Korea came to be forgotten lay the blame entirely at the feet of the home front population.[60] Weary of war and unable to synthesize the many problems and contradictions of the conflict, the American public simply turned away. However, the major civilian institutions producing narratives about Korea—the journalists, academics, moviemakers, and politicians— were not forces for forgetting. They were active in producing and distributing stories about the war. Politicians used Korea for political advantage; journalists and filmmakers used it to generate copy and debate and to praise and criticize the military. Nor, as will become clear below, were veterans' families silencing veterans who wanted to remember Korea. Most, in fact, tried unsuccessfully to get their loved ones to talk.

Thus it was not a dearth of remembrances that effected the so-called forgetting of Korea but rather an absence of affirmative narratives about the war and an abundance of criticism. The constant debates over the conduct of the war, its effects, and POW collaboration deprived the men who fought of a positive narrative about their fighting. Whether one accused the Army or civilians, the education system or military training, the fact remained that victory had not been attained and, from many veterans' perspective, the public would not stop talking about it. For those who fought, the only recourse was to try to put the war behind them and, when challenged, to accuse the public of the very thing they had been charged with: betrayal.

FORGETTING AS BETRAYAL

Were Korea actually a forgotten war, that label would have emerged long after its conclusion, as historians dug up evidence of events no longer present in people's lives and memories. But that is not what happened. The label "forgotten war" emerged early on—in the first months of fighting—and, tellingly, it was military men who coined the phrase. Army general Matthew Ridgway is typically credited with first using the label, but he was not the only one.[61] Writer and former naval officer James Michener called Korea a "lonesome, forgotten war" in an article for the *Saturday Evening Post* in May 1952; four months later, the Army's *Combat Forces Journal* published an editorial entitled "Forgotten Wars," which blamed the public for giving insufficient attention to Korea as well as almost every other war the Army had ever fought.[62] As we will see, it is appropriate that the war's label came from within the armed forces, for the military was the institution most invested both in forgetting Korea and in using charges of forgetting as a weapon against its critics.

The Korean War posed serious problems for the leaderships of the Army, Navy, and Air Force. Combat is not only a proving ground for individuals; it is the final arbiter on each service's funding and acquisition decisions. Unfortunately, many of the procurement choices the services made after World War II proved of little value in Korea. There was no enemy fleet for the Navy to battle and few strategic bombing targets for the Air Force, and most of the Army's leadership viewed Korea as a distraction from a potential war with the Soviets in Europe. Since Korea did little to advance these services' strategic priorities, none of them had any serious interest in preserving its memory. Instead, they all framed the war as a mistake containing no useful lessons for the future.

It is hard to prove forgetting—what is the evidence that something *wasn't* being discussed or remembered?—but some facts are suggestive. Between 1955 and 1963, the *Proceedings of the U.S. Naval Institute,* the locus of professional thought for the Navy, published more than thirty articles on the Navy's experience in World War II. During the same period, it published just seven on the Korean War, two of which were written by Marines. On the fifth and tenth anniversaries of the armistice and invasion, no articles appeared on the war or its lessons.[63] In the few articles that did appear, the war was the "Korean to-do" or the "Korean imbroglio," giving one indication of how the Navy viewed its importance.[64] Less than three years after the armistice, an author writing a 6,000-word essay on the Navy's missions and purpose in Asia devoted just two sentences to Korea.[65] In the only article on the lessons and mistakes of the war, civil-military friction comes again to the fore. The "gravest error" of the war, the author concluded, was the timidity of American politicians.[66]

Korea was equally problematic for the Air Force. At the heart of that institution's stories about itself was the doctrine of strategic bombing, which asserted that wars could be quickly won through massive air bombardment of a nation's war-making industries. However, this doctrine assumed use of the full range of the Air Force's arsenal, including nuclear weapons, which made it inapplicable to the limited war in Korea. Consequently, Air Force officers spent considerable effort reframing Korea as an anomaly in order to preserve their theories about nuclear weapons and air power. As early as 1951, writers for the publication *Air Force* concluded that "the first great lesson from Korea is that this is an unreal war," and so the lessons needed for success in future wars "have not and cannot be learned in Korea."[67] The progression of thought in the Air Force's Basic Doctrine (Air Force Manual 1–2), which was first released in 1954, gives further evidence that Air Force strategists completely disregarded the Korean War experience.[68] Even Air Force academics ignored what had happened during the war. Robert F. Futrell's *The United States Air Force in Korea* (the first and, until recently, only major work on the subject) turned the war into a defense of strategic bombing, a position deeply at odds with the facts.[69] In 1962, the Air Force Academy's History Department compiled a list of student papers by topic. Cadets wrote fifteen papers on strategic bombing or nuclear weapons that year and only two on operations in Korea—the same number of papers cadets wrote on the obscure topic of air operations in Latin America.[70]

Army leaders had their own reasons for wanting to forget Korea. Although the conflict proved one of their basic strategic precepts—that airpower alone could not win a war and that machines could not replace men—many of the Army's strategic thinkers shared the Air Force's belief that Korea was an aberration. "We must guard against the tendency to look upon the Korea fighting as a 'preview of future war,'" argued Army chief of staff J. Lawton Collins in early 1951. "The war in Korea has been a reversion to old-style fighting—more comparable to that of our own Indian frontier days than to modern war.... I do not believe the Korea fighting is typical of future war."[71] These assumptions were shared by much of the senior leadership of the Army throughout the 1950s.[72]

The Army suffered the most criticism over Korea; consequently, its service journals show both avoidance of the topic and a tendency to fight back against the charges leveled against them. The *Combat Forces Journal* published twenty-two articles on Korea in 1952 and fourteen in 1953. In 1955, it published only two.[73] In what little writing there was, the tone was highly defensive, with titles such as "Give Us Back Our Pride" (August 1953) and "Our POWs Are Not Traitors" (October 1953). Letters to the editor were equally argumentative. "Our failure to throw everything we had at the enemy, including atomics, was a moral failure of a flabby, too fat citizenry, fraidy-cat authorities and self-serving allies," wrote one reader in 1960. "*We lost in Korea because some of us didn't have the guts to fight to win.*" "Did we learn in Korea?" asked another reader. "Not no, but Hell no!"[74]

Historians affiliated with the Army also voiced resentment at civilians. Army veteran T. R. Fehrenbach, whose *This Kind of War: A Study in Unpreparedness* would remain a dominant text on the war until the 1980s, was harsh in his descriptions of the Army's performance but placed the bulk of the blame on domestic society: "No American may sneer at them, or what they [the Army] did. . . . They had been raised to believe the world was without tigers, then sent to face those tigers with a stick. On their society must fall the blame."[75] Army historian Brigadier General S. L. A. Marshall made a similar argument. Ten years after the war, he argued, the public's opinions on Korea were still "confused, negative or immature. The common attitude is that Korea didn't count, had little consequence to the national fortunes, [and] taught us nothing." The POW issue, he continued, was the result of scientists and writers "selling false goods, faking their figures . . . [and] waxing fat peddling over and over this dead-end story of young Americans failing themselves and their country. . . . It is an outrageous libel."[76]

The military's resentment toward civilians extended beyond the POW issue and politicians' interference in the war's conduct. Still living with the conceptual frame of World War II, military members expected that civilians would bear hardships on the home front while they fought overseas. Instead, civilians seemed to worry more about their own lives than those of the men abroad. The strikes over steel and other war materials only increased the sense of inequality. "How about all these strikes at home?" complained one service member from Illinois in 1952. "That's all we read about in *The Stars and Stripes*." "This has been declared a national emergency," noted a Marine private first class from Wisconsin. "We don't think those guys have any right to strike. What would they think if we went on strike over here?"[77] Pro-military writers picked up on the theme. As former naval officer James Michener put it:

> Next time you're fretting about the high cost of living, remember the Naval Pilots you'll meet here. . . . [T]hey seem to fight in a vacuum, as if America didn't care a damn. At home we seem even yet unable to

realize that in Korea a tragic few have been nominated to fight the battle for the entire free world. . . . [T]hey are, I am ashamed to say, alone.[78]

This memory of unequal sacrifice persisted long after the war. The "vast majority of Americans prospered as never before in our history, while a relatively few fought the hard battles," wrote an editor for *Army* ten years after the war. "Equality of sacrifice, unattainable, but still a goal in past wars, wasn't seriously attempted during the Korean Conflict."[79]

All of these accusations—that civilians lacked guts, failed to sacrifice, or even failed to remember or acknowledge what the military did in Korea—served a purpose for the armed forces. They allowed the military to answer charges of inadequacy without being overtly political. While retired officers such as Generals Mark Clark and George Stratemeyer could argue that the President or State Department had lost the war, when active-duty officers resorted to such political topics, it carried a price, as both General MacArthur and the Marine officer who published his letter to President Truman learned. Charging the public with forgetting was safer. Apolitical criticism was a less dangerous line of attack—a mild version of the claim that the public and politicians had stabbed the military in the back. Rather than challenging civilian control, this line of argument endorsed it, arguing that since the military fights for and under the authority of the citizenry, it deserves to be recognized and appreciated for its service. Accusing the public of breaking this contract allowed the military to reverse the charges leveled against them: if there was a betrayal during the Korean War, it came from the public or the politicians, not from the military.

KOREA IN THE MEMORY OF THE MARINE CORPS

As a service, the Marine Corps did not share the deep dissatisfaction with Korea felt by the Army, Air Force, and Navy. In fact, for many, the Marines' performance in the war was not an aberration but a continuation of the Corps' long record of battlefield success. Thus, as it had done in World War II, the Corps took great pains to advertise its successes in Korea and used the stories of its enlisted men to do it.

The other services had trouble incorporating Korea into their preexisting conceptual frames. The Marines did not. All during the unification hearings, they had emphasized their ability to deploy ready, capable ground forces at a moment's notice. This ability proved critical in the first months of the Korean War as the Marines raced to Pusan to help halt the North Korean advance. The Corps had also trumpeted its amphibious landing capabilities during unification, a skill that the Army had derided as antiquated.[80] The amphibious assault at Inchon did much to disprove the Army's claims and linked Korean War Marines to those who had fought on Guadalcanal, Tarawa, and Iwo Jima. Stories of the Marines' tenacity in the withdrawal from the Chosin Reservoir boosted the Corps' reputation further, as those were the only positive stories appearing in the press in the otherwise dark days of December 1950. Even the POW issue helped the Marine Corps. While one Marine officer saw his career destroyed by statements he made while a prisoner, overall, Marines survived captivity in higher ratios than did members of the other services, and five Marines earned awards for their conduct in the camps.[81] These facts strengthened the Corps' reputation for physical and moral toughness, giving it a convincing counterargument to the growing belief that America's fighting men were going soft.[82] Consequently, stories about the Marine Corps enjoyed the best mobility on the post-Korea cultural terrain: they advanced fairly easily and uniformly through all the theaters of Korean War memory, gaining legitimacy and encountering little serious opposition.

As in previous years, strong alliances with the press, Hollywood filmmakers, and even a few Army veterans helped augment the Marines' reputation. Civilian journalists produced a steady stream of pro-Marine coverage, much of which ended up in the *Congressional Record,* thanks to the efforts of the Chowder Society.[83] Warner

Bros. produced *Retreat Hell!* (1952) and Allied Artists made *Hold Back the Night* (1956), both of which lionized the Corps' performance in Korea (and also received production support from the Marines). The Marines' congressional coalition was active throughout the war, motivated first by the Corps' strong performance in combat and later by President Truman's "police force" insult.

Books and articles written by Army and Navy veterans gave almost unanimous praise to the Marines in Korea. T. R. Fehrenbach's *This Kind of War* held the Corps up as a shining example of what the nation needed to win the Cold War—and lacked in the other services.[84] Navy veteran Hanson W. Baldwin's "Our Fighting Men Have Gone Soft" gave extensive praise to the Marine POWs, as did the foremost Army critic of the POW crisis, Lieutenant Colonel William E. Mayer.[85] All seemed to endorse the beliefs of Truman's personal observer in Korea, Major General Frank E. Lowe, who reported to the President that "the First Marine Division is the most efficient and courageous combat unit I have ever seen or heard of."[86] When the Senate Subcommittee on Investigations conducted its hearings on POW conduct, it offered its "greatest admiration and credit" to the Marines for resisting their captors and refusing collaboration.[87]

Marine historians, veterans, and reservists also put pen to paper to celebrate the Corps' actions in Korea. The Marines were the first service to put out an official history of the war, completing one volume by 1954 and two more before 1957, when the Navy issued its first and only major work. Unofficial histories by Marines came earlier and were even more praiseful. Major Andrew Geer, a reservist who had rewritten the offensive scene in *Sands of Iwo Jima* and worked with the Chowder Society during the unification fights, published a 400-page paean to the Corps in 1952 entitled *The New Breed: The Story of the U.S. Marines in Korea.*[88] Former Marine Robert Leckie, whose World War II memoir was discussed in Chapter 1, put out three historically minded celebrations of the Corps in Korea in 1960, 1962, and 1963.[89] Chowder member and Marine historian Colonel Robert Debs Heinl's prize-winning history of the Inchon landing,

Victory at High Tide, came out in 1968 and still earns praise from historians four decades later.[90]

A tour through the Marines' professional journal, the *Marine Corps Gazette,* shows that articles on Korea coexisted well with the Corps' earlier stories about itself. Unlike the defensive tone of the Army's journal, the *Gazette*'s articles were triumphant. Lynn Montross' 1953 article "The Man with the Rifle" named Inchon and Chosin as the latest example of the primacy of the infantry since the beginning of Western warfare.[91] Articles on physical training and toughness such as "Don't Kill 'em with Kindness" (1955) and "No Place for Weaklings" (1956) argued that the Marines had proved themselves sufficiently hearty in Korea, and expressed relief and even delight that the nation was finally awakening to the dangers of softness and physical unpreparedness.[92] Even letters to the editor written by junior Marines named Korea as the latest proof that Cold War–era Marines were as good as the "superhuman defender[s]" who had fought in World War II: "From the swampy jungles of Guadalcanal and the volcanic ash of Iwo to Inchon, the Reservoir and the Thirty-Eighth Parallel," wrote one corporal, "the Marines showed the OLD fight, the OLD energy, the OLD experience, and found victory the OLD way—by grit and determination."[93] In nearly every sphere of commemoration, it was this story about the Marines in Korea that prevailed, extending the World War II–era narratives of Marine exceptionalism.

Unless one looks closely. Behind the triumphant narratives are other stories of the Marines in Korea, ones that acknowledge more fully the lasting effects of the war's violence. As in World War II, nearly all of the Marines in Korea were combat troops; very few served in headquarters, supply bases, and other positions of relative safety. As a result, a higher percentage of Marines were exposed to danger than were members of the other services. Of the 130,000 Marines who served in Korea, one in five was wounded or killed, giving the Corps over twice the casualty ratio of the Army and twenty times the ratio of the Navy or Air Force.[94] Even those Marines who were not wounded, like Dick Bahr, had a higher likelihood of witnessing traumatic events, which carried different burdens from those that physical injuries brought.[95]

The psychological trauma experienced by Marines in Korea has not been well explored by historians, but its traces lie evident to those willing to look. David Douglas Duncan's photographs of Marines in *Life*—all taken in the first year of the war and later compiled in a 1951 book—gave the public images that at first glance seemed to be as triumphant as the narratives appearing in print. These would become some of the best-known images of the war, one of which would later become the inspiration for the Korean War Veterans Memorial in Washington, D.C.[96] Because Duncan was himself a former Marine (a combat correspondent in World War II), his images are particularly useful for analysis: they represent the Corps both as it wanted itself portrayed and in intimate terms not usually shown to outsiders. One of Duncan's most famous images was used as the cover photo of his 1951 book *This Is War! A Photonarrative in Three Parts.*[97]

The corporal in the foreground of the photo is a perfect emblem of how the Marines in Korea imagined themselves and, for the most part, presented themselves to the public. Here is the "superhuman defender of the land," the Marine whose toughness and grit are his most obvious attributes. He is determined and experienced. The heat and humidity (regularly over 100 degrees in those first days of fighting in August), the mud, and even the confrontation with death do not deter him.[98] He leans forward with purpose; fear, if present, is not in evidence. He is the pictorial embodiment of what T. R. Fehrenbach would later describe as the "legions" that the nation needed to win the Cold War: "In 1950, a Marine Corps Officer was still an officer, and a sergeant behaved the way good sergeants had behaved since the time of Caesar, expecting no nonsense, allowing none. And Marine leaders had never lost sight of their primary—their only—mission, which was to fight."[99]

However, while the corporal in the foreground tells the Corps' best stories about itself, the young Marine behind him gives some indications of the fissures in the narrative. The man approaching from the rear—a private—is breathing hard, is carrying a heavier weapon, and is wetter, both from sweat and from the foul water of the rice paddy. His gaze is on the corpse in front of him, which the accompanying text explains is an enemy soldier with "most of his head blown away by a Marine bullet."[100] He seems to suffer from the

Marines in Korea, 1950. (David Douglas Duncan and the Harry Ransom Humanities Research Center, The University of Texas at Austin)

heat. The dirt, water, and humid air are likely fogging and fouling his glasses, making it difficult to see the enemy or to spot him through the sights of his weapon. He is hunched over, ready to dive into the mud again if the firing recommences. He looks young, exhausted, and, not surprisingly, afraid.

Yet the text accompanying Duncan's photos erases those differences. The green privates, he tells us, are not like the "battle-innocent young [Army] men who had been soldiering on occupation duty in Japan." Instead, these "tobacco-chewing, raw-knuckled, bristly-headed youngsters in already-faded Khaki . . . had another enormous advantage, one that no one yet has been able to pin down and fully define—they were UNITED STATES MARINES!"[101]

It is appropriate that the young private in Duncan's photo is in the background, because his was a face of the Marine Corps not often shown to the public in the 1950s. In fact, the Marines who went to Korea were not all well-trained, combat-hardened veterans, as both Fehrenbach and Duncan imply. Some were recent draftees and others new reservists who had not yet attended recruit training. Because the leadership of the Marine Corps was intent on getting Marines into the fight as quickly as possible, the minimum requirements for sending reservists into combat were woefully lax. To go to Korea, a reservist needed just one year's service in the Organized Reserve (which involved little more than weekend training sessions at a reserve center) and proof that he had completed two annual training periods of two weeks each.[102] Consequently, some of the Marines who fought in the early part of the war had spent less than two months on active duty before being mobilized for Korea. The lack of training so alarmed some parents that they wrote letters of protest to Congress, prompting the Secretary of Defense to initiate an investigation.[103] Dick Bahr saw the problems firsthand: "Some of the biggest stressors the Marine Corps went through were those untrained reservists. They'd been living on cookies and ice cream and their conditioning was pretty bad. Some of the reservists didn't even know how to put their suspenders on their packs."

For these unprepared Marines in Korea, the Corps' high standards were as much a curse as an inspiration, for they had not yet been trained to meet them but still felt guilt and shame when they failed to do so. As one Marine who fought in those first months recalled, "I never felt the kind of heat I felt in Korea. I just burned up. My hands went numb. I couldn't help myself; I began crying like a baby. I was ashamed. I felt I could crawl into a mouse hole and die, but I couldn't help what was happening to me."[104] Still, the shame of breaking into tears was minor compared to the trauma suffered by another of Duncan's subjects.

The subject of two other photos is also a corporal, a driver whose ambulance had just hit a land mine. Three men were wounded and one, a friend of the driver's who had only accompanied him to help with the wounded, was killed. Upon hearing that his friend had

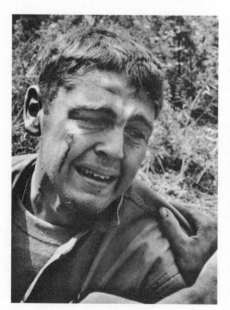

A traumatized Marine in Korea, 1950. (David Douglas Duncan and the Harry Ransom Center, The University of Texas at Austin)

died, the young corporal sat alone on the side of the road, still in shock, trying to force the experience from his mind. The following day he was evacuated to a hospital in Japan, and he was sent home five months later. He had not been wounded; the blood on his cheek was his friend's, and the only injury listed on his casualty card was "MLTPL/ABRSN" (multiple abrasions or scrapes), making it likely that he was evacuated for what was then known as battle fatigue and is today called post-traumatic stress.[105]

Neither of these images appeared in *Life*, although other, less affecting images of the same incident did. From the captions of those photos, we learn that the driver "is crying, not because he is wounded, which he is, but because he thinks it is his fault that another Marine was killed, which it is not."[106] Duncan later called this Marine's tears "one of the secrets of the Marine Corps—the indifference of a man to his own wounds, while openly and brokenheartedly mourning the loss of another."[107] But the fact that Marines cry is no secret at all, either for the Corps or for anyone viewing Duncan's photos. The real secret here is the permanence of the images this young corporal is trying to push out of his mind, and the strong likelihood that those images haunted him for many years after the war. For this Marine, for Dick Bahr, and for hundreds of thousands of other veterans, the sights, sounds, and feelings of the war would remain present in their daily lives long after the fighting stopped. For these men, remembering and forgetting Korea would prove a lifelong struggle.

POST-TRAUMATIC STRESS AND THE BURDENS OF MEMORY

In some ways, violence and trauma were an asset to the Marine Corps in the 1940s and 1950s. Inside the Corps' own cultural field, boot camp's ritualized violence linked prestige to the capacity to suffer, giving novitiates access to the narratives of Marine exceptionalism. Marines' commitments to those stories only grew stronger as they encountered the extreme violence of the Pacific War. The Corps' proficiency with violence enabled their combat successes; in Korea, the ability to withstand hardship eased civilians' concerns that the nation's fighters might be going soft. Even the sophisticated ways Marines talked about death and trauma were an asset, as Frances Newman's birthday party demonstrates. In all of these moments, a nuanced relationship with violence helped keep Marines focused, intense, and effective, both on the battlefield and off.

But Marines' relationship with violence brought burdens too. At the heart of the narratives of Marine exceptionalism was the fiction that Marines could withstand almost any degree of suffering, and that failing to do so was somehow a betrayal of the Corps, both its living members and the dead. For the most part, Marines drew strength from this fiction and from the sense of deep community that it offered. But particularly for those traumatized by war, lingering connections to the dead could be terrifying. The ghosts that visited could haunt as well as comfort.

Psychiatrists noticed this about the Marines as early as World War II. Navy doctors in the Pacific expressed surprise at the "extraordinary amount of guilt" that Marine shell shock victims exhibited, which was accompanied by a "feeling of complete loss of the idealized ego of the Marine Corps." This, they concluded, made Marines more difficult to treat, for "once their defenses had broken, some degree of personality disintegration occurred. . . . The psychiatrists gained the impression that these young men had been given the conception that they must never show fear and that there was a complete loss of personal honor involved in any manifestation of anxiety under combat conditions." This was far less common in the Army, the psychiatrists noted, where those evacuated often showed "no evidence of shame, self-pity or a reluctance to face the other men in their units."[108]

Shame and guilt haunted Korean War Marines as well. While we cannot know whether Duncan's ambulance driver ever managed to live with the images he could not force from his mind, other Korean War veterans have recently begun to talk. Understanding their postwar experiences complicates the largely positive stories about the Marines' service culture and the sense of duty and commitment that it demanded of its members.

Dick Bahr grew up on a Wisconsin farm, dropped out of high school at sixteen, and joined the Marine Corps at seventeen in 1946. After three years on active duty, he returned to civilian life and joined the reserves as a corporal. When the Marine Corps activated its reserves for Korea, Corporal Bahr became an acting sergeant and a squad leader in charge of twelve men in Second Platoon, Baker Company, First Battalion, Seventh Marines. He landed at Inchon, went through the initial conquest of Seoul, and then moved north with the First Marine Division into North Korea. When the Chinese attacked at the Chosin Reservoir on November 27, 1950, Dick's company had roughly 220 men. When they reached safety two weeks later, he counted only thirteen.[109] Dick saw men die in Korea and watched others go insane. Some memories remain burned in his brain to this day: a demolitions engineer being vaporized while defusing explosives, an entire Korean family lying dead in the cold, the face of one of his Marines "tor[n] open from his mouth to his ear" by mortar fire, and another who was shot right between the eyes. For thirty years, Dick would not speak of these things. "I would kinda keep it all to myself. That was the problem that I had to get over—to try to get it out . . . holding it all in made things worse for me."

Dick's memories of Korea are one problem; what he can't remember is another. Like many sufferers of post-traumatic stress, Dick also has gaps in his memory, blank spaces that fill him with guilt and dread. His most troubling blank space concerns an attack on a Chinese machine gun position during the withdrawal from the Chosin Reservoir. Dick remembers charging the enemy, seizing the gun, and turning it on the Chinese infantry. His next memory is of himself kneeling in the snow, with his helmet off and parka open, as the regimental chaplain coaxes him up and tells him to cover up against the cold. His men stand nearby, "looking at me kinda strange." One of his Marines told him later that some in the squad thought he had gone out of his mind and were afraid to approach, because they thought he might kill them. "I don't know what happened in those [blank] spaces," he says, his voice filling with frustration. "And I don't know what I did. Did I do something to my own people or did I do something to the enemy? Why would it be blanked out? . . . Just what did I do?"

After a year in Korea, Dick returned to Wisconsin, but his homecoming was not easy. Most Korean War vets did not come home in large groups; they trickled in one by one, which made it difficult for hometowns to acknowledge their service. Dick came home alone, and his return was more disorienting than most because the war had left him with memory problems. "When I got home, there were a lot of things I didn't remember," he later recalled. "I didn't remember a lot of people that I was supposed to know." He even had trouble finding his own house. He would occasionally mistake people in the street for Marines who had died in the war. Loud noises of any kind bothered him. He felt out of place. "I was afraid to come home," he recalled. "If someone had insulted me or started a fight or something, I really didn't know what I would do to a person. Being a whole year in Korea and just killing people—it kind of leaves you with a tough feeling." He began working as a carpenter, married his girlfriend, Carol, in 1952, and had the first of four daughters in 1953.

Shortly after coming home, the nightmares started. "I'd wake up in the middle of the night. I'd be right there fighting and tearing around in bed and getting so worked up about it and getting so sweated, the wife would have to calm me down, and she would have to change my pajamas because I was so soaked from sweating and from fighting." Carol estimates that the dreams came at least once a week and that they would often end in screaming or thrashing. As soon as their four daughters were grown and moved out of the house, Carol and Dick took separate beds.

When the dreams would come, Dick would have trouble getting back to sleep. It was not so much the content of the dreams, which varied, but their intensity. "I'm actually right there [in Korea] when

I'm getting those nightmares," he explains. "It was kinda scary—well, it still is—to find out that you're in two places at the same time. You're in a dream, and really, you don't know how long it's going to last, but it's so intense sometimes that it's very upsetting when you come out of it." Sometimes he would have to get up and walk around to calm himself down, and on several occasions Carol found him outside in the yard, crying. She tried talking to him, asking him to tell her about the dreams, but he always refused. His reply to her many questions was always the same: "You don't understand. You don't understand."

Dick's feeling that he was in two places at the same time describes well the damage post-traumatic stress disorder (PTSD) does to memory and identity.[110] Identity—much like culture—is really a set of stories that individuals use both to know themselves and to explain themselves to others. Such stories are strategies for living, explains historian J. M. Winter, a way to maintain continuity between past and present, between previous experiences and one's understanding of oneself in the here and now. PTSD occurs when those links between memory and identity are weakened or severed. It is a cognitive dissonance—an inability to integrate the sensory experience of combat into the veteran's life story. When this happens, when experiences cannot be assimilated into a broader sense of self, they do not simply disappear or slip from the frame. They replay compulsively. For some, the memories become embodied, producing physical reactions: a twitch, an altered gait, or an instinctive crouching at even the smallest sound. For others, they replay as nightmares or waking dreams—flashbacks or moments when one mistakes a living stranger for a dead friend. One's sense of self, time, and place destabilizes. Even the most ordinary events—a certain smell in the woods or going to bed at night—can rip the victim out of the present and send him or her back to the moment of trauma. "When that happens," Winter writes, "past identity hijacks or obliterates present identity; and the war resumes again."[111]

Because PTSD is an inability to reconcile traumatic experiences with one's life stories and identity, most psychiatrists today believe the road to healing lies in creating new stories, ones that allow the victim to psychologically metabolize what he or she has experienced. However, this was not well understood in the 1950s, and those who could not talk about their memories often turned to other, less effective coping mechanisms. Dick's primary method of coping with the war within was to keep himself busy. He often worked three different construction jobs at the same time, partly for the money, but also so that he didn't have to think about the things that bothered him. For the first few years, he worked for private contractors by day and built his own house at night with plans he had drawn up himself. Later he joined a union and became a construction foreman; eventually he got a permanent job in the carpentry shop at a Veterans Administration hospital. Even at work, however, the war could resurface. If Dick was startled, his reaction could be dramatic, and some of his coworkers would occasionally torment him by slapping wood on the floor just to make him jump. One time, when a coworker approached him from behind and grabbed his arm, he was so startled that he spat tobacco juice directly into the man's face. "I hit a few guys," he recalled. "The word kinda got passed around just to stay away from this SOB because he's liable to hit you or to spit in your face. That kinda cured a few of them. But they thought this was a big joke that I would be so jumpy . . . I'm so nervous about people." Even when people meant well, as did a minister in his church, Dick did not like being touched. "This one minister we had, she would like to give people hugs and she would put her arms around you. So I had to tell her one time, 'Don't do that, because if you do, I'm liable to hurt you.' . . . [A] lot of times, if the Chinese would try to overrun us, that would be one of the first things they would do, throw their arms around you, and you couldn't do nothing. That was very scary."

Another coping mechanism was alcohol, though Dick was far more controlled in this regard than many other veterans. He drank only on the weekends and stuck mainly to beer, but the alcohol would bring out strong emotions and occasionally cause crises. Carol threatened divorce repeatedly and entreated Dick to go to counseling. He refused. She found it difficult either to go out with Dick or to leave him home alone. "It was hard to leave him home with the kids alone, because I never knew what he was going to do," she remembered. "I worried that maybe he would start drinking or he would somewhat go out of his mind. He never did take anything out on the kids, but I always had that fear. . . . The more he'd drink, the angrier he would get."

Besides periodic temper outbursts, Carol remembers two occasions when Dick had more serious breakdowns. The first and most serious episode occurred in front of their young daughter Dona and required paramedics. "He was sitting on a chair, and he was mumbling, and incoherent, and he'd been drinking while he had been working on the car, and the next thing I know, he threw himself down on the floor. . . . He was thrashing and carrying on and incoherent like he was out of his mind. That's why they had to use the straitjacket because they couldn't get [him] up and just walk out. They got him in the hospital and they gave him some medication." Another time, when Dick's parents were visiting, he had a similar breakdown. A doctor friend living next door—a World War II veteran who also struggled with alcohol and traumatic memories—came over, gave Dick two injections of sedatives, and helped him to bed.

The medical treatment Dick received—sedatives administered by family physicians rather than psychiatrists—was commonplace for veterans suffering from PTSD in the 1950s.[112] Although psychiatrists had been writing about shell shock as early as 1919, the understanding of the illness in the American psychiatric community was still woefully inadequate in the decade after Korea, as were the resources available to veterans.[113] In 1956, there were just 10,000 psychiatrists licensed in the United States; a study published the same year found that there were more than a quarter million World War II veterans alone who either were "in great need" of regular psychiatric treatment or would "benefit considerably" from it.[114] Even this study underestimated the problem.[115] Better studies now judge that between 10 and 15 percent of combat veterans eventually develop significant PTSD symptoms, which means the total number of affected veterans was between 440,000 and 660,000 for World War II and between 86,000 and 130,000 for Korea.[116]

In fact, the numbers for Korea may be even higher. Recent research reveals that Korean War veterans show "significantly more severe PTSD symptoms than the World War II combat veterans," including greater "psychiatric distress," more addiction, a higher number of suicidal thoughts, and greater "psychosocial maladjustment."[117] Korean War vets also exhibit higher rates of anxiety, hostility, and paranoia than World War II vets; one study found they were "more distressed in general than either World War II or Vietnam veterans."[118] Among some VA hospital populations, PTSD rates run as high as 30 percent for Korean War combat vets, compared with only 19 percent for World War II vets and 46 percent for Vietnam veterans.[119]

The reasons for progressively higher PTSD rates among World War II, Korean War, and Vietnam veterans are enormously complex and are inextricably bound up with the fact that beginning in 1980, veterans could receive VA compensation for the condition.[120] Nonetheless, there were cultural reasons Korean War vets experienced more PTSD than World War II veterans, including the persistent civil-military friction that pervaded the home front during and after the war. That friction not only obscured the war's legacy in national narratives but also increased returning veterans' "homecoming stress," which psychiatrists define as "the beliefs and feelings that they [veterans] have not been welcomed back home and not accepted or helped in their readjustment by family and society."[121]

In World War II, civil-military friction was relatively low, as were the levels of veterans' homecoming stress. Long and costly as it was, the war was successful and the public performed its thanks for the veterans' service through a variety of parades and rituals of celebration. Subsequent polling showed that 70 percent of World War II veterans "felt appreciated by Americans upon their return to this country and to civilian life." Korea was different. Only one-third of

Korean War vets felt appreciated upon their return, and for Vietnam, it was less than a quarter.[122] Some psychiatrists now believe that homecoming stress is the strongest predictor—even more so than "combat exposure, childhood and civilian traumas, or stressful life events"—of whether a veteran will fall victim to PTSD.[123]

The reasons for this are obvious. Since PTSD is an inability to reconcile memory and identity, the narratives others tell about veterans and the war can be as helpful or harmful as the veterans' own life stories. In World War II, the dominant stories in civilian society were fundamentally validating and affirmative; during the Korean War and the Vietnam War, they were not. Arguments over war or "police action," charges of collaboration and weakness, and an unsatisfying armistice all created what one psychiatrist called a "rejecting and non-supportive societal homecoming reception," which played a role in "preventing returning veterans from constructively assimilating the meaning of their combat experiences and leading over time to 'repetitive and persistent PTSD symptoms.'"[124] For these veterans, the only recourse was to try to ignore the subject altogether, a task that was ultimately impossible.

Dick's private struggles with the Korean War continued when he retired. In 1998, he applied for and received disability benefits and began attending a VA support group, as did his wife. He began talking about the war, and now travels to schools to discuss his experiences. He formed a local chapter of the "Chosin Few" veterans organization, and even traveled to Korea in 2000 to visit the ground he had fought over so many years before. He is finding an elusive peace and feels he is finally beginning to heal. But symptoms still persist. He continues to get headaches almost every week, and he cannot watch news coverage of the wars in Iraq or Afghanistan. When he goes to funerals for veterans, the rifle shots bother him. "I know they're going to fire, but when they do, it just does something inside of me, I just kinda jump and stiffen up, as you might say, and hold myself." The nightmares still come, but they are less frequent now, and his drinking is under control.

Given the degree of suffering and sacrifice the Marine Corps required of Dick, it is little wonder that he, like Rick Spooner and so many other veterans, still advertises his service affiliation through Marine Corps hats, jackets, neckties, and other pieces of Marine Corps paraphernalia. For him and for others, such explicit advertisements have a largely positive effect: they help turn experiences of trauma into stories of brotherhood, converting pain into love and pride. But perhaps because such traumas never fully depart

Sergeant Dick Bahr, USMC (retired), 2003. Note the Marine Corps hat, bolo tie, shirt, and belt buckle. (Veterans History Project, American Folklife Center, Library of Congress)

from consciousness, they require constant—almost compulsive—inoculation. That, in a sense, is what the tattoos, car stickers, and other trappings of Marine Corps culture offer: protection from memory and a ready defense against a still-lingering war. In a very real way, they help Dick "hold himself" and thus stave off the unraveling that comes from remembering. For traumatized veterans such as Dick, the question is not whether he can continue to live inside the culture of the Corps but whether he will ever be able to live outside it.

In the strange cultural landscape of the 1950s, persistent civil-military friction made Korea America's Forgotten War. The war's legal status and dramatic reversals, Truman's relief of MacArthur, the POW scandal, and the armistice generated accusations and acrimony, which both inhibited the formation of a triumphant national narrative and increased returning veterans' homecoming stress. The civilians did not turn away from the war; the military did. Viewing the war more as an aberration than as a harbinger of future conflict, it worked to ensure that no significant lessons would be taken from it. When confronted with criticism about the war's unsatisfying conclusion, the military used memory as a weapon, charging civilians with failing to remember the very events it worked to erase.

Only the Marine Corps found a way to integrate the war into its preexisting stories about itself. By racing troops to the conflict, expecting much of them in combat, and then publicizing their heroics on the home front, the Marines successfully incorporated Korea into the still-powerful conceptual frame of World War II. Civilian groups also joined the pro-Marine chorus for a variety of reasons: to help the Marines, to embarrass President Truman, to sell newspapers, movie tickets, and books; or to explain what proper conduct in the POW camps was supposed to look like. As a result, the Corps emerged from Korea culturally stronger and with new evidence that the narratives of Marine exceptionalism were true.

The triumphant tales of Inchon and the Chosin Reservoir continue to proliferate in the Marines' cultural field today, sixty years after the war's uneasy conclusion. But they should not remain the only stories in that field; for too long, they have crowded out other, less-pleasant truths of Marines' experiences in the war. For while the Korean War helped the Corps as an institution, it also placed extraordinary demands on the Marines fighting in it. Three moments attest to this: a young and unprepared Marine crying in the summer heat, an ambulance driver blaming himself for the death of a friend, and Dick Bahr's inaccessible memories of his actions during a Chinese attack. In each of these incidents, the dominant emotions are shame and guilt, either for failing to measure up to what was expected of Marines or, in Dick Bahr's case, for not even knowing if he did something to his own men.

This is an aspect of Marine Corps culture that few are willing to acknowledge. While the narratives of Marine exceptionalism may help Dick live with the past today, they also intensified the feelings of guilt that have haunted him for more than half a century. The exaggerated tales of Marines as "superhuman defender[s]" inspired some to perform heroics but also established near-impossible standards of conduct in combat. The same imagined community of Marine ancestors that gave the culture such strength asked too much of the living at times, particularly of the untrained reservists who had not yet attended boot camp. The result for some Marines has been a lifetime of remembering and refighting, a fundamental inability to ever forget Korea.

5

First to Fight in the 1950s

The American people believe . . . that our Corps is downright good for the manhood of our country; that the Marines are masters of a form of indoctrination that without fail converts unoriented young men into proud, self-reliant, stable citizens—men in whose hands they can safely entrust the nation's affairs.

—General Randall Pate to the Marine Officers' Wives Club,
September 17, 1958

And then he hit me, and then he hit me.

—Elizabeth Goricki, May 22, 1955

War trauma did not only affect men such as Dick Bahr who left the Marine Corps and reentered civilian life. It affected the Marines who stayed in the Corps, as well as those joining after Korea, when the Corps was overwhelmingly populated with combat veterans. A culture of violence ran through the Corps in this era: violence against self, against Marine recruits, and against Marines' wives, girlfriends, and children. Even some of the Marines who never went to war had trouble containing the violence the Corps' culture had instilled in them. The Corps' dictum of being "first to fight"—a line in "The Marines' Hymn" and a World War I recruiting slogan still in regular use in the 1950s—too often crossed over into civilian society, with sometimes tragic consequences.

Most Americans are familiar with the professional violence of the Marine Corps—particularly the combat heroics and the rigors of recruit training. Most know little of the unauthorized aggression: beatings given ostensibly in the name of discipline, bar fights, violent crime, incidents of domestic abuse, and other belligerent acts related to alcohol abuse. These were also elements of Marine Corps life in the early Cold War, ones left too long unacknowledged and unexplored.

As with most arguments about abuse, the evidence of it in the Corps is indirect. It was an open secret in this era that enlisted leaders regularly enforced their will with punches and slaps; however, unless the result was a serious injury, these and other transgressions were rarely documented. Nonetheless, a few figures are suggestive. Throughout the 1950s, the Corps had the highest rate of general courts-martial (a rough equivalent to felony trials in a civilian court) as well as the highest punitive discharge rate. Suicide, homicide, and motor vehicle accident death rates were all significantly higher than in the Navy or the broader American population. Furthermore, the factors sociologists have identified as correlates of violent behavior— previous exposure to violence, participation in an aggressive subculture, and high degrees of stress and alcohol use, among others—were all more extreme in the Marine Corps than in the other services or in civilian society. And once the armed services began tracking alcohol consumption three decades later, the Marine Corps has consistently had the highest rates of heavy drinkers and the lowest rates of abstainers, in times of both war and peace.[1]

Even the Marines' most laudatory chroniclers admit that the Corps had problems with alcohol and abuse in the 1950s, but they miss the full scope of the problem. In most histories of this period, the problem of unauthorized violence is confined to one scandal—a single event that spawned an investigation, a court-martial, a spate of institutional reforms, and finally a Hollywood film.[2] In the spring of 1956, Staff Sergeant Matthew C. McKeon, a drill instructor and veteran of World War II and Korea, took his recruit platoon on a night march through the swamps of Parris Island, South Carolina. Though not officially sanctioned for training, night marches in the swamps had long been used by DIs as a way to punish poor performance and improve discipline. This time, however, the swamp was swollen from recent rains and Staff Sergeant McKeon had been drinking on duty. Six recruits drowned in the deep tidal pools of Ribbon Creek. The incident and court-martial that followed received daily coverage in the nation's major papers; the *New York Times* alone wrote sixty-three stories on the trial.[3] On the witness stand, McKeon admitted to drinking whiskey, vodka, and beer the day of the march and to threatening and slapping several recruits before leading them into the swamp. The reason for the slaps, he claimed, was to prepare the recruits for combat. "I wasn't out to hurt him, sir," he later testified about one of the recruits he slapped. "I slapped my own [five-year-old] kid, to be frank with you, harder than I slapped him."[4]

Much has already been written on the Ribbon Creek scandal and the brutal nature of recruit training in the 1950s.[5] However, no accounts discuss the broader culture of violence running through the Corps in this period or the public's thoughts and feelings about that violence. As Staff Sergeant McKeon's testimony suggests, it was not only recruits that Marines hit, and alcohol abuse (a problem in all the services and in the broader civilian society of the 1950s) was often part of the reason why. By 1953, violence had grown so problematic in the Corps that the Commandant directed all commands to maintain files on any incidents of negative publicity, Marine brutality, and murders involving Marine Corps personnel. In the vast majority of incidents contained in these files, alcohol was involved.[6]

Perhaps because of these problems of drinking and violence, the records of this period—the public relations files, letters to the Commandant of the Marine Corps, newspaper articles, and letters to the editor—show few moderate opinions toward the Marine Corps. Two extremes emerge, aligned largely according to gender. The Corps' loudest supporters were primarily men; opposition came most often from women. Supporters saw the Corps as essential for national defense and a necessary corrective for the soft and unmanly elements of 1950s youth culture. Detractors thought the nation suffered not from a lack of masculine toughness but from a surfeit of it. Unbridled aggression, even more than pampering and coddling, was the problem, and a small but vocal minority of women believed that military culture, with its emphasis on violence and drinking, was poisoning the very communities the armed forces were meant to protect.

These two positions did not remain static over time. While criticism of Marine training and violence appeared sporadically in the first half of the decade and reached a peak during the Ribbon Creek trial of 1956, it faded thereafter as celebratory narratives increased. Thus, while the Ribbon Creek incident and subsequent court-martial had short-term negative effects for the Corps, it did not appreciably degrade the Corps' reputation with the American people.[7] In fact, by the end of the decade, both men and women were defending the Corps' violent practices as salutary for the nation, for society, and for young men in particular.

The Corps' interventions in the landscape of civilian culture were crucial enablers of this growing popularity. As they had during World War II, the Marines continued to speak the language of American family life throughout the 1950s and grew increasingly adept at tailoring different messages to men and women. To men, they emphasized the Corps' toughness and combat readiness; to women, they stressed Marines' value as parental role models. Together these two narratives successfully framed the Marine Corps as a service that was rough enough for the battlefield but still appropriate for the kids. By presenting themselves as both fighters and fathers, warriors as well as family men, the Marines were able to conceal practices that deserved fainter praise.

The Corps also formed new alliances with civilian proxies and deepened its connections to Hollywood. The American Heritage Foundation's Freedom Train Tour brought Marines in dress blue uniforms to over 300 cities around the country. The Boy Scouts of America, Walt Disney Company, and a variety of local businesses all supported the Corps' Devil Pups Citizenship Project—a camp for teenagers based out of Camp Pendleton, California. The Marine Corps War Memorial, an immense bronze rendition of the Iwo Jima flag raising funded entirely by private donations, went up in Arlington National Cemetery. Less than a year after Staff Sergeant McKeon was convicted in the Ribbon Creek scandal, actor Jack Webb (an Army Air Forces veteran) directed, produced, and starred in *The*

D.I., a film about boot camp that sought to ease concerns over the violent nature of Marine training.

Good public relations do not explain all, however; Americans' Cold War obsession with virility and strength also made the public more open to the Marines' self-celebrations. As James Gilbert and others have shown, the 1950s were unusual for their "relentless and self-conscious preoccupation with masculinity," which others have called a "crisis of masculinity" or even a "male panic."[8] An overemphasis on toughness, meant to counter deep fears about flagging male vigor, ran through not only film and television but also the most popular social commentaries of the decade, from David Riesman's *The Lonely Crowd* (1950) to Graham Greene's *The Quiet American* (1955) and William H. Whyte's *The Organization Man* (1956). Particularly after Korea, this hypertrophic masculinity not only became the dominant gender model for young American men but also grew increasingly linked to arguments about the Cold War and national survival. Thus, as warnings about weakness and out-of-control youth proliferated in the cultural landscape, the public grew more tolerant of the Marines' misdirected violence.

I trace the Corps' culture of violence through four interactions, ranging from the seemingly insignificant to the criminal and tragic. The first, a quick (and perhaps unintended) moment of verbal nastiness on a public relations tour, shows the Marines' difficulties with alcohol and their propensity to attack when challenged, even in carefully controlled public relations events. The second interaction—the experience of children in the Marine Corps' Devil Pups Citizenship Project—shows how the Marines blurred the lines between physical training and physical abuse not only with recruits but also with boys as young as thirteen. Those distinctions disappear entirely in the third interaction—the recruit training environment of the 1950s—where recruit abuse was rampant and at times deadly. Finally, a moment of extreme abuse in the home shows the worst effects of the culture of violence and the lingering consequences of war. Together, these four interactions reveal the flip side of the Marines' much-celebrated toughness: a habit of being "first to fight," whose effects the country increasingly rationalized away in the name of national security.

THE CULTURE OF VIOLENCE

The Marine Corps' problems with unauthorized violence in the 1950s stemmed from several sources. The trauma of two wars was part of the problem—as will become clear, most of the incidents described in this chapter involved combat veterans, some of whom still struggled with what they experienced on the battlefield. But trauma alone does not suffice as an explanation. The Marines' warrior ethos also contributed to the abuse. The Corps' celebration of toughness and aggression, the demand for absolute submission to authority, and the violence of boot camp may have built excellent fighters, but that fighting was not always used in the nation's defense. Above all else, however, the culprit was alcohol. The drinking habits young Marines learned in the Corps led many to a life of dependence and would eventually give the Corps the highest rates of alcohol abuse in the armed forces.[9]

Claiming that a culture of violence existed in the Marine Corps of the 1950s both states the obvious and invites criticism. To one degree or another, all military services have cultures of violence; all train their members to perform violent acts and use processes of acculturation to break down societal taboos against such acts. Most also explain that violence to civilians using a general narrative of military professionalism that claims well-trained soldiers can fight with fervor one moment and control their aggressive emotions the next. On the battlefield, the Marines were perhaps the most professional practitioners of violence, able to direct it effectively, even when it involved bayoneting a man to death or burning him alive with a flamethrower. But what happened off the battlefield is a different story. The episodes detailed in the following pages highlight some of the fissures in that professionalism narrative by showing that violence is not always so containable. It is, in a sense, contagious: the more contact one has with it, the more likely it is to spread into other environments.

Sociologists have known this for decades. Forty years of research in that field have established correlations between violent behavior and previous exposure to violence. Men, in particular, are far more likely to become violent if they have experienced high degrees of violence in their youth, either by being victims of abuse or by seeing violence practiced on others.[10] Violent behavior is also more likely in individuals who abuse alcohol and in subcultures that tolerate or celebrate violence as an appropriate tool for solving interpersonal problems.[11] Finally, violence is more frequent among people who experience high degrees of stress and live in "authoritarian" households where one parent makes most or all of the family decisions.[12] While experts still disagree on the root causes of violent behavior, almost all of the research endorses a general conclusion that violent behavior is learned primarily through contact with violence, and that violence in one setting or relationship often migrates to (and usually escalates in) another.[13]

These correlating factors have always been more present in the military than in civilian society, as the armed forces' own training literature now admits.[14] However, in the 1950s, they were particularly present in the Marine Corps. As earlier chapters have shown, the Marines had the highest exposure to violence, both in boot camp and in combat. All the services celebrated toughness and aggression, but the narratives of Marine exceptionalism explicitly framed the ability to use and withstand violence as key components of Marine identity. Authoritarianism was also more severe in the Marine Corps, as almost every memoir of recruit training attests.[15] The disciplinary practices learned there were often carried into the enlisted ranks of the 1950s, where challenges to authority that could not be settled by rank were sometimes settled with fists. As a result, Marines became accustomed to conflict resolution strategies that worked within the Corps but not outside it. The more the culture reinforced violence as an acceptable tool for problem solving, the more it became ingrained in the young Marines participating in it.

This does not mean all Marines were destined to have violent lives; indeed, the vast majority kept control of the aggression they had become experts in employing. It is fair to say nonetheless that the Corps had more problems with violence than the other services during the 1950s. Throughout the decade, the Marines' average rate of general courts-martial (the most serious type of court-martial, which was reserved for felony offenses, and usually for violent crimes) was 6.38 per 1,000—more than double the Navy's rate and three times higher than the Air Force's. The Army, which took far more draftees than did the Marines, had a general court-martial rate of just 6 per 1,000.[16] The Marines also had the highest rate of punitive discharges (dishonorable and bad-conduct discharges, which were typically reserved for those convicted in a general court-martial); in 1955, it was three times higher than the Army's.[17] Death rates give a final indication of the Corps' problems with violence and aggressive behavior. Throughout the 1950s, the Marines' average death rate from assaults was more than twice the Navy's rate, and their average suicide rate was significantly higher as well. Except for combat in Korea, the biggest killer of Marines in the 1950s was motor vehicle accidents. They accounted for an average of 165 deaths per year, giving the Corps a vehicular death rate that was 40 percent higher than the Navy's and three times higher than the rate in American society.[18]

Higher court-martial, punitive discharge, and death rates do not mean that the Corps' culture made otherwise nonviolent youth violent, of course. The Marines serving on courts-martial likely had a resistance toward leniency and a cultural predisposition toward harsher sentences than members of the other services. Furthermore, because the Marines marketed themselves as the toughest branch of service, they explicitly sought out young men who were accustomed to using violence and having it used on them. The Corps was also willing to accept some young men with aggression problems in an effort to reform them. The common practice in some civilian communities of giving juvenile offenders a choice between jail or the Marine Corps—though not documented anywhere as an official policy—may help explain why the Marines had more punitive discharges and civil convictions than the other services.[19]

The higher rates do tell us one thing, however. Being a Marine in the 1950s was a life with more exposure to violence than in the other services, even when the nation was at peace. If the last four decades of sociological research can be trusted, this suggests that in the Corps of the 1950s, a service inundated with combat veterans and young Marines eager to emulate them, the violence authorized for the battlefield did not always remain there. It made its way to other Marines on base, to civilians in the bars out in town, and into the home. Writer Pat Conroy, whose semiautobiographical novel *The Great Santini* remains today an iconic depiction of the 1960s Marine Corps, learned this firsthand: "I grew up thinking my father would one day kill me. I never remember a time when I was not afraid of my father's hands."[20]

ALCOHOL ABUSE IN THE 1950S MARINE CORPS

Alcohol abuse was perhaps the most significant factor contributing to unauthorized acts of aggression in the 1950s Marine Corps. The Marines were not alone in this; the entire nation saw rising alcoholism during the 1940s and 1950s, and in World War II, the country's alcoholism rate went up by 13 percent.[21] But whatever problems alcohol caused in American society, they were more severe in the armed forces.[22] A poll taken in 1946 showed that more than half of World War II veterans, both those who had seen combat and those who had not, found themselves "more likely to indulge in alcoholic drink" than they were before entering military service.[23] That same year, a writer for the *New York Times* gave fuller voice to the problem. Of the nation's 45 million drinkers, estimated the *Times,* fully 8 million fell into the category of the "military drinker." "Even the mildest of social drinkers, clothed in a natty Army, Navy, Coast Guard or Air Force uniform, tends to metamorphose into a full-fledged military drinker. In this condition, he will drink as often, as much, and as noisily as possible." The reasons military drinking was so excessive, concluded the author, were threefold:

> There are several reasons which explain the tendency of the military drinker to drink. It is expected of him, once he joins the fighting fraternity, to indulge in excesses. He feels the obligation strongly, wishes to live up to the tradition—and drinks. Further, he is particularly afflicted with boredom, the soldier's occupational disease, and drinks to kill the palling, uneventful hours of war. He drinks, finally, when he is in danger to kill his fears.[24]

Of these three reasons, the first and last—tradition and fear—were the most significant for the Marine Corps. The first edition of the *Marine Officer's Guide,* published in 1956, lists alcohol-related traditions for promotions, farewells, dice games, drawing a sword improperly, or entering a mess without removing one's cap. The section entitled "Social Do's and Don'ts" cautions officers to be discreet when going on a binge. " 'If you must raise hell,' runs an old Marine proverb, 'do it at least a mile away from the flagpole.' "[25] And while all military services had drinking rituals in the 1950s, the unwritten contracts in the Marines' service culture were probably more strenuously enforced. Abstaining from drink in the Marine Corps was not only unmanly; it was, for some, a refusal to participate in the social life of the service. A photo taken by a *Life* photographer at a formal banquet for new lieutenants in 1959 gives some indication of the role alcohol played in the Corps' rituals of community.

As the author of the *Times* article noted, mere participation in the rituals of drink would not suffice. Military fraternities expected their members to "indulge in excesses." This too, like fistfights and the drill instructor's verbal assaults, was a way to establish dominance in the all-male group. In ways not dissimilar to the violence of recruit training, being able to hold one's liquor—to remain in control as the alcohol destabilized both stomach and mind—was a means of demonstrating endurance and strength. In the military, as one psychiatrist noted in 1960, drinking was "somehow linked with sports, guns, strength, sexual prowess, and other things manly."[26]

Framing drinking as either an emblem of strength or a celebration of community masked another purpose: tempering nerves and self-medicating trauma. Because Marine Corps culture placed such emphasis on strength and endurance, it offered members few

A mess night for second lieutenants, 1959. Standing at the piano are General Lemuel C. Shepherd Jr. (left) and Chowder Society member General Merrill B. Twining (right). (Getty Images)

acceptable outlets for the natural emotions produced by combat. Young men learned at an early age that the panic, fury, and grief experienced in war should be suppressed, forgotten, or avoided in conversation. Revisiting traumatic memories aloud—even with one's fellow veterans—risked loosing everyone's demons and was taboo in most circumstances. Consequently, Marines learned to bury their stories and to dilute their emotions with drink. When they could no longer stay silent, the response was usually to do what the Marine Corps had first taught them to do: fight. Many applied this strategy to other emotional conflicts in their lives when they found themselves afraid, confused, or challenged.

No statistics exist for military drinking rates in the 1950s. However, since the services began tracking alcohol consumption in 1980, the Marines have consistently had the most drinkers, the fewest abstainers, and the highest rates of heavy drinkers. In five studies conducted between 1980 and 2002, between 23 and 35 percent of Marines were classified as "heavy drinkers," compared to between 12 and 15 percent for the civilian population sample. The Army's and Navy's rates hovered just below the Marines' (between 14 and 27 percent), and the Air Force had the lowest rates (between 10 and 20 percent). While the Marines' participation in Vietnam undoubtedly contributed to their high drinking rates in the 1980s, the underlying drivers—exposure to trauma, tradition, and the competitive elements of the military fraternity—were equally present among World War II and Korean War veterans. Therefore, it is plausible that the current rates, consistent since 1980, were similar in the 1950s, when alcohol consumption in the military was both more acceptable and less monitored.[27]

A combination of factors, then, contributed to a culture of violence in the Marine Corps of the 1950s. The trauma of two wars generated more friction in the lives and psyches of the Marines of that era, not least because they had the highest rates of combat exposure of any of the armed services. The aggression, stress, and authoritarianism present in all military cultures were particularly explicit and severe in the Marine Corps. Regular violence in the recruit training depots and in the enlisted ranks taught Marines to value strength, to disdain weakness, and to solve problems with their fists. The Marines may also have taken a greater number of violent applicants than the other services, which increased the violence in the Corps and contributed to the service's higher court-martial, punitive discharge, and separation rates. And while all the services treated alcohol consumption as an indicator of manhood and a ritual of community, the Marines, as the service most concerned with such rituals, probably drank more and more heavily than the other services.

FIRST TO FIGHT ON THE FREEDOM TRAIN

Americans had few problems with the Corps' aggressive tendencies during World War II, when the violence was both far away and aimed at appropriate targets. But in the immediate postwar period, the public was less concerned with national security and more concerned with the domestic effects of a large standing military. In this environment, the Marine Corps needed new stories for attracting public support, and above all else, it had to avoid the perception that it was detrimental to American family life.

A critical first step was to deemphasize the role of alcohol. In 1947, the Commandant directed that no Marine publicity would contain pictures of alcoholic beverages and that liquor advertisers could no longer sponsor recruiting ads, a practice that had been common in years previous. (Brewing companies could still provide sponsorships, provided that "only the name of the sponsor appears on the poster or in the advertisement.")[28] In 1948, the Corps refused to provide support for a film about the postwar occupation of China specifically because of its portrayals of excessive drinking and carousing.[29] While approving the script for the hit film *Battle Cry* in 1953, the script screeners insisted that "the impression that seventeen- and eighteen-year-old young men have to get drunk at least once before they can be considered good Marines has to come out."[30]

Despite these efforts, the Corps' problems with alcohol came into public view in the first months of the Cold War and continued throughout the decade. The Freedom Train tour of 1948 offers one example of how Marines worked to refashion their wartime image, and how the darker side of Marine culture came to light, even in the most carefully controlled public relations events.

The idea for the Freedom Train came to U.S. Attorney General Tom C. Clark in May 1947. Convinced that the nation lacked the necessary ideological commitment to fight the Cold War, Clark and a group of wealthy patrons at the privately run American Heritage Foundation called for a national rededication effort that would "emphasize the worth and meaning of American citizenship." The engine for that rededication would be a custom-designed locomotive carrying the nation's most prized and historic documents into cities and towns as a traveling museum exhibit. At every stop, the arrival of the Freedom Train would herald a "week's revival meeting for American democracy," complete with parades, religious ceremonies, and mass recitations of the "Freedom Pledge" by young and old alike. The central message of the Freedom Train was that the nation's democratic ideals were no longer important merely for societal cohesion. They were essential to winning the Cold War.[31]

From September 1947 until January 1949, the train traveled through forty-eight states, stopping in 322 cities and generating mile-long waiting lines. More than 3.5 million people boarded the exhibit, and an estimated 30 million participated in the rededication ceremonies. The largest such ceremony was in Dover, Delaware, where a quarter million people turned out for the parade. In the twenty minutes most viewers spent inside the train, they received an ideological tour through America's best notions of itself. Their first encounter was a display titled "Beginnings," containing a thirteenth-century copy of the Magna Charta and a letter from Christopher Columbus announcing his discovery of America. Displays followed on the Declaration of Independence, the Constitution and Bill of Rights, the Emancipation Proclamation, and the Gettysburg Address. A display entitled "Freedom Triumphs" covered World War II, and a final display, "Flags of Freedom," contained numerous American flags from key battles, including the one raised over Iwo Jima. War papers constituted fully one-quarter of the exhibit's 127 documents.[32]

Attorney General Clark left most of the details of the Freedom Train to the American Heritage Foundation, but on a few points he made decisions himself. One of them was the train's honor guard and security detail, which he insisted should come from the Marine Corps. (His pro-Marine sentiments may have something to do with the fact that his son Ramsey, himself a future attorney general, had served as a Marine in World War II.) When Secretary of the Army Kenneth Royall complained of the favoritism and suggested a rotating guard from all four armed services, he was rebuffed.[33]

The primary duty of the twenty-seven Marines aboard was safeguarding the exhibit, and for that reason, the guards carried rifles or .45 caliber pistols.[34] Newspapers warned prospective saboteurs that the entire security detachment was composed of combat veterans (in fact, there were several Marines in the detail who had never gone overseas), and articles regularly called attention to their height (all were at least five feet eleven inches tall), weight (they averaged 185 pounds), and combat awards.[35] As visitors toured the train, they made their way around Marines standing rigidly at attention next to the most well-known documents. "We have a burglar alarm system, but we don't depend on it," boasted one guard to a newspaper reporter. "Before anything could happen to these documents, somebody would have to kill a couple of Marines."[36]

Outside the train, other Marines served as the exhibit's promoters and guides. These Marines, who wore dress uniforms just like the interior guards, led participants through the train, accompanied prominent guests, and gave more than 200 radio and newspaper interviews.[37] Because waiting times for the exhibit often exceeded several hours, the guides also helped the old and infirm, and would occasionally move disabled visitors to the front of the line. Photos of Marines with children were favorites for many newspapers.

If the guards posted inside the train were overt symbols of American military strength, the Marines posted outside represented the softer power of community cohesion and familial affection. Together, these two images presented the public with a nuanced message about the Marine Corps and Cold War defense. The nation still needed warriors for national security, but in this strange state of quasi-war with the Soviet Union, the entire community would fight the Cold War by being united in support of the state. Dedication to democracy, both individual and collective, was a national security imperative—a duty just like military service. "Freedom is everybody's job," the tour's official theme song explained: "Every Jack and Jill, and every movie queen / The same as any butcher, baker, banker, or Marine!"[38]

Both Marines and their supporters would use this dual image of the Corps throughout the 1950s. To those who worried about national softness and flagging commitment, they presented the image of the train's interior guard—experts in violence who stood prepared to protect the nation's ideals with deadly force. The Marines, in this formulation, were quite literally weapons, forever cocked and ready to kill in the nation's defense. To those who worried about the volatility of such weapons, the Corps presented another image: Marines as fathers and brothers offering a helping hand to women and children. Reinforced by Toys for Tots, the Devil Pups Citizenship Project, and the 1957 film *The D.I.*, this second image worked to erase the very violence that the former image lauded. Together, this twin formulation presented a Marine Corps that could unleash aggression on the battlefield but control it on the home front. The Marines would be first to fight one moment, friend and father the next.

There was also a third type of story told about Marines on the Freedom Train, one that got far less attention than the previous two. Though each of the detachment's twenty-seven Marines was handpicked to present the Corps' best image to the public, not all were well suited to serve as role models for children. Social studies teacher Isobel Kinney saw this firsthand while standing in line with her students in Elmira, New York. "At approximately 12:30 P.M., one of the students was affronted by a technical sergeant of the Marines . . . [who] had come from a tavern across the street," she wrote in a letter of complaint to Headquarters Marine Corps. "The student mentioned above has the misfortune of having had one leg amputated from above the knee and was therefore walking on crutches. This boy does not want to be favored in any way and wished to wait in line with the rest of his friends. . . . It appeared that he [the Marine] had been drinking because after the handicapped boy had refused the offer of the Marine to place him in the front of the line, he became very obnoxious and insulted the boy by telling him that if he were too proud to accept favoritism perhaps he should remove the other leg."[39]

Nor was this the only incident of misconduct on the tour. Though the records reveal no other incident in such detail, the detachment commander's after-action report shows that over the course of the tour, five Marines received reductions in rank for offenses: four from sergeant to corporal and one from corporal to private first class.[40]

The remarkable thing about the incident in Elmira is not that a drunk Marine said something cruel to a disabled boy but that it happened where and when it did—on the Freedom Train and during a time of shrinking defense budgets, when the Marines were doing everything in their power to put forth a positive image of their service to the public. As the Freedom Train detachment was the most visible face of the Corps in 1947–1948, officers screened each prospective member for alcohol, discipline, and misconduct issues before accepting him into the unit. Led by a lieutenant colonel and assisted by a major and a captain, the detachment also had far more leadership and supervision than a typical Marine unit, and the majority of Marines aboard were sergeants or above. That five Marines lost rank on the tour and at least one was drunk on duty indicates that problems of alcohol and misconduct were likely more severe elsewhere in the Corps, where the media's spotlight was less intense.

The Marine guards on the Freedom Train are important for two reasons. As we will see, the positive stories told about them are an early example of the cultural operations used by Marines and their supporters throughout the 1950s. But more than that, the interaction between a drunk Marine and an independent-minded young boy is a subtle indication of a default program in Marine Corps culture—a habit of mind that the Corps and its supporters were eager to conceal. When Marines were thrown outside their comfort zone by challenges to their authority—in this case, a bold answer from a young amputee—their response was often the same as it had been in combat: to fight back.

THE DEVIL PUPS CITIZENSHIP PROJECT

The Freedom Train was not the only opportunity for the Marines to present themselves as both warriors and role models for children in the early Cold War. The Devil Pups Citizenship Project, created in 1953, was another way Marines demonstrated that they could perform a domestic service for American boys and families. Like the Freedom Train, Devil Pups generated enormous positive publicity for the Corps, but the Marines' aggressive habits were present nonetheless and were passed on to children as young as thirteen.

By the mid-1950s, juvenile delinquency and youth violence had become major problems in America. In the decade after World War II, crime by persons under twenty-one increased by 76 percent. Between 1950 and 1960, the number of juveniles in detention centers almost tripled; for fourteen-year-olds, it more than quadrupled. By mid-decade, Attorney General Herbert Brownell predicted that 1 million juvenile offenders would be arrested in the coming year.[41] To address the problem, Congress established the Subcommittee on Juvenile Delinquency in 1953, and thereafter Congress held hearings on the matter every year of the Eisenhower, Kennedy, and Johnson administrations.[42]

Besides Congress' efforts, a wide variety of corporate, nonprofit, and governmental entities devised programs to rehabilitate the nation's boys. The Marine Corps' Devil Pups Citizenship Project was one such program. After learning of a school break-in in 1953, a group of Marines from a local reserve unit in Los Angeles resolved to bring Marine Corps discipline to America's youth, who, they felt, needed less pampering and more "self-control, self-respect, and sense of self-responsibility for one's own actions." A "normal boy can be as rough and tough as any situation calls for yet remain a mannerly gentleman, physically and mentally clean," the program's founders argued. All he needed was training. Delinquency, they asserted, was a national security problem because "guided morals are as important as guided missiles."[43]

The best way to inculcate America's youth with morals while simultaneously keeping them "rough and tough," reasoned the Marines, was by exposure to Marine Corps culture. Taking the name "Devil Pups" (an adaptation of the Marine nickname "Devil Dogs"), they proposed first a five-day camp and later a ten-day program for boys, to be held at Camp Pendleton in Oceanside, California. The Commandant enthusiastically endorsed the idea, and the Walt Disney Company designed the logo—a fiendish version of Mickey Mouse's dog, Pluto, with horns and a pair of hayforks. Boy Scout leaders and community groups nominated prospective Pups, and while the program targeted at-risk youth, applicants had to be "non-delinquent[s]" in order to be accepted. The first year, 1954, the program had more than 400 participants, ages thirteen to seventeen. By 1960, it had raised the minimum age to fourteen and averaged more than a thousand graduates a year. The Devil Pups program is still in existence today and boasts more than 49,000 graduates.[44]

Like the Freedom Train before it, the Devil Pups Project was a joint civil-military endeavor. Marines ran the program; private businesses and municipal organizations supported it and benefited from the good publicity that ensued. Insurance companies and law firms made donations; department stores provided the Pups with uniforms and gym shoes below retail cost; baseball team owners gave out season passes, and the Los Angeles Board of Education loaned the Marines school buses to transport the Pups to Camp Pendleton.[45]

Though it was a combination of military and civilian entities that brought the program into existence, the experience was unapologetically militaristic. For ten days, boys participated in Marine Corps training, ate Marine Corps food, and followed Marine Corps customs and courtesies. They all received military haircuts, wore uniforms, and were required to answer their counselors (all of whom were Marine officers or enlisted men) with the customary "yes, sir" or "no, sir." Though the children never fired weapons, they received training in hand-to-hand combat, rode on top of tanks, sat within inches of Marines firing machine guns, marched in drill formations,

The logo of the Devil Pups Citizenship Project. (Devil Pups Youth Program for America)

and suffered through seemingly endless push-ups and calisthenics. Even the first day was more like an introduction to boot camp than summer camp. As one Devil Pup described it:

> A cold, hateful, indescribably vicious form clamored up to the head of the bus: "I'm your sergeant," it began in a way only a Marine sergeant could. "You're gonna get off this bus now and when you do, you're gonna be running, is that clear?" Period of silence. "Is that clear?" Everyone nods their head. "NOW YOU LISTEN UP HERE," the sergeant rang out red with anger. "When I ask you a question you answer me 'yes sir' or 'no sir,' and you better make it good and loud, do you hear me?" . . . "YES SIR." "You want push ups?" "NO, SIR." "Then you better make it louder." "YES, SIR!!" "All right, get out of here." Zoom, the bus was empty.[46]

There were few, if any, complaints from parents about the military nature of this voluntary program. But much as with the Freedom Train, if one probes below the surface, disturbing moments emerge. Undergirding the entire Devil Pups program was the threat of violence, a scaled-down version of the recruit training program used at Parris Island and San Diego. There is no evidence that the DIs ever hit the young Pups, but the Marines routinely punished disobedience with exercises and verbal assaults. "They really put you through your paces physically," remembers the son of one Marine sergeant who attended the program for two summers. "You learned how to take orders and not talk back, or you'd get your butt kicked."[47] When young Pups did lose control and attacked each other, the Marines taught them how to guide their fists. " 'Oh, the boys had a couple of little spats,' " remarked one Marine captain to a reporter, " 'but we cleared that up with the boxing gloves,' he said with a smile." The young boys took the lessons to heart. While watching the boys march around the camp, a journalist saw one Devil Pup mistakenly step on the heel of another. Immediately the boy in front "wheeled without a word and struck the second boy in the face with his fist. Both kept on marching stony faced and silent. The drill instructor at the head of the unit did not see the incident."[48]

Like the Freedom Train, the Devil Pups Project was a resounding public relations success for the Corps. Presenting the Marine Corps as mentors and big brothers, it did much to advance the idea that Marines were not only tough but knew how to contain toughness and to channel aggression from juvenile delinquency into proper manly citizenship. But underneath that public relations success were martial practices that were inappropriate for children as young as thirteen. Punishing boys with push-ups, boxing matches, and verbal tirades may have bred respect for authority, but it also encouraged boys to believe that anger and violence were necessary elements of manhood and appropriate tools for solving interpersonal problems.

These minor incidents involving the Freedom Train and Devil Pups Project may seem insignificant until one considers that in both cases the Marine Corps was exerting the maximum effort to present the best possible image of itself to the public. Disturbing moments resulted nonetheless. What happened, therefore, in the moments when neither reporters nor civilians were watching?

RECRUIT ABUSE AND MANHOOD IN THE 1950S

For the Marines at the Division of Public Information, recruit training presented the greatest problem for managing the Corps' image in the 1950s. A pattern of abuse plagued the Marine Corps during this era, which, for a time, exacerbated the gendered division of opinion over the Corps' utility in American society. Staff Sergeant McKeon's 1956 Ribbon Creek trial was the most highly publicized event, but by no means was it the only one. In the five years before Ribbon Creek, there were eighty-three court-martial convictions for recruit maltreatment (averaging about sixteen per year); in the twelve months after the Ribbon Creek drownings, there were twenty-three more, including several for DIs who had kicked and choked recruits or hit

them with broom handles, rifles, and swagger sticks.[49] A survey of
27,000 Marines, mostly age twenty-one and younger, conducted one
month after the Ribbon Creek incident showed that "abusive language, hazing and maltreatment" were "prevalent" at the recruit depots, and the number of "improper practices reported had been increasing over the [last ten] years." More than half of the respondents
reported that the DIs used vulgar language, and roughly a third had
seen DIs haze, strike, or kick recruits.[50] A Marine general sent to investigate recruit abuse concluded that a "system of cruel and brutal
treatment" existed at Parris Island. A "drill instructor made a recruit
stand at attention while the instructor struck him repeatedly, breaking his jaw," he wrote to a friend after conducting his investigation.
"When the recruit fell to the deck, the drill instructor kicked him
time after time. This was not an isolated incident . . . this was common everyday treatment which fortunately didn't always put the recruit in the hospital."[51] Other recruits were even less fortunate. One
Marine, who attended boot camp in 1951, remembered what happened when a young recruit was caught smoking:

> The Corporal called everybody to formation in the squad bay and
> then had the little guy sit on a chair on top of a table. Then he had
> somebody put a full pack of lit cigarettes into his mouth. Then he
> put a bucket over the guy's head. Then he put a poncho over that,
> and a blanket over the poncho. We all stood at attention as the DI
> screamed that he wanted to see more smoke coming out from under
> the blanket. The recruit later was taken to the hospital. The DI was
> not punished."[52]

Women noticed the problem in the earliest months of the Korean War. In September 1950, just after the Marines' landing in Inchon, Korea, Mrs. Frank Sorensen of Hartland, Wisconsin, wrote to
the President of the United States about an article on recruit training
she had seen in her local paper. The Marines, she wrote, "want these

boys of ours to be soulless beasts with no personality. Those who live to come home again must enter civilian life. Can they discard their Marine nature like they would take off a coat? . . . If we would give our dogs the same treatment the officers of the Humane Society would prosecute us."[53]

The Divisions of Recruiting and Public Information were not blind to the problem or to the fact that women were complaining more than men. As early as 1951, they had concluded that "as a rule, parental resistance to the Marine Corps begins with mothers, rather than fathers," and that the Corps' publicists needed to "break down this resistance and tell mothers what the Marine Corps has to offer their sons."[54] To help them do so, the Marines returned again to J. Walter Thompson, the same New York agency that had conducted their nationwide public opinion survey back in 1941.[55] Their Madison Avenue consultants advised the Marines to reframe the image of recruit training to make it seem more familial. In one proposal for a photo shoot at Parris Island, they cautioned that "the strict discipline should be placed in an extremely favorable light," and photos of DIs "must not be the tough prototype, [but] rather a fatherly-looking fellow."[56]

The Marine Corps either disagreed with J. Walter Thompson's advice or simply ignored it, because in the summer of 1951 they allowed *Life* magazine unfettered access to Parris Island to write a story on recruit training. The article that followed, "How to Make Marines," focused on one DI and portrayed him as tough but professional.[57] Unfortunately, the feature also contained pictures of recruits crying, standing with buckets over their heads or with neckties in their mouths, and lying unconscious from physical exhaustion. The response from female readers was almost uniformly negative. The "article in *Life* fills me with contempt and utter disgust," wrote one woman. "Why don't they stop acting like childish dictators and treat the young men with respect due a human being?" asked another. The article "is revolting and disgusting," wrote Mrs. R. D. Quinn from

Pittsburgh. "After all the difficult tasks we parents go through to in-still our children with American ideals for decency, freedom and democracy, and then have these young men trained by a 'Nazi Con-centration Camp' sergeant shows, I am sorry to say, the deterioration of America."[58]

When the letters of protest began to appear, the Marine Corps and its supporters counterattacked en masse. Active-duty members and veterans wrote 160 letters to *Life*'s editor defending the Corps' training and demeaning its critics, overwhelming the dozen or so complaints that the story originally generated. "Did you only show the good side of life down there or is it that easy now?" asked one for-mer Marine. "What does she want—men or babies?" another wrote in response to Quinn's letter. "She could use her time to better advan-tage in getting her husband's supper ready. . . . Keep your mouth shut about things you know nothing about and buy a few bonds."[59]

Similar sentiments emerged during the Ribbon Creek trial of 1956 and in other abuse trials that followed. A particularly sensational story hit the papers in early 1957, when several New York newspapers reported that a DI had beaten recruit David Lee Porter with a "steel bar" and forced him to march with sand in his mouth.[60] More angry letters from women followed in hometown and national newspapers, followed by letters of support, usually written by men. "I thought my son was taking military training in order to help prevent cruelty in the world," wrote Mrs. Maybel Darrah of Cadyville, Vermont, in a letter to the editor of her local paper. "If he is just going to be taught how to be cruel to those he may have under him, my God, I want him back home. I didn't let him go to be taught to be a murderer and a sadist."[61] A court-martial convicted the DI shortly thereafter, but the day the court delivered its verdict, Porter was beaten again, this time by his lieutenant (presumably for testifying against his DI). The lieu-tenant too was later court-martialed and discharged from the Marine Corps. A group of mothers with sons in recruit training wrote to a Parris Island military chaplain, desperate for help:

Please try to help those poor Marines, who are pitifully getting beaten up by those drill instructors. Those poor boys are afraid to report them because they are threaten[ed] to keep their mouths shut or else they know what. They are not supposed to put a hand on those boys. . . . We mothers are sick to think of what is going on over there. The training is hard enough for our boys without getting those beatings. Father, you won't get any information out of the boys; they're afraid to talk. Something has to be done. You are the only one who can help them father; we mothers beg you to help them without getting them in any more trouble than they are in.[62]

It makes sense that women would write to chaplains with their complaints, for on the few occasions when criticism did come from men, it was usually from the clergy.[63] On the whole, however, men's reactions to the Porter court-martial and others after Ribbon Creek were as positive as they had been in response to the 1951 *Life* article, if not more so. Fears of emasculation and disdain for weakness ran throughout their editorials and letters to the editor. "No More Nursemaids!" ran the headline on one; "Too Many Cry Babies Joining the Marines" went another.[64] The Marine Corps must not "hold a court-martial every time a drill instructor does something to a raw recruit that his parents should have done long before, but probably neglected," wrote an editor for the *Savannah* (Georgia) *Morning News*. "Who Wants Panty-Waist Marines?" was the title of one notorious extremist's article in the *American Mercury*. "The army, the navy and air force have been viciously emasculated. . . . The U.S. Marine Corps is the last stronghold of the tough, aristocratic, iron-disciplined tradition which is the guts of a real fighting outfit."[65]

The 27,000 Marines surveyed in 1956 also had positive feelings about recruit training, and ideas about manhood were integral to the reasons for those feelings. More than 80 percent thought they had been treated "as recruits should be treated," and this number was even higher among combat veterans. Three-quarters of all respondents rated boot camp as "good training"; tellingly, this number was highest at the recruit depot with the most maltreatment problems. Respondents described the DIs' use of vulgarity as "man's language, the kind of language men use when women and children are not present." While brutality "was universally condemned," fully two-thirds believed the hazing, punches, and kicks were "most often used to correct a mistake or stress a point." Respondents' most common positive sentiment about recruit training was that it taught them discipline and courtesy. As one said, "It taught us to act and think like Marines and not act like wise punks." In a second study conducted a year after Ribbon Creek, recruits agreed that "the best thing about recruit training was that it made better men of them," and that it "could be improved by making it more rigorous."[66]

Given the fact that the Marine Corps, like all military services, was a culture dominated by masculine values, it is not particularly surprising that many men supported it and some women did not. But the vehemence of some men's support—not only defending the Corps but attacking and mocking those who questioned its methods—deserves explanation. Why did women's reasonable protests against abuse generate such strong fear and misogyny? The answer lies in the specific linkages between violence and prestige, which the Marine Corps cultivated in its members and supporters. While all of the armed forces framed their recruit training experience as a rite of passage to adulthood in this era, none used violence in such explicitly ritualized ways as did the Marines. The purpose of that violence was to create a cultural contract between the recruit and the Corps—a charter of identity that linked membership in an elite male institution to the capacity to endure physical hardship and suffering. Therefore, when the Corps' methods came under question by women, so too did the experiential foundation of the narratives of Marine exceptionalism. Attacking the Corps' use of violence was nothing less than an attack on the Marines' identity. The response from the Corps' supporters was to counterattack, using gendered insults as weapons.

There is another reason why men were so adamant that the Corps should remain unadulterated by civilian or feminine values.

Many were passionate about defending the Corps as an all-male pre-serve because it had only recently ceased to be one. Although women had been in the Marine Corps Reserve since 1943, few male Marines had much contact with them during the war, as women were all sta-tioned stateside and almost all of the men went abroad. Peacetime yielded greater contact between the sexes. The Women's Armed Ser-vices Integration Act of 1948 made women full members of the regu-lar component of all the services, and the number of women in the Marine Corps rose from just 167 in 1948 to over 1,700 in 1956. Even though the Marines had the lowest percentage of women in their active-duty forces (less than 1 percent), the presence of women still generated friction.[67] A set of surveys taken in 1952 and 1953 showed that women Marines had the greatest dissatisfaction with life in the armed forces and the lowest reenlistment rates.[68] The Marines also had the highest percentages of women claiming to have "a pretty rot-ten time" in the service and the lowest percentage of women who believed their leaders showed concern for their personal welfare.[69] One general serving in the Marine Corps at that time later admitted that "to tell the truth, the integration of the blacks into the Marine Corps caused less of a ruffle in the Marine Corps than the integra-tion of women."[70]

These polls and the debates over physical abuse in the Corps show that there was a hypermasculine logic at work in the 1950s Ma-rine Corps, one that appealed to many men but few women. Those embracing that logic not only resented women's criticisms of recruit training but also believed violence had a constructive role to play in both national defense and civilian society. The ability to withstand drill instructors' beatings was more than preparation for combat; it was a necessary component of the passage from boyhood to adult-hood. As one supporter explained, if the Corps was "cracking down" on recruits such as David Lee Porter, it was because the nation—and mothers in particular—was giving the Marines "too many young-sters who need cracking down."[71] When women challenged this connection between violence and manhood, the responses ranged from complaints of "emasculation" to calls for women to return to the kitchen.

MANHOOD AND TOUGH LOVE IN *THE D.I.*

While explicit celebrations of the hardships of boot camp worked well with veterans and other men, Marines and their allies also helped construct more nuanced narratives of recruit training through film. Here they drew again on the language of family and tender violence that had worked so well in *Sands of Iwo Jima*, in the Toys for Tots program, and at Frances Newman's birthday party. In the 1957 film *The D.I.*, the Marines didn't challenge women's right to criticize recruit training; instead, they used a woman to defend it. In so doing, the Marines and their civilian proxies reconfigured recruit training as parenting and the DI as the ultimate practitioner of tough love.

The creative force behind *The D.I.* was one of the most well-known voices of masculine toughness in the 1950s: radio and film star Jack Webb, who played the role of Detective Joe Friday on the popular radio program *Dragnet*. An Army Air Forces veteran, Webb had worked with Marines while starring in 20th Century Fox's film *The Halls of Montezuma* (1951) and had become an ardent fan. Shortly after the Ribbon Creek trial, he approached the Corps with an idea for a film; the Corps provided extensive production support.[72] Webb directed and produced the film, which was based on a play written by a former Marine. Webb also starred as the title character, a senior drill instructor named Technical Sergeant Moore.

As the film was a form of damage control for Ribbon Creek, recruit abuse is entirely absent from *The D.I.* Unlike John Wayne in *Sands of Iwo Jima* (1949), Jack Webb's Sergeant Moore yells but never hits, and he drinks tomato juice rather than liquor. In other ways, however, the basic character development in *The D.I.* is similar to that of Sergeant Stryker and Private Conway in *Sands of Iwo Jima*.

Webb's Sergeant Moore is saddled with an immature but intelligent new recruit, Private Owens (played by Don Dubbins, himself a former Marine). No matter what technique Moore uses to encourage Owens to be a good Marine, the young, troubled man complains, resists, and even contemplates swimming through the swamps to escape Parris Island.

Jack Webb stars as the title character in *The D.I.* (1957). Standing at the far left is the problematic complainer, Recruit Owens, played by former Marine Don Dubbins. (*The D.I.,* © Warner Bros. Entertainment, Inc. All Rights Reserved.)

While both films deal with uncooperative young Marines, Sergeant Moore's problems in *The D.I.* are different from Sergeant Stryker's. Moore is not only training men for war but making citizens out of them. When recruits arrive, he explains (in a scene marked "very sensitive" by the Marine Corps script screeners), they are a strange mix of "bookworms" and "hoodlums." Some "look like they could drink blood," and others are "stupid idiots who oughtta be home with their mamas."[73] The job of the DI, Moore goes on to say, is to "make the tough guys nicer and the nice guys a little tougher." Though he has a variety of techniques for training the too-soft and the too-hard, none seems to work on the obstinate Owens. If he cannot change Owens' attitude, warns Moore's superior, Captain Anderson, the Marine Corps will discharge the uncooperative recruit.

In the real Marine Corps—and particularly before Ribbon Creek—a recruit like Owens would have been beaten into submission, either by the DI or, more likely, by his fellow recruits, whom the DI would punish collectively for the mistakes of the one. But in Webb's film, the solution for Private Owens comes from outside the Marine Corps and gives a feminine and familial gloss to the violence of recruit training.

In the film's climatic scene, Captain Anderson and Sergeant Moore meet to decide Private Owens' fate. Captain Anderson is adamant that they discharge him; Sergeant Moore wants more time. Just as Moore is about to capitulate, the two Marines receive a visit from Private Owens' mother (Virginia Gregg) and they learn why her son has been such a poor recruit. Owens' father and brothers had also been Marines, but his father was killed in World War II and both of his brothers in Korea. After losing them, explains Mrs. Owens, she grew too attached to her only remaining son and failed to teach him to be a man. "He must stick this out, Captain. He must," she explains. "I've made many mistakes with him. Too many. He was all I had left and I pampered him. Without realizing it, I made a mama's boy out of him." Both Sergeant Moore and Captain Anderson are doubtful. What, they ask, could they do that they have not already tried? Mrs. Owens offers the answer: "Sergeant, I will tell you what my husband would tell you if he were here now. Rough him up some more. Give it to him. He can take it. He's my son." Luckily, no such violence is required. After Mrs. Owens leaves, Sergeant Moore returns to his platoon. Private Owens, horrified that his mother came to Parris Island and spoke to his DI, instantly becomes a model recruit, and the story ends well for all involved.

A pivotal scene from *The D.I.* The Marines receive a visit from Private Owens' mother, played by Virginia Gregg. Note the image of the Iwo Jima flag raising in the background and the portraits of Marines killed in the Marshall Islands during World War II. (*The D.I.*, © Warner Bros. Entertainment, Inc. All Rights Reserved.)

It is hard to believe that Mrs. Owens' charge to "rough him up some more" represents the opinions of most women toward recruit training in the 1950s. It seems more likely that she is a fictional proxy for the Marine Corps—a way for it to present its own best arguments about itself in reply to the accusations of abuse. With Mrs. Owens as the spokesperson for the Marines' methods, *The D.I.* frames the violence of recruit abuse as the solution to a mother's problem rather than as the problem itself.

And yet there is evidence that as the decade wore on, Americans—both men and women—rehearsed the same cultural logic present in *The D.I.* to explain the need for Marines and their peculiar form of recruit training. Just as the Porter abuse trial was reaching its conclusion in March 1957, one mother wrote that she was "fed up, chagrined, sick to my stomach, and rapidly approaching a slow boil in regard to the accusations against the Marine Corps. . . . The same parents who are yakking now about the mistreatment of their babies will be the first to holler 'you didn't train my boy to protect himself.' "[74] Another mother wrote the Commandant of the Marine Corps to "ask that the Corps does not shelve its methods of discipline which my son and so many young men of the next generation are so sorely in need of."[75] Even after the second court-martial involving Porter's vengeful lieutenant, some women begged the Corps to make its training harder. One of the most passionate supporters, female war correspondent Dickey Chapelle, defended the Corps in an article entitled "Is Momma Running the Marines?"

> So keep up the pressure for tapioca training, Mom, if that's what you want, and that's what you'll get. . . . As for me, if I ever cover another war, whether big or brushfire, I'm going to look for a few old Marines behind whom to go forward—Marines trained before the reform wave of last year. I don't want to get mixed up in any sturm and mishmash near a man who has never before in his life faced hostility greater than a grammatically-worded shout.[76]

Celebrations of Marine toughness grew only more numerous after 1957, spurred on perhaps by Sputnik, the so-called missile gap, and hysterical accusations that the nation's boys were growing soft.[77] When the Corps began reorganizing recruit training to weed out abuse, the Commandant received numerous letters from both men and women complaining that recruit training would become too easy. The Commandant and his subordinates responded by giving numerous speeches assuring the public that boot camp was still sufficiently rough. Parris Island public relations officers found themselves emphasizing repeatedly that "RECRUIT TRAINING HAS NOT BEEN SOFTENED . . . if anything we are moving in the other direction. We are trying to make the training even more rugged and effective."[78] The new training program increased the recruits' physical fitness training and replaced bayonet training with pugil sticks—a form of hand-to-hand combat training where recruits pound each other with large padded sticks instead of attacking padded dummies. And, as the photo of hand-to-hand combat training reveals, such training remained fairly brutal into the early 1960s.

Many Marines today believe that Ribbon Creek created lasting and serious damage to the Corps' reputation. It did not. A careful review of letters and articles about recruit training supports the opposite conclusion: that while women objected more often than men, as a whole, Americans grew more tolerant of the Corps' recruit training practices as the decade continued. Ribbon Creek did generate a spate of negative publicity during the months of the trial, but the Corps' supporters counterattacked, presenting Marine recruit training as a symbol of the idealized, unpampered masculinity they felt the nation still lacked. Pro-Marine editorials increasingly outnumbered criticism in most papers; critical letters to the editor were followed regularly by letters of support. By the end of the decade, most Americans—not just the Marines and their supporters—seemed convinced by the Commandant's claim that the Marines' indoctrination "converts unoriented young men into proud, self-reliant, stable citizens—men in whose hands they can safely entrust the nation's affairs."[79]

But, as will become clear in what follows, the pass America issued the Corps for its violence rationalized away things it should not have. Despite the Commandant's claim, the interpersonal strategies Marines learned in their service were not always the right ones for civilian life, and the bias toward violence could sometimes turn tragic. While recruit training and the culture of the Corps may have prepared men for war, it did far less to prepare them for civilian life. Most did become "proud, self-reliant, stable citizens," but those who did not found few resources within the Corps to help them cope with their

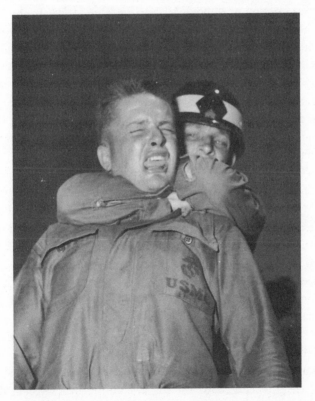

Hand-to-hand combat training, 1962, five years after the Ribbon Creek abuse trial. (United States Marine Corps)

troubles. These men stayed locked in a warrior culture, and when confronted or challenged, they returned to the violent habits that the Corps had nurtured in them.

DOMESTIC VIOLENCE AND THE PORK CHOP MURDER TRIAL

Most of the Corps' negative publicity in the national papers dealt with alcohol and recruit abuse, but in local coverage, the crimes reported were often more violent. Marines were arrested in the 1950s for assaults, rapes, murders, theft, and family violence. Of course, no statistics exist on how many Marines became violent in the home, and there is no way to know with certainty whether the numbers were higher than elsewhere in American society. However, the incidents of crime and abuse were plentiful enough in the five years after Korea that Headquarters began maintaining special files on the murder trials involving active duty and retired Marines.[80] The story of one of those trials, involving a public relations officer from Headquarters Marine Corps, tells of the agony of domestic abuse, both for the victim and for the abuser.

When the police arrived at the Arlington, Virginia, home of Lieutenant Ed Goricki on May 22, 1955, they found him lying on the floor unconscious with a bullet to the chest. His wife, Elizabeth, a Marine veteran herself, hovered over him frantically. "I shot him but he's still alive," she cried to the officer at the door. "Help me."[81] A .22 caliber pistol lay on the dining room table. On the floor and in the other rooms of the house lay broken furniture, blood, and almost twenty empty whiskey bottles. After the ambulance took Ed to the hospital, police tried to question Elizabeth, but she was dazed and in shock. No matter what they asked her, she kept repeating one line: "And then he hit me, and then he hit me."[82] The police took her to the hospital, where she was examined and found to have a blood-alcohol level twice the legal limit. The slight, blond former sergeant in the Marine Corps Reserve also had "bruises of the forehead, shoulders, elbows, and legs; scratches on the arms, a cut lip, puffed jaw, and swelling around the base of the spine."[83] Ed, who was also drunk, died en route to the hospital.

Ed and Elizabeth met in the Marine Corps, which he had joined at age eighteen in 1933 and she shortly after Pearl Harbor. He fought on Iwo Jima and later was commissioned as an officer. When the war ended, both left the Marines, but Ed rejoined soon after and decided to make it his career. Elizabeth went to work at the Veterans Administration in Washington, D.C. The problems in their marriage began as soon as he returned from the Pacific. In July 1946, during an argument, Elizabeth threw a water glass at Ed. He threw a knife and threatened to kill her. They separated shortly thereafter. He tried repeatedly to reconcile with her, but Elizabeth was skeptical. "We'd almost get to the point of getting back together," she later testified at her trial. "Then he'd do something to make me change my mind."[84] In 1947, Ed smashed through two doors and broke into the apartment where Elizabeth lived. She called the police and obtained a restraining order against her husband. They divorced in 1948.

Ed apologized repeatedly and tried to woo Elizabeth back. Though physically much larger than she, he was also two years younger and felt he had to prove to her that he was mature. "He would say that he was so sure that he was an adult by now; that he'd found himself—that he couldn't possibly ever be mean to me again," she testified. "I believed him." They reconciled in 1949 and remarried in 1952. Once they were remarried, the fights and drinking grew worse. Although Elizabeth insisted at her trial that her husband was "wonderful, considerate [and] kind" most of the time, he was prone to "uncontrollable rages" when he would "beat and kick her, smash furniture and dishes, seemingly without reason."[85] Often Ed would not even remember his violence the next morning and would ask Elizabeth how she had gotten bruises on her legs. Elizabeth begged him to go to a psychiatrist, but he refused. "He said if the Marine Corps ever found out he would be ruined. I said we could cash in our stock and go to a private doctor and the Marines didn't have to know . . . [but] he said now he knew what he did, he felt sure he could control himself. He said if he felt angry again, he would go and see a doctor."[86]

On the night Elizabeth shot her husband, her sister and brother-in-law were over for dinner. Ed was "moody" when they arrived, her brother-in-law testified, because he had just learned that he was to be transferred to Japan in the coming month. After all four had had several drinks, Ed grew increasingly belligerent. The arguing turned violent after Ed accused his wife of cooking the pork chops improperly, after which he "sent her reeling with a slap."[87] Then

> he started raising hell about the pork chops. She went to put something on the dining room table and he kicked her about half way across the room. She lay on the floor for a while and then went into the kitchen and they started arguing again at the top of the basement steps. I saw him push her down the steps and I said to my wife "let's get out of here." I didn't want to interfere with a man who was arguing with his wife.[88]

After his in-laws left, Ed continued to beat Elizabeth. At just five feet three inches and 114 pounds, she was no match for a six-foot Marine weighing over 200 pounds. After knocking her down the steps, "he ran down the steps, picked me up and dragged me up the steps," she testified. "He hit me and I don't remember anything more until I was sitting on the floor facing the bathroom."[89] At this point, Elizabeth claims Ed took a pistol from the bedroom, fired it into the air, and then tried to force her to take the gun and to shoot herself. "He kept screaming at me, 'take it, hold it, take it, hold it,'" testified Elizabeth. "He tried to force my hand around the gun. . . . I twisted. . . . That's when the gun went off."[90]

Partly because they were both Marines, the media quickly latched onto the "pork chop murder" and gave it regular coverage. Although the prosecutors offered convincing evidence that the gun could not have discharged by accident, as Elizabeth claimed, the all-male jury deliberated for just five hours before acquitting her on all charges. The news brought Elizabeth little comfort. "Alone with her freedom, she kept staring at the table," wrote a Washington reporter who observed the defendant at the moment of her acquittal. "Then she keeled forward from the waist, her face on her hands propped up on her knees, and her high thin wailing pierced the courtroom."[91]

HELD IN DEATH OF HUSBAND—Mrs. Elizabeth Goricki, shown in the Woman Marine's uniform she formerly wore, has been charged with murder in the shooting of Marine 1st Lt. Edward Goricki after they quarreled about pork chops.

Former Marine Sergeant Elizabeth Goricki, shown here in a 1945 photo, shot her Marine husband after what would later be termed a "domestic quarrel" in their Arlington, Virginia home, in 1955. (United States Marine Corps)

The sad and violent marriage of Ed and Elizabeth Goricki was not the norm for Marine families in the 1950s, but neither was it entirely unique. The year that Ed Goricki died, the Corps' rate for deaths by assault was more than five times that of the Navy.[92] In the twelve months after the Korean War ended, at least seventeen active-duty or discharged Marines found themselves on trial for murder.[93] Much like the violence of Marines returning from World War II, the post–Korean War crimes were at times grisly. One Marine killed a civilian with a samurai sword; another killed his wife and three children with an ax before slitting his own throat. On several occasions, fistfights or bar brawls turned more brutal and resulted in death by gunshot or head injury. One former Marine, after strangling a high school sophomore to death, stated simply that he "had an urge to kill and couldn't control it."[94] Some claimed war trauma as their justification; others blamed alcohol. Dishonorable discharges in the enlisted ranks almost doubled between 1953 and 1954 and rose by another 50 percent in 1955.[95]

The Goricki trial is important not because it is typical of Marines' domestic life—of course it is not—but because it complicates the Marines' oft-rehearsed claim (both then and now) that the Corps is a family as well as an armed service. Since the first weeks of World War II, Marine publicists used familial narratives to idealize the sense of community inside the Marine Corps; Elizabeth Goricki's story shows that the experiences of Marines' real families were not always so positive. How widespread domestic violence was, either in the Marine Corps or civilian society of the 1950s, will never be known. Accurate statistics are impossible to obtain, both because victims usually did not report the crimes and because those who witnessed them, like Elizabeth's own brother-in-law, too often turned their back. Furthermore, the Marine Corps' careful control of its public relations, its skepticism of outsiders, and its male-dominated culture likely kept some of the abuse hidden from view. Indeed, had Elizabeth not shot and killed her husband, her brutal beating that night would have remained nothing more than "a man who was arguing with his wife."

Nor is the Goricki story entirely separable from one of the events that has made the Marines so well known in American society today: the battle of Iwo Jima. Indeed, the picture of Ed Goricki that emerged during his wife's trial is of a man still unable to cope with the trauma he experienced over a decade earlier. Elizabeth testified that Ed had had no violent episodes before the war and that the knife-throwing episode of July 1946 was the first violent act of their marriage.[96] While he may have had a drinking problem before the war, when he returned from the Pacific his friends noticed that his temperament had changed. As his brother-in-law later recalled, "[he] sometimes acted funny and sometimes was all right. I think something happened to him in the war."[97]

Furthermore, Ed's belief that he could not seek psychiatric help without risking his career was accurate. No Marine officer of that era (particularly a public relations officer, who was attuned to the importance of image) would admit to psychiatric problems, let alone seek professional help. Admissions of weakness were anathema to the culture of the Corps, where mental and physical stamina were the hallmarks of leadership. Among Marines, the only broadly accepted strategies for coping with trauma were stoic silence and "raising hell" through the occasional drinking binge. When Ed tried the latter, it loosed the very inhibitions he needed to maintain. His wife's testimony, filled with sorrow and kind words for her dead husband, gives a clue of the demons Ed wrestled with. After years of trying to reconcile with Elizabeth, Ed finally won her back with the promise that he would control his fists. One week after their remarriage, Elizabeth explained, Ed "flew into one of his rages. When it was over, he threw himself down on his bed and wept."[98]

The Gorickis' story is an unusually extreme example of the culture of violence in the Cold War Marine Corps. But in almost every area of Marine Corps life lie other incidents that raise questions about the psychological effects of combat and of Marine training and culture. On the Freedom Train, a sergeant chosen to present the Corps' best image got drunk on duty and lashed out at a young boy. In the Devil Pups program, boys got their "butt[s] kicked" and learned to settle problems with fists instead of words. In recruit training, violence prepared young men for the battlefield but put others in their graves.

For each of these stories, there are, of course, other possible interpretations. Recruit training was brutal in the 1950s, but so too were the habits and lives of many of the young recruits who joined the Corps in the strength-obsessed culture of the early Cold War. And no matter how extreme the use of military training on middle school and high school students in the Devil Pups program may seem today, since the program targeted at-risk youth, there is no way to measure whether it encouraged violence or taught young men how to restrain it. But what of the unnamed Freedom Train guard, whose insult is, in some ways, the most puzzling episode in this chapter? Whether one calls this an incident of violent behavior or just a moment of cruelty is less important than what motivated it in the first place. Why would a Marine, who was presumably invested in narratives of toughness and stoicism, lash out at a young boy who adopted such narratives for himself by refusing special treatment? It is possible that the Marine's remark was just a poorly chosen joke, one appropriate for a fellow Marine on crutches but not a young boy. Or perhaps the technical sergeant, who was almost certainly a combat veteran given his rank and the year, had been drinking on duty for reasons similar to Dick Bahr's or Ed Goricki's: to cope with memories of a war that he could not leave behind. If so, he may have found it difficult even to talk to an amputee. Perhaps his offer of help was a small attempt to assuage a feeling of guilt long buried, and when he was rebuffed, he felt the rejection keenly. If this was the case, it makes sense that when hurt he would attack, for the culture of the Marine Corps, both in and out of combat, had taught him that very tactic.

The two extremes of abuse presented in this chapter—an unkind word by a Freedom Train guard, on one hand, and the horrible violence in the Goricki home, on the other—give a fuller answer to the question posed by Mrs. Sorensen back in 1950. Some Marines could not "discard their Marine nature like they would take off a coat," and that nature brought liabilities as well as the benefits that earlier chapters have discussed.[99] The default programs Marines learned in the Corps—admitting no weakness, attacking when challenged, and using alcohol and violence to resolve or avoid conflicts—came home with them, sometimes with tragic consequences. The cultural indoctrination that served them so well inside the Corps also reduced their ability to operate outside of it. Despite the claims of the Commandant, the Marine Corps did *not* always build men into whose hands the public could entrust the nation's affairs. Its primary obligation was to build warriors, men whose primary impetus in situations of conflict was to be "first to fight."

Throughout the 1950s, the Corps both celebrated that aggressive spirit and endeavored to reframe it using two complementary cultural operations. To those who worried that the nation lacked strength, they continued to present themselves as hardened fighters who kept the nation safe from invasion. To those less concerned with national security, they emphasized the Marines' domestic utility, presenting the Corps as the solution to both juvenile delinquency and flagging masculinity. If not properly trained, they suggested, America's boys might either languish in softness or rage out of control. The Marine Corps was "downright good for the manhood of our country" because it could steer boys between these two extremes, making them manly and tough, yet able to control their aggression. This strategy grew only more effective as the Cold War heated up. As issues of gender and family were written into conversations about citizenship and national security, the Marine Corps appropriated those topics and turned them to their own purposes.

The records of civilians' contact with the Corps in this period suggest that the Marines' cultural operations worked. While some women protested the violence, most Americans tolerated (and in some cases celebrated) it as a necessary component of societal health and national security. Particularly in the late 1950s, as fears over the

Soviets' supposed nuclear advantage grew, the Marines' arguments about toughness seemed increasingly apt. Even after the Ribbon Creek incident and subsequent recruit abuse trials, worries that recruit training was growing too easy outnumbered complaints. As guided morals became as important as guided missiles, the Marine Corps succeeded in presenting itself as experts in both.

6 Rise of the Amphibious Force-in-Readiness

When someone makes a move
Of which we don't approve,
Who is it that always intervenes?
U.N. and O.A.S.,
They have their place, I guess,
But first, send the Marines!

—Tom Lehrer, "Send the Marines," 1965

In 1946, officers at the Air University in Montgomery, Alabama, asked their Marine liaison to give a lecture on the Marine Corps' bureaucracy and organizational structure. Lieutenant Colonel Wilburt S. "Bigfoot" Brown retorted that the Marine Corps had no organizational structure. Rather, he joked, the Marines "stayed in a continual state of disorganization so they could be ready for anything."[1]

In a sense, Colonel Brown's comment was not far from the truth. From the mid-1930s through the end of World War II, the Corps had focused all its thinking and training on one type of military operation: amphibious assaults. In the two decades after the war, they kept this mission and added a host of others: occupation duty in China, disaster relief in Europe, Africa, and Asia, civilian evacuations in Egypt and Japan, peacekeeping and stabilization operations in Lebanon and the Dominican Republic, and major combat operations in Korea and Vietnam. They also began providing Marine security guards to U.S. embassies abroad, served as advisors to foreign corps of marines throughout Asia, and created the nation's first helicopter squadron. At a time when the other services became increasingly specialized, the Corps thrived by being generalists, fighting for an increased role in every type of military operation, no matter how small. This diversification may have seemed like a "continual state of disorganization," but it was farsighted nonetheless. As the need for more diverse military capabilities rose throughout the early Cold War, the Marines proved repeatedly that with the Navy's help, they could react more quickly than the Army and Air Force and provide the president more military options for foreign policy and national defense.

The Corps' cognitive style shaped this adaptation, the Marines' strategic vision, and, in turn, U.S. military capabilities and American foreign policy in the early Cold War. For even though the Corps had almost no role in formulating Cold War military strategy, of all the armed services, it adapted quickest to the type of military operations that the Cold War would bring. While the other services all focused on the most dangerous possible future scenario, the Marines focused on the most likely ones and built multipurpose forces to respond to them. Because of its prescience, the Corps' capabilities expanded yet again, this time across the oceans of the world.

Few Americans today give much thought to the global military networks the United States created in the wake of World War II. Those who do usually think of the string of military bases in Europe and Asia, or the nation's nuclear networks: the broad arrays of sensors, missiles, bombers, and computers that became the most visible symbols of the Cold War.[2] But while those systems succeeded in deterring a total war with the Soviet Union, they played only a small role in the vast majority of military operations occurring between 1947 and 1991. Nuclear weapons proved unusable in Korea and Vietnam and were even more ill-suited to the numerous smaller contingency operations occurring within a hundred miles of a coastline. Those operations depended mostly on maritime networks, namely, the Navy ships that moved forces, equipment, and amphibious military capabilities around the world when crises erupted unexpectedly. The Marines saw the need for such forces in the first year of the Cold War. They subsequently designed and built the nation's most responsive tool for projecting power around the globe: the Marine Air-Ground Task Forces (MAGTFs), known more generally as the amphibious force-in-readiness.

The Marine Corps' ideas about itself, warfare, and the other services are part of the reason the force-in-readiness emerged. Marines strayed from the strategic path hewed by the other services because they feared that doing otherwise would lead to their abolition. Extreme distrust of outsiders spurred them to action; entrenched ideas about technology and bureaucracy shaped the direction they took. Their sense of being surrounded and under threat increased their cohesion and created the necessary conditions for innovation. These cultural traits helped them see the future clearly and adapt to it quickly.

COLD WAR MILITARY OPERATIONS AND THE SPECTRUM OF CONFLICT

In the first three decades of the Cold War, there were two major wars and 215 discrete incidents in which the President used the military in situations short of war. Signaling resolve with nuclear weapons (by repositioning nuclear forces or raising alert levels) occurred nineteen times, constituting just 8 percent of the total incidents. Marine Corps ground combat forces, by comparison, participated in between seventy-seven and ninety-one incidents. Army ground forces (sometimes acting in concert with Marine forces) participated in thirty-nine. Thus, while the Marines never exceeded 9 percent of the total armed forces in this period, the President used them in 35 to 40 percent of all military incidents and in four-fifths of the incidents requiring ground forces. In all but six incidents, the Marines deployed from the Navy's amphibious ships.[3]

The types of military operations the Marines performed are also relevant. Military planners use the terms "range of military operations" or "spectrum of conflict" to plot military missions on a graph from high intensity to low. The largest, most violent operations—such as nuclear and major theater wars—occupy the high-intensity end of the spectrum; peacekeeping and humanitarian operations are some of the missions occupying the low end. In the first two decades of the Cold War, the Marine Corps operated across the entire spectrum of conflict. They performed high-intensity conventional operations in Korea and mid-intensity counterinsurgency operations in Vietnam. At the lowest end of the conflict spectrum, they conducted humanitarian assistance and disaster relief in Greece (1953), Spain (1957), Ceylon (1958), Congo (1961), Turkey (1961), and British Honduras (1961). In concert with the Navy, they performed shows of force off the coasts of Indonesia (1957) and the Dominican Republic (1961), and in Thailand (1962). The Navy and Marines evacuated 300,000 refugees from North Vietnam to South Vietnam in 1955 and 2,000 civilians from Egypt during the 1956 Suez crisis. In the 1958 Lebanon intervention, the Corps put 6,000 Marines ashore complete with tanks, artillery, and air support, all in a matter of hours. Another 25,000 put to sea during the Cuban Missile Crisis, and in the 1965 invasion of the Dominican Republic, the Corps put 2,000 Marines ashore before the first Army airborne units even left the United States.[4]

These events are part of a pattern of conflict that the Marines predicted as early as 1947. Eschewing the other services' preoccupation with nuclear weapons, the Marines designed and deployed, with somewhat reluctant help from the Navy, a global network of sea-based task forces that could provide tailored military forces—in a matter of days and, later, hours—in response to security crises both large and small. More important, the Marines designed their task forces to be scalable: commanders could dial up or dial down the capabilities and degree of violence as the situation deteriorated or improved. This rheostatic, sea-based force-in-readiness remains the Corps' principal contribution to national defense today.

Neither the President nor the three larger services showed much interest in the Marines' plans for an amphibious force-in-readiness when the Cold War started. All were focused instead on a potential nuclear war with the Soviet Union. The Marines saw things differently. They never completely disregarded nuclear warfare, but on balance, they had a more nuanced vision of the role of the military in foreign affairs. They viewed the Cold War strategy of containment more broadly, arguing that the armed forces should actively support foreign policy rather than merely react violently when diplomacy failed. Such active support required a more robust notion of what the military calls "power projection," one that projected men, resources, and capabilities overseas in addition to missiles, bombers, and violence. This expanded role for the military in the conduct of foreign affairs would only grow more accepted as the Cold War progressed. And while the rise of the amphibious force-in-readiness had largely salutary effects for the Marine Corps, its effects on the nation and the world have been much more ambiguous. For as the Marines' short-of-war military capabilities increased, so too did the President's willingness to use the Corps in conflicts peripheral to U.S. national security. What former secretary of defense Robert M. Gates has called a "creeping militarization of foreign policy" has its roots in the Cold War.[5] The rise of the amphibious force-in-readiness is part of that militarization.

"NUKES WITH EVERYTHING": THE EARLY COLD WAR STRATEGIC CONSENSUS

Using the Marine Corps as a sea-based force-in-readiness was neither predetermined nor even likely in the first years of the Cold War. In the late 1940s, the greatest threat to U.S. interests was the Soviets' ability to conquer Western Europe in a land campaign. If that war came, American military strategists decided, the U.S. Air Force would initiate an atomic blitz. The Navy would then evacuate forces from Europe and defend key shipping lanes. Following a period of mobilization, the Army would retake Europe in a ground campaign. The only role for the Marine Corps' light, amphibious forces in the first emergency war plan was peripheral defense. They would occupy Iceland and the Azores and evacuate civilians from the Middle East.[6]

Since the Marines had no voice in war planning or on the Joint Chiefs of Staff, they could do nothing to increase their responsibilities.

Once the Soviets obtained nuclear weapons in 1949, the Marine Corps seemed even less relevant—a point the Army made repeatedly in the unification fights. Amphibious landings required ships to converge near a hostile shore and remain in place while discharging and supporting the landing forces. If the enemy used nuclear weapons, whole waves of troops would be vaporized and the fleet would be either sunk or irradiated. This fact convinced the Navy to shift its focus away from amphibious operations and toward nuclear warfare.[7]

As the Soviets' nuclear capabilities grew, so too did the American services' fascination with nuclear technologies. The Army, Navy, and Air Force all jockeyed for nuclear missions, for research dollars, and even, it would seem, for the most heroic names for the new weapons. The Air Force developed the Matador, Thor, and Atlas missile programs; the Army countered with the Jupiter and Hercules missiles. The Navy developed the less mythically named Regulus and Polaris missiles but also built nuclear-powered submarines, aircraft carriers, cruisers, and frigates. The Navy's motto in the early Cold War, joked one naval historian, seemed to be "nukes with everything."[8]

These turf wars over nuclear weapons are less important for the divisions they reveal between the services than for the shared assumptions animating them. In fact, the three larger services competed for nuclear missions precisely because they all agreed on the basic outlines of Cold War conflict. Throughout the latter part of the 1940s and the early 1950s, there was a strategic consensus in Army, Navy, and Air Force that any future war would be nuclear and that the most useful military tools were the most violent ones. By building a redundant, responsive nuclear capability, they believed the military would be both ready for war and able to keep the peace.

Events soon proved these assumptions false. The Korean War was the first piece of evidence that Cold War conflict would not necessarily be nuclear and that readiness required on-call forces able to deploy and fight almost immediately. Later crises in the Middle East,

Southeast Asia, and the Caribbean gave further evidence that America could not protect its interests in the Cold War through the threat of nuclear annihilation alone. The Army, Navy, and Air Force were all slow to take the lesson. The overwhelming consensus regarding Korea in the larger services was that it was an aberration, one offering no lessons for the types of conflict to come. Instead of designing forces for such conflicts, strategists from the larger services argued, the United States should simply avoid limited non-nuclear wars altogether.[9] While the Army would gradually move away from this position after 1954, it continued to make nuclear warfare its priority in training, research and development, and force design throughout the 1950s. Consequently, throughout the early Cold War, the Army, Navy, and Air Force all focused on a single, apocalyptic scenario but ignored countless others that were more likely, if less destructive.

President Dwight D. Eisenhower was a major part of the reason why. Convinced that even small-scale contingency operations could quickly escalate out of control, the President decided the best way to prevent war was to make every conflict with the Soviets a choice between negotiation and annihilation. His strategy of massive retaliation forced all disputes onto the highest end of the conflict spectrum, which, he reasoned correctly, would both reduce defense spending and limit his opponents' risk taking.[10] To make the nuclear deterrent credible, Eisenhower ordered the development of tactical nuclear weapons—small warheads mounted on mines, rockets, and artillery rounds for use in a ground campaign. Under Eisenhower, the services' nuclear arsenals grew from 1,161 nuclear weapons in 1953 to more than 12,000 in 1959. To decrease defense costs, Eisenhower cut manpower in the conventional forces. The Army suffered the worst cuts; the Marine Corps, thanks to its friends in Congress, fared far better. But while Eisenhower's reliance on the nuclear deterrent did contain the Soviets, it did little to control other actors on the Cold War periphery. Short-of-war military incidents increased steadily throughout Eisenhower's presidency, from three incidents in 1953 to eleven in 1959. (They would peak in the Johnson administration at twenty incidents per year.) Among these were several major incidents in which nuclear weapons were useless: the 1956 Suez crisis, the 1958 Lebanon landing, and later, destabilization in several states in Southeast Asia and the Caribbean. In these and in countless smaller operations, the larger services' focus on nuclear warfare left them ill-equipped and poorly trained to respond.[11]

This rise in non-nuclear crises is partially attributable to the strange paradox of nuclear weapons. By effectively deterring an all-out general war, nuclear weapons increased the likelihood of conflicts in which they could not be used: the smaller, limited wars occurring outside Europe.[12] While Eisenhower's strategy was frugal and effective in deterring the major Communist powers, it also unbalanced the nation's military forces, making them less ready for the types of conflicts they would face in the Cold War. Throughout the 1950s, the three larger services all developed countless weapons that they could never use and failed to build forces, doctrine, and tactics that they could. By 1958, the Air Force had developed plans to drop nuclear warheads on more than 3,000 targets in the Soviet Union, but it could not provide timely transportation for the Army during the Lebanon intervention.[13] The Navy also gave short shrift to conventional capabilities but built nuclear-tipped depth charges, nuclear antisubmarine torpedoes, and nuclear antiaircraft missiles.[14] Nuclear weapons dropped from carrier planes and, later, launched from submarines gave the Navy a steady source of funding and a central role in Cold War strategy but also shifted the Navy's priorities away from the Marines and non-nuclear crises. Throughout the 1950s, argues one prominent naval historian, the Navy "prepared almost exclusively for a general war with the Soviet Union and embraced a central role for atomic weapons in that war."[15]

The Army did the same. Instead of building capable forces for limited wars, the Army developed thousands of tactical nuclear weapons, including atomic cannons, the Honest John and Little John nuclear rockets, and the Davy Crockett nuclear recoilless rifle (a weapon that most likely could not have been used safely in combat).

By 1961, research on missiles accounted for 47 percent of the Army's research and development budget; the combined funding for vehicles and aircraft totaled just 10 percent.[16] Other statistics give convincing evidence of where the Army's priorities lay in the later 1950s. Between 1958 and 1960, the Army increased the hours of instruction on nuclear warfare for its senior officers by 55 percent. The number of articles on nuclear warfare in *Military Review* grew fourfold in the second half of the 1950s compared to the first half.[17] Nor did the Army expect its emphasis on nuclear weapons to change. As historian Paul C. Jussel has argued, Army strategists in 1955 assumed that "nuclear weapons, nuclear use, and nuclear war were part and parcel of the conduct of operations for the period 1960–1970."[18] Faced with preparing three separate forces for nuclear war, conventional war, and short-of-war contingencies, the Army focused almost exclusively on the nuclear force. That decision made the creation of general-purpose forces that could function as a force-in-readiness "unattainable."[19]

Nothing shows the Army's muddled strategic vision better than the reorganization of its infantry units into "pentomic" divisions, an effort that began in 1956 and was abandoned in 1961. It was, by Army generals' own admission, a multimillion-dollar blunder.[20] Ostensibly designed for use on either a nuclear or non-nuclear battlefield, the pentomic forces were incapable of fighting effectively on either. To avoid losing thousands of men to a single atomic blast, the pentomic reorganization broke each infantry division down into five independently operating groups, which could spread out over the battlefield. Supported by nuclear artillery rounds, the independent battle groups would then storm across a battlefield still shimmering from the air-delivered atomic blitz and destroy the remaining enemy forces. Nuclear firepower would make maneuver less important; as a result, the pentomic divisions would use frontal assaults to maximize speed, which was little more than a return to the least imaginative tactics of World War I but with the added destructive capabilities of nuclear weapons.[21] "Every time I think of the . . . pentomic division,

I shudder," one Army general later commented. "Thank God we never had to go to war with it."[22]

At roughly the same time as the Army began converting to pentomic divisions, it also tried to muscle into the Marines' growing niche as a force-in-readiness. In 1958 (seven years after the Marines began designing its air-ground task forces), the Army established the Strategic Army Corps (STRAC), a four-division force designed specifically for short-of-war contingencies. But STRAC was doomed from the start. While its stated purpose was to provide forces for worldwide deployment, all four STRAC divisions were simultaneously tasked with reinforcing NATO if the Soviets attacked, thus tying them inextricably to events in Europe. Furthermore, because the Army had limited aviation assets, STRAC depended on the Air Force for transportation, which caused persistent friction and problems. Finally, the political and logistical constraints of using foreign airspace and airports to bring in forces created endless headaches for the Army and the State Department.[23]

Budget cuts soon forced STRAC to reduce its manpower from four divisions to three, and quarrels with the Air Force caused regular transportation problems. The Pentagon merged STRAC into another command in 1961. STRAC forces participated in only one major contingency operation before Vietnam: the 1965 intervention in the Dominican Republic, where their performance was less than ideal. STRAC's mission withered further during Vietnam, and by the early 1980s, the idea of "specially trained 'short-of-war' formations" in the Army "had clearly fallen by the wayside."[24]

Historian Samuel P. Huntington has argued that during Eisenhower's first term, "the army emerged as the principal supporter of limited war programs."[25] In fact, the Marines were. While the Army began voicing objections to the nation's overreliance on nuclear weapons in the mid-1950s, it never translated its theoretical dissatisfaction into a workable force-in-readiness capability. The Marine Corps did. Because the Marines never fell under the spell of nuclear weapons, they were the only service focused seriously on non-nuclear contingencies from the outset of the Cold War. This focus helped the Corps corner the market on rapid-response operations even after the Army and Air Force began recognizing their growing frequency and importance.

THE ORIGINS OF THE AMPHIBIOUS FORCE-IN-READINESS

The notion of a scalable, highly mobile reaction force was not new in the first years of the Cold War, but it was not particularly popular. George F. Kennan called for the Marines to fill just such a role in 1947 and again in 1949.[26] In 1950, Paul Nitze, Kennan's successor at the State Department, also hinted at the need for a force-in-readiness when he warned in NSC-68 that the United States relied too much on atomic weapons and lacked mobile conventional forces to counter local Soviet moves.[27] These warnings fell on deaf ears. Before the Korean War broke out, President Truman was primarily concerned with limiting military spending and saw little need to expand the military's capabilities beyond its clear advantage in nuclear armaments.

Perennially concerned with institutional survival, the Marine Corps viewed atomic weapons as more of a threat than a capability. A Marine general observing the 1946 atomic tests at Bikini atoll advised the Commandant to consider atomic weapons "a very serious and urgent matter" for the Marine Corps, because they would likely render obsolete the Corps' raison d'être—amphibious operations.[28] A year later, another prominent Marine general boasted that the Corps had already reorganized itself to become a military "fire department" that could quell local conflicts short of nuclear war by arriving immediately and establishing conditions for follow-on forces if necessary.[29] In 1948, future Commandant of the Marine Corps Robert E. Cushman gave fuller voice to these ideas in an article in the *Marine Corps Gazette*:

> When local disturbances occur which it is to our interest to suppress, does anyone seriously suggest that we "atomize" the offenders, the

hapless bystanders, and the surrounding countryside? No, but we certainly can employ the Fleet and its included Fleet Marine Forces for the purpose of taking measures suited to the peacetime task, ranging from a show of force to offensive action of a limited nature as required by the local situation. Landings by Marines will surely figure largely in such naval action.[30]

The Marine Corps view, consistent throughout the Cold War, was that if left unchecked, local disturbances would escalate into larger, and possibly nuclear, conflicts. The answer, therefore, was to have a diverse set of military tools for suppressing minor disturbances in order to prevent escalation. Controlling the low end of the conflict spectrum would decrease the likelihood of operations on the high end.

Inherent in this vision was a notion of containment and strategic readiness different from that proposed by President Eisenhower or the other services. The threat of nuclear annihilation might deter the Soviets, but it would not ensure stability. Decolonization, natural disasters, and "local disturbances" required a different kind of military power projection. Instead of just delivering missiles and violence, the military needed to project *capabilities* ashore—men, equipment, and resources—and to grow, shrink, or change those capabilities as the situation required.[31] Military power, in this formulation, operated in the interstices of war and peace, bolstering foreign policy with a wide range of incentives and threats. Despite President Eisenhower's initial skepticism of this more interventionist approach, he sent the Marines ashore ten times in nine countries during his two terms, in operations ranging from disaster relief to peacekeeping and stabilization.[32]

What President Eisenhower used with reticence, President Kennedy embraced formally. And while it was a retired chief of staff of the army who popularized the term "flexible response," the animating assumption of General Maxwell D. Taylor's and Kennedy's strategy was what the Marine Corps had been saying since 1947: the nation needed small, highly mobile forces to support diplomacy with a wide range of military tools. By the time President Kennedy took office, the Marines had already built the forces that flexible response required.

The Marines' first formal enunciation of the need for a scalable force-in-readiness came in a 1948 Marine Corps Board report entitled "Organization of the Fleet Marine Force: War and Peace."[33] In it, planners broke with the conventional wisdom of all the other services by calling the likelihood of a nuclear war in the next ten years "remote."[34] Instead, they argued that "there probably will be frequent requirements during the next ten years for 'peacetime' or 'short of war' naval and military operations. These requirements will vary from a mere show of force to an assault landing of sizable forces against hostile resistance." Because the likelihood of such operations was "almost certain," the military must prepare for regular operations in "areas of unstable government, countries torn by civil wars or revolt, nations suffering economic depression [and] areas possessing great strategical importance."[35]

The Navy and Marine Corps, the report continued, were ideal for such operations. These "units provide a highly flexible, mobile and versatile means for intervention in situations short of war," it argued. "Such task forces are capable of applying every gradation of pressure from a mere show of force to the actual commitment, if necessary, of a ground force of combined arms, fully supported by aircraft and naval gunfire."[36] That same year, a force of 1,000 Marines, complete with vehicles, aircraft, and supplies, began deploying regularly to the Mediterranean aboard Navy ships. Staying afloat with the Navy for six months at a time, these Marines formed the first operational MAGTF of the Cold War. But because its air and ground elements had separate staffs and commanders, coordination was slow and its capabilities were limited.[37] In June 1950, the Corps put all air, ground, and support forces under a single commander, and the MAGTF's ability to react to changing conditions increased exponentially.[38]

The next step forward in MAGTF development came in October 1950, just months into the Korean War. Incorrectly anticipating an imminent cessation of hostilities, the commanding general of all Marine forces in the Pacific submitted a plan for a larger and more capable MAGTF that could help preserve peace in the Western Pacific. Even once the Korean War ended, he argued, "it is reasonable to assume that the overall situation in the Western Pacific will remain unstable." Situations would arise "demand[ing] the immediate dispatch of a balanced amphibious force-in-readiness" capable of performing operations extending "all the way from peaceful occupation and installation of defenses to the short-notice conduct of a full scale amphibious assault, including close air support." The study then outlined the proposed structure of the force, its training requirements, and its likely missions. The proposed MAGTF was nine times the size of the Mediterranean MAGTF created two years earlier. It would contain an infantry regiment, an artillery battalion, a tank company, engineers, and a service support element with trucks, maintenance, and supply units. The air element would contain helicopters, jets, and prop-driven planes. Total personnel numbered close to 9,000 Marines.[39]

The Corps would have to wait until 1960 before a MAGTF would float continuously in the Pacific, but the 1950 study outlined the force's composition and basic purpose.[40] It emphasized immediate readiness, not to deliver nuclear weapons, but to put men and equipment ashore for a variety of purposes. Like the 1948 study, it rejected a firm division between war and peace, and argued instead that the best way to keep peace was by arriving immediately and with a variety of tools.

The recommendations in these and other studies soon became Marine Corps policy. In January 1953, the Corps created, as a permanent unit, the First Provisional Marine Air-Ground Task Force, based in Hawaii. Three months later, the Commandant formed the Advanced Research Group to analyze problems of particular concern to the Marine Corps. The group's first task was "to develop a concept of future (within the next ten years) amphibious operations that will require maximum utilization of the Fleet Marine Forces as a mobile force-in-readiness."[41] In December 1953, the Commandant ordered the entire Second Marine Division, Second Air Wing, and assorted Force Troops—totaling roughly half the Corps' operating forces—to adopt the MAGTF organizational structure.[42] A year later, he further ordered that in all situations of training, planning, and actual operations, Marine air and ground forces "will habitually operate as a single operational command."[43] Thereafter, whenever Marines deployed outside the United States in large numbers, they did so under a single MAGTF commander who controlled the subordinate air, ground, and service support elements. One year after Korea, when the Army chief of staff was still arguing that "the day when wars had limited effects is past," the Marine Corps had built the force structure for responding to the non-nuclear, limited conflicts and contingencies that would dominate the Cold War.[44]

HELICOPTERS AND NUCLEAR WEAPONS

The Marines did not ignore nuclear weapons entirely; in fact, they stocked a small number of tactical nuclear weapons and conducted some nuclear training. However, the principal technology they developed for nuclear combat—the helicopter—proved most useful for the non-nuclear battlefield. And even as they claimed (unconvincingly) that they could fight on a nuclear battlefield, Marine strategists also cautioned in numerous studies that limited wars were the more likely future conflicts.[45]

The Corps' primary concern with nuclear weapons was how to avoid being annihilated by them during an amphibious assault. Their proposed solution in 1946 was helicopters—a nascent technology that could then lift no more than a pilot and two passengers. If the amount of weight a helicopter could carry could be increased, the Marines reasoned, they would be able to move an entire division from ship to shore without exposing the fleet to nuclear attack.[46] In

1947, they created the nation's first experimental helicopter squadron (HMX-1, which now operates the fleet of Marine One helicopters for the President of the United States) and authored the first tentative doctrine for using helicopters in an amphibious assault.[47] In Korea, they were the first service to use helicopters to transport and resupply combat troops. When Army officers authored their service's first doctrine for employing helicopters, they copied much of it from the Marines.[48]

The helicopter never proved the panacea for nuclear assaults that the Corps originally envisioned it to be. By 1956, the most modern helicopters still could not lift the weight the Marines required, and the Navy's reticence in purchasing them and building helicopter-capable ships posed other problems. As a result, the Corps abandoned the idea of an all-helicopter division assault in 1957. However, the Marines' efforts to research and develop helicopters had not been in vain as the Army's pentomic divisions were. As the amount of weight they could lift increased, helicopters became one of the Cold War military's most important tools of power projection. Freed from the constraints of runways, basing rights, and even landing beaches, helicopters could move men and equipment from ship to shore much quicker than landing craft, and also could transport forces deep inland. They could hop over formidable terrain, give commanders better observation of the battlefield, and distribute military assets in ways unimaginable in World War II. In addition to projecting military power, helicopters could also evacuate civilians, rescue the wounded, and deliver water, food, and humanitarian aid. While the Marines were not the only service working to develop helicopters in the early Cold War, they were routinely ahead of their counterparts in the other services. In the end, the technologies that resulted have proved far more useful—to both militaries and civilians—than the other services' thousands of nuclear weapons.[49]

Even as the Corps dabbled in nuclear conflict, when the time came to choose between the nuclear and conventional missions, the Corps correctly chose the latter. The 1956 Hogaboom Board prompted a complete reorganization of the Marine Corps' operating forces and explicitly privileged low- and mid-intensity conflicts over nuclear warfare.[50] Coming at the very moment when the Army was transitioning to the ill-fated pentomic divisions, the Corps' new structure would remain virtually unchanged for the remainder of the Cold War.

Earlier studies in 1948 and 1955 had already named limited war as the most likely future conflict; the Hogaboom Board report endorsed those findings and went beyond them.[51] It warned again that nuclear war with the Soviet Union was unlikely, and that the Corps' greatest utility lay in the proxy wars and contingency operations that would occur on the Cold War periphery. To prepare the Marine Corps for those missions, the board made the infantry division lighter, decreased the personnel in the division headquarters, and removed the tank battalion and heavy artillery. No longer would the Corps try to land a full division via helicopter; instead, should Marine forces go ashore against a nuclear-armed foe, most of the troops would be delivered by landing craft and amphibious tractors, much as they had been in World War II and Korea. The Hogaboom Board also transferred the Corps' "Honest John" nuclear-capable rockets out of the infantry divisions in the expectation that their use was unlikely. The Marine Corps' operating forces were now far more mobile, streamlined, and adaptive but less capable in high-intensity combat and extremely vulnerable in a nuclear assault.

Thus, by the time President Kennedy took office, the Marine Corps had fully implemented a concept it had been developing since the first year of the Cold War. MAGTFs operated in three oceans, with two providing a continuous presence in the Mediterranean and Western Pacific, and a third operating sporadically in the Caribbean. In 1962, Marine Corps Order 3120.3, "Organization of Marine Air-Ground Task Forces," made only minor changes to the force structure and gave the MAGTFs the names they use today: Marine Expeditionary Units (MEUs), organized around a reinforced infantry battalion; Marine Expeditionary Brigades (MEBs), built around a regiment; and Marine Expeditionary Forces (MEFs), built around a division.[52] Each was designed for limited, independent operations but could also be absorbed into the next-larger MAGTF should operations escalate. As short-of-war incidents increased in the 1960s, the Marines' innovations proved both useful and prescient.

USING THE FORCE-IN-READINESS

Once the MAGTFs became operational, the very presidents who had been reluctant to develop them sent them into action repeatedly. The first time the Marines assembled a reinforced regiment for Korea in 1950, they did it in eleven days. During the Cuban Missile Crisis, they put four times as many troops to sea in just two weeks. In the 1958 Lebanon intervention and the 1965 invasion of the Dominican Republic, the Marines put their first waves ashore within twenty-four hours of receiving their orders.

In these and other contingencies, the Marine Corps operated throughout the globe and across the range of military operations. They gave support to hurricane, flood, famine, and earthquake victims on three different continents and several island nations. When Great Britain, France, and Israel launched a surprise attack on the Suez Canal in 1956, a battalion of Marines landed the next day and evacuated more than 2,000 civilians.[53] In 1962, President Kennedy sent 3,500 Marines into Thailand to deter Communist forces in neighboring Laos.[54] Other Marines toured Africa and South America with the Navy on goodwill tours. What had been a highly specialized amphibious assault force in World War II was now a military jack-of-all-trades that helped assure allies, bolster security partnerships, evacuate civilians, and react promptly to chaotic events on the Cold War periphery.

Military historians have largely ignored these limited military interventions because they involved relatively small numbers of forces. But the three largest operations—the 1958 Lebanon intervention, the Cuban Missile Crisis, and the 1965 invasion of the Dominican Republic—each involved several thousand troops. These interventions also cemented the Corps' new role in national defense, making them the force of choice for short-of-war contingencies.

On July 14, 1958, following a coup in Iraq, Lebanese president Camille Chamoun announced that his government could fall to pro-Egyptian and Syrian rebels if an American peacekeeping force did

"We Get Around," a recruiting poster from the late 1950s, marks the Marines' transformation from an amphibious assault force to an amphibious force-in-readiness. (United States Marine Corps)

not arrive in the next two days.[55] Although the Army and Air Force had already designated specific units for such a contingency, no force would have landed inside the forty-eight-hour time line had it not been for the Marines. The first Marines hit the beach within fifteen hours of receiving their orders; when the operation began, four companies were ashore within twenty minutes. A second battalion landed a day later, and after five days there were almost 6,000 Marines in Lebanon, complete with helicopters, tanks, and artillery. Though the Army was ordered to land twenty-four hours after the first Marines hit the beach, problems delayed the arrival for four days. All 6,000 Marines were ashore before the first Army airborne units arrived in Lebanon.

The Marine landing was not perfect: tanks arrived without sufficient ammunition, and several landing craft got stuck on a sandbar.[56] However, the Army's troubles at this and other interventions were far more debilitating, despite the fact that it had been planning for a possible contingency operation in the Levant for over two years.[57] What worked on paper failed in practice. Different Army units drew up separate plans for the deployment; coordination with the Air Force was almost nonexistent. The day of the alert, the deploying unit still had not received an Air Force liaison or been told what type of planes they would use. The 1,500 men of Force Alpha— the first unit designated to deploy—had to be swapped out so that they could participate in an exercise. Greece and Austria denied the Air Force overflight rights; congestion at the airport in Turkey caused other problems, and when the Army units finally arrived at the airport in Beirut, they could not find a forklift to unload their planes.[58] A final complication ensued when the Navy requested that the Army send its Honest John rockets without nuclear warheads because of the political sensitivity of the weapons. The Army resisted, but in the end, the Joint Chiefs of Staff directed that no nuclear weapons be landed in Lebanon.[59]

The Air Force's own attempt at a force-in-readiness—the Composite Air Strike Force (CASF)—had even more problems. Orders called for the first CASF planes to arrive in Turkey within forty-eight hours of receiving the alert. Less than half the planes arrived within the forty-eight-hour window, and five days passed before the entire force was on the ground. When the first squadron of fighters launched, one plane crashed, seven aborted, and only four arrived in Turkey on time. Obstructions on runways, refueling difficulties, incomplete qualifications for the crews, and last-minute substitutions caused other problems, as did additional airspace restrictions imposed by Israel and Saudi Arabia. Finally, had the Air Force encountered any resistance when it flew into Lebanon, the results might have been disastrous, as the majority of the air crews "lacked experience in conventional weapons delivery." Few had any strafing experience or had ever launched rockets or dropped conventional bombs. However, nearly all the crews were qualified to drop nuclear weapons.[60]

The Army's and Air Force's troubles during the Lebanon operation give a good picture of those services' preparations for nonnuclear operations in the late 1950s. While both services had forces designated for such operations, neither could respond as effectively as the Navy and Marine Corps. Despite extensive and detailed planning, Army and Air Force units were slowed by bureaucratic difficulties and lacked basic equipment and sound deployment procedures. Their services' emphasis on nuclear weapons only further complicated operations.

Lebanon settled whatever debate remained over the utility of the Marine Corps as a force-in-readiness. In the following years, the Corps took on an even more central role in operations requiring the immediate deployment of ground forces. The Cuban Missile Crisis was the largest such operation to date; there, the Corps put a full Marine Expeditionary Force of 25,000 Marines to sea in less than two weeks. When the first Battalion Landing Team was alerted for deployment to Cuba, it was ready in twelve hours.[61] The President activated a Marine Expeditionary Brigade of 6,200 Marines five days later with orders to depart within ninety-six hours. They left ahead of schedule. All of the Marines' air assets arrived on station quicker than the operation order required. Eleven days after the naval quarantine of Cuba began, more than 25,000 Marines were at Guantánamo Bay, Cuba, or en route with supplies and equipment for fifteen days of sustained combat.[62] This response was almost three times quicker than the 1950 division activation for Korea and included more air assets and combat service support. However, the Corps' emphasis on the lower end of the conflict spectrum was not without risk. Had the Cubans used nuclear weapons against the Marines, the Joint Chiefs of Staff estimated that the Corps would have suffered 8,000 casualties.[63]

Nothing demonstrated the scalable nature of the MAGTFs better than the 1965 intervention in the Dominican Republic. When a military coup prompted widespread revolt and fighting in the tiny Caribbean nation, the President ordered the Marines ashore to protect American citizens. The Corps moved more than 500 Marines from ship to shore by helicopter in just five hours and evacuated almost 700 civilians. When the violence escalated, 1,500 more went ashore with mechanized vehicles and tanks while the Army's airborne forces were still preparing to deploy. Once the President changed the mission from evacuating civilians to stabilizing the country, the Corps increased its presence again, eventually deploying an entire Marine Expeditionary Brigade of 8,000 Marines with their own helicopters and fighter aircraft.[64]

The Army's 82nd Airborne Division would eventually provide the majority of forces for the Dominican intervention, but they suffered many of the same problems experienced in Lebanon. Chief among these were an inflexible bureaucracy and poor coordination. When the alert order first reached the 82nd Airborne Division, hours of delay ensued because the alert had not come through the proper channels.[65] The numerous layers of command between the President and the deploying forces created confusion and persistent friction. An ongoing Army–Air Force military exercise delayed the Army's departure, partly because a general initially refused to cancel a parachute demonstration. The Army's plans for the Dominican intervention still used the old pentomic division configuration (which should have been discarded four years earlier), forcing Army logisticians to rewrite lists of units and equipment when they should have been loading both on planes. When the troops landed at the San Isidro airport, they once again lacked the basic tools for unloading and derigging their equipment. The men hacked the tough nylon parachute rigging apart with axes and offloaded their gear by hand, which damaged some of the airplanes and exhausted everyone involved.[66]

Just before the Army and Marine forces began stabilizing the Dominican Republic, the United States began its long, difficult ground war in Vietnam. On March 8, 1965, a Marine Battalion Landing Team splashed across the beaches of Da Nang, providing the first nonadvisory ground forces of the Vietnam War. Initially deployed to provide airfield security, the Marine forces would grow to a reinforced division and air wing of 25,000 by the end of the summer.

Even though many historians now consider the costly attempt to stabilize Vietnam with military forces a mistake, the Marines' force-in-readiness gave President Johnson what he and all subsequent Presidents have wanted and continued to use: a wider variety of military tools for communicating America's intentions, commitments, and demands to friends and adversaries alike.[67] To do this in the nuclear era, the military required something the earliest proponents of containment had argued for but which only the Marines produced: "vertical flexibility"—the ability to move rapidly up and down the spectrum of conflict and to provide a targeted force for everything from disaster relief to a full-scale invasion.[68] President Eisenhower initially opposed this militarization of U.S. foreign policy, arguing that increasing capabilities at the low end of the conflict spectrum would only encourage the use of such forces. Vietnam may have validated this concern, but few presidents since have heeded Eisenhower's warning. Since its inception, the amphibious force-in-readiness has seen its utility grow steadily, even after the Soviet Union declined and collapsed.

While the Navy and Marine Corps could perform some short-of-war contingency operations even before the development of MAGTFs, the amphibious force-in-readiness was nonetheless a new capability. With the development of combined air-ground teams, helicopters, and streamlined planning procedures, the Navy and Marine Corps could now project military power quicker and deeper onto land than previous amphibious operations had allowed. More important, they could tailor their forces and equipment and grow or shrink their capabilities as the situation required. This expanded the President's range of options, allowing him to use military forces more often and in more diverse ways. By the start of the Kennedy administration, and increasingly under President Johnson, active military intervention on the Cold War periphery had become a habitual practice. The Marines' force-in-readiness was a fundamental enabler of that habit.

CULTURAL FOUNDATIONS OF THE AMPHIBIOUS FORCE-IN-READINESS

The amphibious force-in-readiness did not materialize by accident. It emerged from the Marines' service culture, and in particular from their fear of institutional abolition and their skepticism of nuclear weapons and related technologies. Far more than the other services, the Marines resisted the consensus about a coming nuclear war. Even as they experimented with nuclear tactics, they remained deeply ambivalent about the weapons themselves, and resented the increased specialization, bureaucracy, and scientific mind-set that such weapons brought to conflict. These cultural components did not dictate the Corps' path in the Cold War—war plans, budgets, and interservice politics mattered too—but they helped push the Corps toward non-nuclear operations, lower-intensity combat, and the innovative organizational structure of the MAGTF.

It may seem counterintuitive that the Marines' culture would affect their movement away from high-intensity combat. After all, an institution's culture grows out of its members' shared experiences, and almost all Marines' practical knowledge of warfare in the early Cold War came from the large, high-intensity operations of World

War II and Korea. The memory and legacy of these two wars pervaded the culture of the Corps in the 1950s, establishing a common set of assumptions about warfare and the Marines' role in it. Chief among these was the idea that the Marines belonged on the *highest* end of the conflict spectrum—that their greatest added value to national defense was their sheer toughness and ability to prevail in the most violent situations. Disaster relief, civilian evacuations and peacekeeping, should not have been congruous with this understanding of warfare.

It was not only the legacies of World War II and Korea that should have hindered their progress. Other cultural traits described in the previous pages should have further committed the Corps to a vision of future warfare that looked like the past. Compared to the other services, the Marines had far stricter discipline and greater investment in rank and status hierarchies—hardly traits that should have promoted innovation or unconventional thinking. Their culture's deep adherence to tradition and emphasis on history should have been additional liabilities. How could an institution so firmly rooted in the past see the future so clearly?

The Marines were farsighted and innovative because deep ideological strains drove them to be so. The most important of these was a persistent mistrust of the other services and the President. This fear did not only exist at the highest levels of the Corps leadership. It was ubiquitous. From generals to privates, the Marines drew strength from the notion that they were persecuted by the other, larger services. Enlisted contributors to the *Gazette* warned that "our Corps is fighting for its life."[69] Marine Corps historians and public relations experts recorded every slight against the Corps and forwarded copies to newspapers and their friends in Congress.[70] Marine generals believed the Joint Chiefs of Staff purposely designed early war plans not only to defend the nation but also to dismantle the Corps.[71] Throughout the ranks, there was agreement that the Corps "is, and always has been, a David-like fighting unit that stands in readiness to engage Goliath-like enemies."[72] More often than not, the Goliath was neither the Soviets nor Communists worldwide. It was the other services.

Most important, the senior members of the very boards and study groups that drove the Corps' doctrinal innovations shared these views. In the Commandant's inner circles (the members of the Hogaboom Board, the Chowder Society, the Policy Analysis Division, and the Advanced Research Group), the very officers adapting the Corps to the force-in-readiness mission did so explicitly as a way "to protect the Marine Corps from the depredations of the other services."[73] Brigadier General Samuel Shaw, a Chowder Society member and former director of the Policy Analysis Division, believed the Corps was "the little man in a barroom brawl [that must] tolerate nothing that hurts the Corps."[74] This was different—in degree, if not in substance—from what motivated the other services. The Army pursued "better combat efficiency," Brigadier General Don Hittle later remarked. "With us, it was something much more deep. It became really an article of faith that they were trying to destroy us."[75]

This sense of persecution had several effects on the Corps' adaptation and innovation in the early Cold War. First, it created cohesion and minimized extended debates over the value of change. With something constantly threatening the Corps, there was little room for the intraservice factionalism that plagued the larger services. The pages of the Army's *Infantry Journal* and *Combat Forces Journal* are rife with such intraservice debates over, among other things, whether the infantry should have special uniforms, who should rate the Combat Infantrymen's Badge, and which units should receive combat pay.[76] Disputes between the different ship and airplane communities created regular friction within the Navy and Air Force.[77] While there was some intraservice friction inside the Marine Corps, it was noticeably less.[78] A firm belief that outsiders were threatening the future of their service kept Marines imbued with what one called "the necessary spiritual and mental cohesion" to present a unified front to their rivals.[79]

Fears of encroaching outsiders also kept the Marines' love of tradition in perspective and allowed new ideas to move up and down the chain of command. For all their attention to the past, the Marines were remarkably open to change in the early Cold War. They not only changed their service's mission but also abolished certain ranks and uniform items, created new units, and completely reorganized both the operating forces and the staff structure at Headquarters Marine Corps.[80] While celebrations of tradition were regular features in their service journals, so too were warnings of the dangers of relying too heavily on it.[81] When tradition-obsessed officers argued that too much change threatened the survival of the Corps, more-junior Marines acknowledged the threat but disputed the solution.[82] "Right now, our Corps is fighting for its life. Our most lethal weapon in this fight [against the other services] is the proof that we are ready to accept the challenge of every changing modernization," wrote a sergeant in response to a lieutenant colonel's article in the *Marine Corps Gazette*. "We can tear ourselves away from the 'Old Corps' way of doing things and keep our Marine Corps always on the advance. This can only be done by accepting new rules, customs, and traditions and placing the old ones carefully under museum glass to be viewed on Marine Corps birthdays, remembered and respected."[83]

Besides soliciting ideas from junior Marines and tolerating dissent, the Corps also returned to the Chowder Society's tactics of spying and stealing information from the other services. As one of the Corps' directors of Research and Development explained, "We had liaison officers everywhere. We picked their [the other services'] pockets blind all the time. We would steal more ideas as fast as we could go. If they were not smart enough to do it to us, that was their fault."[84]

The Army had a harder time departing from the status quo and encouraging innovation to rise from the ranks. "The loneliest man in the military is the man with the new idea," complained an Army colonel in 1959. The "best ideas don't reach fruition through command channels. The very nature of our military relationship actively works against radically new ideas." The Army needed "an organizational climate where individuals feel motivated to think creatively," the colonel continued, but the Army's culture was openly hostile to creativity. "The single concept of 'you must go through channels' ever present at all levels in the military, is perhaps the greatest single barrier to effectiveness and efficiency of management that was ever self-inflicted by man."[85] The Army's difficulties with official channels in the Lebanon and Dominican Republic interventions would confirm the colonel's warning.

Part of the Army's problem was its size. Being so much larger than the Marine Corps, the Army had multiple layers of command, each imposing its own desire for control and information on the lower units. An Army battalion staff entering combat might find itself drafting reports for its regiment, division, and corps, and even for the Army General Staff. But this problem of size was aggravated by the fact that the Army took few steps to lessen its bureaucracy. "Each general and special staff officer all the way down the line tries to amplify and expand his own department," complained one battalion commander in 1942. "We are actually swamped with typed and mimeographed literature. . . . I have had six clerks busy day and night since we received our typewriters."[86] As Cold War technology made the military more specialized and data-oriented, these problems only got worse. The Army required "entirely too many detailed reports," an Army general told a Marine colonel in Korea. "Staffs requiring reports down to, and including, daily patrol reports, were asinine. . . . [T]he staff must be the servant of command and not the master."[87]

Like any large organization, the Marines had bureaucracy and administration too. But unlike the Army, they were simply more likely to avoid, deride, or ignore it. From the late 1940s onward, the pages of the *Gazette* are replete with attacks against "administration zealots" and the "behemoth-like" administrative "frills" and "shackles" that prevented leaders from gaining genuine knowledge of their subordinates.[88] Chowder member and Marine historian Robert Debs Heinl was one of the most vociferous critics. As he wrote in 1949, "The weight of monolithic, impersonal, overly detailed regulations, written and enforced by career administrators does more to crush the exercise of individual discretion than any other factor in today's armed services."[89] But Heinl was not alone. Even the Commandant of the Marine Corps felt strongly enough on the subject to include it in his annual report to the secretary of the Navy: "We must not fall into the deadly habit of thinking of Marines as file jackets or machine record cards. They must not be treated or administered as a group of mysterious numbers. They are warm living men."[90] The Military Occupational Specialty (MOS) classification system, which assigned jobs to Marines according to a skill evaluation, received particularly harsh criticism. "Battles are fought with the heart, not with the head, and the 'misfit' can fight with as great an inspiration as the 'perfect choice,'" wrote one captain in 1958. "The MOS classification system is a product of the administrative mind, not the fighting mind. . . . [I]t performs no positive function at all, except to serve as a model to those who prize administrative method above all else."[91]

This distaste for "administrative method" extended to the machines that were central to it, none more so than the IBM punch card computers that sorted Marines and their skills according to different Specialization Serial Numbers (SSNs). These machines, argued Marine technophobes, not only inhibited leadership but destroyed tradition and enslaved the mind. "IBM juggernauts [are] crushing the Muster Roll Section," shrieked Heinl in 1949. They are "plunging gunnery sergeants, marine gunners, field musics, and all the other time-honored ratings [job assignments] into the Lethean anonymity of the SSN."[92] "In the age of mechanization, we have become slaves to the IBM machine," wrote another officer in 1958. "The machines dictate when and where you will be transferred and affect every aspect of a serviceman's life. It has regimented our thinking in the field of human relations."[93] Even efficiency itself came under attack. The preoccupation with "management efficiency," wrote one captain, is "the great occupational disease of military organizations."[94] It destroys initiative, substitutes management for leadership, and mistakenly tries to rationalize warfare. "The typical Marine is gone," lamented a staff sergeant in 1951, "killed by the very efficiency he strove to attain."[95]

Of course, the belief that bureaucracy, administration, and management efficiency were producing a weak-willed society of "organization men" was not limited to the Marine Corps. It was widespread in American society in the latter 1950s. It is worth noting, however, that the very text that gave society that term came from the pen of a Marine. Before William H. Whyte wrote *The Organization Man*, he served as a Marine lieutenant in World War II, and his now-classic critique of fifties culture explores in detail the same criticisms made by Marine officers. Whyte rails against the stultifying effects of bureaucracy and the misguided notion that scientific management will produce good leaders or effective corporations. He attacks assembly-line automation, administration experts, increased career specialization and classification systems.[96] He uses the Army and the Navy as examples of the dangers of conformity.[97] And although *The Organization Man* makes no explicit mention of the Marine Corps, a later work by Whyte makes clear that he saw the Corps as the precise opposite of the flaccid, bureaucratic culture he found so damaging to civilian society.[98]

At the root of the Corps' resistance to computers, automated administration, and bureaucracy were the machines that so many in the Cold War military were seduced by: nuclear weapons. And although it suffered fewer manpower cuts than the Army, the Marine Corps, more than any other service, was afraid that nuclear weapons were replacing the human element in warfare. "Atomic bombs, guided missiles, supersonic aircraft, electronic devices—these are what the public has been led to believe are the materials of modern warfare," complained one lieutenant in 1952. "Overlooked in the shouting is the basic ingredient—man, the one who must come to grips with the enemy and overcome him if victory is to be realized."[99] "The administrative demands alone of this new machine are enormous—the IBMs and the data computers haven't solved this problem," wrote another officer in 1960.[100] Similar disdain was evident in the most senior ranks of the Corps' leadership. The Marine Corps provided the best deterrent to war, the Commandant explained in 1957, because it was human, present, and visible—"like the policeman on the corner." A nuclear weapon, on the other hand "can only destroy. . . . As a deterrent, it is like the electric chair. . . . The first H-bomb exploded in war may mark the beginning of the end of civilization as we know it."[101]

One of the reasons the Corps was so uneasy with nuclear weapons was because it was a light infantry force filled with veterans of World War II and Korea—men who knew well what munitions dropped from the sky could do to the human body. "Only an aviator can ever say . . . that 'the burst of the bombs was like the unfolding of the petals of flowers,'" wrote one contributor to the *Gazette* in 1952. The infantryman finds "before his eyes only too graphic a picture of the effects of his and the enemy's marksmanship."[102] The Corps' limited tests with nuclear weapons—where troops were exposed to a nuclear blast to show they could still assault a nuclear beachhead—likely only increased their service's unease with the weapons. Even though the Marines were positioned four kilometers from the blast, the explosion still ignited trees less than 200 meters from their foxholes. "I instinctively closed my eyes as the blinding light hit," one of the Marines later reported, "yet I could still see the pebbles and small rocks around my feet. Nothing could be done to get away from it."[103]

The Marines' dystopic visions of technology and bureaucracy were all a reaction to what historian Paul N. Edwards has called the "closed world" discourse of national security—a way of viewing military conflict through the prism of computers, technology, and automated systems.[104] Brought on by the technological requirements of nuclear weapons, the closed world assumed warfare could be known, managed, and mastered through systems analysis, operational research, and precise techniques of centralized, automated control. It privileged technological management over leadership, specialists over generalists, and quantitative administrative methods over personal relationships. These assumptions dominated thinking about national defense in the 1950s and early 1960s and, in the opinion of Edwards and other scholars, contributed directly to the debacle in Vietnam.[105]

Historians tracing the cultural effects of nuclear weapons on the services have argued that the Air Force and Navy were the most enamored of the closed world and the Army the least so.[106] But even in the Army, there was regular endorsement of the closed world's core principles of specialization, quantitative methods, computers, and efficiency. The pages of *Infantry Journal* and *Combat Forces Journal* (which, of all the Army's journals, should have shown the most cultural similarity to the Marine Corps' publications) demonstrate this well. "The critics who want more shooters and fewer specialists are flying in the face of history," wrote the editors of *Combat Forces Journal* in 1952.

> The question the critics should ask is not whether we have too many specialists in uniform, but whether we have enough specialists assigned to the right units. . . . [S]imilar questions should be asked about the machines these specialists operate. Have we enough of them? . . . What other new machines do we need that scientists and engineers can produce?[107]

One year later, another officer wrote a paean to computers; called "Robot Generals," it looked hopefully toward the very future the Marine Corps feared:

> The computer may mean the maximum utilization of our manpower, by freeing many administrative and staff people for other duties. . . . In the endless struggle for military superiority, the relative speed of advancement of "robot generals" will become a vital test of military

leadership by bringing more manpower to the front lines and permitting more efficient tactics.[108]

The Army was also regularly preoccupied with quantitative methods and calculating efficiency. In the late 1940s, as Marines were deriding efficiency as a disease, authors in the *Infantry Journal* called for "further application of scientific efficiency to military methods."[109] In 1946, the journal added a regular column entitled "Science and War"; two years later, the editors opined that science should be applied "to the great human equations of war and peace" to predict which nations would become belligerent, measuring not only war potential but human anger and aggression.[110] Warfare, for the Army, was more of a science than an art, and this philosophy was even more entrenched in the more technological Navy and Air Force.

These passages from the Marines' and Army's service journals reveal a philosophical disagreement over the role of technology and bureaucracy in warfare. The Army—and to a much greater extent, the Navy and Air Force—became increasingly technophiliac, celebrating machines, centralized bureaucracies, and the closed world. Combat, to these organizations, was calculable, quantifiable, and predictable. Not so for the Marines. It was an animating assumption in the Corps—originating perhaps in the close and horrific combat of World War II and Korea—that warfare was more Dionysian than Apollonian, a fundamentally chaotic and emotion-driven activity rather than something rational, intellectual, and controllable.[111] Viewing combat as more of an art than a science pushed Marines away from technologies that strove to calculate, predict, and organize armed conflict.

This was not true everywhere in the Corps. Marine pilots loved their planes and helicopters much as Air Force pilots did; the Corps' few administrators and accountants believed deeply in the value of IBM machines and sound bureaucracy.[112] But as a service, the Marine Corps concerned itself less with trying to centralize control of information, and more with building forces and procedures that could operate with incomplete data. The Marines celebrated generalists over specialists, adaptation and improvisation over official channels and regulations. They embraced war (and interservice warfare) as fundamentally unpredictable, an activity where spirit counted as much, or more, as reason and efficiency. In this mindset, man was the principal determinant of victory, and personal relationships knit the group together in ways no IBM machine could comprehend.

Technology was not absent from this cognitive style, but it played a lesser role than in the other services. The principal focus remained the warm bonds of the family of the Corps; technology, if celebrated at all, had to be incorporated into this larger familial schema. Nowhere is this more evident than in the Corps' best-known paean to their favorite machine, "The Rifleman's Creed," written by Major General William H. Rupertus during World War II:

> This is my rifle. There are many like it, but this one is mine. My rifle is my best friend. . . . My rifle is human, even as I, because it is my life. Thus, I will learn it as a brother. I will learn its weaknesses, its strength, its parts, its accessories, its sights, and its barrel. . . . I will keep my rifle clean and ready, even as I am clean and ready. We will become part of each other.[113]

Another example, one rife with Freudian possibility, is a recruiting poster from the early 1960s, entitled "This Rifle Needs a Man!"

As these two examples demonstrate, the Marine Corps did not reject all technology—indeed, no military service would. But the Corps' particularly strong resistance to nuclear technology, administration, and bureaucracy kept it from falling into the closed-world mind-set that engulfed the other services. The Marines kept their focus on individuals and on human-centered narratives in ways the larger services did not. In the Army's imagination, military machines might produce robot generals and spreadsheets that quantified emotion. In the Marine Corps' fantasies, rifles were not machines; they were friends, brothers, and even soul mates.

The Marines' cultural attributes were more than mere character traits of their organization. They had effects on the Corps' strategic development and its role in national defense. Fear and mistrust of the other services helped the Corps overcome the conventional

"This Rifle Needs a Man," a recruiting poster from the early 1960s. Like "The Rifleman's Creed," this advertisement framed the Marines' relationship with technology within the logic of human relationships and family. (United States Marine Corps)

wisdom about Cold War conflict and to pursue a different course. Suspicion of technology and dystopic visions of push-button warfare pushed the Corps away from nuclear combat and the highest end of the conflict spectrum. Disdain of administration kept them from becoming overly specialized or prisoners of their own bureaucracy, challenges the other services struggled with throughout the Cold War. A driving fear of abolition kept the Corps energized and focused on creating a lasting niche for itself in the nation's national security architecture.

This cognitive style did not affect only the Marine Corps or the United States. It had effects throughout the globe. In the decade after World War II, the United States built a range of transnational military networks all designed to counter the Communist threat and to spread American influence around the world. While the larger services focused most of their efforts on the timely delivery of nuclear destruction, the Marines practiced power projection of a different sort. In concert with the Navy, they developed ways to deliver softer types of power ranging from aid and influence to peacekeepers and global policemen. These forces not only helped militarize American foreign policy, they became the bricks and mortar of America's Cold War empire.[114]

Of course, the Marine Corps did not make the decisions to use the force-in-readiness repeatedly in the Cold War; that responsibility rested ultimately with the President. However, more than any other service, the Marines created effective military tools for interacting with weak or struggling states, and thus increased the military's role in those interactions. The result over time was a steady blurring of the lines between war and peace, military operations and foreign relations. While many of the interventions—the disaster relief missions in particular—proved beneficial for all involved, others were more problematic. The invited intervention into Lebanon encountered few problems with the rebel forces but almost devolved into a battle between the Marines and the Lebanese Army, who were supposed to be on the same side.[115] When President Johnson ordered forces into the Dominican Republic, ostensibly to evacuate American civilians, they stayed for more than a year and encountered increasing resentment from Dominican civilians.[116] Using the military to stabilize weak states may have created partnerships between governments, but it also generated friction at lower levels. And while the Marines deserve credit for speed, efficiency, and professionalism in Lebanon and the Dominican Republic, one wonders if those operations also helped convince President Johnson and Secretary of Defense Robert McNamara that the same could be done in Vietnam.

In the end, there are a number of ironies in the Marine Corps' strategic trajectory in the period after World War II. The service that was least preoccupied with quantifying and calculating Cold War conflict had the clearest understanding of the forces needed for it. The service that was least enthusiastic about technology and machines did the most to develop the helicopter, which has outlasted the utility of most of the nuclear technologies the other services developed. The service that disdained efficiency and kept itself in a "continual state of disorganization" proved the most efficient at responding to crises. And, finally, although the Corps' innovations were undertaken primarily in the name of institutional survival, the forces that resulted have had wide-ranging effects on the nation and the world. Less than twenty years after nuclear weapons had ostensibly made the Marine Corps irrelevant, its force-in-readiness had become a principal military tool of American foreign relations and national defense.

Marines in 1965 looking back on the previous twenty-five years had good reasons for pride. The Corps had almost quadrupled in size since 1941 and had survived the attempts of two Presidents to lessen its role in national defense. Civilian allies in Hollywood and the press had orchestrated a steady stream of good publicity for the Corps, which culminated in an honorary Academy Award in 1962 for the documentary film *A Force-in-Readiness*. A robust congressional coalition had ensured the Corps' place in national defense with legislative protections; the Marines' performance in numerous short-of-war contingencies had validated Congress' actions. Most important, the Marines had proved themselves essential in two major wars and now enjoyed a reputation among the public as the most elite and rugged of the nation's armed services.

Another war had already begun. As they had in World War II, Marines would serve in Vietnam in numbers disproportionate to the other services, with almost half of the entire Marine Corps deploying to the country during the years of American involvement.[1] As in World War II and Korea, the Marines again suffered the highest casualty ratios. After ten years of fighting, 13,000 Marines had been killed and another 51,000 had been wounded, not counting post-conflict psychiatric casualties. Marines accounted for roughly a third of all American casualties in the war.[2]

The ten years of unsuccessful fighting and the domestic unrest it produced dramatically lessened the Marine Corps' cultural capital and did the same to the other services. It also wreaked havoc within the Corps, making the late 1970s the most challenging period in its modern history. Drugs and racial conflict plagued all the services, but by 1979, the Marine Corps' illegal drug use rates were the highest.[3] The military's reputation in America descended to new lows. Civil-military friction persisted throughout the decade, keeping the psychological wounds of Vietnam open and raw in ways far worse than after Korea. Criticism of militarization pervaded popular culture and academia, with even former Commandant of the Marine Corps General David M. Shoup joining the rising chorus.[4] In film, the military veteran became a disturbed and dangerous antihero, exemplified best by Robert De Niro's portrayal of a psychotic former Marine in Martin Scorsese's *Taxi Driver* (1976) and Sylvester Stallone's depiction of traumatized Army veteran John Rambo in *First Blood* (1983).

The events of the late 1960s and 1970s seem to suggest that Americans resisted the Cold War's militarization of politics and culture rather than acquiescing to it. That resistance was only temporary, however. In the early 1980s, the armed services rebounded, helped in no small part by the muscular, nostalgic rhetoric of a President with extensive experience in Hollywood but no firsthand knowledge of warfare. The armed services rekindled their relationships with the entertainment industries that had languished during Vietnam, and after a few false starts, the Army found its voice again with its "be all you can be" recruiting drive.[5] All the services benefited from the near-doubling of defense spending that occurred in the Reagan years.[6] Films such as *An Officer and a Gentleman* (1982), *Heartbreak Ridge* (1986), and *Top Gun* (1986) helped erase the lingering image of De Niro's psychotic Marine of a decade earlier. Even films that didn't receive military support worked to rehabilitate the armed forces' image, none more so than the sequels to *First Blood*, which allowed Stallone's John Rambo to go from losing in America to winning in Vietnam and Afghanistan. Chuck Norris' *Missing in Action* and its sequels performed a similar reversal. It may have taken the Gulf War to finally kick what President George H. W. Bush called "the Vietnam syndrome," but many Americans were already primed to do so, for they had been enjoying several years of cinematic fantasies that used fictional victories to bury the ghosts of defeat.[7]

Since the end of the Cold War, the Marines have occupied an even greater place in America's stories about its military, mostly by serving as the inspiration for several excellent books and films. Aaron Sorkin's *A Few Good Men* (1992) earned four Academy Award nominations, won the People's Choice Award for drama, and garnered another award for top box office gross. James Bradley's sensitive biography of his father and the other five Iwo Jima flag raisers, *Flags of Our Fathers* (2000), spent forty-six weeks on the *New York Times* bestseller list and six weeks in the top spot. Clint Eastwood adapted Bradley's book into an award-winning film in 2006, and made a second film the same year, *Letters from Iwo Jima,* which won an Oscar and sixteen other awards.

Since the invasions of Afghanistan and Iraq, books and films by and about Marines have continued to appear in numbers disproportionate to the Corps' small size in the Department of Defense. HBO has produced two high-budget miniseries on the Corps: *Generation Kill* (2008), based on *Rolling Stone* reporter Evan Wright's book of the same name, and *The Pacific* (2010), based on some of the Marine memoirs discussed in Chapter 1 of this book. Even Ken Burns' PBS series *The War* (2007), which was ostensibly about the entire American experience in World War II, gave disproportionate emphasis to the Marine Corps. Three films released in 2009 emphasized Marines' combat trauma or grief: *Taking Chance, Brothers,* and *Avatar,* which won three Academy Awards and became the highest-grossing film in North American history. Most of these films rehearse the same narratives of Marine exceptionalism of the World War II generation, and consequently, the Corps' cultural capital continues to grow apace.

The Marines have also grown more important in national defense since the end of the Cold War. As the United States shifted from deterring the Soviet Union to policing the global commons, the Army, Navy, and Air Force all found themselves saddled with Cold War weapons systems and outdated missions, but the Marines' force-in-readiness became only more useful. In the 1990s, a time some historians point to as a decade of military complacency, Marine Corps deployments increased.[8] From 1991 to 1994, Marine Air-Ground Task Forces participated in eleven contingency operations, ranging from disaster relief in Liberia and Somalia to high-intensity combat in Kuwait.[9] In the twenty years after the Berlin Wall fell, Marine amphibious forces have participated in 101 separate military operations occurring in thirty-five different countries. On average, Marines conduct operations in four different countries per year, not counting classified operations. Approximately 43,000 Marines are serving overseas today in Afghanistan, Iraq, aboard ships, or in forward deployed bases in the Middle East, Africa, Europe, or the Pacific.[10]

Manpower and budget trends offer further evidence of the Marines' increasing utility and power. Since 1992, the active-duty military has shrunk 21 percent, with the Navy and Air Force seeing double-digit declines. The Marine Corps has been the only service to see its numbers increase.[11] During the same period, the Corps' budget has almost tripled.[12] Even more than in the Cold War, the United States today has a habit of enforcing global order by sending in the Marines.

The central claim of this book has been that the Marines' service culture helped them build the political and public relations infrastructure that would eventually bring them to their present heights. Between 1941 and 1965, I have argued, the Marine Corps constructed enduring networks of support with the American public, the media, and Congress. The Corps' cohesion—a sense of commitment unparalleled in any of the three larger services—was a principal enabler for these developments. That commitment began in recruit training, where ritualistic violence knit the group together in a symbolic order that equated suffering with prestige and gave members access to an imagined family larger than their own biological one. The island warfare of the Pacific validated the narratives of Marine exceptionalism, as did the Korean War and the constant interservice strife of the early Cold War. Together, these experiences convinced Marines that the stories they learned in boot camp were true: the Corps was different, unique, and better than any other military service in the world. They also reinforced an already existing strain within Marine culture: a propensity to mistrust outsiders and to view interservice friction as evidence of a master plan to reduce or destroy the Marine Corps.

This sense of being under siege did not isolate Marines from American society; in fact, it helped them extend and expand their networks into surrounding cultural fields. Hypervigilance spurred them to read the cultural terrain constantly and to adapt their messages to different audiences. As Americans suffered hardship and loss in World War II, the Marines emphasized familial themes and extended their promises of community to the families of the fallen. In the postwar period, they used strategies of tender violence to domesticate their image for a war-weary public. After Korea, they made further adjustments, presenting themselves as tough but benevolent role models for boys, which allowed them to capitalize on the nation's fears of softness and juvenile delinquency. All of these maneuvers yielded a network of civilian admirers who both supported the Marine Corps and, at times, appropriated its stories for themselves.

With Congress and national security experts, Marines in Washington, D.C., used different but equally effective cultural politics. Transforming complex arguments about the defense establishment into simple and at times hysterical claims, they presented the Corps and the nation as victims of the Army's militarism. Accompanying these claims was a host of lobbying tactics that did exactly what the Corps claimed to detest, expanding military power in the government and diminishing the President's civilian control over the armed forces. The result by 1965 was a Marine Corps more firmly established in politics and national defense than at any previous moment in its history.

Flexibility, dynamism, and mistrust also characterized the Corps' interactions inside the Department of Defense, where they fought the other services constantly for resources, missions, and respect. Largely because they feared for their service's survival, the Marines' senior strategists broke with conventional wisdom shared by the other three services. They rejected the closed world and nuclear warfare, focusing instead on tactics, doctrine, and technology that were useful in the interstices of war and peace. The utility of such capabilities became apparent almost immediately, and the President has used the amphibious force-in-readiness ever since as one of the principal tools for maintaining American global hegemony.

All of these developments owed something to culture. The Marines' intense commitment to their service, their ability to build coalitions, their effective but questionable political tactics, and their growing role in national defense all came about because the Corps had a cognitive style different from that of the other services. But that cognitive style had negative attributes as well. On the battlefield, Marine Corps culture was both a blessing and a curse. While it generated strong feelings of devotion and mutual obligation, it also linked men's sense of self-worth to combat performance in ways more intense than in the other services. Marines who broke down on the battlefield felt more shame, blamed themselves more often, and experienced greater degrees of "personality disintegration" than did the Army's infantry. Even those who performed well in combat, such as Dick Bahr, were sometimes beset with guilt or unable to relax, even with their closest family members. Furthermore, the social habits imparted to Marines—distrust of outsiders, a reactive and offensive mind-set, and alcohol use as a seminal component of manhood—did not always produce healthy relationships outside the nearly all-male community of the Corps. Some Marines carried the habit of being "first to fight" off the battlefield and into their civilian lives.

A few broader conclusions may be drawn from this study about military history and the Marine Corps today. First, *Underdogs* has expanded upon a point long understood by military theorists but rediscovered in every war: culture matters in military affairs. As Sun Tzu first reminded military leaders several thousand years ago, a strong sense of unit morale or esprit de corps is essential for victory, and failure to understand what motivates one's enemy is a recipe for defeat.[13] But for too long, studies of military culture have stopped at these relatively obvious points. It is axiomatic that a successful military institution "requires stories as well as guns," but few historians have tried to explain in detail how those stories operated anywhere but on the battlefield.[14] This, coupled with a general hostility to the military inside American studies and cultural studies, has left important areas of American cultural life unexplored or misunderstood.

The preceding chapters have sought to marry the best practices of military and cultural history and to show how habits of mind shaped much more than battlefield conduct. While Marine Corps culture certainly mattered in combat, it also shaped the service's public relations and political activities, Marine families, and the Corps' strategic direction. It provided ways for Marines to understand themselves and their actions on the battlefield and in the many cultural fields in which they operated. It was a dominant force in members' lives and essential for the day-to-day functioning of the Corps.

This study has also shown that what President Truman called a "propaganda machine" was really a collection of alliances that linked the Corps to its veterans, to Marine families, and to a number of civilians with little or no formal connection to the Marine Corps. These civilians not only participated in advancing the Corps' reputation but also at times played a central role. Indeed, the most well-known culture products generated about the Marine Corps in this era—the photo of the Iwo Jima flag raising, *Sands of Iwo Jima,* and *The D.I.*— were all created by civilians. Likewise, some of the most important members of the congressional coalition were not Marines: Representative Clare Hoffman, the Corps' savior during the unification fights, never served in the military at all, and other pro-Marine senators and representatives were veterans of other services. Even the letter that provoked the "propaganda machine" comment in the first place came from the pen of an Army veteran. While the Marines actively nurtured these coalitions, they did not control them. Civilians made common cause with the Marines for a variety of reasons, oftentimes to advance their own agendas.[15] Similar civil-military coalitions exist today and are a driving force behind the ongoing militarization of American culture. They deserve further study.

This book has also called for more attention to the aftermath of war and to the ways that this country's repeated pattern of military conflict has shaped Americans' lives. The conventional cost-benefit analysis for conducting military operations has always focused on physical casualties: the potential number of bodies broken or lives destroyed in the fighting. As I have shown here, that calculus is incomplete, for the psychological wounds of war often appear years later and continue to injure the living long after the fighting stops. There are today approximately 23 million veterans in American society, of whom roughly a third have experienced traumatic events in war: exposure to the dead, dying, or wounded.[16] If even the most conservative estimates are correct, between 10 and 15 percent of those combat veterans will experience symptoms of post-traumatic stress—between 782,000 and 1.2 million casualties of war that are not counted on the official rolls.[17] These veterans, as well as the estimated 200,000 who have suffered traumatic brain injuries over the last decade, must not be forgotten as the present wars recede into the past. They—and their spouses, children, and parents—deserve the attention of historians, for the burdens such families bear are carried for generations.[18]

Today, male veterans are committing suicide at twice the rate of civilians, and female veterans are at even greater risk. In the active-duty forces, the services that have had the most contact with the wars in Iraq and Afghanistan also have the highest suicide rates. In 2009, Army and Marine rates were more than double that of civilian society, and since 2001, suicides across the entire Department of Defense have increased by 71 percent. Senior military leaders have named post-traumatic stress, traumatic brain injuries, and the stresses of ten years of constant deployments as some of the reasons for the increase. These deaths are also casualties of war, ones that many Americans are still not willing to acknowledge fully.[19]

Finally, *Underdogs* has shown that while the stereotypical images of United States Marines are partly true, they do not give a complete and accurate picture of Marine Corps life in midcentury America. Some Marines were stoic, hardened, and disciplined in combat, but the same men could also break down and cry at parades, in their beds at night, and even after beating their wives. Indeed, of the ten incidents involving crying Marines chronicled in this study, only four occurred on the battlefield. The other six occurred in combat's aftermath—in the home, in the courtroom, or on the street.[20] It is to these noncombat realms that military historians should take their investigations of military culture next.

This exploration of those realms has shown that labels such as "military culture" or "civil-military relations" are too broad for understanding the actions and ideas of the various armed services. While the Marines of the early Cold War were neither homogeneous nor an entirely exceptional culture, as they claimed, their ways of thinking and living were sufficiently different in three ways to warrant distinction from the other services.

First, more than the other armed services, the Marines of this era were romantics. As Navy leaders warned President Eisenhower during unification, the Marines were "emotional"—they lived more in the world of feelings than logic, privileging spirit, history, and mythology over factors that were more material and scientific.[21]

They viewed war as an unpredictable and fundamentally human activity, which led them further away from the mechanization and quantitative techniques of information management that suffused the closed world in that era. This temperament made Marines relatively comfortable with culture and chaos and with adapting to uncertain environments rather than attempting to predict and control them. This, like so much in the Marines' cultural universe, stemmed from their institution's long history of perceived persecution. Science and logic were not irrelevant to the Marine Corps; they were just less useful in its primary preoccupation—the art of survival.

Second, while the Marine Corps survived and even thrived in this period, its members did not do so without anger and violence. More so perhaps than any other American subculture then in existence, Marines led a life with regular exposure to trauma. Violence empowered the stories told in recruit training, giving narratives about suffering the authority that comes with experience. Trauma cemented the bonds formed in recruit training and energized the underlying paranoia and distrust that were already present in the culture. Violence also followed some Marines home, reigniting wars in their minds that sometimes spilled over onto families.

Third, Marines' sense of commitment and devotion came very rarely from state-centered narratives about patriotism or country. Rather, Marines' bonds of kinship concerned a smaller imagined community, the Corps itself, which drew regularly from the language of religion and family. The famous litany of a Marine's priorities of affiliation in Aaron Sorkin's film *A Few Good Men*—"unit, Corps, God, country"—may have been Sorkin's own invention, but it reflects the correct order of Marines' commitments nonetheless. Country comes fourth, after one's fellow Marines and the broader imagined "family" of the Corps.

This emphasis on community helps explain why Marines have remained so high in the public's esteem since World War II. For, as the feelings of young Frances Newman, actor Jack Webb, and a host of politicians, journalists, and ordinary citizens demonstrate, the culture of the Corps was not only attractive to its members. It was, to a certain degree, exportable; it gave the American people something that they valued. I have suggested here that the standard explanations of what makes Marines impressive—their toughness, courage, and battlefield success—are only half the story. The Marines' culture also had intimate, nostalgic, and familial elements that they advertised and occasionally offered to the public. They gave their members (and some civilians too) what we might call a mediating community between family and nation—a network of affiliation that adapted the deep feelings of biological kin to a larger group of individuals. Veterans such as Rick Spooner and Dick Bahr, mothers such as Jean "the Marines' Mom" De Marranza, and countless other Americans all valued its ability to bridge the gap between family and nation-state and to give people a deeper sense of belonging than modern liberal society's emphasis on individuality allows. That sense of family remains palpably present in the Marine Corps today.[22]

The Marines' constant emphasis on the past, their history, and tradition is another reason for their sustained civilian support. Because the Corps' internal cohesion has always been so dependent on past-focused narratives—on being loyal not just to living Marines but to the ancestors and legends binding them all together—Marines have become expert at mobilizing that language in their public utterances.[23] They never reject future-focused narratives, but they emphasize them less, preferring the warm and constant comfort of their (sometimes partly fictionalized) past. These nostalgic narratives were useful to many in midcentury America and remain so today, particularly for those mourning the dead or fearing an uncertain future. To these Americans, the Marines offer a conservative counternarrative to society's unceasing celebrations of individualism, materialism, and the promises of tomorrow.

More than anything else, however, it has been the internal bonds of affection that explain the Corps' cohesion in both the past and the present. Those bonds have been strengthened by an ideology of elitism, superiority, and paranoia—elements that run through the still-powerful narratives of Marine exceptionalism today. That ideology, which shares some similarities with narratives of American exceptionalism, has kept the Marines forever on the attack and reactive in ways both good and bad. Their sense of being a "David-like fighting unit" engaging "Goliath-like enemies" is a principal reason for their present-day success.

Abbreviations

CC   Combat correspondent

DI   Drill instructor

GPO   Government Printing Office

HAF   Historical Amphibious File

HBP   Hanson W. Baldwin Papers, Manuscripts and Archives, Yale
        University, New Haven, Connecticut

HD   Marine Corps History Division, Marine Corps University,
        Quantico, Virginia

HQMC   Headquarters, U.S. Marine Corps

LOC   Library of Congress, Washington, DC

MAGTF   Marine-Air Ground Task Force

MCA   Marine Corps Archives, Quantico, Virginia

MCOHC   Marine Corps Oral History Collection, Quantico, Virginia

MHQ   Military History Quarterly

NARA   National Archives and Records Administration, College Park,
        Maryland

NCO   Non-commissioned officer

PPC   Personal Papers Collection

TOA   Total Obligational Authority

Notes

Introduction

1. J. Walter Thompson Company, "United States Marine Corps Nation-Wide Survey, November 1941," 13–16, HD subject file "Selective Service 1861–1965," MCA.
2. Though the Air Force would not become a separate service until 1947, I refer to the Army, Navy, Air Force, and Marines as the "four armed services" throughout this book. The Coast Guard, which then resided in the Department of the Treasury and is now a part of the Department of Homeland Security, is not included.
3. I use story, narrative, and culture throughout as synonyms for discourse, which one historian has described as "historically specific, coordinated sets of meanings . . . expressed through beliefs, habits, vocabularies, representations, and institutional practices . . . that, taken together, serve to articulate what will count as knowledge and succeed as power in any given culture." See Laura Wexler, *Tender Violence: Domestic Visions in an Age of U.S. Imperialism* (Chapel Hill: University of North Carolina Press, 2000), 53. See also Edward W. Said, *Orientalism* (New York: Vintage, 1978), 94; Michel Foucault, *The Archaeology of Knowledge and the Discourse on Language* (New York: Pantheon, 1972), 116–117.
4. For one such comparison, see Craig M. Cameron, *American Samurai: Myth, Imagination, and the Conduct of Battle in the First Marine Division, 1941–1951* (New York: Cambridge University Press, 1994). While the title suggests a comparison to the Japanese, much of Cameron's study makes problematic comparisons between the Marine Corps and the German Waffen-Schutzstaffel (SS) in World War II. For a looser

analogy, see James A. Warren, *American Spartans: The U.S. Marines: A Combat History from Iwo Jima to Iraq* (New York: Free Press, 2005). The best work on the Corps' contemporary culture is Thomas E. Ricks, *Making the Corps* (New York: Scribner, 1997).

5. One of the better explorations of the cultural similarities between militaries across millennia is John A. Lynn, *Battle: A History of Combat and Culture* (Boulder, CO: Westview Press, 2003). Less successful is Martin Van Creveld, *The Culture of War* (Novato, CA: Presidio Press, 2008).

6. I use the word "modern" generically here, meaning the present-day Marine Corps. The principal characteristics of the Corps today are its force-in-readiness mission, its aggressive public relations infrastructure, its deep-seated political influence, and its elite position in American society. While another author dates the modern Marine Corps to World War I, the organization that fought at Belleau Wood had none of these characteristics yet. See Alan Axelrod, *Miracle at Belleau Wood: The Birth of the Modern U.S. Marine Corps* (Guilford, CT: Lyons Press, 2007), 226–229.

7. For evidence of the Corps' contemporary prestige, see Gallup Poll, May 18, 2001, question 37; Gallup Poll, April 22, 2002, question 49; Gallup Poll, May 21, 2004, question 22; and Gallup Poll, June 9, 2011, question 16, all available at http://brain.gallup.com (accessed April 20, 2012).

8. Among the Marines to have held prominent roles in national security leadership are secretaries of state George P. Shultz and James A. Baker III; Joint Chiefs of Staff chairman Peter Pace and vice chairman James E. Cartwright; national security advisors Robert C. McFarlane and James L. Jones (who also served as supreme Allied commander of Europe and combatant commander of United States European Command); and Senators John W. Warner and James "Jim" Webb, both of whom also served as secretary of the Navy. Anthony C. Zinni served as the combatant commander of United States Central Command; James E. Cartwright served as combatant commander of United States Strategic Command; James N. Mattis served as combatant commander of United States Joint Forces Command and Central Command; Charles E. Wilhelm and Peter Pace both served as the Combatant Commander of United States Southern Command.

9. Department of Defense, Defense Manpower Data Center, "Active Duty Military Strength by Service," available at http://siadapp.dmdc.osd.mil /personnel/MILITARY/miltop.htm (accessed March 4, 2012).

10. From 1971 to 1990, Marine amphibious forces participated in 43 separate contingency operations. Since 1989, they have participated in 101 operations, not counting classified operations, exercises, or disaster relief on U.S. soil. Cold War data is found in Adam B. Siegel, *The Use of Naval Forces in the Post-War Era: U.S. Navy and U.S. Marine Corps Crisis Response Activity, 1946–1991* (Alexandria, VA: Center for Naval Analyses, 1991), 37–52. For the period after 1990, see United States Marine Corps, *Amphibious Operations in the 21st Century* (Quantico, VA: Marine Corps Combat Development Command, 2009), 2. For a breakdown of operations by year and type, see Marine Corps Strategic Vision Group, "U.S. Amphibious Operations, 1990–2009," January 19, 2010, copy in author's possession.

11. Captain Phillip N. Pierce, "The Marine Corps' Fourth Estate," *Marine Corps Gazette* 30 (September 1946): 51.

12. The poem "Brass-Button Queens" was written by Captain Earl J. Wilson, USMC, and reprinted in *Time*, May 1, 1944, 66.

13. This tendency to view one's community as an exceptional, embattled, morally superior group surrounded by a hostile environment has a long history in American thought and culture. See Richard Slotkin, *Gunfighter Nation: The Myth of the Frontier in Twentieth-Century America* (New York: Atheneum, 1992), 10–26; Michael Denning, *Culture in the Age of Three Worlds* (London: Verso, 2004), 180–183; Anders Stephanson, *Manifest Destiny: American Expansion and the Empire of Right* (New York: Hill and Wang, 1994), 4–12.

14. The most comprehensive investigation of fundamentalist cultures is Martin E. Marty and R. Scott Appleby, eds., *The Fundamentalism Project*, 5 vols. (Chicago: University of Chicago Press, 1991–1993). See in particular vol. 1, *Fundamentalisms Observed*, i–x, 817–832; vol. 2, *Fundamentalism and Society*, 3–4; and vol. 5, *Fundamentalisms Comprehended*, 11–68. See also Martin E. Marty and R. Scott Appleby, *The Glory and the Power: The Fundamentalist Challenge to the Modern World* (Boston: Beacon Press, 1992), 15, 30, 35; R. Scott Appleby and Martin E. Marty, "Fundamentalism," *Foreign Policy* 122 (January–February 2002): 16.

15. Inside the Marine Corps, "Semper Fi" also had an ironic usage, meaning, in effect, "You're on your own; I'm taking care of myself." See Henry Berry, *Semper Fi, Mac: Living Memories of the U.S. Marines in World War II* (New York: Arbor House, 1982), 13.

16. Institutional agility, a deep commitment to transcendent narratives, and a conflicted relationship with modern technology are additional traits that the Marine Corps shares with fundamentalist cultures. See Marty and Appleby, *The Glory and the Power,* 1–35.

17. President Truman's remark to the Commandant of the Marine Corps is found in Victor H. Krulak, *First to Fight: An Inside View of the U.S. Marine Corps* (Annapolis, MD: Naval Institute Press, 1999), 51.

18. The "propaganda machine" comment is found in a letter to Representative Gordon L. McDonough of California and is reprinted in 81st Cong., 2nd Sess., *Congressional Record* 96 (September 15, 1950): 14952.

19. General Clifton B. Cates, USMC, oral history, 225–226, MCOHC, MCA.

20. For a few representative comments, see Gerald P. Averill, *Mustang: A Combat Marine* (Novato, CA: Presidio Press, 1987), 3; Master Sergeant C. V. Crumb, "The New and the Old," *Marine Corps Gazette* 40 (November 1956): 64–67; Major J. L. Tobin, "Morale," *Marine Corps Gazette* 38 (November 1954): 42–43; Krulak, *First to Fight,* xvi. For comments by civilians, see Chapter 2.

21. Michael G. Kammen, *Mystic Chords of Memory: The Transformation of Tradition in American Culture* (New York: Knopf, 1991), 3–14, 513–514, 702.

22. An excellent analysis of the cultures of these three services is Carl H. Builder, *The Masks of War: American Military Styles in Strategy and Analysis* (Baltimore: Johns Hopkins University Press, 1989). Unfortunately, Builder's study ignores the Marine Corps.

23. Casualty ratios and combat participation ratios for all the services are available at Department of Defense, Defense Manpower Data Center, http://siadapp.dmdc.osd.mil (accessed September 22, 2009).

24. Further evidence that Americans created the label lies in the fact that in German, the compound noun "devil dogs" is *Teufelshunde,* not *Teufel Hunden.* The term appeared in numerous U.S. newspapers starting in late April 1918. For just two examples, see "Teufel Hunden: German

Name for U.S. Marines," *Lacrosse* (WI) *Tribune and Leader-Press,* April 27, 1918, 1; "Huns Call Marines Teufel Hunden or Better, 'Devil Dogs,'" *Newark* (OH) *Advocate,* April 27, 1918, 1.

25. The Corps claims (and still celebrates) November 10, 1775, as its birthday, even though the two battalions of Marines authorized by the Continental Congress on that date were never raised. The creative use of facts in this claim is discussed in Allan Reed Millett, *Semper Fidelis: The History of the United States Marine Corps* (New York: Free Press, 1991), 6–9. Triumphant and problematic accounts of the Marines' performance in the American Revolution, War of 1812, Mexican War, and Civil War may be found in Robert Debs Heinl Jr., *Soldiers of the Sea: The United States Marine Corps, 1775–1962* (Annapolis, MD: Naval Institute Press, 1962), 3–69, and J. Robert Moskin, *The U.S. Marine Corps Story,* 2nd ed. (New York: McGraw-Hill, 1987), 24–76. For a more balanced and scholarly account, see Millett, *Semper Fidelis,* ch. 1–4.

26. Heinl, *Soldiers of the Sea,* 33. The numerous efforts to diminish the Corps are well catalogued in Robert Debs Heinl Jr., "The Cat with More Than Nine Lives," *Proceedings of the U.S. Naval Institute,* June 1954, 658–671; Millett, *Semper Fidelis,* 52–115; Jack Shulimson, *The Marine Corps' Search for a Mission, 1880–1898,* Modern War Studies (Lawrence: University Press of Kansas, 1993), 15–18, 47, 99, 130–165.

27. The history of the Corps' legal status inside the Navy Department is well explained in Hamilton M. Hoyler, "Legal Status of the Marine Corps," *Marine Corps Gazette* 34 (November 1950): 4–18.

28. Heinl, "The Cat with More than Nine Lives," 671; Robert Sherrod, "Get the Marines," unpublished article, January 13, 1950, HD subject file "Unification," MCA.

29. Shulimson, *The Marine Corps' Search for a Mission,* 147.

30. Heinl, "The Cat with More than Nine Lives," 671; Sherrod, "Get the Marines," 3.

31. While the Marines did fight bravely in World War I, they also suffered horrendous casualties: 15 percent of the Marines participating in the war were wounded or killed, compared to 6 percent in the Army. See "Principal Wars in Which the United States Participated: U.S. Military Personnel Serving and Casualties," available at http://siadapp.dmdc .osd.mil (accessed September 22, 2009). For detailed assessments of the

Marines' performance in World War I, see Millett, *Semper Fidelis,* 298–311; Edwin H. Simmons and Joseph H. Alexander, *Through the Wheat: The U.S. Marines in World War I* (Annapolis, MD: Naval Institute Press, 2008).

32. The censoring error that occurred just after the Battle of Belleau Wood is discussed in Robert George Lindsay, *This High Name: Public Relations and the U.S. Marine Corps* (Madison: University of Wisconsin Press, 1956), 31–34; Millett, *Semper Fidelis,* 302–303.

33. The Marines' performance as "State Department troops" in the interwar period is discussed in Max Boot, *The Savage Wars of Peace: Small Wars and the Rise of American Power* (New York: Basic Books, 2003), 69–99, 156–181, 231–285; Leo J. Daugherty III, *The Marine Corps and the State Department: Enduring Partners in United States Foreign Policy* (Jefferson, NC: McFarland, 2009), 39–59; Millett, *Semper Fidelis,* 147–236. On the Marines' experience in Haiti, see Hans Schmidt, *The United States Occupation of Haiti, 1915–1934* (New Brunswick, NJ: Rutgers University Press, 1971); Mary A. Renda, *Taking Haiti: Military Occupation and the Culture of U.S. Imperialism, 1915–1940* (Chapel Hill: University of North Carolina Press, 2001).

34. J. Walter Thompson Company, "United States Marine Corps Nation-Wide Survey, November 1941," 13–14, HD subject file "Selective Service 1861–1965," MCA.

35. Interservice rivalry and innovation are discussed in detail in Krulak, *First to Fight,* 67–110.

36. The metaphor of military forces as an oil stain or inkblot was first used by French general Hubert Lyautey to describe a military strategy for what is now called counterinsurgency. See Louis Hubert Gonzalve Lyautey, *Du Rôle Colonial de l'Armée* (Paris: Armand Colin, 1900). See also the discussion of Lyautey's notion of "indirect rule" in William A. Hoisington Jr., *Lyautey and the French Conquest of Morocco* (New York: St. Martin's Press, 1995), 6–7, 19–20.

37. I define "militarization" generically, as the increasing prestige a society affords to military members, metaphors, tools, and war stories. This term should not be confused with "militarism," which invites inappropriate comparison to Germany and Japan in World War II. For further discussion of militarization, see Michael S. Sherry, *In the Shadow of*

War: The United States since the 1930s (New Haven: Yale University Press, 1995), xi–xii. The best recent work on the subject is Andrew J. Bacevich, *The New American Militarism: How Americans Are Seduced by War* (New York: Oxford University Press, 2005). See also Andrew J. Bacevich, ed., *The Long War: A New History of U.S. National Security Policy since World War II* (New York: Columbia University Press, 2007), vii–xiv; Richard H. Kohn, "The Dangers of Militarization in an Endless War on Terror," *Journal of Military History* 73 (January 2009): 177–208.

38. Scott Sigmund Gartner, "National Defense Outlays and Veterans' Benefits: 1915–1995," 146–154, in Susan B. Carter et al., eds., *Historical Statistics of the United States* (New York: Cambridge University Press, 2006.

39. In fact, those developments are more generally considered militarism, not militarization. On balance, the United States has assiduously avoided militarism; even in the Cold War, no garrison state ever emerged. See Aaron L. Friedberg, *In the Shadow of the Garrison State: America's Anti-Statism and Its Cold War Grand Strategy* (Princeton, NJ: Princeton University Press, 2000), 1–8, 340–351. See also Volker R. Berghahn, *Militarism: The History of an International Debate, 1861–1979* (New York: St. Martin's Press, 1982), 105–124. The seminal work on militarism remains Alfred Vagts, *A History of Militarism: Civilian and Military* (New York: Meridian Books, 1959), 11–32.

40. This definition is an adaptation of Michael Sherry's belief that militarization is "the process by which war and national security became consuming anxieties and provided the memories, models, and metaphors that shaped broad areas of national life." See Sherry, *In the Shadow of War*, xi.

41. On gender and family life, see Elaine Tyler May, *Homeward Bound: American Families in the Cold War Era* (New York: Basic Books, 1999). On masculinity, see James Burkhart Gilbert, *Men in the Middle: Searching for Masculinity in the 1950s* (Chicago: University of Chicago Press, 2005), and Kyle A. Cuordileone, *Manhood and American Political Culture in the Cold War* (New York: Routledge, 2005). On homosexuality, see David K. Johnson, *The Lavender Scare: The Cold War Persecution of Gays and Lesbians in the Federal Government* (Chicago: University of

Chicago Press, 2004). On race, see Mary L. Dudziak, *Cold War Civil Rights: Race and the Image of American Democracy,* Politics and Society in Twentieth-Century America (Princeton, NJ: Princeton University Press, 2000).

42. One exception, but a deeply flawed one, is Cameron, *American Samurai.* Another attempt, equally unsatisfying for historians, is Frank Marutollo, *Organizational Behavior in the Marine Corps: Three Interpretations* (New York: Praeger, 1990).

43. The seminal early works in the field of civil-military relations all occurred in the field of political science and sociology. See, in particular, Samuel Andrew Stouffer et al., *Studies in Social Psychology in World War II*, vol. 1, *The American Soldier: Adjustment during Army Life* (Princeton, NJ: Princeton University Press, 1949); Samuel P. Huntington, *The Soldier and the State: The Theory and Politics of Civil-Military Relations* (Cambridge, MA: Belknap Press, 1959); and Morris Janowitz, *The Professional Soldier, a Social and Political Portrait* (Glencoe, IL: Free Press, 1960).

44. The best application of the language of military tactics and strategy to the study of culture is Michel Foucault, *Society Must Be Defended: Lectures at the Collége de France, 1975–1976* (New York: Picador, 1997), xvii–xxii, 15–16, 24–41.

45. Antonio Gramsci calls this process of managing consent "cultural hegemony." The best explanation of it is T. J. Jackson Lears, "The Concept of Cultural Hegemony: Problems and Possibilities," *American Historical Review* 90 (June 1985): 567–593.

46. The notion of the "cultural field" is explained in Pierre Bourdieu, *The Field of Cultural Production: Essays on Art and Literature* (New York: Columbia University Press, 1993), 29–73. I use Bourdieu's term more as an earthy metaphor than as a theoretical model for the Marines' cultural operations. See also Michel Foucault, *Society Must Be Defended,* xvii–xxii; Michel Foucault, *Power/Knowledge: Selected Interviews and Other Writings, 1972–1977* (New York: Pantheon, 1980), 77.

47. The idea of culture as the stories we tell ourselves about ourselves is adapted from Clifford Geertz, *The Interpretation of Cultures: Selected Essays* (New York: Basic Books, 1973), 448–453.

48. The notion of culture as a set of commitments comes from Warren Susman, *Culture and Commitment, 1929-1945* (New York: G. Braziller, 1973), 1-24. An excellent discussion of the different attempts by scholars of American studies to define culture is found in Michael Denning, *Culture in the Age of Three Worlds* (London: Verso, 2004), 75-147.

49. This is my paraphrase of Immanuel Wallerstein's definition of culture. See Immanuel Maurice Wallerstein, *The Essential Wallerstein* (New York: New Press, 2000), 265.

50. While Anderson is most interested in the specific relationships between print culture and nationalism, his central point about community as an imagined construct applies to groups other than the nation-state as well. See Benedict R. Anderson, *Imagined Communities: Reflections on the Origin and Spread of Nationalism* (London: Verso, 1983), 5-7.

51. For a detailed explanation of the notion of how ideology shapes the material world, see Louis Althusser, "Ideology and Ideological State Apparatuses," in Julie Rivkin and Michael Ryan, eds., *Literary Theory: An Anthology* (Malden, MA: Blackwell, 1998), 294-304.

52. Isabel V. Hull, *Absolute Destruction: Military Culture and the Practices of War in Imperial Germany* (Ithaca, NY: Cornell University Press, 2005), 2, 94-98. See also Wayne E. Lee, "Mind and Matter—Cultural Analysis in American Military History: A Look at the State of the Field," *Journal of American History* 93 (March 2007): 1116-1142.

53. I am grateful to Jean-Christophe Agnew for this metaphor.

54. The concept of "tender violence" is taken from Laura Wexler, *Tender Violence: Domestic Visions in an Age of U.S. Imperialism,* Cultural Studies of the United States (Chapel Hill: University of North Carolina Press, 2000), 52-53.

1. A Harsh and Spiritual Unity

1. All quotes from Major Richard T. Spooner come from an interview by the author, Quantico, VA, January 29, 2007, unless otherwise specified. Interview transcript in author's possession.

2. Spooner interview, 15. See also Major Rick Spooner, *The Spirit of Semper Fidelis: Reflections from the Bottom of an Old Canteen Cup*

(Williamstown, NJ: Phillips Publications, 2005); Major Richard Spooner, *A Marine Anthology: In the Spirit of Semper Fidelis* (Williamstown, NJ: Phillips Publications, 2010).

3. A similar point is made in Craig M. Cameron, *American Samurai: Myth, Imagination, and the Conduct of Battle in the First Marine Division, 1941–1951* (New York: Cambridge University Press, 1994), 138–156.

4. For more on the theory of symbolic exchange, see Jean Baudrillard, *Symbolic Exchange and Death* (London: Sage Publications, 1993), 1–43.

5. Lieutenant Colonel John H. Magruder III, USMC, "A Touch of Tradition," *Marine Corps Gazette* 43 (November 1959): 43.

6. The Marines suffered 5,616 casualties from December 1941 to February 1943. Between June 1944 and June 1945, they suffered 71,000 more. For Marine casualties by battle, see United States Marine Corps, *History of U.S. Marine Corps Operations in World War II* (Washington, DC: GPO, 1958–1971), 1:395, 2:587, 3:636, 4:797, 5:884. For total casualties by service, see Department of Defense, "Principal Wars in Which the United States Participated, U.S. Military Personnel Serving and Casualties," http://siadapp.dmdc.osd.mil/personnel/CASUALTY/WCPRINCIPAL .pdf (accessed January 8, 2009).

7. The Navy was roughly seven times as large; the Army (which then included the Army Air Forces) was almost ten times as large. See Department of Defense, Statistical Information Analysis Division, *Selected Manpower Statistics, Fiscal Year 2005* (Washington, DC: Defense Manpower Data Center, 2005), 42, 51, available at http://siadapp.dmdc.osd .mil/personnel/M01/fy05/m01fy05.pdf (accessed May 8, 2012).

8. Cameron, *American Samurai,* 52; Allan Reed Millett, *Semper Fidelis: The History of the United States Marine Corps* (New York: Free Press, 1991), 178–263.

9. Benedict R. Anderson, *Imagined Communities: Reflections on the Origin and Spread of Nationalism* (London: Verso, 1983), 5–6.

10. Department of Defense, *Selected Manpower Statistics,* 42.

11. U.S. Bureau of Naval Personnel, *Register of Commissioned and Warrant Officers of the United States Navy and Marine Corps* (Washington, DC: GPO, 1945), 594. For Army general officer figures, see United States Selective Service System, *Selective Service and Victory: The Fourth Report of the Director of Selective Service* (Washington, DC: GPO, 1948), 621. Army figures include the Army Air Forces.

12. The best example of this recruiting strategy was the Corps' "Semper Fidelis" recruiting poster from 1943, which featured a World War II Marine surrounded by Marines of previous eras, including a Continental Marine from the eighteenth century. However, this and other references to the Corps' volunteer image ignored the fact that the Marines took approximately 7,000 draftees during World War I. See Robert George Lindsay, *This High Name: Public Relations and the U.S. Marine Corps* (Madison: University of Wisconsin Press, 1956), 24.

13. Department of Defense, Directorate for Information Operations and Reports (DIOR), *Selected Manpower Statistics* (Washington, DC: The Pentagon, 1980), 80.

14. Millett, *Semper Fidelis*, 360.

15. Ibid., 374. For annual data on the number of seventeen-year-olds serving during World War II, see "Age Distribution, Marine Corps Male Enlisted Personnel," in "Personnel Distributions" binder, HD statistics section, MCA. Nearly every Marine memoir of World War II also mentions underage Marines who lied about their age to join. The most famous of these was Private First Class Jack Lucas, who enlisted at age fourteen and won the Medal of Honor on Iwo Jima. See Jack Lucas and D. K. Drum, *Indestructible: The Unforgettable Story of a Marine Hero at the Battle of Iwo Jima* (Waterville, ME: Thorndike Press, 2006). For other references to underage enlistees, see George Lince, *Too Young the Heroes: A World War II Marine's Account of Facing a Veteran Enemy at Guadalcanal, the Solomons and Okinawa* (Jefferson, NC: McFarland, 1997), 3–11; Kerry Lane, *Guadalcanal Marine* (Jackson: University Press of Mississippi, 2004), 3–6.

16. For a detailed explanation of how the Corps adapted to Executive Order 9279, see "Induction and Enlistment of Men Received through the Selective Service System," HD subject file "Selective Service," Reference Branch, MCA.

17. The Marine Corps accepted 188,989 draftees during World War II. See United States Selective Service System, *Special Monograph No. 16: Problems of Selective Service*, vol. 3, *Appendices D–I* (Washington, DC: GPO, 1952), 193. For the number who joined completely involuntarily, see Millett, *Semper Fidelis*, 374.

18. A total of 11,260,000 personnel served in the Army and Army Air Forces during World War II; 7,952,606 were inducted via the Selective

Service System. See Selective Service System, *Selective Service and Victory,* 605. For total personnel, see "Principal Wars in Which the United States Participated." For induction statistics of all services, see Selective Service System, *Problems of Selective Service,* 193.

19. The South provided 30.3 percent of all the military personnel who served during World War II and comprised 31.3 percent of the U.S. population in 1940 (and 32.2 percent in 1945). The South provided just 27.8 percent of the Marines who served in World War II. Pennsylvania was the most overrepresented state. It accounted for 8.5 percent of the Marines who served in World War II but just 7.5 percent of the U.S. population in 1940 (and just 7 percent in 1945). For total military personnel by state, see Selective Service System, *Problems of Selective Service,* 190. For total Marine Corps personnel by state, see "Marine Corps Personnel, December 1941–July 1945," E107, Information Division Correspondence 1946–1950, box 10, statistics file, RG 127, NARA. Census data is available at www.census.gov (accessed January 8, 2009). For 1945 population data, see United States Public Health Service, *Vital Statistics of the United States, 1945,* Part I (Washington, DC: GPO, 1947), table 6.

20. The Marines probably concentrated their liaison efforts at the large urban induction centers, which helps explain the disparity. For another explanation of why industrial areas sent more recruits to the Marines than rural areas, see Peter Karsten, *The Military in America: From the Colonial Era to the Present* (New York: Free Press, 1986), 337. Of the ten most rural states in 1940 (Mississippi, North Dakota, Arkansas, South Carolina, South Dakota, North Carolina, West Virginia, Kentucky, Alabama, and New Mexico), only West Virginia was overrepresented in the World War II Marine Corps. See "Marine Corps Personnel, December 1941–July 1945," E107, box 10, statistics file, RG 127, NARA. Census data available at www.census.gov (accessed January 8, 2009).

21. A total of 19,168 African Americans served in the Marine Corps in World War II. Assigned to labor and defense battalions, they saw combat on Saipan, Guam, Peleliu, Iwo Jima, and Okinawa, and suffered nearly 100 combat casualties. See Henry I. Shaw and Ralph W. Donnelly, *Blacks in the Marine Corps* (Washington, DC: History and Museums Division,

HQMC, 2002), 29–46, 48; Millett, *Semper Fidelis*, 374–375; Melton A. McLaurin, *The Marines of Montford Point: America's First Black Marines* (Chapel Hill: University of North Carolina Press, 2007).

22. A total of 18,460 women served in the Marine Corps Reserve during World War II, mostly in administrative, clerical, and technical positions, at Headquarters Marine Corps. See Pat Meid, *Marine Corps Women's Reserve in World War II* (Washington, DC: Historical Branch, HQMC, 1968), 55. See also Peter A. Soderbergh, *Women Marines: The World War II Era* (Westport, CT: Praeger, 1992).

23. A total of 9.57 million men were either inducted or enlisted in the Army between 1940 and 1945. Of these, only 1.85 million were age twenty-one or younger by June 1945. See Selective Service System, *Selective Service and Victory*, 605.

24. By August 1945, 193,936 enlisted Marines were age twenty-one or younger out of a total Marine Corps (officer and enlisted) of 485,113. See "Age Distribution, Enlisted Personnel on Active Duty 1 Aug 45," HD subject file "Strength and Distribution 1930–1949," MCA. Approximately 2,500 officers were also age twenty-one or below in August 1945. This figure is estimated from the number of officers listed in the age distribution tables from September 1944 in "Personnel Distributions" binder, HD statistics section, MCA.

25. U.S. Bureau of Naval Personnel, *Register of Commissioned and Warrant Officers of the United States Navy and Marine Corps* (Washington, DC: GPO, 1942), 734–807.

26. The Army's challenges with draftees are explored in Samuel Andrew Stouffer et al., *Studies in Social Psychology in World War II*, vol. 1, *The American Soldier: Adjustment during Army Life* (Princeton, NJ: Princeton University Press, 1949), 66–68.

27. As one Army officer explained, "What ships are to sailors, divisions are to soldiers. The Marine Corps, smaller, more compact, and less burdened with necessary housekeeping duties, is more fortunate; it can maintain its pride in the whole corps. In the army, basic esprit is tied to the division." See Major Thomas H. Farnsworth, "The Division," *United States Army Combat Forces Journal* 2 (August 1951): 18.

28. The attitudes of Army draftees are discussed in detail in Stouffer, *The American Soldier*, 1:54–81.

29. For a discussion of the "democratic army" narrative, see Benjamin L. Alpers, "This Is the Army: Imagining a Democratic Military in World War II," *Journal of American History* 85 (June 1998): 129–163.

30. Ibid., 138–139. See also Benjamin L. Alpers, *Dictators, Democracy, and American Public Culture: Envisioning the Totalitarian Enemy, 1920s–1950s,* Cultural Studies of the United States (Chapel Hill: University of North Carolina Press, 2003).

31. Stouffer, *The American Soldier,* 1:59–68, 74, 212, 449.

32. Commandant's Training Directive to the Recruit Depots, cited in a manuscript by Kenneth W. Condit, "Marine Corps Ground Training in World War II" (Washington, DC: Historical Branch, HQMC, 1956), 170.

33. Lee B. Kennett, *G.I.: The American Soldier in World War II* (New York: C. Scribner's Sons, 1987), 42. The Army's training philosophy during World War II is also discussed in B. N. Harlow, "Training for Military Service: Organizing for Total War," *Annals of the American Academy of Political and Social Science* 220 (March 1942): 45–48; R. R. Palmer, *The Procurement and Training of Ground Combat Troops* (Washington, DC: Historical Division, Department of the Army, 1948), 442–455; Alpers, "This Is the Army," 129–163.

34. Palmer, *Procurement and Training,* 444–446.

35. General Krulak served as the commander of Marine Corps Recruit Depot San Diego in 1960, though the processes he describes are well documented in Marines' memoirs of World War II. Victor H. Krulak, *First to Fight: An Inside View of the U.S. Marine Corps* (Annapolis, MD: Naval Institute Press, 1999), 161. See also Robert Leckie, *Helmet for My Pillow* (New York: Random House, 1957), 8–9; Paul H. Douglas, *In the Fullness of Time: The Memoirs of Paul H. Douglas* (New York: Harcourt Brace Jovanovich, 1972), 112.

36. For a detailed explanation of the stages of separation, liminality, and incorporation involved in rites of passage, see Arnold van Gennep, *The Rites of Passage* (London: Routledge and Kegan Paul, 1960).

37. Krulak, *First to Fight,* 167.

38. William Raymond Manchester, *Goodbye, Darkness: A Memoir of the Pacific War* (Boston: Little, Brown, 1980), 122.

39. Ibid.

40. Condit, "Marine Corps Ground Training," 165.

41. Douglas, *In the Fullness of Time,* 112. Paul Douglas was awarded a Bronze Star for bravery on Peleliu and served in the Senate from 1949 to 1967.

42. Condit, "Marine Corps Ground Training," 172.

43. Training schedules did not separate out drill from other garrison subjects, so precise hours of drill are impossible to calculate. This figure comes from one Marine's recollection of boot camp at Parris Island. See Gerald P. Averill, *Mustang: A Combat Marine* (Novato, CA: Presidio Press, 1987), 17.

44. E. J. Kahn Jr., "The Army Life," in *The New Yorker Book of War Pieces* (New York: Reynal and Hitchcock, 1947), 108; Palmer, *Procurement and Training,* 444–445.

45. For a skeptical perspective on recruit training, see S. G. Silcox, *A Hillbilly Marine* (Quantico, VA: Library of the Marine Corps, 1977), 76. More positive portrayals are found in Lince, *Too Young the Heroes,* 3–28; E. B. Sledge, *With the Old Breed, at Peleliu and Okinawa* (Novato, CA: Presidio Press, 1981); Averill, *Mustang,* 3–12; Samuel E. Stavisky, *Marine Combat Correspondent: World War II in the Pacific* (New York: Ivy Books, 1999), 9–25.

46. Spooner interview, 2, 21.

47. Leckie, *Helmet for My Pillow,* 6, 13.

48. Dan Levin, *From the Battlefield: Dispatches of a World War II Marine* (Annapolis, MD: Naval Institute Press, 1995), 3.

49. Manchester, *Goodbye, Darkness,* 120, 122–123.

50. J. Ted Hartman, *Tank Driver: With the 11th Armored from the Battle of the Bulge to VE Day* (Bloomington: Indiana University Press, 2003), 6–13, 26; T. Moffatt Burriss, *Strike and Hold: A Memoir of the 82nd Airborne in World War II* (Washington, DC: Brassey's, 2000), 15–20; John D. McKenzie, *On Time, on Target: The World War II Memoir of a Paratrooper in the 82nd Airborne* (Novato, CA: Presidio Press, 2000), 1–6, 37–53.

51. Stouffer, *The American Soldier,* 78.

52. Clyde Hill Metcalf, *The Marine Corps Reader* (New York: G. P. Putnam's Sons, 1944), 41.

53. United States Marine Corps, "Leadership," 1, William H. Whyte Papers, PPC, box 3, folder 1, MCA.

54. Levin, *From the Battlefield*, 117.

55. Lieutenant Colonel John H. Magruder III, "A Touch of Tradition," *Marine Corps Gazette* 43 (November 1959): 43. The second quote comes from remarks by General Vernon E. Megee, USMC, at the Dallas, Texas, Marine Corps Birthday Ball, reprinted in *Marine Corps Gazette* 49 (January 1965): 18.

56. Averill, *Mustang*, 3.

57. The importance of the "primary group" in establishing norms and standards of conduct in warfare is discussed in Stouffer, *The American Soldier*, 2:130–142. The importance of the primary group to Marines in the Pacific is discussed in Cameron, *American Samurai*, 192–201.

58. J. M. Winter and Emmanuel Sivan, *War and Remembrance in the Twentieth Century*, Studies in the Social and Cultural History of Modern Warfare (Cambridge, UK: Cambridge University Press, 1999), 40–60. Winter focuses mostly on the benefits of fictive kinship for mediating bereavement, a point I explore in Chapter 2.

59. "A Marine Never Dies," in Metcalf, *The Marine Corps Reader*, 93–98.

60. Corporal Gary C. Cooper, USMC, "Guideposts for Leadership," *Marine Corps Gazette* 44 (July 1960): 35.

61. See "Post of the Corps: Camp Geiger," *Leatherneck* 50 (August 1967): 71. See also Captain Kendall S. Schaefer, USMC, "No Man's Ghost," *Marine Corps Gazette* 54 (January 1970): 42. A variation of the same slogan appeared on the masthead of the *Parris Island Boot* newspaper in the 1940s and in the opening sequence of the 1957 film *The D.I.*, which is discussed in Chapter 5.

62. Spooner, *The Spirit of Semper Fidelis*, 251.

63. Lucas, *Indestructible*, 33.

64. Émile Durkheim was the first to argue that a system of belief need not contain affirmations of God or the supernatural to be a religion. Rather, the defining characteristic of a religion is its ability to tie individuals together in a single moral community through "a unified system of beliefs and practices relative to sacred things." This "functionalist" definition of religion applies well to the Marine Corps. Durkheim's discussion of the principal feelings religions inspire, which he terms "collective effervescence," also bears striking similarities to the Marine Corps notion of *esprit de corps*, which Rick Spooner calls "a magical feeling" and Rob-

ert Leckie called an "intangible mystique." See Émile Durkheim, *The Elementary Forms of Religious Life* (New York: Free Press, 1995), 44, 220–241, 424–429; Leckie, *Helmet for My Pillow*, 6.

65. The likely etymological roots of the English word "religion" are the Latin words *religare* (to bind together) and *religo* (obligation, bond). *Oxford English Dictionary*, 2nd ed. (2005), s.v. "religion."

66. Leckie, *Helmet for My Pillow*, 6.

67. A total of 97 percent of all officers and 90 percent of all enlisted Marines served overseas during World War II. See "Reference Service Log," HD subject file "Wars, World War II," MCA.

68. There were three operational theaters of the Pacific: China-Burma-India, Southwest Pacific Area, and Pacific Ocean Area. My discussion of the "Pacific theater" refers to both the Southwest Pacific Area and the Pacific Ocean Area.

69. A service's casualty ratio is the total battle casualties divided by the number who served between December 1941 and December 1945. This includes battle deaths and wounds but excludes most combat fatigue cases as well as non-battle deaths from disease or accidents. The Marine Corps suffered 86,940 casualties in World War II. The Army suffered 800,735 casualties and had a casualty ratio of 7 percent. The Navy suffered 74,728 casualties and had a casualty ratio of 1.2 percent. For all casualties, see "Principal Wars in Which the United States Participated."

70. Comparative casualty figures are given in Robert S. Burrell, *The Ghosts of Iwo Jima* (College Station, TX: Texas A&M Press, 2006), 84; Dower, *War without Mercy*, 299.

71. Comments about the Army's poor performance abound in the personal papers of World War II Marines. See the comments of George E. Aho in "Fighting on Guadalcanal," 6, Samuel Cosman Papers, PPC, MCA. See also the letters of Lieutenant Richard Kennard to family, February 22, March 8, and October 8, 1944; February 24, April 24, and May 18, 1945. For views on the Navy and Army Air Forces, see letters from June 3 and September 12, 1945, all in box 1, folders 9–27, Kennard PPC, MCA.

72. Only the Middle East theater had higher rates. See William S. Mullins and Albert J. Glass, eds., *Neuropsychiatry in World War II*, vol. 2,

Overseas Theaters (Washington, DC: Office of the Surgeon General, Department of the Army, 1973), 1008; Gilbert W. Beebe and Michael E. DeBakey, *Battle Casualties* (Springfield, IL: Thomas, 1952), 69.

73. United States Army Medical Department, *Medical Statistics in World War II* (Washington, DC: Office of the Surgeon General, Department of the Army, 1975), 738, 746.

74. The use of atabrine to treat malaria was also part of the problem, as it could produce a condition called atabrine psychosis. This point is made in Mullins and Glass, *Neuropsychiatry in World War II*, 2:1017–1021. Psychiatric admission rates by theater are listed on 1015–1020.

75. Kennett, *G.I.*, 156, 184.

76. The definitive work on the influence of race in the Pacific War is John W. Dower, *War without Mercy: Race and Power in the Pacific War* (New York: Pantheon Books, 1986). See also Kennett, *G.I.*, 162–171.

77. David M. Kennedy, *Freedom from Fear*, Oxford History of the United States (New York: Oxford University Press, 2004), 813; Kennett, *G.I.*, 184.

78. Richard Tregaskis, *Guadalcanal Diary* (New York: Random House, 1943), 15–16.

79. 1st Marine Division Intelligence Section Directive, September 26, 1943, Samuel Cosman Papers, PPC, MCA.

80. "Honor after Death," *Time*, June 26, 1944, 88. On mailing body parts home, see also Richard Kennard to family, February 20, 1944, box 1, file 9, Kennard PPC, MCA.

81. The landing and the nighttime Battle of Savo Island is covered in Ronald H. Spector, *Eagle against the Sun: The American War with Japan* (New York: Free Press, 1985), 193–195. For Marines' thoughts on Guadalcanal, see Leckie, *Helmet for my Pillow*, 108; Stanley E. Smith, *The United States Marine Corps in World War II: The One-Volume History, from Wake to Tsingtao* (New York: Random House, 1969), 202.

82. Combat fatigue—which earlier generations called shell shock and the Army and Navy called psychoneurosis—should not be confused with post-traumatic stress, which is discussed in Chapter 4. A total of 6,842 Marines were labeled as combat fatigue cases during World War II. For a list of all combat fatigue cases by battle, see "U.S. Marine Corps Casualties," series I, box 18, file 919, HBP. See also "Battle Casualties by

State of Residence and Type of Casualty," "Personnel Distribution" binder, HD statistics section, MCA, which lists 6,413 cases of combat fatigue. Some of the official monographs produced by the Historical Section, HQMC, also list combat fatigue cases. See Captain James R. Stockman, *The Battle for Tarawa* (Washington, DC: Historical Section, HQMC, 1947), 72; Whitman S. Bartley, *Iwo Jima: Amphibious Epic* (Washington, DC: Historical Branch, HQMC, 1954), 221; Chas. S. Nichols and Henry I. Shaw, *Okinawa: Victory in the Pacific* (Washington, DC: Historical Branch, HQMC, 1955), 308. None of these tallies reflects the full sum of combat fatigue cases, however, because a number of units labeled psychiatric casualties as victims of "blast concussion" and routed them through medical channels rather than psychiatric ones. See Cameron, *American Samurai,* 157–165.

83. Allan Reed Millett, *In Many a Strife: General Gerald C. Thomas and the U.S. Marine Corps, 1917–1956* (Annapolis, MD: Naval Institute Press, 1993), 213.

84. These battles are covered in Millett, *Semper Fidelis,* 379–385; Spector, *Eagle against the Sun,* 223–248. See also Lieutenant Colonel Frank O. Hough and Major John A. Crown, *The Campaign on New Britain* (Washington, DC: Historical Branch, HQMC, 1952).

85. The Marines suffered 23,203 physical casualties on Iwo Jima and 19,460 on Okinawa. These figures do not include an additional 3,716 cases of combat fatigue. See United States Marine Corps, *History of U.S. Marine Corps Operations in World War II,* 4:797, 5:884; "U.S. Marine Corps Casualties," HPB.

86. United States Marine Corps, *History of U.S. Marine Corps Operations in World War II,* vol. 4, *Western Pacific Operations* (Washington, DC: Historical Division, HQMC, 1968), 489–490. For a similar disagreement during the Peleliu operation, see ibid., 104.

87. Jeter Allen Isely and Philip Axtell Crowl, *The U.S. Marines and Amphibious War: Its Theory and Its Practice in the Pacific* (Princeton, NJ: Princeton University Press, 1951), 11–12, 251, 338. See also Robert S. Burrell, *The Ghosts of Iwo Jima* (College Station: Texas A&M University Press, 2006), 18–19.

88. United States Marine Corps, *History of U.S. Marine Corps Operations in World War II,* vol. 3, *Central Pacific Drive* (Washington, DC: Historical

Branch, HQMC, 1966), 636. An additional sixteen men were labeled combat fatigue cases. See "U.S. Marine Corps Casualties," HBP; a similar number is listed in Stockman, *The Battle for Tarawa*, 72.

89. "Our Will to Die Won Tarawa, Says General," *Chicago Daily Tribune*, November 30, 1943, 4.

90. United States Marine Corps, *Central Pacific Drive*, 97.

91. Ibid.

92. Millett, *Semper Fidelis*, 400–403; United States Marine Corps, *Central Pacific Drive*, 207.

93. Millett, *Semper Fidelis*, 402.

94. United States Marine Corps, *Central Pacific Drive*, 636; "U.S. Marine Corps Casualties," HBP.

95. United States Marine Corps, *Central Pacific Drive*, 317–320.

96. Cameron, *American Samurai*, 144.

97. Levin, *From the Battlefield*, 117.

98. Lieutenant Richard Kennard to father, February 22, 1944, Folder 9, Kennard Papers, PPC, MCA.

99. Diary of Platoon Sergeant Thomas R. O'Neill, entry for August 21, 1944, 33, folder 2, O'Neill Papers, PPC, MCA (hereafter cited as O'Neill diary).

100. Ronald H. Spector, *Eagle against the Sun*, 145, 187.

101. Levin, *From the Battlefield*, 84–85. See also Lieutenant Richard Kennard to family, February 24, 1945, box 1, folder 22, PPC, MCA.

102. Leckie, *Helmet for My Pillow*, 311.

103. Ibid., 98–99.

104. Robert Sherrod, "It Was Sickening to Watch," *Time*, March 5, 1945, 26.

105. O'Neill diary, entry for July 25, 1944, 15, O'Neill PPC, MCA.

106. "U.S. Marine Corps Casualties," HBP.

107. Ibid.

108. A total of 1,336 Marines were killed on Peleliu and 5,450 were wounded. See United States Marine Corps, *History of U.S. Marine Corps Operations in World War II*, vol. 4, *Western Pacific Operations* (Washington, DC: Historical Division, HQMC, 1968), 797. The most compelling memoir of the battle is Sledge, *With the Old Breed*.

109. *Western Pacific Operations*, 797.

110. "Description of Battle by 2ndLT Robert A. Schless, B-2-25," March 20, 1945, 15, Iwo Jima Collection, MCA.

111. Ibid.

112. Sledge, *With the Old Breed,* 264; "U.S. Marine Corps Casualties," HBP. Official Historical Branch monographs list the number of combat fatigue cases at 2,648 on Iwo Jima and 1,645 on Okinawa. See Whitman S. Bartley, *Iwo Jima: Amphibious Epic,* 221; Nichols and Shaw, *Okinawa: Victory in the Pacific,* 308. For a detailed discussion of Iwo's casualties, see Burrell, *The Ghosts of Iwo Jima,* 80–91.

113. For psychiatrists' perspective on the Marines, see Mullins and Glass, eds., *Neuropsychiatry in World War II,* 2:610–611, 664.

114. David Tucker Brown Jr., *Marine from Virginia: Letters 1941–1945* (Chapel Hill: University of North Carolina Press, 1947), 66.

115. Schless, "Description of Battle," 16.

116. Levin, *From the Battlefield,* 133.

117. Fully fifty-two of the Marines' eighty-two medals were awarded posthumously. A complete list of World War II Medal of Honor recipients may be found in George Lang, Raymond L. Collins, and Gerard F. White, *Medal of Honor Recipients, 1863–1994* (New York: Facts on File, 1995), 2:605–655.

118. Schless, "Description of Battle," 19, Iwo Jima Collection, MCA.

119. Lieutenant Richard Kennard to family, April 24, 1945, Folder 24, Kennard PPC, MCA.

120. Captain Bonnie Little's quote is contained in W. O. Maxwell, letter to the editor, *Time,* April 17, 1944, 4.

121. R. Alton Lee, "The Army Mutiny of 1946," *Journal of American History* 53 (December 1966): 555–571.

122. "Department of War Review of Public Relations," April 30, 1946, 5, E107 Information Division Correspondence 1946–1950, box 3, "Army" file, RG 127, NARA.

123. Colonel Maverick (pseud.), "Here's Looking at You," *Infantry Journal* 58 (May 1946): 8.

124. Hanson W. Baldwin, "The GI and the Brass," *Infantry Journal* 58 (May 1946): 13.

125. Cameron, *American Samurai,* 15–20.

2. The Privates' War and the Home Front in the 1940s

1. Frances Newman to Major General Clifton B. Cates, June 22, 1945, E107 Information Division Correspondence 1946–1950, box 13, "1835 Commandant" file, RG 127, NARA. For newspaper coverage of the party, see "Cinderella Story" and other clippings in Clifton Bledsoe Cates Papers, PPC, box 2, "4th Marine Division Letters" file, MCA.

2. Untitled article in the Knoxville (TN) *New Sentinel,* June 13, 1945, Cates PPC, box 2, "4th Marine Division Letters" file, MCA. This is also a quote from Frances' first letter to the general. See Frances Newman to C. B. Cates, April 24, 1945, E107, box 13, "1835 Commandant" file, RG 127, NARA.

3. "Orchid from Iwo Jima," *Christian Science Monitor,* June 27, 1945, Cates PPC, box 2, "4th Marine Division Letters" file, MCA.

4. Frances Newman to C. B. Cates, June 22, 1945, E107, box 13, "1835 Commandant" file, RG 127, NARA.

5. The best works on Marine public relations in World War II are Robert George Lindsay, *This High Name: Public Relations and the U.S. Marine Corps* (Madison: University of Wisconsin Press, 1956), 53–67, and Bemis M. Frank, *Denig's Demons and How They Grew: The Story of Marine Corps Combat Correspondents, Photographers and Artists* (Washington, DC: Marine Corps Combat Correspondents and Photographers Association, 1967). See also Captain Phillip N. Pierce, "The Marine Corps' Fourth Estate," *Marine Corps Gazette* 30 (September 1946): 48–53. A number of memoirs by combat correspondents are also useful. See, in particular, Samuel E. Stavisky, *Marine Combat Correspondent: World War II in the Pacific* (New York: Ivy Books, 1999); Dan Levin, *From the Battlefield: Dispatches of a World War II Marine* (Annapolis, MD: Naval Institute Press, 1995); Jim Griffing Lucas, *Combat Correspondent* (New York: Reynal and Hitchcock, 1944); Alvin M. Josephy, *The Long and the Short and the Tall: The Story of a Marine Combat Unit in the Pacific* (New York: A. A. Knopf, 1946); and Garry M. Cameron, *Last to Know, First to Go: The United States Marine Corps' Combat Correspondents* (Capistrano Beach, CA: Charger Books, 1988).

6. Even though it is a memoir, the best treatment of the photograph and bond tour is James Bradley and Ron Powers, *Flags of Our Fathers* (New

York: Bantam Books, 2000). See also Karal Ann Marling and John Wetenhall, *Iwo Jima: Monuments, Memories, and the American Hero* (Cambridge, MA: Harvard University Press, 1991); Robert S. Burrell, *The Ghosts of Iwo Jima* (College Station: Texas A&M University Press, 2006), 129–196.

7. The history of the image and its many reproductions is explored in Marling and Wetenhall, *Iwo Jima*, 102–242.

8. John Bradley's and Ira Hayes' discomfort on the bond tour is detailed in Bradley and Powers, *Flags of Our Fathers*, 285–295.

9. A full explanation of the use of private obligation to persuade Americans to fight in World War II can be found in Robert B. Westbrook, *Why We Fought: Forging American Obligations in World War II* (Washington, DC: Smithsonian Books, 2004), 40–91.

10. Richard Polenberg, *War and Society: The United States, 1941–1945* (Philadelphia: J. B. Lippincott, 1972), 79, 138, 145, 148–150. See also William M. Tuttle, *Daddy's Gone to War: The Second World War in the Lives of America's Children* (New York: Oxford University Press, 1993), 219–220.

11. In the last six months of 1944, Army casualties alone were over 50,000 per month. See Lee Kennett, *G.I.: The American Soldier in World War II* (New York: C. Scribner's Sons, 1987), 174–175. For a summary of Navy and Marine Corps casualties in the same period, see John W. Dower, *War without Mercy: Race and Power in the Pacific War* (New York: Pantheon Books, 1986), 300. See also U.S. Navy Bureau of Medicine and Surgery, *History of the Medical Department of the United States Navy in World War II*, vol. 3, *The Statistics of Diseases and Injuries* (Washington, DC: GPO, 1950), 159–160.

12. Anonymous letter to Secretary of the Navy James V. Forrestal, March 22, 1945, Records of Secretary of the Navy James V. Forrestal, box 104, file 57-4-6, RG 80, NARA.

13. Lindsay, *This High Name*, 50, 53, 55.

14. Ibid., 53.

15. Perry R. Duis, "No Time for Privacy: WWII and Chicago Families," in Lewis A. Erenberg and Susan E. Hirsch, eds., *The War in American Culture: Society and Consciousness during World War II* (Chicago: University of Chicago Press, 1996), 34.

16. J. Walter Thompson Company, "United States Marine Corps Nation-Wide Survey, November 1941," 13–16, HD subject file "Selective Service 1861–1955," MCA. The survey involved more than 2,000 boys and parents selected to form a geographic, economic, and educational cross-section of the country.

17. Ibid., 17.

18. Allan Reed Millett, *Semper Fidelis: The History of the United States Marine Corps* (New York: Free Press, 1991), 348.

19. For a fine overview of the battle of Wake Island, see Ronald H. Spector, *Eagle against the Sun: The American War with Japan* (New York: Free Press, 1985), 102–106.

20. Lindsay, *This High Name*, 55. The major works written by Lieutenant Thomason's father, John W. Thomason, are *Fix Bayonets!* (New York: C. Scribner's Sons, 1927); *Red Pants and Other Stories* (New York: C. Scribner's Sons, 1927); *Marines and Others* (New York: Scribner, 1929); and *And a Few Marines* (New York: C. Scribner's Sons, 1943).

21. Walter Trohan, "President Hails Heroic Marine Stand at Wake," *Chicago Daily Tribune*, December 13, 1941, 6; "Far Eastern Battle," *New York Times*, December 28, 1941, E2.

22. Samuel T. Williamson, "From Montezuma's Halls to Wake Island; Wherever He Has Fought the United States Marine Has Added a Bit to His Now Towering Reputation," *New York Times Sunday Magazine*, January 25, 1942, 10. See also Samuel T. Williamson, "The Fighting Marine—Why He's a Fighter," *New York Times Sunday Magazine*, August 16, 1942, SM6.

23. "What Faith?" *Time*, August 17, 1942, 46.

24. Emmet Lavery, "The Enemy in Perspective," *Commonweal*, November 19, 1943, cited in Westbrook, *Why We Fought*, 33.

25. For just a few examples, see Edward T. Folliard, "Marines Gallantly Hold Wake," *Washington Post*, December 12, 1941, 1; "Far Eastern Battle," *New York Times*, December 28, 1941, E1; "Wake Island, a Bright Page in Our History," *Los Angeles Times*, December 29, 1941, A4; Samuel T. Williamson, "From Montezuma's Halls to Wake Island," *New York Times Sunday Magazine*, January 25, 1942, 10.

26. Editorial, "Wake," *Washington Post*, December 25, 1941, 10. For a similar sentiment, see President Franklin Delano Roosevelt's comments on

Wake in "Message to Congress on the State of the Union," *Chicago Tribune,* January 7, 1942, 4.

27. Hanson W. Baldwin, "Parris Island Fast in Making Marines," *New York Times,* August 17, 1942, 11.

28. Robert Sherrod, "After Two Years," *Time,* December 27, 1943, 31.

29. Frank, *Denig's Demons,* 4–5.

30. "Thirteen Capitol Reporters Become Marine Combat Correspondents," HD subject file "Combat Correspondents 440–80 (1)," MCA.

31. Frank, *Denig's Demons,* 49.

32. Department of the Navy Office of Public Relations, "Public Relations Bulletin," June 10, 1943, HD subject file "Public Relations, Navy," 1, 3, MCA.

33. "Army Public Relations," in "Proceedings of the 1st Annual Naval Public Relations Officers' Conference, July 28–31, 1941, Washington, D.C.," 11, HD subject file "Public Relations, Navy," MCA.

34. Ibid., 10–15. See also George H. Roeder, *The Censored War: American Visual Experience during World War Two* (New Haven: Yale University Press, 1993), 92.

35. For Army accreditation figures, see Colonel R. Ernest Dupuy, USA, "War News and the Press," *Military Review,* August 1943, 5. By November 1943, the Navy Department had accredited only 112 civilian journalists to cover the Navy overseas and was issuing temporary credentials at a rate of seven per month. Roughly half received credentials to be aboard ship. See "112 War Correspondents Covering Navy," Department of Navy press release, November 2, 1943, HD subject file "Combat Correspondents, Memo," MCA.

36. Robert Landry to *Life* pictures editor Wilson Hicks, n.d., cited in Roeder, *The Censored War,* 92.

37. Production and distribution logs of the stories submitted and published, by correspondent and by month, from 1942 to 1946 may be found in HD subject file "Combat Correspondents" (three folders), MCA, and in "Division of Public Information, Production and Distribution Logs," box 3, "CC Bulletin" file, RG 127, NARA. The number of CCs in uniform in August 1943 is listed in *Combat Correspondents Memorandum* 2, no. 14 (August 1943), HD subject file "Combat Correspondents (3)," MCA.

38. See linage surveys in *Combat Correspondents Memorandum* 2, no. 14 (August 1943), and 3, no. 7 (May 1944), HD subject file "Combat Correspondents (3)," MCA.

39. "Proceedings of the 1st Annual Naval Public Relations Officers' Conference, 28–31 July 1941, Washington, D.C.," 10, HD subject file "Public Relations, Navy," MCA.

40. A good summary of the different service cultures, which discusses the Army's emphasis on the profession of arms and the Navy and Air Force's obsessions with technology, can be found in Carl H. Builder, *The Masks of War: American Military Styles in Strategy and Analysis* (Baltimore, MD: Johns Hopkins University Press, 1989), ch. 1–3. For a few indications of the Army's focus on the "view from the map," see Hanson W. Baldwin, "Philippines Delaying Foe: Japanese Strategy Believed to Aim at Extending Thin Defense Lines," *New York Times*, December 13, 1941, 4; James B. Reston, "MacArthur Beats Off Two Divisions," *New York Times*, February 3, 1942, 1.

41. Coverage of the Battle of Midway demonstrates well the technocentric tone of Navy and Army Air Forces reporting. See "The Fightingest Ship," *Time*, September 28, 1942, 36–37; Clark Lee, "Call Torpedo, Diver Planes Key to Sea War," *Chicago Daily Tribune*, June 27, 1942, 1; Frank Tremaine, "Army Flyers Tell of Midway Flight," *Los Angeles Times*, June 12, 1942, 1.

42. "Official Style Book for Marine Corps Public Relations Officers and Combat Correspondents," 11, HD subject file "Combat Correspondents Memo," MCA. Emphasis in original.

43. See comments of the managing editor of the *Albany* (NY) *Times-Union* and other editors in "Memo to General Denig," 4, in "Division of Public Information, General Corr. 1942–1950," box 1, "Clip Sheets" file, RG 127, NARA. See also *Combat Correspondents Memorandum* 3, no. 16 (October 1944): 5, "Combat Correspondents (3)," MCA.

44. *Combat Correspondents Memorandum* 2, no. 19 (December 1943): 6, HD subject file "Combat Correspondents (3)," MCA.

45. Memorandum, "Combat Correspondents, Assignment for," June 4, 1943, HD subject file "440–80 Combat Correspondents (2)," MCA.

46. *Combat Correspondents Memorandum* 2, no. 12 (July 1943): 6, HD subject file "Combat Correspondents (3)," MCA.

47. See the linage survey in *Combat Correspondents Memorandum* 3, no. 7 (May, 1944): 8, HD subject file "Combat Correspondents (3)," MCA; Lindsay, *This High Name*, 63; Cameron, *Last to Know*, 31.

48. "Halls of Montezuma," script 9, II-1, June 7, 1942, Radio Scripts 1933–1945, box 1, "4: Halls of Montezuma, 1942" file, RG 127, NARA.

49. *Combat Correspondents Memorandum* 3, no. 17 (October 1944): 2, HD subject file "Combat Correspondents (3)," MCA.

50. *Combat Correspondents Memorandum* 2, no. 3 (February 1943): 6. For a description of life as a female CC, including a light-hearted poem about life in Washington, DC, see *Combat Correspondents Memorandum* 2, no. 16 (October 1943): 4–5, HD subject file "Combat Correspondents (3)," MCA.

51. *Combat Correspondents Memorandum* 2, no. 19 (December 1943): 7, HD subject file "Combat Correspondents (3)," MCA .

52. *Combat Correspondents Memorandum* 3, no. 1 (January 1944): 9–10, HD subject file "Combat Correspondents (3)," MCA.

53. *Combat Correspondents Memorandum* 4, no. 1 (January 1945): 4–5, HD subject file "Combat Correspondents (3)," MCA.

54. *CC Bulletin* 4, no. 9 (July 1945), "Division of Public Info Production and Distribution Logs," box 3, "CC Bulletin" file, RG 127, NARA.

55. *CC Bulletin* 4, no. 8 (June 1945), "Division of Public Info Production and Distribution Logs," box 3, "CC Bulletin" file, RG 127, NARA.

56. *CC Bulletin* 4, no. 7 (May 1945), "Division of Public Info Production and Distribution Logs," box 3, "CC Bulletin" file, RG 127, NARA.

57. "Guide to Navy Public Relations," 23, HD Subject file "Public Relations, Navy," MCA.

58. Ibid., 19.

59. The CCs had great respect for Ernie Pyle particularly because he shared their goal of reporting on the experiences of the enlisted men. See Captain Phillip N. Pierce, "The Marine Corps' Fourth Estate," *Marine Corps Gazette* 30 (September 1946): 48.

60. See *Combat Correspondents Memorandum* 3, no. 12 (July 1944): 4, HD subject file "Combat Correspondents (3), MCA.

61. Kennett, *G.I.*, 174–175. See also Roeder, *The Censored War*, 33, which cites a War Department statistic that American soldiers died at a rate of one every three minutes. These numbers are just for the Army and

Army Air Forces. For Navy and Marine Corps deaths by month, see U.S. Navy, *The Statistics of Diseases and Injuries,* 178–179.

62. Mrs. L. W. Lotspeich to Secretary of the Navy James V. Forrestal, March 9, 1945, box 104, file 57-4-6, RG 80, NARA. The letter was quoted in "No Stopping," *Time,* March 26, 1945, 19, and it prompted more than a dozen critical letters to the secretary of the Navy, mostly from mothers, all of which are found in the same file.

63. Mrs. George Lambina to Secretary of the Navy James V. Forrestal, March 19, 1945, box 104, file 57-4-6, RG 80, NARA.

64. Frances Newman to Mrs. Cates, June 8, 1945, E107, box 13, "1835 Commandant" file, RG 127, NARA.

65. C. B. Cates to Frances Newman, May 5, 1945, E107, box 13, "1835 Commandant" file, RG 127, NARA.

66. Frances Newman to C. B. Cates, April 24, 1945, E107, box 13, "1835 Commandant" file, RG 127, NARA.

67. Ibid.

68. C. B. Cates to Frances Newman, May 5, 1945, E107, box 13, "1835 Commandant" file, RG 127, NARA.

69. Comic strip from *Washington* (DC) *Sunday Star,* September 2, 1945, Cates scrapbook, Cates PPC, box 1, MCA. The details of the many events the Marines planned for Frances are found in her letters to General Cates and in the correspondence between General Cates and Mayor Charles L. Bolan, all in E107, box 13, "1835 Commandant" file, RG 127, NARA. For additional clippings on the party, see Cates PPC, box 2, "Fourth Marine Division letters" file and HD biographical file "Clifton Cates," MCA.

70. Mrs. W. C. Baty to C. B. Cates, June 28, 1945, Cates PPC, box 10, "Misc. Letters" file, MCA.

71. James Fowler, "Kid Sister of Iwo Marines Dances with a Heavy Heart," Cates PPC, box 2, "Fourth Marine Division 1942" file, MCA.

72. C. B. Cates to family, June 23, 1945, Cates PPC, box 2, "Fourth Marine Division, 1942" file, MCA.

73. Meldred I. Kelly to C. B. Cates, June 17, 1945, Cates PPC, box 10, "Misc. Letters" file, MCA.

74. The sign in General Denig's office is noted in Millett, *Semper Fidelis,* 390–391.

75. Frances Newman to C. B. Cates, April 24, 1945, E107, box 13, "1835 Commandant" file, RG 127, NARA.

76. Frances Newman to Mrs. Cates, June 8, 1945, E107, box 13, "1835 Commandant" file, RG 127, NARA.

77. Frances Newman to C. B. Cates, June 22, 1945, E107, box 13, "1835 Commandant" file, RG 127, NARA.

78. Ibid.

79. Ibid.

80. The final line of "The Marines' Hymn" is "If the army and the navy ever look on Heaven's scenes / They will find the streets are guarded by United States Marines." Frances' reference to the hymn is in her letter to C. B. Cates, April 24, 1945, E107, box 13, "1835 Commandant" file, RG 127, NARA.

81. C. B. Cates to family, June 27 and July 8, 1945, Cates PPC, box 2, "Fourth Marine Division 1942" file, MCA.

82. Margaret Shannon, "Orchids for Frances: Kid Sister to Broadcast on 'We the People' Hour," *Atlanta Journal,* June 14, 1945, 1, and "Brave Girl's Birthday Date," unnamed newspaper, both in Cates PPC, box 2, "Fourth Marine Division 1942" file, MCA.

83. Carl Hilstrom, "Death Claims Marines' Friend in Three Wars," *Navy Times,* May 29, 1968, 48, HD biographical file "Jean De Marranza," MCA.

84. Jean De Marranza to General A. A. Vandegrift, October 30, 1946, E107, box 12, file "1670-30-5 MC Birthday (1)," RG 127, NARA. Emphasis in original.

85. Jean De Marranza to General A. A. Vandegrift, November 9, 1947, E107, box 12, file "1670-30-5 MC Birthday (1)," RG 127, NARA.

86. Westbrook, *Why We Fought,* 40–91.

87. Laura Wexler, *Tender Violence: Domestic Visions in an Age of U.S. Imperialism, Cultural Studies of the United States* (Chapel Hill: University of North Carolina Press, 2000), 6–14.

88. Hans Pols, "War Neurosis, Adjustment Problems in Veterans and an Ill Nation: The Disciplinary Project of American Psychiatry during and after World War II," *Osiris* 22 (2007): 82–92.

89. Tuttle, *Daddy's Gone to War,* 217.

90. Veterans Administration hospitals had 42,281 psychiatric beds in 1944. By 1948, the number had grown to 56,101. See Hugh Rockoff, "Operating Beds in Medical Centers of the U.S. Department of Veterans Affairs, by Type of Bed: 1936–1997," table Ed431–436, in Susan B. Carter et al., eds., *Historical Statistics of the United States, Earliest Times to the Present,* millennial ed. (New York: Cambridge University Press, 2006). On disability payments, see John Morton Blum, *V Was for Victory: Politics and American Culture during World War II* (New York: Harcourt Brace Jovanovich, 1976), 335.

91. Douglas Eckberg, "Suicides and Homicides, by Race and Ethnicity: 1910–1997," table Ec199–236 in Susan B. Carter et al., eds., *Historical Statistics of the United States, Earliest Times to the Present,* millennial ed. (New York: Cambridge University Press, 2006).

92. "'Toss of Coin' Robbery Jails Veteran and Wife," *Los Angeles Times,* November 21, 1945, 9; "Battered Bride from Motel to Be Quizzed," *Los Angeles Times,* January 1, 1947, 8; "Ungrateful Robbers Want More Service," *Los Angeles Times,* September 8, 1947, 5; "Testimony Holds Kidnap Suspect," *Los Angeles Times,* April 9, 1948, 5.

93. "Love Blast Perils Three; Police Capture Ex-Marine," *Los Angeles Times,* February 2, 1946, 3; "Another Woman Slain, Victim of Mutilation Killer," *Los Angeles Times,* February 11, 1947, 2; "Los Angeles Briefs," *Los Angeles Times,* December 30, 1947, A16; "Police Hold Ex-Marine for Killing Roommate," *Los Angeles Times,* January 15, 1948, A3.

94. "Marine Shoots Self in Suicide Attempt," *Los Angeles Times,* October 4, 1945, A3; "Ex-Marine Dies from Shot Fired at Wife's Bedside," *Los Angeles Times,* November 13, 1945, A2; "Thunderstorm Held Cause of G.I. Suicide," *Los Angeles Times,* June 10, 1946, 2; "City Briefs," *Los Angeles Times,* December 12, 1946, 11; "Poison Kills Girl; Fiance May Live," *Los Angeles Times,* June 28, 1947, 4;

95. "Toys for Tots: A Community Relations Program of the Marine Corps Reserve," 7, HD subject file "Toys for Tots," MCA.

96. "Toys for Tots: A Community Relations Program, 1956," HD subject file "Toys for Tots," 2–3, MCA.

97. "Toys for Tots News Material: Sample Release Number 3," HD subject file "Toys for Tots," MCA.

98. "Toys for Tots Fact Sheet: 1952," HD subject file "Toys for Tots," MCA.

99. "How to Get the Most out of a Toys for Tots Campaign," 7–12, HD subject file "Toys for Tots," MCA.

100. "Toys for Tots: A Community Relations Program of the Marine Corps Reserve," 2, HD subject file "Toys for Tots," MCA.

101. "Toys for Tots News Material: Sample Release 3," HD subject file "Toys for Tots," MCA.

102. "Toys for Tots: A Community Relations Program of the Marine Corps Reserve," 2, HD subject file "Toys for Tots," MCA.

103. Lawrence H. Suid, *Guts and Glory: The Making of the American Military Image in Film*, rev. ed. (Lexington: University Press of Kentucky, 2002), 97.

104. Brigadier General W. E. Riley to Mr. Robert Denton, May 20, 1948, E107, box 13, "1835 Commandant" file, RG 127, NARA.

105. Suid, *Guts and Glory*, 119.

106. Marling and Wetenhall, *Iwo Jima: Monuments, Memories, and the American Hero*, 128.

107. The producer's claim that the Marines had no substantive input on the script is found in Lawrence Suid's interview with Edmund Grainger, April 30, 1975, typed transcript, 6, HD subject file "Movies, Sands of Iwo Jima," MCA.

108. The Marine Corps' production notes for the film are found in E107, box 24, "Movie, Sands of Iwo Jima" file, RG 127, NARA. See also Major Andrew C. Geer to Director of Public Information, "Notes on the Moving Picture Sands of Iwo Jima," July 19, 1949, and Brigadier General J. T. Seldon to Republic Pictures, June 8, 1949, all in E107, box 24, "Movie, Sands of Iwo Jima" file, RG 127, NARA.

109. See the script screener's comments for scene 207 in E107, box 24, "Movie, Sands of Iwo Jima" file, RG 127, NARA. A later version of the scene (which also was not used) had Stryker pushing Mary and exiting angrily. See Major Andrew Geer's copy of the "Sands of Iwo Jima Final Shooting Script," June 16, 1949, 73, scene 207, in E102 HQ Supt Correspondence, 1950–1958, box 81, "A7 SAF: Sands of Iwo Jima" file, RG 127, NARA.

110. Major Andrew C. Geer to Director of Public Information, "Notes on the Moving Picture Sands of Iwo Jima," July 19, 1949, E107, box 24, "Movie, Sands of Iwo Jima" file, RG 127, NARA.

111. Author's interview with Major Norm Hatch, USMC, April 1, 2006. Transcript in author's possession.
112. On this point, see Marling and Wetenhall, *Iwo Jima: Monuments, Memories, and the American Hero*, 137.
113. See Major Andrew Geer's copy of the "Sands of Iwo Jima Final Shooting Script," June 16, 1949, in E102 HQ Supt Correspondence, 1950–1958, box 81, "A7 SAF: Sands of Iwo Jima" file, RG 127, NARA.
114. John Bodnar, "Saving Private Ryan and Postwar Memory in America," *American Historical Review* 106 (2001): 815; Marling and Wetenhall, *Iwo Jima: Monuments, Memories, and the American Hero*, 138.
115. "Exploitation Manual: 'Sands of Iwo Jima,'" E107, box 24, "Movie Sands of Iwo Jima" file, RG 127, NARA.
116. Captain E. A. Hedahl to Commandant of the Marine Corps, "Marine Corps Presentation of Sportsmanship Award, Plan for," June 1, 1949, E107, box 2, "Thompson, J. Walter (1)" file, RG 127, NARA.
117. "Exploitation Manual 'Sands of Iwo Jima,'" E107, box 24, "Movie Sands of Iwo Jima" file, RG 127, NARA.
118. Ibid.
119. Suid, *Guts and Glory*, 122.
120. Lieutenant Colonel Donovan Yeuell, USA, "An Army That Can Fight," *Infantry Journal* 63 (December 1948): 6.

3. The Politicians and the Guerrillas

1. Paul H. Douglas, *In the Fullness of Time: The Memoirs of Paul H. Douglas* (New York: Harcourt Brace Jovanovich, 1972), 347–348.
2. Lt. Col. James D. Hittle, "The Marine Corps and Its Struggle for Survival," 1948, HD subject file "Unification," MCA. The most detailed discussion of the Marines' unification battles is Gordon W. Keiser, *The U.S. Marine Corps and Defense Unification 1944–47: The Politics of Survival* (Washington, DC: National Defense University Press, 1982). See also, Allan R. Millett, *In Many a Strife: General Gerald C. Thomas and the U.S. Marine Corps, 1917–1956* (Annapolis, MD: Naval Institute Press, 1993), 245–284; Victor H. Krulak, *First to Fight: An Inside View of the U.S. Marine Corps* (Annapolis, MD: Naval Institute Press, 1999), 1–51; Allan Reed Millett, *Semper Fidelis: The History of the United States Marine Corps* (New York: Free Press, 1991), 445–474, 496–507, 541–543;

Jon T. Hoffman, *Once a Legend: "Red Mike" Edson of the Marine Raiders* (Novato, CA: Presidio Press, 1994), 333–380. For an unpublished account by the future publisher of the *New York Times,* see 1st Lt. Arthur Ochs Sulzberger, "Unification and the Marine Corps," 1953, HD subject file "Unification," MCA.

3. "Text of President's Statement on Defense," *New York Times,* May 29, 1958, 8.

4. The three attempts occurred in the battles over the defense budget in fiscal years 1956, 1958, and 1959. See "USMC Fact Sheet," series III, box 72, "Navy-USMC" file, HBP. See also Millett, *Semper Fidelis,* 521–533.

5. The Marine Corps grew from 74,279 to 170,621 in the 1950s—an increase of 130 percent. This was the largest proportional increase of all the services. During the same period, the Air Force's end strength grew by 98 percent, the Navy's by 62 percent, and the Army's by 47 percent. Active duty force levels from 1789 to the present are available online through Department of Defense, Defense Manpower Data Center, Statistical Information and Analysis Division, *Selected Manpower Statistics Fiscal Year 2005,* table 2-11, http://siadapp.dmdc.osd.mil/personnel /M01/fy05/m01fy05.pdf (accessed August 1, 2009).

6. Only the Air Force saw larger proportional growth in its budget. From 1948 to 1960, the Air Force's budget increased by 331 percent, the Marines' increased by 216 percent, the Army's increased by 212 percent, and the Navy's (which also included all Marine Corps funds) increased by 162 percent. Marine Corps budget figures for 1948 are taken from Senate Committee on Appropriations, *Department of the Navy Appropriation Bill, 1949,* 80th Cong., 2d Sess., June 14, 1949, Committee Report 1621, 17. For the 1960 data, see United States Senate, *Department of Defense Appropriation Bill, 1961,* 86th Cong., 2d Sess., June 10, 1960, 44–47. For the period after 1962, see also "Historical Green Dollar Appropriation Data," n.d., HD subject file "Budget," MCA. For total appropriations for the other services, see Office of the Under Secretary of Defense (Comptroller), *National Defense Budget Estimates for FY 2013,* table 6-3, "Department of Defense TOA by Military Department," 73–74, available at http://comptroller.defense.gov/defbudget/fy2013/FY13 _Green_Book.pdf (accessed June 2, 2012).

7. This was also a relative increase in the Marine Corps' share of naval aviation. In 1950, Marine Corps aviation constituted 15 percent of the

Navy's total aviation allowance of 5,582 platforms. In 1965, Marine Corps aviation constituted 20 percent of the Navy's total aviation allowance of 6,066 platforms. See Department of the Navy, Office of the Chief of Naval Operations, "Naval Aeronautical Organization," archived by year, Aviation branch, Archives, Naval History and Heritage Command, Washington Naval Yard, Washington, DC.

8. The total number of amphibious ships grew from 79 in 1950 to 113 in 1960 and to a high of 159 in 1966. This was also a relative increase in the share of ships designed primarily for the Marines' usage. In 1950, amphibious ships constituted 12 percent of the Navy's total active ships; in 1966, they constituted 17 percent of total active ships. While the Navy used a variety of factors to determine the number and type of ships to build, Marine Corps lobbying also influenced it and the Congress. See "U.S. Navy Active Ship Force Levels, 1886–Present," www.history.navy.mil/branches/org9-4.htm (accessed May 5, 2012).

9. On this point, see Thomas G. Paterson, "Presidential Foreign Policy, Public Opinion and the Congress: The Truman Years," *Diplomatic History* 3, no. 1 (1979): 4, 18; Samuel P. Huntington, *The Common Defense: Strategic Programs in National Politics* (New York: Columbia University Press, 1961), 126–129, 133–134, 241; Edward A. Kolodziej, *The Uncommon Defense and Congress 1945–1963* (Columbus: Ohio University Press, 1966), 484–486, 516.

10. Kolodziej, *The Uncommon Defense,* 350–351, 358–362; Morris Janowitz, *The Professional Soldier: A Social and Political Portrait* (Glencoe, IL: Free Press, 1960), 348–350.

11. Oral history transcript of Colonel Robert Debs Heinl Jr., 389, MCOHC, MCA (hereafter Heinl oral history). Heinl also penned one of the most oft-read histories of the Marine Corps, which gives his perspective on the unification fights. See Robert Debs Heinl Jr., *Soldiers of the Sea: The United States Marine Corps 1775–1962* (Annapolis, MD: Naval Institute Press, 1962), 510–536. See also Edwin H. Simmons, *The United States Marines: A History,* 4th ed. (Annapolis, MD: Naval Institute Press, 2003), 191–192.

12. See Major J. C. Fegan, "Ex-Marines Now Members of Congress," *Marine Corps Gazette* 11 (March 1926): 32–35, and "Former Devil Dogs Now Lawmakers," *Washington Evening Star,* May 25, 1937, both in HD subject file "Personalities," MCA.

13. For the armed-service affiliations of members of Congress, see "Advanced Member Analysis," CQ Press Congress Collection, Congressional Quarterly Electronic Library, available at http://library.cqpress.com/congress (accessed August 1, 2009).

14. Another midwestern congressman, Melvin J. Maas (R-Minn.), left the House of Representatives in 1945, but continued to serve in the Marine Corps Reserve and became a powerful behind-the-scenes lobbyist for the Corps until his retirement in 1952. See HD biographical file "Melvin J. Maas," MCA.

15. The professors were Paul Douglas, a professor of economics at the University of Chicago, and Mike Mansfield, a professor of East Asian and Latin American studies at the University of Montana. The war heroes were Marine Raider James Roosevelt (D-Calif.) and James P. S. Devereux (R-Md.), the commander of the Marine garrison on Wake Island.

16. The dual-service veterans were Michael J. Mansfield (D-Mo.), Thomas J. Murray (D-Tenn.), Robert C. Wilson (R-Calif.), and Delbert L. Latta (R-Ohio).

17. For Paul Douglas' career in the Marine Corps and the Senate, see Douglas, *In the Fullness of Time,* 111–124; Roger Biles, *Crusading Liberal: Paul H. Douglas of Illinois* (DeKalb, IL: Northern Illinois University Press, 2002), 39–42. For Senator Mansfield's career, see Don Oberdorfer, *Senator Mansfield: The Extraordinary Life of a Great Statesman and Diplomat* (Washington, DC: Smithsonian Books, 2003), 1–2, 24–28,.

18. Ed Koterba, "Flood Flags Marines," *Evening Bulletin* (Philadelphia, PA), April 15, 1959, 23, in HD subject file "Marine Corps Personalities," MCA.

19. The names of former Marines who worked on congressional staffs are listed in HD subject file "Personalities," MCA. The Marines on the Senate staffs were Lieutenant Colonels George S. Green, Richard J. O'Melia, and Justice M. Chambers, all USMCR. Chambers served on Senate Armed Services, Green was on the Senate Judiciary Committee, and O'Melia served on the Senate Committee on Government Operations.

20. Lieutenant Colonel Russ Blandford was Counsel to the House Armed Services Committee; Lieutenant Colonel Aubrey A. Gunnels, USMCR, served as a professional staff member of the House Appropriations Committee.

21. Senator Saltonstall's assistants were Major John B. Fisher, USMCR, and First Lieutenant Charles W. Colson, USMCR. Senator Styles Bridges' assistant was Lieutenant Colonel Chester M. Wiggan, USMCR. Senator Humphrey's assistant was Captain Max Kampleman, USMCR. See HD subject file "Personalities," MCA.

22. Oral history transcript of Colonel Russell Blandford, USMCR, 7, MCOHC, MCA (hereafter Blandford oral history).

23. "Congressional Marines Group Articles of Organization and Roster," HD subject file "Personalities," MCA.

24. Ibid., 39.

25. For an example of the Navy's attempts to protect its funding and missions, see the discussion of OP-23 in Jeffrey G. Barlow, *Revolt of the Admirals: The Fight for Naval Aviation, 1945–1950* (Washington, DC: Ross and Perry, 2001), 237–243. See also Brigadier General Samuel R. Shaw, USMC, oral history, 220–242, MCOHC, MCA (hereafter Shaw oral history).

26. Sixteen percent of the World War II veterans elected as freshman congressmen in 1946 were either active-duty or retired Marines. Marines also made up 4 percent of the total military personnel who served during World War II. High Morrow, "GI Beachhead in Congress," *Saturday Evening Post,* July 12, 1947, 26. See also "Advanced Member Analysis," CQ Press Congress Collection; Department of Defense, "Principal Wars in Which the United States Participated, U.S. Military Personnel Serving and Casualties," available at http://siadapp.dmdc.osd.mil/personnel/CASUALTY/WCPRINCIPAL.pdf (accessed May 8, 2012).

27. Department of Defense, "Principal Wars"; Morrow, "GI Beachhead in Congress," 121.

28. Morrow, "GI Beachhead."

29. Ibid.

30. Urban Van Sustern cited in Michael O'Brien, "Young Joe McCarthy: 1908–1944," *Wisconsin Magazine of History* 63 (Spring 1980): 218. See this and other articles on McCarthy's career in HD biographical file "Joseph R. McCarthy," MCA. The best accounting of McCarthy's military service is Thomas C. Reeves, *The Life and Times of Joe McCarthy: A Biography* (Lanham, MD: Madison Books, 1997), 45–61. See also Michael O'Brien, "Robert Fleming, Senator McCarthy and the Myth of the Marine Hero," *Journalism Quarterly* 50 (Spring 1973): 48–53.

31. Reeves, *Life and Times,* 42–43; O'Brien, "Young Joe McCarthy," 218–219.

32. Reeves, *Life and Times,* 51.

33. Ibid., 47–48, 51–52. Even hagiographic accounts of Senator McCarthy's career admit that he "puffed up his service record and used this for political advantage." See M. Stanton Evans, *Blacklisted by History: The Untold Story of Senator Joe McCarthy and His Fight against American's Enemies* (New York: Crown Forum, 2007), 31.

34. Reeves, *Life and Times,* 47; O'Brien, "Young Joe McCarthy," 220–221.

35. Reeves, *Life and Times,* 46, 50.

36. O'Brien, "Young Joe McCarthy," 222; Reeves, *Life and Times,* 53–54.

37. O'Brien, "Young Joe McCarthy," 225–227; Reeves, *Life and Times,* 56–57.

38. Reeves, *Life and Times,* 48, 60.

39. Ibid., 52. See also Editorial, "The Meaning of Medals," *Christian Science Monitor,* January 7, 1953, 16.

40. Senator George A. Smathers, interviewed by Donald A. Ritchie, August 1, 1989, Interview I: "The Road to Congress," transcript, 13–14, Senate Oral History Program, Senate Historical Office, Washington, DC, available at www.senate.gov/artandhistory/history/resources/pdf/Smathers_interview_1.pdf (accessed August 1, 2009).

41. Heinl oral history, 387.

42. Good overviews of the Chowder Society and their activities are found in Frank Martullo, "A Good Bowl of Chowder Saved the Marine Corps Following World War II," *Marine Corps Gazette* 62 (December 1978): 22–33; Krulak, *First to Fight,* 17–66; Millett, *In Many a Strife,* 245–259; Millett, *Semper Fidelis,* 456–474; Hoffman, *Once a Legend,* 333–381. See also Robert Coram, *Brute: The Life of Victor Krulak, U.S. Marine* (New York: Back Bay Books, 2010), 158–178.

43. Gerald C. Thomas fought Cacos in Haiti in 1920; Merritt A. Edson fought Sandino's forces in Nicaragua from 1928 to 1929. See Millett, *In Many a Strife,* 74–84; Hoffman, *Once a Legend,* 47–94; Merritt A. Edson, "The Coco Patrol," *Marine Corps Gazette* 20, no. 4 (1936): 40–41, 60–72.

44. Military historians and analysts group these traits under a variety of different labels to include "fourth-generation warfare," "irregular warfare," and "asymmetric warfare." See, for example, Thomas X. Hammes,

"Insurgency: Modern Warfare Evolves into a Fourth Generation," *Strategic Forum* 214 (2005): 2–4; John A. Nagl, *Learning to Eat Soup with a Knife: Counterinsurgency Lessons from Malaya and Vietnam* (Chicago: University of Chicago Press, 2002), 15–16, 25; Rod Thornton, *Asymmetric Warfare: Threat and Response in the Twenty-First Century* (Malden, MA: Polity Press, 2007), 19–20. All of these authors stress insurgents' focus on media and popular opinion, their decentralized organization, and their use of asymmetric tactics. Of course, a major difference is that all of the Chowder Society's efforts were nonviolent. For a discussion on whether such tactics are a form of warfare, see Michel Foucault and Colin Gordon, *Power/Knowledge: Selected Interviews and Other Writings, 1972–1977* (New York: Pantheon Books, 1980), 123; Michel Foucault, *Society Must Be Defended: Lectures at the Collège de France, 1975–76* (New York: Picador, 2003), 15–31.

45. Heinl oral history, 379.

46. Hoffman, *Once a Legend*, 363.

47. Oral history transcript of General Merrill B. Twining, USMC, 274, MCOHC, MCA (hereafter Twining oral history).

48. Krulak, *First to Fight*, 49; Merrill B. Twining to Bemis Frank, n.d., "Last Days of the Chowder Society," 2, in HD biographical file "J. D. Hittle," MCA.

49. Other prominent Marine Quakers include Major General Smedley D. Butler and Senator Paul Douglas. See HD biographical files for both, MCA. See also Roger Butterfield and Frank Gibney, "The Twining Tradition," *Life*, August 26, 1957, 104–122.

50. Heinl oral history, 377.

51. Hoffman, *Once a Legend*, 123. Edson's long experience in fighting insurgencies and writing about them helps explain why the Chowder Society shared so many traits with them. For one indication that Edson viewed Chowder's efforts within the lens of combat, see Merritt A. Edson, "Memorandum for Admiral Sherman," March 20, 1946, in Personal Papers of Merritt A. Edson, box 22, "OP-30" file, Manuscript Division, Library of Congress, Washington, D.C. (hereafter Edson Papers).

52. Diary of Merritt A. Edson, entry for May 16, 1947, Edson Papers, box 56 (hereafter Edson diary, 1947).

53. General Edson's suicide is discussed in detail in Hoffman, *Once a Legend*, 403–413.

54. The single best work on defense unification is Demetrios Caraley, *The Politics of Military Unification: A Study of Conflict and the Policy Process* (New York: Columbia University Press, 1966). Unification is also discussed in detail in Paul Y. Hammond, *Organizing for Defense: The American Military Establishment in the Twentieth Century* (Princeton, NJ: Princeton University Press, 1961), 186–370; Steven L. Reardon, *History of the Office of the Secretary of Defense*, vol. 1, *The Formative Years, 1947–1950* (Washington, DC: Department of Defense Historical Office, 1984), 1–50, 385–402; Laurence J. Legere, *Unification of the Armed Forces* (New York: Garland Publishing, 1988), 267–442; Curtis William Tarr, "Unification of America's Armed Forces: A Century and a Half of Conflict, 1789–1947," Ph.D. diss., Stanford University, 1962, 205–230.

55. The Army coalition's positions are outlined in Caraley, *Politics of Military Unification*, 56–85; Keiser, *U.S. Marine Corps and Defense Unification*, 40–43.

56. The Navy's priorities are well explored in Barlow, *Revolt of the Admirals*, 23–63; Caraley, *Politics of Military Unification*, 86–110; Keiser, *U.S. Marine Corps and Defense Unification*, 43–45.

57. The Marines' worries are detailed in Keiser, *U.S. Marine Corps and Defense Unification*, 45–47; Millett, *Semper Fidelis*, 456–460; Krulak, *First to Fight*, 17–38; Hittle, "The Marine Corps and Its Struggle for Survival," 2–3.

58. Gallup poll, October 17, 1945, Survey 358, question qn8b, available at www.brain.gallup.com (accessed August 1, 2009). For additional evidence of the public's and press' initial support of a single unified department, see Caraley, *Politics of Military Unification*, 38, 242, 296, f. 58.

59. These events are described in Caraley, *Politics of Military Unification*, 153–154; Barlow, *Revolt of the Admirals*, 42–43; Keiser, *U.S. Marine Corps and Defense Unification*, 67–72. The Forrestal-Patterson letter is reprinted in full in Alice C. Cole, ed., *The Department of Defense: Documents on Establishment and Organization, 1944–1978* (Washington, DC: Office of the Secretary of Defense, Historical Office, 1978), 31–33.

60. Shaw oral history, 134. See also Heinl oral history, 361–362, 403; Twining oral history, 302.

61. Krulak, *First to Fight*, 1–52, 50–55; Martullo, "A Good Bowl of Chowder."

62. ALNAV 21, January 16, 1947, cited in Hoffman, *Once a Legend*, 336.

63. U.S. Navy Regulations Chapter 12, Section 3, Article 1252, in Edson Papers, box 15, "HQMC Correspondence" file, Manuscript Division, LOC.

64. The brief Edson distributed to Congress is found in Edson Papers, box 14, file 114, Manuscript Division, LOC. The list of people Edson distributed the brief to is on the inside cover of his 1947 diary.

65. Edson diary, 1947, entry for April 28.

66. Caraley, *Politics of Military Unification*, 317, f. 73.

67. Krulak, *First to Fight*, 49; Twining to Frank, "Last Days of the Chowder Society," HD biographical file, "J. D. Hittle," MCA. On violating orders from the Commandant and Secretary of the Navy, see oral history transcript of Brigadier General James D. Hittle, USMC, 311, MCOHC, MCA (hereafter Hittle oral history); Heinl oral history, 398; Edson diary, 1947, entries for April 29 ("small group of four or five Marine officers"), April 30 ("warn the termites to watch their step"), May 7 ("dirty work"), May 9 ("CMC was boiling"), May 14 ("Nimitz had called CMC"), and May 17 ("confidential dispatch"), LOC.

68. Edson diary, 1947, entry for May 9.

69. Edson diary, 1947, entries for May 2 ("Met McClamara at the Willard"), May 14 ("CMC might give me a verbal admonition"), and May 17.

70. Keiser, *Politics of Survival*, 97. A similar quote appears in Caraley, *Politics of Military Unification*, 229. The fullest discussion of the reversal in Clare Hoffman's committee is in Hittle, "The Marine Corps and Its Struggle for Survival," 3–24, HD biographical file "J. D. Hittle," MCA. See also Krulak, *First to Fight*, 45–51; Millett, *Semper Fidelis*, 462–464; Twining oral history, 300–303.

71. Marshall Andrews, "Marine Corps Keeps Present Status in Revised Measure," *Washington Post*, June 5, 1947, 1.

72. Hittle, "The Marine Corps and Its Struggle for Survival," 20; Caraley, *Politics of Military Unification*, 232. Besides General Edson's theft of the JCS 1478 papers, Major Lyford Hutchens' activities during the unification fights were probably the furthest from the letter of the law. For veiled references to his activities, see Heinl oral history, 370; Blandford oral history, 23–24; Shaw oral history, 133; Hittle oral history, 495; and oral history transcript of Lieutenant General Victor H. Krulak, USMC, 108, MCOHC, MCA.

73. Keiser, *The Politics of Survival*, 111–113; Krulak, *First to Fight*, 51; Tarr, "Unification of America's Armed Forces," 273–274.

74. Ibid., 229; Keiser, *Politics of Survival,* 98–99.

75. Heinl oral history, 393.

76. For Lieutenant Colonel Heinl's admission that he hid "hot" files in the historical section, see Heinl oral history, 430–431.

77. Ibid., 430.

78. Hittle oral history, 299. Sam Shaw was the member investigated as a "suspicious person." See Shaw oral history, 242.

79. Blandford oral history, 24.

80. Heinl oral history, 379.

81. The best recent work on the B-36 hearings and related scandals is Jeffrey G. Barlow, *Revolt of the Admirals: The Fight for Naval Aviation, 1945–1950* (Washington, DC: Ross and Perry, 2001). See also Paul Y. Hammond, *Super Carriers and B-36 Bombers: Appropriations, Strategy, and Politics* (Indianapolis: Bobbs-Merrill, 1963). The description of OP-23 comes from Drew Pearson, "Admirals Running Handout Mill," *Washington Post,* October 19, 1949, cited in Barlow, *Revolt of the Admirals,* 277. For a description of the raid on OP-23, see Shaw oral history, 220–242.

82. The Marine liaison to OP-23 during the Revolt of the Admirals was Chowder member Samuel R. Shaw.

83. The amendments also converted the National Military Establishment into the Department of Defense and strengthened the secretary of defense's authority, created a chairman of the Joint Chiefs of Staff, and increased the size of the Joint Staff. For a detailed explanation of the 1949 amendments, see Reardon, *The Formative Years,* 50–56.

84. This description of asymmetry is adapted from John Lewis Gaddis, *Strategies of Containment: A Critical Appraisal of Postwar American National Security Policy* (New York: Oxford University Press, 1982), 61.

85. Many of the Policy Analysis Division's working files are still classified, but may be found in E1077, "Policy Analysis Division Speech Files of the Commandant and Subordinate Staff Officers 1951–1972," RG 127, NARA. See also HD subject file "Policy Analysis Division," MCA.

86. "History of the Policy Analysis Division" and "Chief of Staff's Brief of the Policy Analysis Division," January 18, 1961, both in HD subject file "Policy Analysis Division," MCA.

87. Dwight David Eisenhower to Congress, April 3, 1958, cited in Cole, ed., *The Department of Defense,* 183. For a detailed explanation of the 1958

Defense Reorganization Act, see Robert J. Watson, *History of the Office of the Secretary of Defense*, vol. 4, *Into the Missile Age, 1956–1960* (Washington, DC: Office of Secretary of Defense, 1997), 243–291.

88. Commandant's notes from National Security Council Meeting, March 27, 1958, 2, "E1039 Records Relating to Postwar Military Planning and Organization 1945–1980," box 5, "Sec Gates" file (1 of 2), RG 127, NARA.

89. Hittle oral history, 337–339.

90. Ibid., 340–345.

91. Watson, *Into the Missile Age*, 262.

92. Ibid., 264–275.

93. General Dwight David Eisenhower, cited in Caraley, *Politics of Military Unification*, 70.

94. Caraley, *Politics of Military Unification*, 49.

95. A good summary of the many positions advanced by the Navy during unification can be found in ibid., 86–122. See also "What's All the Shouting About?," pamphlet of the Citizen's Committee for National Security, 1946, HD subject file "Unification-Reorganization," MCA.

96. This phrase is General Edson's and is taken from the unification brief he distributed around Congress. See Edson unification brief, 23, Edson Papers, box 14, file 114, LOC (hereafter Edson unification brief). See also Major General Merritt A. Edson, "Power Hungry Men in Uniform," *Collier's*, August 27, 1949, 16–17.

97. For an excellent explanation of the antistatist impulses in both Congress and American Cold War strategy, see Aaron L. Friedberg, *In the Shadow of the Garrison State: America's Anti-Statism and Its Cold War Grand Strategy*, Princeton Studies in International History and Politics (Princeton, NJ: Princeton University Press, 2000). See also Arthur M. Schlesinger, *The Imperial Presidency* (Boston: Houghton Mifflin, 2004).

98. Edson unification brief, 22.

99. General A. A. Vandegrift, testimony to Congress, Senate, Committee on Naval Affairs, *Hearings Before the Committee on Naval Affairs, United States Senate, on S. 2044*, 79th Cong., 2nd Sess., May 6, 1946, 118–119.

100. Bemis Frank, "A Giant Passes: General Merrill B. Twining 1902–1996," *Fortitudine*, Summer 1996, 6, in HD subject file "Merrill B. Twining," MCA.

101. Edson unification brief, 29.

102. Heinl oral history, 389.

103. Edson unification brief, 3, 23; Edson, "Power Hungry Men in Uniform," 16–17.

104. Merwin was the editor of the Bloomington (IL) *Daily Pantagraph* and, later, of the *Minneapolis* (MN) *Star*. More of Merwin's rhymes are found in HD subject files "Unification Reorganization Clippings #3" and "Unification Reorganization Newspapers 1946–1954," MCA.

105. Address of Bertram J. Murphy, national judge advocate of the Marine Corps League, June 18, 1949, 1–2, HD subject file "Unification: Miscellaneous Documents," MCA.

106. Brigadier General V. J. McCaul to J. Walter Thompson Company, October 7, 1952, E54 Information Division Correspondence 1951–1952, box 1, "A7-1-1 Marine Corps Methods and Plans" file, RG 127, NARA.

107. General A. A. Vandegrift testimony to Congress, Senate, Committee on Naval Affairs, *Hearings Before the Committee on Naval Affairs, United States Senate, on S. 2044,* 79th Cong., 2nd Sess., May 6, 1946, 105.

108. Address of Bertram J. Murphy, National Judge Advocate of the Marine Corps League, June 18, 1949, in HD subject file "Unification: Miscellaneous Documents," MCA.

109. "Save the Marines," *Duluth* (MN) *News Tribune,* April 29, 1949, in E107 Information Division Correspondence 1946–1950, box 24, file "Supporters, Marine Corps, Loyal," RG 127, NARA; Richard Tregaskis, "The Marine Corps Fights for Its Life," *Saturday Evening Post,* February 5, 1949, 21, 104–106.

110. Francis Kilgore to President Truman, February 8, 1949, E107 Information Division Correspondence 1946–1950, box 24, "Supporters, Marine Corps, Loyal" file, RG 127, NARA.

111. The "United States General Staff system," Hittle argues, "has features of French, British, and Prussian doctrine, [with] the French characteristics predominating." J. D. Hittle, *The Military Staff, Its History and Development* (Harrisburg, PA: Military Service Division, 1961), 299.

112. Senator Edward Robertson of Wyoming, 80th Cong., 1st Sess., *Congressional Record* 93, pt. 14 (July 7, 1947), 8308.

113. Caraley, *Politics of Military Unification,* 130.

114. Representative Gerald Ford of Michigan, 81st Cong., 1st Sess., *Congressional Record* 95 (August 2, 1949), 10609.

115. Representative Clare Hoffman of Michigan, 81st Cong., 1st Sess., *Congressional Record* 95 (August 2, 1949), 10604.

116. Brigadier General James D. Hittle, USMC, oral history interview tapes, September 29, 1972, tape 11408, 20 min. 45 sec., MCOHC, MCA.

117. Edson unification brief, 3, 5. Emphasis in original.

118. Editor, *Saturday Evening Post,* to Andrew Geer, May 16, 1949, in Edson Papers, box 13, "Lyford Hutchens" file, Manuscript Division, LOC.

119. "Prussian Fears and Russian Threats," *Wall Street Journal,* April 21, 1958, 8.

120. Kenneth W. Condit, *A Brief History of Headquarters Marine Corps Staff Organization* (Washington, DC: Historical Division, Headquarters, U.S. Marine Corps, 1970), 26–34.

121. General Clifton B. Cates, cited in Allan Reed Millett and Jack Shulimson, eds., *Commandants of the Marine Corps* (Annapolis, MD: Naval Institute Press, 2004), 324.

122. For just a few celebratory accounts of the Marines' performance in Korea, see T. R. Fehrenbach, *This Kind of War: A Study in Unpreparedness* (New York: Macmillan, 1963), 188–197, 241–251, 237–253, 351–374; Clay Blair, *The Forgotten War: America in Korea, 1950–1953* (Annapolis: Naval Institute Press, 1987), 194, 252–253; Max Hastings, *The Korean War* (London: M. Joseph, 1987), 99–114, 147–164. For a more detailed treatment of the Marines' actions, see Millett, *Semper Fidelis,* 475–517; Allan R. Millett, *The War for Korea, 1950–1951: They Came from the North* (Lawrence: University of Kansas Press, 2010), 215–231, 250–256, 339–351.

123. Harry S. Truman to Representative Gordon L. McDonough, August 29, 1950, cited in Millett and Shulimson, eds., *Commandants of the Marine Corps,* 323. The descriptions of Congressman McDonough come from Franklin D. Mitchell, "An Act of Presidential Indiscretion: Harry S. Truman, Congressman McDonough, and the Marine Corps Incident of 1950," *Presidential Studies Quarterly* 11, no. 4 (1981): 567.

124. This and other letters were read into the record by Representative Gordon L. McDonough of California, 81st Cong., 2nd Sess., *Congressional Record* 96 (September 15, 1950), 14593.

125. The final price was $2,500. McDonough also used the incident to energize his political base during the fall campaign, and he won reelection with 87 percent of the vote. See Mitchell, "An Act of Presidential Indiscretion," 570.

126. The story of the Marines mailing the President their Purple Hearts is reprinted in the *Appendix to the Congressional Record* 97, 82nd Cong., 1st Sess. (1951), A373. For the reaction of the Marine Corps League to the President's apology, see Don Oleson, "Marines Like Apology, Yell, 'Read It Again,'" *Washington Post*, September 7, 1950, 1.

127. Allan R. Millett, "Harry's Police Force," *MHQ: The Quarterly Journal of Military History* 13, no. 1 (2000): 72–81.

128. Huntington, *The Common Defense*, 140.

129. General Cates admitted, "There wasn't any question about that. We did everything in the world to get our friends behind us. And the former Marines and friends that had served with the Marine Corps—correspondents and things—they poured it on Congress and on the White House—letters and telegrams." See oral history transcript of General Clifton B. Cates, USMC, 225–226, MCOHC, MCA.

130. President Dwight David Eisenhower to Congress, April 30, 1953, cited in Cole, ed., *Department of Defense*, 151. Articles opposing the reorganization by Hanson W. Baldwin, Arthur Ochs Sulzberger, and others are contained in HD subject file "Unification Reorganization Newspapers 1946–1954," MCA.

131. Carl Vinson, quoted in John A. Goldsmith, "Congress Gets Ike's Defense Shakeup Bill," *Washington Post*, April 17, 1958, 1.

132. See Garnett D. Horner, "Irritability Leaves Newsmen Puzzled," *Washington Evening Star*, April 24, 1958, A-6; Jerry Greene, "One Unified Service? Ike Looses Angry Barrage," *Daily News* (New York), April 24, 1958, 6, both in HD subject file "Unification clippings, April–Aug 1958," MCA.

133. On this point, see Thomas G. Paterson, "Presidential Foreign Policy, Public Opinion and the Congress: The Truman Years," *Diplomatic History* 3, no. 1 (1979): 4, 18; Huntington, *The Common Defense*, 123–135, 241; Kolodziej, *The Uncommon Defense*, 484–486, 516.

134. Blandford oral history, 17, MCOHC, MCA.

135. Heinl oral history, 387.

4. Forgetting Korea

1. The name "Chosin," which is how most Marines refer to the reservoir today, is an adaptation of the Japanese name "Chosen." In Korean, the name is "Changjing." See Allan R. Millett, *Their War for Korea:*

American, Asian, and European Combatants and Civilians (Washington, DC: Brassey's, 2002), 203.

2. Allan Reed Millett, *Semper Fidelis: The History of the United States Marine Corps* (New York: Free Press, 1991), 493. For detailed descriptions of the battle, see Allan R. Millett, *The War for Korea, 1950–1951: They Came from the North* (Lawrence: University Press of Kansas, 2010), 334–355; Clay Blair, *The Forgotten War: America in Korea, 1950–1953* (Annapolis: Naval Institute Press, 1987), 508–521; Max Hastings, *The Korean War* (London: M. Joseph, 1987), 147–164; John Toland, *In Mortal Combat: Korea, 1950–1953* (New York: Quill, 1991), 289–352; Lynn Montross and Captain Nicholas A. Canzona, USMC, *U.S. Marine Operations in Korea, 1950–1953*, vol. 3, *The Chosin Reservoir Campaign* (Washington, DC: Historical Branch, HQMC, 1957). There is also an excellent collection of news articles on the battle in the HD subject files "Chosin Clippings—Korean War," MCA.

3. Between October 26 and December 15, 718 Marines were killed, 192 were missing in action, and 3,508 were wounded. Another 7,313 suffered frostbite. The Commander of the Chinese forces, General Peng Duhai, estimated his losses for the entire operation (against the Army, Marines, and South Korean forces) at 30,000 killed from enemy fire and 50,000 lost to the cold. Marine ground forces and aviation probably caused around 10,000 of these casualties. Marine casualties are taken from Montross and Canzona, *U.S. Marine Operations in Korea*, 3:351. Chinese casualties are summarized in Millett, *The War for Korea, 1950–1951*, 356. For other Marine estimates of Chinese casualties, see Charles R. Smith, *U.S. Marines in the Korean War* (Washington, DC: History Division, USMC, 2007), 330; Edwin Howard Simmons, *The U.S. Marines: A History* (Annapolis: Naval Institute Press, 1998), 207; Hastings, *The Korean War*, 164.

4. All quotes from Dick, Carol, and Dona Bahr come from interviews conducted between May 7 and June 3, 2008. Recordings and transcripts in author's possession.

5. The most well-known book of that title is Blair, *The Forgotten War*, but Blair's was not the first, nor is it the only one. More than twenty other histories, memoirs, and documentaries contain "forgotten war"

in their titles as well, and the first usage of the label dates to 1952. Bruce Cumings explains the label and its power in *War and Television* (London: Verso, 1992), 129–172. The best exploration of the label is found in James R. Kerin Jr., "The Korean War and American Memory," Ph.D. diss., University of Pennsylvania, 1994, 42–76.

6. Korean War battle deaths and total wounded are listed in Department of Defense, "Principal Wars in Which the United States Participated, U.S. Military Personnel Serving and Casualties," http://siadapp.dmdc .osd.mil/personnel/CASUALTY/WCPRINCIPAL.pdf (accessed January 8, 2009).

7. This point has been made in Cumings, *War and Television*, 145–149; Paul M. Edwards, *To Acknowledge a War: The Korean War in American Memory* (Westport, CT: Greenwood Press, 2000), 15–39; Kerin, "The Korean War and American Memory," 42; William Stuek, "In Search of Essences: Labelling the Korean War," in Philip West and Suh Ji-moon, *Remembering the "Forgotten War": The Korean War through Literature and Art* (Armonk, NY: M. E. Sharpe, 2001), 187–202.

8. This common fallacy of attributing memory to nation-states is discussed in J. M. Winter, *Remembering War: The Great War between Memory and History in the Twentieth Century* (New Haven: Yale University Press, 2006), 4.

9. The notion that Korea has been "repressed" is discussed in Cumings, *War and Television*, 148, and in Paul M. Edwards, *A Guide to Films on the Korean War*, Bibliographies and Indexes in American History (Westport, CT: Greenwood Press, 1997), 45. For a useful discussion of why psychological terms should not be used in memory studies, see Wulf Kansteiner, "Finding Meaning in Memory: A Methodological Critique of Collective Memory Studies," *History and Theory* 41 (May 2002): 192–193.

10. The distinctions between memory and remembrance are set out in J. M. Winter and Emmanuel Sivan, *War and Remembrance in the Twentieth Century*, Studies in the Social and Cultural History of Modern Warfare (New York: Cambridge University Press, 1999), 1–39; Winter, *Remembering War*, 1–12. For specific discussions on the Korean War and memory, see Joanna Bourke, "Introduction: Remembering

War," *Journal of Contemporary History* 39 (October 2004): 473–485; Kansteiner, "Finding Meaning in Memory," 192–193.

11. These theories are discussed in Edwards, *To Acknowledge a War,* 11–39; Cumings, *War and Television,* 145–50; Kerin, "Korean War and American Memory" 42–84, 363–371; West, *Remembering the Forgotten War,* 110–136.

12. The term "unreal war" comes from W. J. Bryan Dorn and O. K. Armstrong, "The Great Lessons of Korea," *Air Force* 34 (May 1951): 29–30.

13. The best summary of Korean War veterans' psychiatric trends is Edward W. McCranie and Leon A. Hyer, "Posttraumatic Stress Disorder Symptoms in Korean Conflict and World War II Combat Veterans Seeking Outpatient Treatment," *Journal of Traumatic Stress* 13 (July 2000): 430, 434. For comparisons between Korea, World War II, and Vietnam, see Alan Fontana and Robert Rosenheck, "Traumatic War Stressors and Psychiatric Symptoms among World War II, Korean, and Vietnam War Veterans," *Psychology and Aging* 9 (1994): 27–33. See also Dudley David Blake et al., "Prevalence of PTSD Symptoms in Combat Veterans Seeking Medical Treatment," *Journal of Traumatic Stress* 3 (January 1990): 15–27.

14. The idea that cognition occurs through a series of frameworks or "frames" is discussed in depth in Erving Goffman, *Frame Analysis: An Essay on the Organization of Experience* (New York: Harper and Row, 1974), 1–39.

15. Edwards, *To Acknowledge a War,* 27–39. See also Cumings, *War and Television,* 145–154; West, *Remembering the Forgotten War,* 187–202.

16. Edwards, *To Acknowledge a War,* 30–31.

17. John E. Mueller, *War, Presidents, and Public Opinion* (New York: Wiley, 1973), 171.

18. Executive-legislative relations at the beginning of the war are discussed in detail in Ronald James Caridi, "The G.O.P. and the Korean War," *Pacific Historical Review* 37 (November 1968): 423–443, and in Charles A. Lofgren, "Mr. Truman's War: A Debate and Its Aftermath," *Review of Politics* 31 (April 1969): 223–241.

19. Gallup Poll number 466, question 17 (October 1950) and Gallup Poll 486, question 2a (February 1952), available at http://brain.gallup.com (accessed August 1, 2009).

20. Editorial, "Impeach Truman," *Chicago Daily Tribune,* April 12, 1951, 1; editorial, "MacArthur Says, 'Treason'—Truman Answers, 'Liar,'" *Hartford Courant,* October 21, 1951, A2.

21. The three quotes by former President Herbert Hoover, Representative Dewey Short, and President Truman, respectively, appear in David Halberstam, *The Fifties* (New York: Villard, 1993), 114–115.

22. Mueller, *War, Presidents, and Public Opinion,* 47.

23. House Committee on Veterans Affairs, *Historical Statistics of the Veteran Population, 1865–1960,* 87th Cong., 1st Sess., 1961, Committee Print 69, 15–21.

24. Mueller, *War, Presidents, and Public Opinion,* 229, 103.

25. A nationwide poll taken in July 1951 asked what course of action the nation should follow in Korea. The most popular answer, which accounted for 24 percent of responses, was "no answer, don't know, couldn't say." The next most popular answer, "all Communists withdraw and stay out," received only 13.3 percent. See Gallup Poll 477, question 7, July 6, 1951, available at www.gallup.com (accessed August 1, 2009). The prominence of "don't know" as an answer to the problem of Korea is further validated in polls of March 1951 and November 1952 cited in Mueller, *War, Presidents, and Public Opinion,* 76, 80.

26. General Mark W. Clark, USA, "Truth about Korea," *Collier's,* March 5, 1954, 44–49; "You Can't Win If Diplomats Interfere," *U.S. News and World Report,* August 20, 1954, 75–81; General James A. Van Fleet, USA, "The Truth about Korea," *Reader's Digest,* July 1953, 1–16; Colonel Shillelagh (pseud.), "Civil Control in Danger," *Combat Forces Journal* 4 (January 1954): 22–24.

27. Lieutenant General George E. Stratemeyer, USAF, testimony in Congress, Senate, Committee on the Judiciary, *The Korean War and Related Matters: Report of the Subcommittee to Investigate the Administration of the Internal Security Act and Other Internal Security Laws,* 84th Cong., 1st Sess. (January 21, 1955), 10. See also "Verdict on Korea," *Chicago Daily Tribune,* January 1, 1955, 8; Clark, "You Can't Win If Diplomats Interfere" and Van Fleet, "Truth about Korea."

28. Editorial, "MacArthur Says 'Treason'—Truman Answers 'Liar,'" *Hartford Courant,* October 21, 1951, A2.

29. Colonel Shillelagh, "Civil Control in Danger," 22.

30. "Corps to Punish Marine for Korea Protest," *New York Herald Tribune*, August 10, 1951; "Marine Raps Truman in Newspaper Letter," *Washington Post*, August 10, 1951, both in HD subject file "Discipline," MCA.

31. John Foster Dulles, "Text of Dulles' Speech before U.N.," *Los Angeles Times*, June 25, 1955, 4.

32. Austin Stevens, "Clark Warns Foe on Truce Breach," *New York Times*, August 7, 1953, 1.

33. This undated cartoon appears in Norval E. Packwood, *Leatherhead in Korea* (Quantico, VA: Marine Corps Gazette, 1952), 79.

34. Edwards, *A Guide to Films on the Korean War*, 109–110; Robert J. Lentz, *Korean War Filmography: 91 English Language Features through 2000* (Jefferson, NC: McFarland, 2002).

35. "Recall Truce in Korean War," *Chicago Daily Tribune*, July 27, 1954, 5.

36. "Remember Korea," *Time*, February 7, 1955, 15; editorial, "Our Forgotten Allies," *Washington Daily News*, July 28, 1955, cited in *Appendix to the Congressional Record*, 84th Cong., 1st Sess. (1955), A5598.

37. R. Alden, "Korea Remembered: Notes on a Strange War," *New York Times Magazine*, June 21, 1959, SM10; Walter Simmons, "Korean War: Uncatalogued Gallery of Images," *Chicago Daily Tribune*, June 25, 1960, 10.

38. Editorial, "Korea: Eight Years After," *New York Times*, June 25, 1958, 28.

39. "A Place of Ten Million Words," *Time*, August 2, 1963, 21.

40. Gordon W. Prange, "Korea: Beyond Its Tragedy, a Symbol," *Washington Post*, July 27, 1958, E6.

41. On Dien Bien Phu, see Walter Lippmann, "Proof and Bluff," *Hartford Courant*, May 25, 1954, 12. On Formosa, see Chalmers M. Roberts, "Question for Ike: War for Quemoy?" *Washington Post*, September 11, 1954, 8; on Sputnik, see Joseph Alsop, "That Pre-Korean Smell," *Hartford Courant*, October 16, 1957, 18.

42. Eugene Kinkead, "A Reporter at Large: The Study of Something New in History," *New Yorker*, October 26, 1957, 102–153; Eugene Kinkead, *In Every War but One* (New York: Norton, 1959). See also William E. Mayer, "Why Did So Many G.I. Captives Cave In?" *U.S. News and World Report*, February 24, 1956, 56–72. Both Mayer and Kinkead are discussed at length in H. H. Wubben, "American Prisoners of War in Korea: A Second Look at the 'Something New in History' Theme,"

American Quarterly 22 (Spring 1970): 3–19; Peter Karsten, "The American Democratic Citizen Soldier: Triumph or Disaster?" *Military Affairs* 30 (Spring 1966): 34–40; and Richard Severo and Lewis Milford, *The Wages of War: When America's Soldiers Came Home—from Valley Forge to Vietnam* (New York: Simon and Schuster, 1989), 316–344.

43. For figures on POW courts-martial, see "POW Collaboration Charges Exploded," *Army–Navy–Air Force Register and Defense Times*, April 16, 1960, reprinted in the *Appendix to the Congressional Record*, 86th Cong., 2nd Sess. (1960), A3799.

44. The different academic theories explaining why POWs collaborated is explored well in Ron Theodore Robin, *The Making of the Cold War Enemy: Culture and Politics in the Military-Intellectual Complex* (Princeton, NJ: Princeton University Press, 2001), 162–181.

45. Mayer, "Why Did So Many G.I. Captives Cave In?," 60–62.

46. Ibid., 60–62, 66.

47. Admiral Rickover's comments are discussed in Severo and Milford, *The Wages of War*, 338. Major Clarence L. Anderson is quoted at length in Eugene Kinkead, "Something New," 138.

48. Kinkead, "Something New," 102; Kinkead, *In Every War but One*, 16.

49. Kinkead, "Something New," 145.

50. Hanson W. Baldwin, "Our Fighting Men Have Gone Soft," *Saturday Evening Post*, August 8, 1959, 13; Bernice Vollick, letter to the editor, *Saturday Evening Post*, September 12, 1959, 4.

51. For more on this argument, see Wubben, "American Prisoners of War in Korea," 7–8; Robin, *The Making of the Cold War Enemy*, 162–181.

52. On education reformers and the Boy Scouts, see Wubben, "American Prisoners of War in Korea," 8. On the use of the softness narrative in arguments supporting racial segregation, see Baldwin, "Our Fighting Men Have Gone Soft," 82.

53. This point is discussed at length in Severo and Milford, *The Wages of War*, 317–44.

54. A chronological list of Korean War films appears in Edwards, *A Guide to Films on the Korean War*, 109–110, 33–38.

55. These films are summarized and discussed in ibid., 1–47; West, *Remembering the Forgotten War*, 110–136; Lawrence H. Suid, *Guts and Glory: The Making of the American Military Image in Film*, rev. ed. (Lexington:

University Press of Kentucky, 2002), 136–142. The making of *Pork Chop Hill* is discussed in detail in Colin Young, "The Old Dependables," *Film Quarterly* 13 (Autumn 1959): 11–13.

56. Lists of congressional hearings and the full text of most Committee Reports on Korea can be found at LexisNexis Congressional, online database, available at http://web.lexis-nexis.com/congcomp (accessed August 1, 2009).

57. Congress, House, Representative Walter Judd of Minnesota, *Congressional Record*, 83rd Cong., 2nd Sess. (July 15, 1954), 10645.

58. "Eisenhower Never Has Ended War," *Sacramento Bee*, March 7, 1960, cited in *Appendix to the Congressional Record*, 86th Cong., 2nd Sess. (1960), A2622.

59. "Nixon, Kennedy Cram Host of Issues into Gloves-Off Debate," *Hartford Courant*, October 8, 1960, 1.

60. Edwards, *To Acknowledge a War*, 11–39; Cumings, *War and Television*, 145–150; Halberstam, *The Fifties*, 73; Kerin, "The Korean War and American Memory," 42–84.

61. Halberstam, *The Fifties*, 73; Edwards, *To Acknowledge a War*, 15.

62. James Michener, "The Forgotten Heroes of Korea," *Saturday Evening Post*, May 10, 1952, 19–21, 124–128; editorial, "Forgotten Wars," *Combat Forces Journal* 2 (September 1952): 12.

63. Index for *U.S. Naval Institute Proceedings* (Annapolis, MD: Naval Institute Press), 1955–1963.

64. Commander F. E. Bitting, USN, "It's Everybody's Business," *U.S. Naval Institute Proceedings* 81 (November 1955): 1189.

65. Maurice H. Hellner, "Sea Power and the Struggle for Asia," *U.S. Naval Institute Proceedings* 82 (April 1956): 353–361.

66. Malcolm W. Cagle, "Errors of the Korean War," *U.S. Naval Institute Proceedings* 84 (March 1958): 34.

67. Dorn and Armstrong, "The Great Lessons of Korea."

68. Although in draft by 1953, the document explaining the Air Force's role in national defense gives no consideration to limited war until its 1959 revision, when it concludes that "the best preparation for limited war is proper preparation for general war." See Department of the Air Force, *Air Force Manual 1–2: United States Air Force Basic Doctrine* (Washington, DC: GPO, 1954, 1955, 1959), ch. 2.

69. Robert Frank Futrell, *The United States Air Force in Korea, 1950–1953* (New York: Duell, 1961). A useful corrective to Futrell is Conrad C. Crane, *American Airpower Strategy in Korea, 1950–1953*, Modern War Studies (Lawrence: University Press of Kansas, 2000).

70. I am grateful to Lieutenant Colonel Ed Kaplan, USAF, for the Air Force articles and lists of papers written by Air Force cadets in 1962.

71. General J. Lawton Collins, USA, "New Approaches to World Peace," *Combat Forces Journal* 2 (January 1951): 17–20.

72. This point is made in David Howell Petraeus, "The American Military and the Lessons of Vietnam: A Study of Military Influence and the Use of Force in the Post-Vietnam Era," Ph.D. diss., Princeton University, 1987, 39–42.

73. See indexes for *Combat Forces Journal* (Washington, DC: Association of the United States Army), 1952, 1953, 1955.

74. Letters by H. T. Sorbean and Chief Warrant Officer Conlon, USA, "Army Letters," *Army* 11 (August 1960): 6, 10. Emphasis in original.

75. T. R. Fehrenbach, *This Kind of War: A Study in Unpreparedness* (New York: Macmillan, 1963), 123, 426–438. See also J. Lawton Collins, *War in Peacetime: The History and Lessons of Korea* (Boston: Houghton Mifflin, 1969), 66–85.

76. Brigadier General S. L. A. Marshall, USA, "Big Little War," *Army* 10 (June 1960): 24–25.

77. Walter Simmons, "Marines Feel the Home Front Lets Them Down," *Chicago Daily Tribune*, April 20, 1952, 16.

78. James Michener, "The Forgotten Heroes of Korea," 19, 126.

79. Editorial, "No Banners, No Bugles, Just Fighting," *Army* 10 (June 1960): 20.

80. General Omar Bradley's statements on amphibious operations can be found in House Committee on Armed Services, *The National Defense Program—Hearings on Unification and Strategy*, 81st Cong., 1st Sess. (October 1949), 521.

81. The Marine Corps POW experience is discussed in James Angus MacDonald, "The Problems of U.S. Marine Corps Prisoners of War in Korea," M.A. thesis, University of Maryland, 1961. See also Baldwin, "Our Fighting Men Have Gone Soft," 13. The Marine officer whose career was destroyed was Colonel Frank W. Schwable. His case is discussed in

Allan R. Millett, *In Many a Strife: General Gerald C. Thomas and the U.S. Marine Corps, 1917–1956* (Annapolis: Naval Institute Press, 1993), 325–326. See also "Text of Inquiry Findings on Marine Col. Schwable," *New York Times,* April 28, 1954, 16.

82. For news coverage on Marine POWs, see HD subject files "POW Clippings" (3 folders), MCA.

83. *Appendix to the Congressional Record,* 82nd Cong., 1st Sess., (1951), A1326, A3514, A3810. For a large collection of stories generated by Marine Combat Correspondents in Korea, see E1068, Division of Information Publicity Articles Relating to the 1st Marine Division in Korea, boxes 1–4, RG 127, NARA.

84. Fehrenbach, *This Kind of War: A Study in Unpreparedness,* 188.

85. Baldwin, "Our Fighting Men Have Gone Soft," 14; Mayer, cited in MacDonald, "The Problems of U.S. Marine Corps Prisoners of War in Korea," 237, n. 1.

86. Major General Frank E. Lowe, USA to H. S. Truman, April 30, 1951, cited in Millett, *Semper Fidelis,* 498.

87. Senate Subcommittee on Investigations, *POW Hearings,* Report no. 2832, cited in MacDonald, "The Problems of U.S. Marine Corps Prisoners of War in Korea," 237. For news coverage on Marine POWs, see HD Subject Files "POW Clippings" (3 folders) in Marine Corps History Division, Quantico, Virginia.

88. Andrew Clare Geer, *The New Breed: The Story of the U.S. Marines in Korea* (New York: Harper, 1952).

89. Robert Leckie, *Conflict: The History of the Korean War, 1950–53* (New York: Putnam, 1962); Robert Leckie, *The March to Glory* (Cleveland: World, 1960); Robert Leckie, *The War in Korea, 1950–1953* (New York: Random House, 1963).

90. Robert Debs Heinl Jr., *Victory at High Tide: The Inchon-Seoul Campaign* (Philadelphia: Lippincott, 1968). See also Robert Debs Heinl, *Soldiers of the Sea: The United States Marine Corps* (Annapolis: Naval Institute Press, 1962), 536–591.

91. Lynn Montross, "The Man with the Rifle," serialized in three parts in *Marine Corps Gazette,* November 1953, December 1953, and January 1954.

92. Captain W. J. Davis, USMC, "Don't Kill Them with Kindness," *Marine Corps Gazette* 39 (September 1955): 64–68; Lieutenant Colonel R. E.

Carey, USMC, "No Place for Weaklings," *Marine Corps Gazette* 40 (April 1956): 36–40.

93. Corporal G. K. Power, "Postscript to Prickett's Old Corps," *Marine Corps Gazette* 40 (August 1956): 58. Emphasis in original.

94. The Marines had 4,267 killed and 23,744 wounded in Korea, giving them a casualty ratio (total in-theater casualties / total who served in theater) of 22 percent. This does not include nonbattle deaths. The Army's casualty ratio was 9 percent; the Navy's and Air Force's were each less than 1 percent. The Army had the most casualties overall: 105,327 of the 1.2 million soldiers who served in the theater were wounded or killed in hostile action. See Department of Defense, Defense Manpower Data Center, "Korean War—Casualty Summary," http://siadapp.dmdc.osd .mil/personnel/CASUALTY/korea.pdf (accessed September 1, 2009).

95. Although the Army had the highest percentage of troops in theater (41 percent of all Army personnel on active duty between June 1950 and August 1953), this number included all support troops located in Japan and in rear areas, where the chance of experiencing trauma was decidedly lower. The Marine Corps had the second-highest percentage of troops in theater: 31 percent, followed by the Navy (23 percent) and the Air Force (19 percent). See Department of Defense, "Korean War Casualty—Summary."

96. The memorial, which consists of bronze statues of infantry in formation, was inspired by a Duncan photograph of Marine infantry, according to one of the architects. The most likely image is David Douglas Duncan, *This Is War! A Photo Narrative in Three Parts* (New York: Harper, 1951), 40. Barbara Gamarekian, "Architects Clash over Korean War Memorial," *New York Times,* December 15, 1990, 17. For a critical reading of the memorial, see Millett, *Their War for Korea,* xv–xxi.

97. Duncan, *This Is War!,* cover.

98. The temperatures in the first weeks of the Marines' landing are cited in James Bell, "The General Gambles," *Life,* August 21, 1950, 19.

99. Fehrenbach, *This Kind of War: A Study in Unpreparedness,* 188.

100. Duncan, *This Is War!,* 27.

101. Ibid., 25. Emphasis in original.

102. The requirements for deployment to Korea are spelled out in General C. B. Cates to Secretary of Defense, "Report to the Secretary of Defense

on the Training and Assignment to Duty of Marine Corps Reserves," December 20, 1950, E107 Information Division Correspondence 1946–1950, box 13, "1835—Commandant (2)" file, RG 127, NARA. See also E107, box 23, "Korea (1)" file, RG 127, NARA. After the initial deployment of the 1st Marine Division, the Corps added an intensive eight-week predeployment training program, but that did not commence until late 1950.

103. Ibid.

104. Unnamed Marine from the 1st Provisional Marine Brigade, cited in Smith, *U.S. Marines in the Korean War,* 28. See also Millett, *Their War for Korea,* 204–205.

105. Neither battle fatigue or psychoneurosis was often listed on casualty cards in the Marine Corps, because of the high stigma attached to the illness. On the driver's casualty card, the "nature of wound" box also has the word "edit" handwritten next to the typed entry "MLTPL/ABRSN," giving some indication that this was not an appropriate entry for evacuation. All USMC casualty cards are held at Marine Corps History Division, MCA, and are arranged alphabetically by war.

106. "Jeep Hits Mine, Casualties: One Dead, Three Wounded," *Life,* October 9, 1950, 32.

107. Duncan, *This Is War!,* 103.

108. William S. Mullins and Albert J. Glass, eds., *Neuropsychiatry in World War II,* vol. 2, *Overseas Theaters* (Washington, DC: Office of the Surgeon General, Department of the Army, 1973), 664, 1064. These conclusions are validated further in Norman Quintus Brill and Gilbert Wheeler Beebe, *A Follow-up Study of War Neuroses* (Washington, DC: GPO, 1956), 172.

109. The company's strength by the end of the withdrawal was actually slightly higher: one officer, twenty-six enlisted Marines. See Millett, *The War for Korea, 1950–1951,* 343.

110. My description of PTSD comes from Winter, *Remembering War,* 52–76. For further explorations of the effects of traumatic experiences on memory, see Cathy Caruth, *Unclaimed Experience: Trauma, Narrative, and History* (Baltimore: Johns Hopkins University Press, 1996). Of particular use is B. A. van der Kolk and Onno van der Hart's "The Intrusive Past: The Flexibility of Memory and the Engraving of Trauma," in

Cathy Caruth, ed., *Trauma: Explorations in Memory* (Baltimore: Johns Hopkins University Press, 1995), 158–182.

111. Winter, *Remembering War*, 75.

112. A 1956 study showed that of World War II veterans previously diagnosed with "neuropsychosis" (the term then used for PTSD), only 35 percent received any medical treatment for psychiatric issues in the five years after the war, and only 15 percent received treatment from psychiatrists. For those not already diagnosed, such as Dick Bahr, the likelihood of seeing a psychiatrist was even lower. See Brill and Beebe, *A Follow-up Study of War Neuroses*, 190.

113. The notion of shell shock as an inability to integrate the sense experience of combat in the life story was first identified in Elmer Ernest Southard, *Shell-Shock and Other Neuropsychiatric Problems Presented in Five Hundred and Eighty-Nine Case Histories from the War Literature, 1914–1918* (Boston: W. M. Leonard, 1919). Sigmund Freud also correctly identified several components of the illness in 1917, but most of these findings were not incorporated into the DSM-1. See Winter, *Remembering War*, 67–68; John P. Wilson, "The Historical Evolution of PTSD Diagnostic Criteria: From Freud to DSM-IV," *Journal of Traumatic Stress* 7 (1994): 681–698.

114. On the number of practicing psychiatrists in 1956, see Gerald N. Grob, "Origins of DSM-I: A Study in Appearance and Reality," *American Journal of Psychiatry* 148 (1991): 428. For the number of World War II vets needing psychiatric treatment, see Brill and Beebe, *A Follow-up Study of War Neuroses*, 132, 35–36.

115. Brill and Beebe's study only included veterans already diagnosed when they were still in the service; the authors made no attempt to estimate how many would later develop symptoms. Furthermore, the study only addressed World War II veterans, leaving out veterans from World War I, the interwar interventions in the Caribbean, and the Korean War.

116. For a summary of the literature on PTSD rates across three wars, see Blake et al., "Prevalence of PTSD Symptoms," 24. A later study estimates that there were 4,434,697 veterans of World War II and 862,901 of Korea who had prolonged exposure to combat. See Robert Rosenheck and Alan Fontana, "Long-Term Sequelae of Combat in World

War II, Korea and Vietnam: A Comparative Study," in Robert J. Ur-
sano, Brian G. McCaughey, and Carol S. Fullerton, eds., *Individual and
Community Responses to Trauma and Disaster: The Structure of Human Chaos* (New York: Cambridge University Press, 1994), 337–338.

117. McCranie and Hyer, "Posttraumatic Stress Disorder Symptoms," 430–
431; Blake et al., "Prevalence of PTSD Symptoms," 24; Fontana and
Rosenheck, "Traumatic War Stressors and Psychiatric Symptoms,"
30–32.

118. Blake et al., "Prevalence of PTSD Symptoms," 15, 22, 30.

119. Ibid., 22. McCranie and Hyer studied only "treatment-seeking" psychiatric patients and found Korean War PTSD rates as high as 43 percent
compared to 29 percent for World War II veterans. Fontana and Rosenheck do not give overall PTSD rates but confirm that Korean War vets
had "higher distress and suicidality" than other veterans.

120. PTSD became a "service-connected" disability in October 1980, giving
a monetary incentive to veterans to claim the symptoms. See B. G. Bur-
kett and Glenna Whitley, *Stolen Valor: How the Vietnam Generation
Was Robbed of Its Heroes and Its History* (Dallas: Verity Press, 1998),
158–160.

121. David Read Johnson et al., "The Impact of the Homecoming Reception
on the Development of Posttraumatic Stress Disorder: The West Haven
Homecoming Stress Scale (WHHSS)," *Journal of Traumatic Stress* 10
(1997): 259–277.

122. G. H. Elder and E. C. Clipp, "Combat Experience and Emotional
Health: Impairment and Resilience in Later Life," *Journal of Personality* 57 (1989): 313.

123. Johnson et al., "Impact of the Homecoming Reception," 259.

124. McCranie and Hyer, "Posttraumatic Stress Disorder Symptoms," 437.

5. First to Fight in the 1950s

1. Court-martial, discharge, and drinking rates are all discussed in this
chapter. For Navy and Marine Corps rates for suicides, homicides, and
motor vehicle accidents, see Department of the Navy, *Annual Report of
the Surgeon General of the United States Navy to the Secretary of the
Navy* (Washington, DC: Bureau of Medicine and Surgery, 1950–1959),

tables 37–48, "Death Rates, Injuries and Poisonings, by Causative Agents." Civilian rates are found in Douglas Eckberg, "Reported Suicides and Suicide Rates by Sex and Mode of Death: 1900–1997," table Ec182–189; "Reported Homicides and Homicide Rates, 1900–1997," table Ec190–198; and Louis P. Cain, "Motor Vehicle Deaths and Death Rates, by Age, 1913–1996," table Df457–472, all in Susan B. Carter et al., eds., *Historical Statistics of the United States, Earliest Times to the Present*, millennial ed. (New York: Cambridge University Press, 2006).

2. The problem of unauthorized violence in the 1950s is addressed in Robert Debs Heinl Jr., *Soldiers of the Sea: The United States Marine Corps* (Annapolis, MD: Naval Institute Press, 1962), 593–594; Victor H. Krulak, *First to Fight: An Inside View of the U.S. Marine Corps* (Annapolis, MD: Naval Institute Press, 1984), 168–170; Edwin H. Simmons, *The United States Marines: A History* (Annapolis, MD: Naval Institute Press, 1998), 213. The film *The D.I.* is discussed in Lawrence H. Suid, *Guts and Glory: The Making of the American Military Image in Film*, rev. ed. (Lexington: University Press of Kentucky, 2002), 129, 374, 490.

3. W. B. McKean, "Panic in the Marine Corps," *Cavalier* 8 (June 1959): 20–23, 54–59, in HD subject file "Newspaper and Magazine Coverage of McKeon Death March," MCA.

4. John C. Stevens, *Court-Martial at Parris Island: The Ribbon Creek Incident* (Annapolis, MD: Naval Institute Press, 1999), 24.

5. The best scholarly treatment of Ribbon Creek is Keith V. Fleming, *The U.S. Marine Corps in Crisis: Ribbon Creek and Recruit Training* (Columbia: University of South Carolina Press, 1990). Another useful account, rich with detail but weak on objectivity, is William Baggarley McKean, *Ribbon Creek* (New York: Dial Press, 1958). The most favorable depiction of the accused is Stevens, *Court-Martial at Parris Island*. Allan Reed Millett covers the issue judiciously in *Semper Fidelis: The History of the United States Marine Corps* (New York: Free Press, 1991), 528–532.

6. Descriptions and press clippings of Marine Corps murders, brutality, and arrests are contained in HD subject files "Marine Brutality" (two folders) and "Murders, MC Personnel Involved" (two folders), MCA. See also HD subject files "Courts-martial" and "Discipline." Additional files on negative publicity in RG 127, NARA, are numerous. The order requiring recruiting districts to forward all incidents of negative

publicity to the Division of Public Information (MC Memo 74-53, October 1953) is found in E3 Correspondence and Subject Files, 1953, box 1, "A7-1/2 Adverse" file, RG 127. See also E3, box 3, A10-1/3 "Newspapers" file; E54 Information Division Correspondence 1951–1952, box 2, "A10-1/2 Magazines, Life Mag. Complaints" file; and E54, box 6, "P8-4 Complaints, Grievances Petitions" file, RG 127.

7. Keith Fleming's excellent study of Ribbon Creek confirms this, though he gives it insufficient attention. See Fleming, *The Marine Corps in Crisis*, 81; Millett, *Semper Fidelis*, 532.

8. The best overview of the issue of masculinity in the 1950s is James Burkhart Gilbert, *Men in the Middle: Searching for Masculinity in the 1950s* (Chicago: University of Chicago Press, 2005). The quote comes from page 2. See also Kyle A. Cuordileone, *Manhood and American Political Culture in the Cold War* (New York: Routledge, 2005), 134–145.

9. Sociologists did not begin compiling military drinking rates until the late 1970s, but all comparative studies since then have shown the Marines to have the highest drinking rates. Five comprehensive studies conducted between 1980 and 1992 are summarized in Robert M. Bray et al., *1992 Worldwide Survey of Substance Abuse and Health Behaviors among Military Personnel* (Washington, DC: Office of the Coordinator, Drug Enforcement Policy and Support, The Pentagon, 1992), 4-2-4-40. For the most recent data, see Robert M. Bray et al., *2002 Department of Defense Survey of Health-Related Behaviors among Military Personnel* (Research Triangle Park, NC: RTI International, 2003), tables 4.1, 4.2, D.3–D.6.

10. For a review of the "cycle of violence" literature, see Richard J. Gelles and Claire Pedrick Cronell, *Intimate Violence in Families*, 2nd ed., Family Studies Text Series (Newbury Park, CA: Sage Publications, 1990), 75–76; Mary Lystad, ed., *Violence in the Home: Interdisciplinary Perspectives* (New York: Brunner/Mazel, 1986), 61–63, 114–115.

11. For the connections to alcohol, see Gelles and Cronell, *Intimate Violence in Families*, 18–19, 74, and Lystad, *Violence in the Home*, 61, 88. For discussions of the "subculture of violence" theory, see Lystad, *Violence in the Home*, 100–101. The original theory was focused mostly on racial, socioeconomic, or regional subcultures but has since been extended to occupational and social subcultures.

12. For the correlation between violence and stress, see Murray A. Straus, Richard Gelles, and Suzanne K. Steinmetz, *Behind Closed Doors: Violence in the American Family* (New York: Doubleday, 1980), 197, cited in Mary Edwards Wertsch, *Military Brats: Legacies of Childhood inside the Fortress* (New York: Harmony Books, 1991), 227, 438, n. 2. For the discussion of authoritarianism, see figure 4.2, "Marital Power," in Gelles and Cronell, *Intimate Violence in Families,* 76–77; Wertsch, *Military Brats,* 19–26.

13. Sociologist Daniel Glaser addresses this topic specifically in "Violence in the Society" in Mary Lystad, ed., *Violence in the Home,* 22–25.

14. See United States Air Force, *Family Violence Prevention Resource Guide: For Air Force Helping Professionals* (Washington, DC: Air Force Family Matters, 1987), I-98–I-99.

15. The term "authoritarianism" describes a set of traits well known to military members, including "conventional behavior, submissiveness to authority, exaggerated notions of masculinity and femininity, extreme emphasis on discipline, heavy reliance on external authority for support of one's belief system," and other traits described in John P. Kirscht and Ronald C. Dillehay, *Dimensions of Authoritarianism: A Review of Research and Theory* (Lexington: University of Kentucky Press, 1967), 72. See also Wertsch, *Military Brats,* 19–26.

16. During the 1950s, the average general court-martial rate across all four branches of the U.S. military was 3.94 per 1,000. Courts-martial raw data and rates are listed by year and by service in Appendices 2–5 of Elizabeth Lutes Hillman, "Cold War Crime and American Military Culture: Courts-Martial in the United States Armed Forces, 1951–1973," Ph.D. diss., Yale University, 2001, 409–423.

17. Throughout the 1950s, the Marine Corps' average punitive discharge rate (comprising both bad conduct and dishonorable discharges) was 8.3 per 1,000, while the Navy's was only 5.8. In 1955, the Army issued 3,561 dishonorable discharges and 1,351 bad conduct discharges for a punitive discharge rate of 4.4 per thousand; the Marine Corps' rate that year was 13.6 per thousand. For Navy and Marine Corps punitive discharge rates, see "NAVPERS 15658: Navy and Marine Corps Military Personnel Statistics," Records of the Bureau of Naval Personnel, Summary of Periodic Statistic Reports on Military Personnel 1943–1971,

RG 24, NARA (hereafter NAVPERS 15658). The reports are filed by year. Punitive discharge rates for the Army and total DOD are also summarized in "5000 Discharged Each Year as Less than Honorable," *Air Force Times,* February 14, 1959, 17, and in "Bad Conduct, Undesirable Discharges Put at 36,000," *Air Force Times,* October 27, 1956, 11.

18. From 1950 to 1959, the Marines' average rates for suicides and deaths from "assaults by others" were 11.5 and 5.2 per 100,000, respectively. The Navy's rates were 8.3 and 2.5 per 100,000; the rates in civilian society were 10.3 and 4.7 per 100,000. The Marines' motor vehicle death rate was 84 per 100,000; the Navy's rate was 60 per 100,000, and the rate in civilian society was 23 per 100,000. These figures are for active-duty service members only. See Department of the Navy, *Annual Report of the Surgeon General of the United States Navy* (1950–1959), tables 37–48. For civilian data, see Eckberg, "Reported Suicides, 1900–1997," "Reported Homicides, 1900–1997," and "Motor Vehicle Deaths and Death Rates, by Age, 1913–1996," in *Historical Statistics of the United States.*

19. One interesting fictional account of the "jail or the Marine Corps" option in the 1950s is described in Charles F. Johnson, *Steve Fletcher, U.S. Marine: A Story of Recruit Training in the Marine Corps* (New York: Holt, Rinehart and Winston, 1957).

20. Wertsch, *Military Brats,* xix. For a semiautobiographical account of life in the Conroy household in the 1960s, see Pat Conroy, *The Great Santini* (Boston: Houghton Mifflin, 1976).

21. For increasing alcoholism rates during the war, see J. Hirsh, "Alcoholism, a Neglected Malady," *New York Times Magazine,* April 10, 1949, SM14. For rising alcoholism rates throughout the 1950s, see Louis Cassels, "Five Million Alcoholics Neglected by Nation," *Washington Post,* July 19, 1957, A20; "Alcoholism Put Third as Disease," *New York Times,* April 2, 1958, 24; "Alcoholism Is Nation's No. 3 Health Problem," *Science News Letter* 76 (August 8, 1959), 82. Drinking habits are discussed in detail in Don Cahalan, Ira H. Cisin, and Helen M. Crossley, *American Drinking Practices: A National Study of Drinking Behavior and Attitudes,* Monographs of the Rutgers Center of Alcohol Studies (New Brunswick, NJ: Publications Division, Rutgers Center of Alcohol Studies, 1969), 18–20; the linkage between heavy drinking and expressions of anger is discussed on p. 153. For more analytical investigations of the connections

among drinking, belligerence, and violent behavior, see Don Cahalan and Robin Room, *Problem Drinking among American Men* (New Brunswick, NJ: Publications Division, Rutgers Center of Alcohol Studies, 1974), 4, 6–8, 23. See also Lori Rotskoff, *Love on the Rocks: Men, Women, and Alcohol in Post–World War II America* (Chapel Hill: University of North Carolina Press, 2002), 90–91.

22. Over the last thirty years, seven separate studies of alcohol use in the military have confirmed that in times of both peace and war, servicemen and women consistently drink more, and more frequently, than civilians, even when adjusted for age and other demographic factors. The earliest studies of military drinking are D. Cahalan et al., *A Study to Measure the Extent and Pattern of Alcohol Use and Abuse in the U.S. Army* (San Diego: Report of Naval Medical Neuropsychiatric Research Unit, 1973), and D. Cahalan and I. H. Cisin, *Analysis of Drinking Behavior and Attitudes by Race* (College Park, MD: Report of Bureau of Social Science Research, 1975), both summarized in M. A. Schuckit, *Alcohol Problems in the United States Armed Forces* (San Diego: Naval Health Research Center, 1976), 9–11. Five more comprehensive studies conducted between 1980 and 1992 are summarized in Bray et al., *1992 Worldwide Survey*, 4-2-4-40; Bray et al., "2002 Department of Defense Survey," tables 4.1, 4.2, D.3–D.6.

23. Leo P. Crespi and G. Schofield Shapleigh, "'The' Veteran: A Myth," *Public Opinion Quarterly* 10 (Autumn 1946): 369. See also William M. Tuttle, *Daddy's Gone to War: The Second World War in the Lives of America's Children* (New York: Oxford University Press, 1993), 218–220.

24. Edith Efron, "Who Drinks, Why and How?" *New York Times Magazine,* April 14, 1946, 103.

25. Gerald Carthrae Thomas, *The Marine Officer's Guide* (Annapolis, MD: Naval Institute Press, 1956), 475–476.

26. "Psychiatrist Hits Attitude of Military on Alcoholism," *Air Force Times,* August 6, 1960, 20. For a surprising example of excessive drinking by a serving secretary of defense in the 1950s, see General Merrill B. Twining oral history, 360, MCOHC, MCA.

27. Bray et al., *1992 Worldwide Survey*, 4-6-4-18, D.3–D.12. The 2002 data showed the highest rates, with 35 percent of Marines being classified as heavy drinkers compared to just 15 percent in the civilian population

and 27 percent in the overall DOD population. See Bray et al., "2002 Department of Defense Survey," tables 4.1, 4.2, D.3–D.6.

28. "Sponsorship of Billboard Posters and Other Advertisements by Liquor Companies," March 5, 1947, E107 "Information Division Correspondence 1947–1950" (hereafter E107), box 2, "Advertising" file, RG 127, NARA.

29. See correspondence on *Never the Twain Shall Meet* and other films in E107, box 16, "Photo and Pictures, Motion, Other (1)" file, RG 127, NARA.

30. Lt. Col. Clair E. Towne to Mr. George M. Dorsey, Warner Bros., October 16, 1953, HD subject file "Movies, Battle Cry," MCA.

31. For information on the Marine Corps' participation in the Freedom Train, see E107, box 1, "Freedom Train" (two files), RG 127 and E56 and E58, "Freedom Train" (six boxes), RG 64, which includes a large scrapbook of newspaper clippings on the tour. See also HD subject file "Freedom Train," MCA. The quotes come from "Public Service Parlay Called at White House," *Chicago Tribune*, May 31, 1947, 3.

32. The statistics on the tour's popularity are taken from Department of the Navy, "Marine Corps Detachment Commended by Heritage Foundation," January 31, 1949, HD subject file "Freedom Train," MCA. See also Sergeant Jorge Vallejo, "Freedom Train: 1947," *Marines*, March 1988, 23–24, and "Freedom Train Tours America," *National Geographic Magazine* 96 (October 1949): 539.

33. See the correspondence between Secretary of War Royall and Secretary of the Navy Sullivan in E107, box 1, "Freedom Train (1)" file, RG 127, NARA.

34. Vallejo, "Freedom Train: 1947," 24.

35. Gilbert Bailey, "Why They Throng to the Freedom Train," *New York Times*, January 25, 1948, SM18. See also "U.S. Marines Guard Nation's Priceless Relics," unnamed newspaper, October 20, 1947, E58, box 6, "Freedom Train Scrapbook," RG 64, NARA.

36. Gilbert Bailey, "Why They Throng to the Freedom Train," SM18.

37. Commanding Officer, Marine Detachment to Commandant of the Marine Corps, "Report of Freedom Train," October 28, 1948, E107, box 1, "Freedom Train (2)" file, RG 127, NARA.

38. Dick Maxwell and Tommy Filas, "Freedom Is Everybody's Job," E58 "Freedom Train," box 6, "music documents" file, RG 64, NARA. The

best work on how notions of home and family became national security concerns in the Cold War is Elaine Tyler May, *Homeward Bound: American Families in the Cold War Era* (New York: Basic Books, 1988).

39. Miss Isobel Kinney to Whom It May Concern, November 11, 1948, E107, Box 1, "Freedom Train (1 of 2)" file, RG 127, NARA.

40. Colonel R. F. Scott to Commandant of Marine Corps, "After Action Report," E107, box 1, "Freedom Train (2 of 2)" file, RG 127, NARA.

41. Statistics on juvenile delinquency from 1946 to 1956 can be found in Richard Sutch, "Juvenile Court Cases Disposed, by Type of Offense: 1940–1997," table Ec1319–1340, and Douglas Eckberg, "Persons in Custody in Training Schools for Juvenile Delinquents and in Detention Centers, by Sex, Race, Ethnicity, and Age: 1950–1990," table Ec358–401, both in Carter et al., *Historical Statistics of the United States, Earliest Times to the Present.* For the quote by Attorney General Brownell, see Benjamin Fine, *1,000,000 Delinquents* (London: V. Gollancz, 1956), 1–30.

42. Lists and full-text reports of the congressional hearings on juvenile delinquency are available through the Lexis-Nexis Congressional online database, http://web.lexis-nexis.com/congcomp (accessed August 1, 2009).

43. United States Marine Corps Reserve VTU-12(s), "Report on Citizenship Project 'Devil Pups,' 1955," December 31, 1955, 1, in E102 Headquarters Support Correspondence 1950–1958 (hereafter E102), box 78, "Apr–Jun 1957" file, RG 127, NARA. The quote on "guided missiles" comes from Lt. Col. Richard F. Hyland to Director 12th USMC R&R District, "Report on Devil Pups Citizenship Project 1958-59-60," December 31, 1960,1, in HD subject file "Devil Pups," MCA. The most comprehensive files on the Devil Pups Citizenship Project are contained in E102, box 84, "A7: Devil Pups" file; box 78, "April–June 1957" file; box 79, "Jan–Jul 1956" file, and "Jan–Jul 1958" file, RG 127, NARA. See also HD subject file "Devil Pups," MCA.

44. "Report on Devil Pups Citizenship Project 1958–59–60" and assorted newspaper clippings and brochures in HD subject file "Devil Pups," MCA.

45. Reserve Volunteer Training Unit 12-5(s), "Report on Citizenship Project 'Devil Pups' 1955," 4 in E102, Box 78, "Apr-Jun-57," NARA.

46. Jim Wright, "I Was a Teenage Devil Pup," ca. 1960, HD subject file "Devil Pups," MCA. Emphasis in original. For evidence of the Pups' close contact with tanks and machine guns, see the pictures at the end of "Report on Citizenship Project Devil Pups, 1955," and "Report on Devil Pups Citizenship Project 1958–59–60," December 31, 1960, MCA.

47. Wertsch, *Military Brats*, 5.

48. Robert Perman, "Devil Dogs Spark Sturdy 'Offspring,'" *Kansas City Times*, August 21, 1958, 36.

49. See "Comparison of Types of Maltreatment Offenses Resulting in Conviction," in Greene PPC, box 94, "956 Maltreatment" file, MCA. For additional primary sources on Ribbon Creek and the problems of recruit abuse, see Greene PPC, boxes 89–103; HD subject files "Ribbon Creek," "McKeon Death March: Newspaper and Magazine coverage," and HD biographical file "McKeon, Matthew C.," MCA.

50. Headquarters, United States Marine Corps, "Recruit Training Survey, July 1956," 4–5, 13–31, series III, box 72, HBP.

51. Wallace M. Greene Jr. to Robert Debs Heinl, October 21, 1960, Greene PPC, box 94, "959 McKeon" file, MCA.

52. Eddie Adams, cited in Larry Smith, *The Few and the Proud: Marine Corps Drill Instructors in Their Own Words* (New York: W. W. Norton, 2006), 109.

53. Mrs. Frank Sorensen to President Harry S. Truman, September 21, 1950, E107, box 10, "1535–75 Recruiting," file, RG 127, NARA.

54. Information Booklet, "How to Use TV," June 20, 1951, 14, in E54, Information Division Correspondence, box 1, "A7-2-2 Television (1)" file, RG 127, NARA. See also United States Marine Corps, *Telling the Marine Corps Story* (Washington, DC: GPO, 1963), 3.5–3.6.

55. Two thick files detailing the work done for the Marine Corps by the J. Walter Thompson Company in the 1940s are found in E107 Information Division Correspondence 1946–1950, box 2, RG 127, NARA.

56. J. Walter Thompson Company to Brigadier General W. E. Riley, January 2, 1948, E107, box 2, "J. Walter Thompson (1)" file, RG 127, NARA.

57. Mark Kauffman, "How to Make Marines," *Life*, October 8, 1951, 141–151.

58. Mrs. Frank Fink to the Commandant of the Marine Corps, October 15, 1951; Mrs. Plankin to the President of the United States, October 8, 1951, and Mrs. R. D. Quinn to the Commandant of the Marine Corps, Octo-

ber 9, 1951, all in E54, Information Division Correspondence, box 2, "A10-1/2 Magazines, Life Mag. Complaints" file, RG 127, NARA.

59. *Life* weekly letters summary in E54, Information Division Correspondence, box 2, "A10-1/2 Magazines, Life Mag. Complaints" file, RG 127, NARA.

60. "Marine Says He Kept Hat on, Was Beaten," *New York Herald Tribune*, February 7, 1957, 1; "Vt. VFW Wants Facts on Marine Treatment," *Burlington Free Press*, February 8, 1957, and other articles in HD subject file "Brutality, Marine (1)," MCA. The reference to a "steel bar" was an exaggeration, one that explains some of the anger by the pro-Marine writers. The Marine was almost certainly hit with a swagger stick, an example of which is found in actor Jack Webb's hand in the photos from *The D.I.*

61. Maybel Darrah to the Editor, *Plattsburgh Press-Republican*, February 11, 1957, 3. A clipping of the letter and several pro-Marine retorts to Ms. Darrah are found in HD subject file "Brutality, Marine (1)," MCA.

62. Anonymous letter, "A Group of Mothers" to Father Marus F. Cook, undated, in Greene PPC, box 94, "957 Investigations" file, MCA.

63. For one example of criticism from the clergy, see Rev. Clinton M. Blake Jr.'s letter to Senator Charles W. Tobey, October 8, 1951, in E54, Information Division Correspondence, box 2, "A10-1/2 Magazines, Life Mag. Complaints" file, RG 127, NARA.

64. Vincenzo B. V. Dipippo, "No More Nursemaids," *Providence* (RI) *Journal,* March 9, 1957; editorial, "Too Many Cry Babies Joining the Marines," *Shreveport* (LA) *Times*, March 10, 1957, B-2, both in HD subject file "Marine Brutality (1)," MCA.

65. Lincoln Rockwell, "Who Wants Panty-waist Marines?" *American Mercury,* April 1957, 120. A decade later, Rockwell, a former naval officer and the leader of the American Nazi Party, was shot and killed by fellow Nazi John Patler, who was a former Marine.

66. Headquarters, United States Marine Corps, "Recruit Training Survey, July 1956," 3, 6, 7, 14, 18, 36, series III, box 72, HBP. For the 1958 survey, see Headquarters Marine Corps, Procedures Analysis Branch, "What Marines Think of Recruit Training after a Year of Service, March 1958," 3, 13, series III, box 72, HBP. See also Headquarters, United States Marine Corps, "Reactions of Recruits to Recruit Training, December

1956," 1–18, in Greene PPC, box 48, file 484, MCA. Keith Fleming discusses the role of violence in male rites of passage in *The U.S. Marine Corps in Crisis*, 5.

67. Statistics of the number of women in the different branches of the armed forces are listed in Department of Defense, Directorate for Information Operations and Reports (DIOR), *Selected Manpower Statistics* (Washington, DC: The Pentagon, 1980), 118.

68. Fully 60 percent of women Marines claimed they wouldn't reenlist, compared to just 46 percent of women in the Army and 49 percent of women in the Air Force. These figures are listed in a series of studies on women's opinions toward military life done by the Attitudes Research Branch, Office of Armed Forces Information and Education. For reenlistment rates, see "Enlisted Women in the Services I: Attitudes of Enlisted Women in the Regular Service toward Reenlistment (April–May 1952)," 95–97 in E102, HQ Support Correspondence 1950–1958, box 353, "Enlistment May–Oct 1952" file, RG 127, NARA.

69. "Enlisted Women in the Services III: Some Satisfactions and Dissatisfactions of Service Life (April–May 1952)," 95, E102, box 354, "Enlistment (Aug–Dec 1953)" file, RG 127, NARA.

70. Oral history of Lieutenant General Ormond R. Simpson USMC, 191, MCOHC, MCA.

71. "Too Many Cry Babies Joining the Marines."

72. Files detailing the Marine Corps' participation in *The D.I.* are found both in the National Archives and in the Reference Branch of the Marine Corps History Division, MCA. See, in particular, HD subject file "Movies—The D.I.," MCA. A complete shooting script with annotations by the Marine script screener is found in E102, box 86, "SAF Movie, The DI" file, RG 127, NARA.

73. "The D.I., Shooting Script, Final," 18, E102, box 86, "SAF Movie, The DI," NARA.

74. Mrs. Jeannette A. Walls, "Reader Sees Marine Complaining Done by Sissy Yankees," *Richmond* (VA) *Times-Dispatch*, March 6, 1957, 16.

75. Mrs. Virginia Greer to the Commandant of the Marine Corps, cited in General Randolph McCall Pate, USMC, "What's with the Marines?" *American Weekly*, June 9, 1957, reprinted in *Congressional Record* 103, part 13 (June 11, 1957): A4570.

76. Dickey Chapelle, "Is Momma Running the Marines?" *Shreveport* (LA) *Journal*, August 1, 1957, B-2.

77. See the many letters and articles on this topic in HD subject file "Newspaper and Magazine Coverage of McKeon Death March," and HD biographical file "McKeon, Matthew C.," MCA.

78. Pate, "What's with the Marines?," A4571. See also "Report of the Commandant of the Marine Corps to the House Armed Services Committee, 30 January 1957," Greene PPC, box 48, file 484, MCA; Commandant of the Marine Corps to All General Officers, "Recruit Training (Green Letter No. 8-57)," February 27, 1957, Greene PPC Box 484, file 484, MCA. The quote from the public relations officer is from Informational Services Officer to Chief of Staff, "Query from Peter Hackes, NBC," August 1, 1956, E102, box 79, "Aug–Dec 56," NARA.

79. "Address of General Randall McC. Pate, Commandant of the Marine Corps to the Marine Officers' Wives," September 17, 1958, E1077 Policy Analysis Division Speech Files of the Commandant and Subordinate Staff Officers 1951–1972, box 3, file 1, RG 127, NARA. Much of the material from this speech, including the quotation cited earlier, comes from Victor H. Krulak's letter to the Commandant of October 30, 1957, cited in Victor H. Krulak, *First to Fight: An Inside View of the U.S. Marine Corps* (Annapolis, MD: Naval Institute Press, 1999), xv.

80. See the assorted clippings on Marine murders in HD subject files "Murders, MC Personnel Involved (1)" and "Murders, MC Personnel Involved (2)," MCA. Thirty-one Marines were tried for murder in the five years after Korea, mostly for killing spouses, children, or girlfriends. Of this number, more than half occurred in the twelve months following the armistice. Of course, this list is by no means comprehensive. The coverage of all these crimes highlighted the accused's connection to the Marine Corps, which explains why the Marine Corps kept the clippings. Additional files on crimes other than murders during the same time period are found in HD subject file "Courts Martial," MCA.

81. John Briney, "Officer Says Wife Cried: I Shot Him," *Washington Post*, November 16, 1955, 3. All coverage of the Goricki trial is contained in the HD subject files "Murders, MC Personnel Involved (2)" and HD biographical file "Edward Goricki," MCA.

82. "Marine Slain," unnamed newspaper, May 23, 1955, 1, in HD subject file "Murder, MC Personnel Involved (2)," MCA.

83. Jean White, "Kin Testify How Goricki Beat Wife," *Washington Post*, November 19, 1955, 25.

84. John Briney, "Widow Sobs Love for Slain Goricki," *Washington Post*, November 22, 1955, 3.

85. Ibid., 1.

86. Don Maclean, "Goricki Case Heads for Jury," *Washington Daily News*, November 22, 1955, 5.

87. "Prosecution Nears End in Trial of Mrs. Goricki," *Washington Evening Star*, November 18, 1955, 19.

88. "Wife Charged in Chop Death," *Washington Daily News*, May 23, 1955, 5.

89. Briney, "Widow Sobs Love for Slain Goricki," 1. The height and weight data come from "Prosecution Nears End in Trial of Mrs. Goricki," 19.

90. Ibid.

91. Richard Rodgers, "Goricki Widow Sobs as Jury Acquits Her," unnamed Washington newspaper, November 22, 1955, HD subject file "Murders, Marine Corps Personnel Involved (2)," MCA.

92. In 1955, the Marines' death from assault rate was 3.4 per 100,000, and the Navy's was 0.7 per 100,000. These figures are for active-duty service members only. See Department of the Navy, *Annual Report of the Surgeon General of the United States Navy* (Washington, DC: Bureau of Medicine and Surgery, 1955), 138.

93. Newspaper clippings on Marine murders are found in HD subject files "Murders, MC Personnel Involved (1)" and "Murders, MC Personnel Involved (2)," MCA.

94. "Twenty Year Old Ex-Marine Admits Strangling," *Oklahoma City Times*, February 12, 1954, HD subject file "Murders—MC Personnel Involved (2)," MCA.

95. Marine Corps enlisted dishonorable discharges rose from 43 in 1953 to 82 in 1954 and to 127 in 1955. In the Navy's enlisted ranks (which contained three times as many personnel), dishonorable discharges decreased from 75 in 1953 to 62 in 1954 before rising to 76 in 1955. See NAVPERS 15658, FY1953–1955, RG 24, NARA.

96. Briney, "Widow Sobs Love for Slain Goricki," 1.

97. "Marine Slain, Wife Is Held in Arlington Jail," *Washington Evening Star*, May 23, 1955, HD subject file "Murder, MC Personnel Involved (2)," MCA.

98. Briney, "Widow Sobs Love for Slain Goricki," 3.

99. Mrs. Frank Sorensen to President Harry S. Truman, September 21, 1950, E107, box 10, "1535–75 Recruiting" file, RG 127, NARA.

6. Rise of the Amphibious Force-in-Readiness

1. Edwin H. Simmons, "Bigfoot Brown," *Marine Corps Gazette* 57 (September 1973): 26.

2. These Cold War nuclear networks are discussed in Lawrence Freedman, *The Evolution of Nuclear Strategy*, 3rd ed. (New York: Palgrave Macmillan, 2003). For a cultural analysis of Cold War networks, see Paul M. Edwards, *The Closed World: Computers and the Politics of Discourse in Cold War America* (Cambridge, MA: MIT Press, 1996).

3. A detailed analysis of the many military incidents that occurred between January 1, 1946, and December 31, 1975, may be found in Barry M. Blechman and Stephen S. Kaplan, *Force without War: U.S. Armed Forces as a Political Instrument* (Washington, DC: Brookings Institution, 1978), 23–57. Naval incidents receive more detailed attention in Adam B. Siegel, *The Use of Naval Forces in the Post-War Era: U.S. Navy and U.S. Marine Corps Crisis Response Activity, 1946–1990* (Alexandria, VA: Center for Naval Analyses, 1991), 7–40.

4. Blechman and Kaplan's figures do not include disaster relief missions. For a full accounting of Marine Corps interventions (including disaster relief) from 1946 to 1971, see Ralph W. Donnelly, Gabrielle M. Neufeld, and Carolyn A. Tyson, *A Chronology of the United States Marine Corps* (Washington, DC: Historical Division, HQMC, 1971), 3:29–53, 4:1–37. See also Siegel, *Use of Naval Forces in the Post-War Era*, 17–52.

5. For Secretary of Defense Robert M. Gates' comment on the "creeping militarization" of U.S. foreign policy, see Ann Scott Tyson, "Gates Warns of Militarized Policy," *Washington Post*, July 16, 2008, 6.

6. Succinct explanations of the Short Range Emergency War Plan (HALFMOON) are found in Kenneth W. Condit, *History of the Joint Chiefs of*

Staff: The Joint Chiefs of Staff and National Policy, vol. 2, *1947–1949* (Washington, DC: Office of Joint History, Office of the Chairman of the Joint Chiefs of Staff, 1986), 156–158; Freedman, *The Evolution of Nuclear Strategy,* 51–53. The Marines' role is discussed in Thomas H. Etzold and John Lewis Gaddis, eds., *Containment: Documents on American Policy and Strategy, 1945–1950* (New York: Columbia University Press, 1978), 321.

7. On the Navy's thinking on nuclear weapons, see Jeffrey G. Barlow, *Revolt of the Admirals: The Fight for Naval Aviation, 1945–1950* (Washington, DC: Ross and Perry, 2001), 72–80, 106–130. See also George W. Baer, *One Hundred Years of Sea Power: The U.S. Navy, 1890–1990* (Palo Alto, CA: Stanford University Press, 1994), 349–362; Elliot V. Converse III, *History of Acquisition in the Department of Defense,* vol. 1, *Rearming for the Cold War, 1945–1950* (Washington, DC: Department of Defense Historical Office, 2012), 320–359.

8. Stephen Howarth, *To Shining Sea: A History of the United States Navy, 1775–1991* (New York: Random House, 1991), 495. A succinct summary of the different services' missile programs is found in Robert J. Watson, *History of the Office of the Secretary of Defense,* vol. 4, *Into the Missile Age, 1956–1960* (Washington, DC: Historical Office of the Secretary of Defense, 1997), 157–201.

9. The Navy's response to Korea is detailed in Baer, *One Hundred Years of Sea Power,* 332–334. The Army's post-Korea "never again club," which argued that the United States should avoid future limited wars, is discussed in David Howell Petraeus, "The American Military and the Lessons of Vietnam: A Study of Military Influence and the Use of Force in the Post-Vietnam Era," Ph.D. diss., Princeton University, 1987, 35–43.

10. John Lewis Gaddis, *Strategies of Containment: A Critical Appraisal of Postwar American National Security Policy* (New York: Oxford University Press, 1982), 148–152, 164–167, 178–179.

11. The growth of the nuclear arsenal is discussed in Allan Reed Millett and Peter Maslowski, *For the Common Defense: A Military History of the United States of America* (New York: Free Press, 1984), 541. The various short-of-war incidents in the Eisenhower, Kennedy, and Johnson presidencies are discussed in Blechman and Kaplan, *Force without War,* 26–32. The inapplicability of massive retaliation to local, non-

nuclear conflicts is discussed in Gaddis, *Strategies of Containment*, 175–179.

12. Gaddis, *Strategies of Containment*. The notion of the paradox of nuclear weapons is also explored in Baer, *One Hundred Years of Sea Power*, 345.

13. The Navy estimated that destroying just 10 percent of those targets "was sufficient to destroy all of Russia." See David Alan Rosenberg, "The Origins of Overkill: Nuclear Weapons and American Strategy, 1945–1960," *International Security* 7 (Spring 1983): 50, 56. The Air Force's difficulties during the Lebanon intervention are discussed in David A. Byrd, "Lebanon Crisis: Operation Blue Bat," in A. Timothy Warnock, ed., *Short of War: Major USAF Contingency Operations, 1947–1997* (Washington, DC: Air Force History and Museums Program and Air University Press, 2000), 11–21. See also Roger J. Spiller, *"Not War but like War": The American Intervention in Lebanon*, Leavenworth Papers (Fort Leavenworth, KS: Combat Studies Institute, U.S. Army Command and General Staff College, 1981), 29–34.

14. Howarth, *To Shining Sea*, 495; Baer, *One Hundred Years of Sea Power*, 349.

15. Baer, *One Hundred Years of Sea Power*, 339.

16. On the Army's acquisition of various tactical nuclear weapons, see Converse, *Rearming for the Cold War*, 592–603. Research dollars for 1961 are discussed on p. 602. See also, A. J. Bacevich, *The Pentomic Era: The U.S. Army between Korea and Vietnam* (Washington, DC: National Defense University Press, 1986), 71–102. The single best work on the Army's inability to prepare for both nuclear warfare and short-of-war contingencies is Ingo Trauschweizer, *The Cold War U.S. Army* (Lawrence: University of Kansas Press, 2008).

17. In 1958, students at the Command and General Staff College received 387 hours of instruction on nuclear combat. That number grew to 600 hours by 1960. This and the data on *Military Review* articles are found in Robert T. Davis, *The Challenge of Adaptation: The U.S. Army in the Aftermath of Conflict, 1953–2000* (Fort Leavenworth, KS: Combat Studies Institute Press, 2008), 27.

18. Paul C. Jussel, "Intimidating the World: The United States Atomic Army, 1945–1960," Ph.D. diss., The Ohio State University, 2004, 91.

19. Trauschweizer, *The Cold War U.S. Army*, 1, 48–113.

20. Detailed criticisms of the Pentomic concept are found in Bacevich, *The Pentomic Era*, 103–157; Davis, *Challenge of Adaptation*, 11–32; Robert A. Doughty, *The Evolution of U.S. Army Tactical Doctrine, 1946–76* (Fort Leavenworth, KS: Combat Studies Institute, US Army Command and General Staff College, 1979), 18–19. The most charitable analysis of the pentomic reorganization comes from Jussel, "Intimidating the World," 206–213.

21. The comparison to World War I frontal assault tactics comes from Bacevich, *The Pentomic Era*, 108–110.

22. General Paul L. Freeman USA (Ret'd) cited in ibid., 135.

23. A brief overview of the Strategic Army Corps may be found in A. J. Birtle, *U.S. Army Counterinsurgency and Contingency Operations Doctrine, 1942–1976* (Washington, DC: Center of Military History, 2006), 198–204. See also Trauschweizer, *The Cold War U.S. Army,* 94–95, 99.

24. Birtle, *U.S. Army Counterinsurgency and Contingency Operations Doctrine,* 216. See also Spiller, *Not War but like War,* 26–32; Samuel P. Huntington, *The Common Defense: Strategic Programs in National Politics* (New York: Columbia University Press, 1961), 352–353.

25. Huntington, *The Common Defense,* 344.

26. Kennan's position is well documented in George F. Kennan, *Memoirs, 1925–1950* (London: Hutchinson, 1968), 311–312. See also Gaddis, *Strategies of Containment,* 39, 97–98; Huntington, *The Common Defense,* 41.

27. NSC-68, which was the most comprehensive statement of Cold War defense policy yet penned in 1950, is discussed in detail in Gaddis, *Strategies of Containment,* 89–126. The text of NSC-68 is found in Etzold and Gaddis, eds., *Containment,* 385–442. See, in particular, p. 434.

28. For excerpts from Lieutenant General Roy S. Geiger's report on the Bikini tests, see Lieutenant Colonel Kenneth J. Clifford, *Progress and Purpose: A Developmental History of the United States Marine Corps, 1900–1970* (Washington, DC: History and Museums Division, HQMC, 1973), 71. See also Richard S. Hodgson, "The Atom Bomb Comes into Focus," *Marine Corps Gazette* 30 (October 1946): 22.

29. Major General Pedro A. Del Valle, "Post War Organization of the Marine Corps," *Military Review* 27 (November 1947): 8–11. See also General A. A. Vandegrift with Robert B. Asprey, *Once a Marine* (New York: W. W. Norton, 1964), 319.

30. Lieutenant Colonel Robert E. Cushman, "Where Do We Go from Here?" *Marine Corps Gazette* 32 (May 1948): 12.

31. For evidence of this broader notion of containment, see General Randall McC. Pate, "Remarks to Naval War College," March 4, 1957, box 2, file 1, 14–15; "War in the Nuclear Age: Remarks to the Naval Research Committee Symposium," June 9, 1958, box 2, file 7; "Suggested Questions and Answers for Taped Interview on CBS," box 2, file 2, all in E1077 "Policy Analysis Division Speech Files of the Commandant 1951–1972," RG 127, NARA.

32. The ten interventions are Greece (disaster relief, 1953), North Vietnam (refugee evacuations, 1955), Egypt (civilian evacuations, 1956), Morocco (stabilization operations, 1956), Spain (disaster relief, 1957), Ceylon (disaster relief, 1958), Lebanon (peacekeeping and stabilization, 1958), Taiwan (show of force during the second Taiwan Strait Crisis, 1958), Cuba (show of force, 1959), and Morocco (disaster relief, 1960). These do not include the show-of-force operations off Indonesia (1957) and Venezuela (1958), when the Marines did not actually land on foreign soil. These events are detailed in Donnelly, Neufeld, and Tyson, *Chronology of the United States Marine Corps,* 3:26–48.

33. United States Marine Corps, "Marine Corps Board Report: Organization of the Fleet Marine Force: War and Peace 1 December 1948," Studies and Reports Collection, box 1, "War and Peace" file, MCA (hereafter "Marine Corps Board Report: War and Peace").

34. Ibid., 29.

35. Ibid., 19, 24, 28–30.

36. Ibid., 19.

37. The deployment of the first MAGTF is recorded in Donnelly, Neufeld, and Tyson, *Chronology of the United States Marine Corps,* 3:5. See also John G. Norris, "Marines Sail for Europe," *Washington Post,* January 6, 1948, 1.

38. This change was made during the First Provisional Brigade's hasty deployment to Korea. Planners later detailed the benefits of the adjustment in Fleet Marine Forces Pacific, "FMFPAC Staff Study: Establishment of a Balanced Fleet Marine Force Air Ground Force in the Western Pacific," October 19, 1950, 1–2, HAF document 742, box 41, MCA.

39. Ibid., 1–2. Troop composition is spelled out in Annex A, "Detailed Troop List," 1–5.

40. Battalion and regimental landing teams had embarked with the Seventh Fleet periodically starting in 1955, but the continuous embarkation of a reinforced battalion with an aviation element did not occur until the Special Landing Force was created in 1960. These events are detailed in Donnelly, Neufeld, and Tyson, *Chronology of the U.S. Marine Corps*, 3:34, 36, 42, 46–47. See also the discussion of Operation Spearhead in "Marine Corps 1960: The Marine Corps Association Newsletter," *Marine Corps Gazette* 44 (September 1960): A3.

41. CMC to director, Marine Corps Schools, April 22, 1953, "1953–1954 Advanced Research Groups, Assignment of Basic Projects to," E1039, Records Relating to Postwar Military Planning and Organization 1945–1980, box 10, "2: ARG 1952–1954" file, RG 127, NARA. For the group's final report, see ARG I, "Analysis of Marine Corps Concept of Landing Force" box 1, "Advanced Research Group 1953–1955" file, Studies and Reports Collection, MCA.

42. Commandant of the Marine Corps to Commanding General FMF Atlantic, "Activation of the 2nd Marine Air Ground Task Force FMF," December 20, 1953, HAF document 687, box 38, MCA.

43. Commandant of the Marine Corps, "The Marine Air-Ground Concept," November 9, 1954, HAF document 686, box 38, MCA. This is also discussed at length in ARG III, "Air-Ground Relations," box 1, "Project III" file, Studies and Reports Collection, MCA.

44. Huntington, *The Common Defense*, 345. For the full article, see General Matthew B. Ridgway, "The Army's Role in National Defense," *Army Information Digest*, May 1954, 21–30.

45. The reports that prioritized limited war over nuclear war are "Marine Corps Board Report: War and Peace" (1948), "Board to Study the Composition and Functions of Marine Corps Aviation" (Smith Board), 1955, and "FMF Organization and Composition Board" (Hogaboom Board), 1956, all available in the Studies and Reports Collection, MCA.

46. The concept of vertical envelopment is explained succinctly in Allan Reed Millett, *Semper Fidelis: The History of the United States Marine Corps* (New York: Free Press, 1991), 452–456, 524–525. See also ARG I, "Analysis of Marine Corps Concept of Landing Force," 2–20, MCA.

47. Clifford, *Progress and Purpose,* 71–78; Millett, *Semper Fidelis,* 452–456; Eugene W. Rawlins, *Marines and Helicopters, 1946–1962* (Washington, DC: History and Museums Division, HQMC, 1976), 19–30.

48. Rawlins, *Marines and Helicopters,* 26. For a detailed comparison of the two services' efforts to develop the helicopter, see Carl John Horne III, "Military Innovation and the Helicopter: A Comparison of Development in the United States Army and Marine Corps, 1945–1965," Ph.D. diss., Ohio State University, 2003, 98–100, 131–135, 248–251, 334–340.

49. An excellent study of the Marine Corps' innovations with helicopters is James Anthony Ginther Jr., "Keith Barr McKutcheon: Integrating Aviation into the United States Marine Corps, 1937–1971," Ph.D. diss., Texas Tech University, 1999, 53–114.

50. The full name of the Hogaboom Board was the FMF Organization and Composition Board. A succinct explanation of the board's reforms is found in Millett, *Semper Fidelis,* 525–527. The report was published in sections in the *Marine Corps Gazette* in April, May, June, and July 1957. The full report may also be found in Studies and Reports Collection, MCA.

51. It makes sense that the 1956 board endorsed the conclusions of the 1948 "Marine Corps Board Report: War and Peace," for General Hogaboom chaired both boards. See also Lieutenant General V. E. Megee's speech to the American Legion, January 20, 1956, which states unequivocally that "limited warfare is the most likely form of warfare in the future." This and other speeches noting the likelihood of more limited wars are found in E1077, "Policy Analysis Division Speech Files of the Commandant and Subordinate Staff Officers 1951–1972," box 1, file 1,RG 127, NARA.

52. This order is the usual one cited as the official start date of the Marine Corps MAGTFs. I have shown here that the concept was actually conceived and implemented a decade earlier. See MCO 3120.3, "Organization of Marine Air-Ground Task Forces," December 27, 1962, HAF document 907, box 54, MCA.

53. Siegel, *Use of Naval Forces in the Post-War Era,* 23–24; Donnelly, Neufeld, and Tyson, *Chronology of the U.S. Marine Corps,* 3:34; Millett, *Semper Fidelis,* 539.

54. Siegel, *Use of Naval Forces in the Post-War Era*, 30; Donnelly, Neufeld, and Tyson, *Chronology of the U.S. Marine Corps*, 3:56; Millett, *Semper Fidelis*, 554.

55. A good overview to the diplomatic events of the crisis may be found in Salim Yaqub, *Containing Arab Nationalism: The Eisenhower Doctrine and the Middle East*, New Cold War History (Chapel Hill: University of North Carolina Press, 2004), 205–237. The most detailed explanation of the military operation is found in Jack Shulimson, *Marines in Lebanon, 1958*, Marine Corps Historical Reference Pamphlet (Washington, DC: Historical Branch, G-3 Division Headquarters, 1966). See also Blechman and Kaplan, *Force without War*, 222–257.

56. The Marines' problems with the landing are detailed in Shulimson, *Marines in Lebanon, 1958*, 16–17. See also Spiller, *Not War but like War*, 20; Brigadier General S. S. Wade, USMC, "Operation Bluebat," *Marine Corps Gazette* 43 (July 1959): 10–23; Lieutenant Colonel Harry A. Hadd, USMC, "Who's a Rebel? *Marine Corps Gazette* 46 (March 1962): 50–54.

57. Spiller, *Not War but like War*, 7–9.

58. The Army's problems in the Lebanon operation are found in ibid., 12–14, 26–38.

59. "USAREUR Lessons Learned," n.p., cited in ibid., 37.

60. Ibid., 32–33. See also Warnock, *Short of War*, 11–21.

61. Major John M. Young, *When the Russians Blinked: The U.S. Maritime Response to the Cuban Missile Crisis*, Occasional Paper Series (Washington, DC: History and Museums Division, HQMC, 1990), 127.

62. A fine explanation of the Marines' activities in the Cuban Missile Crisis is found in ibid., 114–166. A detailed time line is included on pp. 225–236.

63. This offers further evidence that the Marine Corps could not have ever conducted an actual amphibious landing against a nuclear-armed foe. See Millett, *Semper Fidelis*, 556.

64. A detailed time line and explanation of Marine activities in the Dominican intervention is found in Jack K. Ringler and Henry I. Shaw Jr., *U.S. Marine Corps Operations in the Dominican Republic, April–June 1965*, Occasional Paper Series (Washington, DC: Historical Division, HQMC, 1970), 83–108. See also Millett, *Semper Fidelis*, 557–558.

65. Lawrence A. Yates, *Power Pack: U.S. Intervention in the Dominican Republic, 1965–1966*, Leavenworth Papers (Fort Leavenworth, KS: Combat Studies Institute, 1988), 57.

66. The Army's problems in the Dominican landings are well detailed in ibid., 55–71.

67. A detailed condemnation of the folly of Vietnam may be found in Gaddis, *Strategies of Containment*, 237–273. See also George C. Herring, *America's Longest War: The United States and Vietnam, 1950–1975* (New York: McGraw-Hill, 2002); Michael S. Hunt, *Lyndon Johnson's War: America's Cold War Crusade in Vietnam, 1945–1968* (New York: Hill and Wang, 1996).

68. The notion of "vertical flexibility"—being able to operate "up and down the spectrum of military capabilities, ranging from peacetime deterrence through nuclear war"—is explained in Gaddis, *Strategies of Containment*, 101.

69. Sergeant Thomas R. Harper, USMC, letter in "Message Center," *Marine Corps Gazette* 33 (September 1949): 2.

70. Harold M. Hyman, "When Congress Considered Abolishing the Marine Corps: An Interpretation," *Marine Corps Gazette* 43 (April 1959): 54–56.

71. Oral history of General Merrill B. Twining, 314, MCOHC, MCA.

72. Lieutenant Colonel Dennis D. Nicholson, USMC, "The Security of Stability," *Marine Corps Gazette* 43 (April 1959): 12.

73. Oral history of Major General Norman J. Anderson, USMC, 122, MCOHC, MCA. Anderson was a member of the Hogaboom Board and a director of the Policy Analysis Division.

74. Oral history of Brigadier General Samuel R. Shaw, USMC, 155, MCOHC, MCA.

75. Oral history of Brigadier General James Donald Hittle, tape 11408A, 5 minutes, 30 seconds, MCOHC, MCA.

76. Arguments over specialized badges and uniforms are found throughout the Army's service journals, particularly in the letters to the editor. For a representative sample, see Captain Willis C. Rowe, "To the Everlasting Glory of the Infantry," *Infantry Journal* 58 (March 1946): 22–26; Captain John D. McDonough, "Combat Artilleryman Badge" and "Come on

Up," *Combat Forces Journal* 2 (September 1951): 1, 7; "What's Wrong with the Infantry?" *Combat Forces Journal* 2 (January 1953): 23.

77. Intraservice friction in the Navy and Air Force is discussed in Carl H. Builder, *The Masks of War: American Military Styles in Strategy and Analysis* (Baltimore: Johns Hopkins University Press, 1989), 24–27.

78. Intraservice friction in the Marine Corps was usually between aviators and ground officers, between regular and reserve Marines, and occasionally over the perceived dominance of First Marine Division officers in Corps leadership. None of it, however, matched the friction present in the other services.

79. Major Andrew C. Geer to director, Division of Reserve, December 13, 1948, E24 Correspondence Files of the Office of the Commandant and HQ Supt Div files 1939–1950, box 25, "2195: Publicity" file, RG 127, NARA.

80. Succinct explanations of the Corps' changes during the first decade of the Cold War are found in Clifford, *Progress and Purpose*, 79–94; Millett, *Semper Fidelis*, 518–559.

81. For a few examples, see Lieutenant Colonel John H. Magruder III, USMC, "A Touch of Tradition," *Marine Corps Gazette* 43 (November 1959): 43; General R. Mc.C Pate, USMC, "A Birthday Message from the Commandant," *Leatherneck* 42 (November 1959): 15; Robert Leckie, *Helmet for My Pillow* (New York: Random House, 1957), 133.

82. For some of the most pro-tradition writings, see John Corbin (pseud.), "The Thin Line of Tradition II," *Marine Corps Gazette* 32 (April 1948): 8–13; Lieutenant Colonel Robert Debs Heinl Jr., USMC, "The Thin Line of Tradition III," *Marine Corps Gazette* 33 (July 1949): 46–52. For a plea to balance tradition against future requirements, see Lieutenant Colonel Donald R. Carter, "High Button Shoes," *Marine Corps Gazette* 33 (October 1949): 29.

83. Sergeant Thomas R. Harper, USMCR, "The Changing Corps," *Marine Corps Gazette* 33 (September 1949): 2; see also Master Sergeant John J. Morgan, "The Outlook," *Marine Corps Gazette* 38 (January 1954): 27.

84. Shaw oral history, 377, MCOHC, MCA.

85. Lieutenant Colonel C. F. Austin, USA, "The Loneliest Man in the Military," *Marine Corps Gazette* 43 (September 1959): 54–55.

86. Bell I. Wiley, "The Building and Training of Infantry Divisions: Obstacles to Effective Training," *Infantry Journal* 62 (April 1948): 43.

87. Pacific Fleet Evaluation Group, "Interview with Major General Lowe," December 8, 1950, E1077 Policy Analysis Division Speech Files, box 4, file 3, RG 127, NARA.

88. For a representative sample, see Heinl, "The Thin Line of Tradition III," 46–52; Major D. D. Nicholson Jr., USMC, "Administrative Frills," *Marine Corps Gazette* 39 (May 1955): 30–32; Captain T. K. Thomas, USMC, "Privates for General Service," *Marine Corps Gazette* 42 (February 1958): 28–31; and Lieutenant Colonel F. C. Bacon, USMC, "Strike Off Those Administrative Shackles," *Marine Corps Gazette* 42 (October 1958): 14–16.

89. Colonel Robert Debs Heinl Jr., USMC, "Special Trust and Confidence," *Marine Corps Gazette* 40 (November 1956): 33.

90. United States Marine Corps, *Annual Report of the Commandant of the Marine Corps to the Secretary of the Navy for Fiscal Year 1954* (Washington, DC: GPO, 1954), I-5.

91. Thomas, "Privates for General Service," 30–31.

92. Heinl, "The Thin Line of Tradition II," 12.

93. "Captain E. W. Haughey, USMC, "Machine Age," *Marine Corps Gazette* 42 (May 1958): 8.

94. Thomas, "Privates for General Service," 30.

95. Staff Sergeant Charles E. Gore, USMC, "The Typical Marine Is Gone," *Marine Corps Gazette* 35 (September 1951): 58.

96. William Hollingsworth Whyte, *The Organization Man* (Philadelphia: University of Pennsylvania Press, 2002). The strongest criticism of bureaucracy appears on 63–78. The discussions of "scientism" and scientific management are found on 23–32. Whyte's discussion of automation and classification appears on pp. 78 and 401.

97. Ibid.; the criticisms of the Navy appear on 54, and via a reading of *The Caine Mutiny* on 243–248, while criticism of the Army appears on 256.

98. See William Hollingsworth Whyte, *A Time of War: Remembering Guadalcanal, a Battle without Maps* (New York: Fordham University Press, 2000), 11–16. The dust cover of the first edition of *The Organization Man* did say that Whyte was "educated at Princeton and in the

United States Marine Corps at Guadalcanal." Whyte, *Organization Man*, x–xii.

99. First Lieutenant R. F. Van Cantfort, USMC, "The Human Element," *Marine Corps Gazette* 36 (August 1952): 14. See also First Lieutenant Lawrence V. Ryan, USMC, "Nobody Wants to Be a Fighting Man," *Marine Corps Gazette* 36 (April 1952): 35–37.

100. Lieutenant Colonel F. M. Johnson, USMC, "Lest We Forget," *Marine Corps Gazette* 44 (January 1960): 22.

101. General R. McC. Pate, address at the Naval War College, March 4, 1957, E1077 Policy Analysis Division Speech Files of the Commandant 1951–1972, box 2, "Speeches March–April 1957" file, RG 127, NARA.

102. Ryan, "Nobody Wants to Be a Fighting Man," 35.

103. A good description of the Desert Rock exercises is found in Roy E. Heinecke, "Desert Rock V," *Leatherneck* 36 (July 1953): 35. Further evidence that the Corps kept its focus on the force-in-readiness even as it dabbled in nuclear warfare is found in its first attempt at atomic doctrine, which argued in 1955 that "in some situations non-atomic weapons will continue to be the only means appropriate to accomplish the mission. Consequently, reliance upon the atomic capability must not result in a deterioration of our ability to conduct effective operations without atomic fire support." See Landing Force Bulletin 2 (revised), "Interim Doctrine for the Conduct of Tactical Atomic Warfare 1955," 1–1, HAF document 442, box 21, MCA.

104. Paul N. Edwards, *The Closed World: Computers and the Politics of Discourse in Cold War America* (Cambridge, MA: MIT Press, 1996), 12–13. Marine Corps culture bears many of the attributes of the closed world's antithesis, the "green world," which Edwards adapts from the literary criticism of Northrop Frye and explains on 13.

105. Ibid., 134–145. See also Martin Van Creveld, *Command in War* (Cambridge, MA: Harvard University Press, 1985), 232–275; R. W. Komer, *Bureaucracy at War: U.S. Performance in the Vietnam Conflict* (Boulder, CO: Westview Press, 1986), 16, 70–78, 88, 148–149.

106. A good overview of the different services' relationship to technology is found in Builder, *Masks of War*, 3–43. See also Morris Janowitz, *The Professional Soldier, a Social and Political Portrait* (Glencoe, IL: Free Press, 1960), 21–28, 31–36. Neither of these studies gives more than cursory attention to the Marine Corps.

107. Editorial, "Machines and Men," *Combat Forces Journal* 3 (October 1952): 9.

108. Major Leslie G. Calahan, USA, "Robot Generals," *Combat Forces Journal* 3 (April 1953): 30–32. See also Colonel Reuben Horchow, USA, "Classification Didn't Kill the Noncom," *Infantry Journal* 60 (June 1947): 20–21.

109. Editorial, "The Infantryman of Tomorrow," *Infantry Journal* 60 (March 1947): 7.

110. See the *Infantry Journal*'s monthly column "Science and War," introduced in 1946 and continuing through the period. The quote comes from "Mathematics of War and Peace," *Infantry Journal* 62 (March 1948): 4–5.

111. For a full explanation of Apollonian and Dionysian traits, see Friedrich Nietzsche, *The Birth of Tragedy and The Case for Wagner,* trans. Walter Kaufman (New York: Vintage Books, 1967), 33–144.

112. There are a few celebrations of machines and computers in the *Marine Corps Gazette,* but they are far outweighed by criticisms. See, for example, Captain Bill L. Parham, USMC, "Machines Fill the Billet," *Marine Corps Gazette* 37 (July 1953): 52–57.

113. The full text of the "The Rifleman's Creed" appears in "My Rifle," *Leatherneck* 32 (March 1949): 2.

114. For a nuanced explanation of America's Cold War empire, see John Lewis Gaddis, *We Now Know: Rethinking Cold War History* (New York: Oxford University Press, 1997), 27.

115. Jack Shulimson, *Marines in Lebanon, 1958,* 16–21; Spiller, *Not War but like War,* 24–25. The use of the Marines also generated friction between the military and the State Department. Even before the operation began, the U.S. ambassador to Lebanon tried to get the landing canceled and later requested modifications to the Marines' orders and movements, most of which were ignored or overruled. See Yaqub, *Containing Arab Nationalism,* 228–229; Spiller, *Not War but like War,* 22; Hadd, "Who's a Rebel?," 52–53.

116. One of the harshest assessments of the U.S. intervention in Lebanon came from the recently retired Commandant of the Marine Corps. See General David M. Shoup, "The New American Militarism," *Atlantic Monthly,* April 1969, 51–56.

Conclusion

1. Forty-nine percent of the entire Marine Corps served in South Vietnam during the years 1955–1975. During the same period, 40 percent of the Army served in South Vietnam. Navy and Air Force percentages are even lower. See Department of Defense, Defense Manpower Data Center, "Vietnam Conflict Casualty Summary, as of May 16, 2008," http://siadapp.dmdc.osd.mil/personnel/CASUALTY/vietnam.pdf (accessed September 1, 2009).

2. Seventeen percent of all Marines who served in Vietnam were wounded or killed, compared to 7 percent in the Army, 3 percent in the Navy, and less than 1 percent in the Air Force. These numbers do not include the 10,786 non-battle deaths incurred by the services in the Vietnam theater of operations. See Department of Defense, Defense Manpower Data Center, "Vietnam Conflict Casualty Summary, as of May 16, 2008," available at http://siadapp.dmdc.osd.mil/personnel/CASUALTY /vietnam.pdf (accessed August 1, 2009).

3. House of Representatives, Select Committee on Narcotics Abuse and Control, *Drug Abuse in the Armed Forces of the United States: Oversight Update*, 96th Cong, 1st Sess., 1979, SCNAC-96-1-13, 70, 80–85.

4. See General David M. Shoup, USMC, "The New American Militarism," *Atlantic Monthly*, April 1969, 51–56. See also General Shoup's preface to James A. Donovan, *Militarism, U.S.A.* (New York: Scribner, 1970); Howard Jablon, *David M. Shoup: A Warrior against War*, Biographies in American Foreign Policy (Lanham, MD: Rowman and Littlefield, 2005), 99–117.

5. For a fine overview of the Army's rehabilitation, see Beth Bailey, *America's Army: Making the All-Volunteer Force* (Cambridge, MA: Harvard University Press, 2009).

6. The U.S. government spent $157.5 billion on national defense in 1981. In 1988, it spent $290.4 billion—an increase of 84 percent. See Office of the Under Secretary of Defense (Comptroller), *National Defense Budget Estimates for FY 2013*, table 7-1, "Total Federal Outlays," 246, available at http://comptroller.defense.gov/defbudget/fy2013/FY13_Green_Book .pdf (accessed May 8, 2012).

7. E. J. Dionne, "Kicking the Vietnam Syndrome: Victory Sweeps away U.S. Doomed-to-Failure Feeling," *Washington Post,* March 4, 1991, 1. The effects of films such as *Top Gun* and the *Rambo* trilogy are discussed in Andrew J. Bacevich, *The New American Militarism: How Americans Are Seduced by War* (New York: Oxford University Press, 2005), 97–121.

8. At the height of the Cold War, Marine Corps infantry battalions spent 43 percent of their time deployed away from their home station. In the first half decade after the Cold War, that number jumped to 57 percent. See Lieutenant Commander Joseph M. Flynn, USN, "The Marine Corps Budget and Contingency Operations: Is the Funding Adequate to the Mission?" M.A. thesis, Army Command and General Staff College, Fort Leavenworth, KS, 1994, 70–71. For accusations of complacency, see Donald Kagan and Frederick W. Kagan, *While America Sleeps: Self-Delusion, Military Weakness, and the Threat to Peace Today* (New York: St. Martin's Press, 2000).

9. The Marine Corps also conducted contingency operations in Iraq, Bangladesh, the Philippines, Micronesia, Guam, Cuba, Saudi Arabia, and Kuwait. See Flynn, "The Marine Corps Budget and Contingency Operations," 3.

10. The statistics on operations do not include exercises, operations on U.S. soil (such as hurricane relief), or operations not involving amphibious forces. See U.S. Marine Corps Strategic Vision Group, "US Amphibious Operations 1990–2009," January 19, 2010, copy in author's possession. See also United States Marine Corps, *Amphibious Operations in the 21st Century* (Quantico, VA: Marine Corps Combat Development Command, 2009), 2. For the location of Marine forces by country, see Department of Defense, "Active Duty Military Personnel Strengths by Regional Area and Country," December 31, 2011, available at http://siadapp.dmdc.osd.mil/personnel/MILITARY/history/hst1112.pdf (accessed June 2, 2012).

11. From 1992 to 2012, all the services except the Marine Corps have seen their active-duty numbers decrease. The Navy's shrank 40 percent; the Air Force's, 29 percent; and the Army's, 8 percent. The Marine Corps' active duty manpower has increased by 10 percent. See Department of

Defense, Defense Manpower Data Center, Statistical Information and Analysis Division, *Selected Manpower Statistics,* http://siadapp.dmdc .osd.mil (accessed August 1, 2009). For 2012 manpower data, see *National Defense Budget Estimates for FY 2013,* table 3-2.

12. Between 1992 and 2012, the Marine Corps Total Obligation Authority (TOA) rose from $9.7 billion to $28.27 billion—an increase of 191 percent. This number does not include funding for aviation or military construction, all of which came from the Navy Department's budget. During the same period, the TOA for the entire Department of Defense increased 128 percent. See Comptroller, *National Defense Budget Estimates for FY 2013,* table 6-1, "Department of Defense TOA, by Title." Marine Corps TOA is available in three-year increments in table 6-6.

13. These points are found throughout Sun Tzu, *The Art of War,* trans. Samuel B. Griffith (New York: Oxford University Press, 1963). See in particular Sun Tzu's explanation of "moral forces," 63–64, 108, 121–122.

14. Mary A. Renda, paraphrasing Edward W. Said, made this point about the Marines in *Taking Haiti: Military Occupation and the Culture of U.S. Imperialism, 1915–1940* (Chapel Hill: University of North Carolina Press, 2001), 9. See also Edward W. Said, *Culture and Imperialism* (New York: Alfred A. Knopf, 1994), xi–14.

15. For further appropriations by civilians of the Iwo Jima flag-raising image, including in advertisements for Spam and in numerous political cartoons, see Karal Ann Marling and John Wetenhall, *Iwo Jima: Monuments, Memories, and the American Hero* (Cambridge, MA: Harvard University Press, 1991), 195–220.

16. Westat, "National Survey of Veterans, Active Duty Service Members, Demobilized National Guard and Reserve Members," October 18, 2010, available at www.va.gov/vetdata/docs/SurveysAndStudies/NVSSurvey FinalWeightedReport.pdf (accessed September 22, 2011), 53, 59. These numbers do not include homeless veterans.

17. The Department of Veterans Affairs projected statistics for post-traumatic stress are considerably higher. See "How Common Is PTSD?" www.ptsd.va.gov/public/pages/how-common-is-ptsd.asp (accessed September 22, 2011).

18. Statistics on traumatic brain injury are available by year at the Defense and Veterans Brain Injury Center, http://dvbic.org/TBI-Numbers.aspx

(accessed September 22, 2011). These numbers include injuries sustained in and out of combat.

19. In 2009, the Marine Corps' suicide rate was 24 per 100,000. The Army's rate was 22; the Air Force's was 15.5, and the Navy's was 13.3. The rate in civilian society was 10 per 100,000. For the statistics and statements by military leaders, see United States Senate, Committee on Armed Services, "The Progress in Preventing Military Suicides," June 22, 2010 (Washington, DC: GPO, 2010), 6–7, 20–24, 60. The data on the suicide rates in the veteran population comes from Anthony Swofford, "We Pretend the Vets Don't Even Exist," *Newsweek*, May 28, 2012, 29–30.

20. The battlefield incidents are Privates Duravelo and Watts on Guam, shell-shock cases on Iwo Jima, the overheated Marine in Korea, and the traumatized ambulance driver photographed by David Douglas Duncan. The other six stories were Rick Spooner watching a Marine Corps parade; General Clifton Cates reading Frances Newman's letter; Dick Bahr crying in his bed; Dick Bahr crying in his backyard; Lieutenant Ed Goricki after beating his wife; and Elizabeth Goricki upon being acquitted of her husband's murder.

21. Robert J. Watson, *History of the Office of the Secretary of Defense*, vol. 4, *Into the Missile Age, 1956–1960* (Washington, DC: Historical Office, Office of the Secretary of Defense, 1997), 262.

22. For a contemporary example of the bonds the Corps generates, see Lieutenant Colonel Michael R. Strobl, "Taking Chance," *Marine Corps Gazette* 88 (July 2004): 42–47. Strobl's autobiographical account of escorting the body of a fallen Marine home was made into an excellent film starring Kevin Bacon in 2009.

23. For a contemporary example, see the 2002 recruiting commercial "The Climb," wherein a struggling Marine recruit is helped to the top of the mountain by a shimmering, ethereal Marine ghost from World War II.

Acknowledgments

Numerous people and institutions supported me during the writing of this book. In New Haven, I owe the greatest debt to John Lewis Gaddis, Paul Kennedy, and the entire exceptional scholarly community that is International Security Studies at Yale. John's unyielding insistence on clear, succinct writing brought on the occasional flashback to Officer Candidate School, but his training, like OCS, made me a better thinker, writer, and teacher. In the history and American studies programs at Yale, I benefited from the advice and counsel of extraordinary faculty. Jean-Christophe Agnew gave me more time and support than any advisor should, and taught me how to think and write about culture. Jay Winter opened my eyes to the marvelous field of war and memory and to the sensitivity and humility that writing about trauma requires. Michael Denning, Laura Wexler, and Paul Gilroy introduced me to much of the theory that has informed this work, and conversations with John Mack Faragher, David W. Blight, Joanne B. Freeman, and Beverly Gage helped shape the project in the early stages.

At Harvard University Press, Kathleen McDermott and Andrew Kinney shepherded the project through numerous obstacles, including my deployment to Afghanistan. Michael S. Sherry, Melani McAlister, and Beth Bailey all read the entire manuscript and offered helpful suggestions, as did Ronald H. Spector, Alex Roland, and Allan R. Millett. Sue Warga was a master copyeditor, and Gregory Kornbluh and Margaux Leonard handled all of the book's publicity. I am grateful to them all.

At the Marine Corps History Division and Marine Corps Archives, diligent archivists and experts in Marine Corps history contributed mightily to this project. I owe the greatest debts to Annette Amerman, Bob Aquilina, Danny Crawford, Jim Ginther, Charles D. Melson, J. Michael Miller, Charles P. Neimeyer, and Kara Newcomer. In College Park, Maryland,

Barry Zerby at the National Archives and Records Administration was an indispensable resource, as was Dave Giordano. At the Naval History and Heritage Command, Sarandis Papadopoulos always had time for a research question or a chat, which made the hours of work in the archives much more pleasant.

I owe thanks to several colleagues who endured long hours of hearing me drone on endlessly about Marine Corps culture. Michael Cotey Morgan and Kate Epstein suffered the worst of this, though Jenifer Van Vleck, Sahr Conway-Lanz, Benjamin Madley, and Victor McFarland trail closely behind. Jonathan Reed Winkler was a mentor in more ways than one. Molly Worthen, Gretchen Heefner, Charlie Edel, Charles Keith, Helen Zoe Veit, Katie Scharf, Geraldo Cadava, Adam Arenson, Nandini Deo, and Khurram Hussain all helped me hone my ideas and kept me inspired with their own work and friendship.

My fellow historians at the United States Naval Academy helped me think more critically about my subject matter, and the History Department works-in-progress seminar gave me a chance to test out new material. Richard P. Abels, Daniel M. Masterson, Frederick S. Harrod, Craig Symonds, David P. Peeler, Nancy W. Ellenberger, and Stephen D. Wrage were constant sources of advice and good humor, and research librarian Barbara Manvel helped me track down elusive statistics. No one could ask for better colleagues or friends.

A number of active-duty and retired Marines shared their stories with me along the way, some of them deeply personal and painful. Major Rick Spooner made the trips down to Quantico a pleasure, and Norm Hatch helped me understand the Marine Corps' public relations in World War II. A special word of thanks goes to Sergeant Dick Bahr, his wife, Carol, and their daughter Dona Zori for the many interviews they sat through.

A number of foundations also gave me financial support during the writing of this book, including the Marine Corps Heritage Foundation, the Yale Center for the Study of Globalization, the Smith Richardson Foundation, the Brady-Johnson Program in Grand Strategy, and the Naval Academy Research Council. I gratefully acknowledge them all. My thanks also to David Douglas Duncan, Tom Lehrer, Norval Packwood, the Naval Institute Press, Devil Pups Inc., and the *Marine Corps Gazette* for permission to reprint their materials in this book.